EUROPE, COLD WAR AND COEXISTENCE
1953–1965

CASS SERIES: COLD WAR HISTORY
Series Editor: Odd Arne Westad
ISSN: 1471-3829

In the new history of the Cold War that has been forming since 1989, many of the established truths about the international conflict that shaped the latter half of the twentieth century have come up for revision. The present series is an attempt to make available interpretations and materials that will help further the development of this new history, and it will concentrate in particular on publishing expositions of key historical issues and critical surveys of newly available sources.

1. *Reviewing the Cold War: Approaches, Interpretations,Theory*
   Odd Arne Westad (ed.)

2. *Rethinking Theory and History in the Cold War*
   Richard Saull

3. *British and American Anticommunism before the Cold War*
   Marrku Ruotsila

4. *Europe, Cold War and Coexistence, 1953–1965*
   Wilfred Loth (ed.)

5. *The Last Decade of the Cold War: From Conflict Escalation to Conflict Transformation*
   Olav Njølstad (ed.)

EUROPE, COLD WAR AND COEXISTENCE
1953–1965

Editor:
WILFRIED LOTH
University of Essen

FRANK CASS
LONDON • PORTLAND, OR

First published in 2004 in Great Britain by
FRANK CASS PUBLISHERS
Crown House, 47 Chase Side, Southgate
London N14 5BP

and in the United States of America by
FRANK CASS PUBLISHERS
c/o ISBS, 920 NE 58th Avenue, Suite 300
Portland, Oregon, 97213-3786

Website: www.frankcass.com

British Library Cataloguing in Publication Data

Europe, Cold War and coexistence, 1953–1965. –
(Cass series. Cold War history; 4)
1. Cold War 2. Europe – Politics and government – 1945 –
3. Europe – Foreign relations – 1945
I. Loth, Wilfried
327.4'009045

ISBN 0-7146-5465-5 (cloth)
ISBN 0-7146-8465-1 (paper)
ISSN 1471-3829

Library of Congress Cataloging-in-Publication Data

Europe, Cold War and coexistence, 1953–1965 / editor, Wilfried Loth.
    p.   cm. – (Cass series–Cold War history; 4)
Includes bibliographical references and index.
    ISBN 0-7146-5465-5 – ISBN 0-7146-8465-1 (paper)
1. Cold War. 2. Communist strategy. 3. World politics–1955–1965.
4. National security–Europe. 5. Soviet Union–Foreign
relations–Europe, Western. 6. Europe, Western–Foreign
relations–Soviet Union. 7. Europe–Politics and government–1945– .
I. Loth, Wilfried. II. Title. III. Series
    D843.E836 2004
    90.82'5–dc21   2003055328

Typeset in 10.5/12 pt Times by Cambridge Photosetting Services
Printed in Great Britain by MPG Books Ltd, Victoria Square, Bodmin, Cornwall

Contents

Series Editor's Preface

The European origins of détente have long been a key research area for those historians who believe that the Cold War was more than just a superpower conflict. By attempting to find the reasons why European leaders developed their own concepts of the need for confidence-building and stability between the military blocs roughly in parallel with those that emerged in the United States and the Soviet Union, European Cold War historians want to stress both the autonomy and the inter-relationship between continental and superpower causes in the new 1960s direction in international politics. This re-evaluation is a significant project, because it promises a new and better understanding of what was perhaps the crucial turning point in Cold War history.

The present volume concentrates on explaining why, in many different West European countries, the period from the mid-1950s to the mid-1960s saw attempts at improving relations across the Iron Curtain. Most of these attempts may have been sporadic and contradictory, and there are only a few cases where the policies left a lasting legacy. But the beginning of a reconsideration of the methods that could be used in inter-bloc diplomacy signalled a willingness – on the side of some European policymakers – to move beyond the hard-line Cold War confrontation of the Stalin era.

Many of the means by which a reduction of tension could be achieved were – in the minds of key leaders – economic rather than political. By the mid-1950s the long-awaited West European post-war economic recovery had started, and it was thought that the new economic potential of the West had something to offer to the Soviet-controlled states in Eastern Europe. Perhaps even more importantly, economic progress increased the self-confidence of West European leaders, in the sense that they not only seemed to win the confrontation with Communism in their own countries, but also that their systems would be able to out-produce and out-compete the socialist economies of the East (something that had been in no way given in the first post-war decade).

Second, there were the new Soviet European policies that emerged immediately after Stalin's death in 1953. In Moscow, everyone in the new leadership agreed that the Soviet Union needed to decrease the tension with Western Europe, in part in order to get European assistance in their attempts at an even more significant détente with the United States, but also because of long-term hopes of detaching key West European countries from the Atlantic alliance. Generally, the Soviet overtures were seen as much more significant by European leaders than by the US administration of Dwight D. Eisenhower, and – as this volume shows – even the 1956 Soviet invasion of Hungary did not significantly reduce the hopes for an improved East–West relationship.

Third, during the second Cold War decade some of the key countries of Western Europe had started finding their own voice in international affairs. As the immediate impact of the last war receded, a number of leaders on both sides of the bourgeois–socialist divide began sensing that avoiding a new war in Europe was as much their responsibility as that of the superpowers. To many, the attempts at forging large-scale plans for European economic cooperation were steps in that direction, by pointing to how Germany and Italy – former enemy countries – could become integrated peacefully into a larger European economic context that also had political dimensions. Then, under Charles de Gaulle, there was the re-emergence of a self-consciously independent French foreign policy, which – as it slowly wound its way out from the disastrous attempts at keeping its empire – became a forerunner for a greater independence for Europe both in political and in defence matters.

Ironically, as this volume shows, the gradual recognition within Europe that the transatlantic alliance was here to stay contributed significantly to the willingness of West European leaders to engage in moves towards a European détente. As long as the fear remained that Washington could disengage from a Europe that was becoming increasingly more prosperous and therefore, seemingly, better equipped to cover its own defence needs, leaders in Paris, Bonn and, for that matter, in London, felt that engaging in any diplomacy with the East on their own was an unnecessarily risky business. Dispelling the notion of an American withdrawal was a slow process, and it could be argued that it was not complete until the new Democratic administration of John F. Kennedy signalled a renewed commitment to Europe in 1961–62.

In a book like this, where the main purpose is to seek the origins of something that came into full bloom much later, especially with Willy Brandt's *Ostpolitik* during the late 1960s and early 1970s, there is always a danger of reading history backwards. My sense is that the contributors have avoided that trap, especially because so many of them are aiming at telling the story of why the early attempts at détente failed. Still, for the reader it is probably useful to reflect for himself or herself on the period presented here in terms of that later era, and to ask questions about what had to change in order for Western Europe to play the much more active role in determining the future of the continent that it filled in the third decade of the Cold War.

Odd Arne Westad
Series Editor

Notes on Contributors

Eckart Conze is Privatdozent at the Institute for Contemporary History of the University of Tübingen (Germany). Main fields of research: international history (eighteenth to twentieth centuries), history of the Federal Republic of Germany, history of aristocracy and elites.

Ralph Dietl is Visiting Fellow at the Department of War Studies of King's College London. Main fields of research: Cold War history, European Integration history, Western European Union, European arms cooperation.

Elena Dundovich is Research Fellow at the Faculty of Political Sciences of the University of Florence (Italy). She is specialist on Soviet history in the 1930s and in the 1970s. She currently works with the International History Section of Studies on State in the Faculty of Political Science in Florence.

Marilena Gala is Research Fellow in History of International Relations at the Faculty of Political Sciences of the University of Florence (Italy). Since 2001 she has been teaching one of the courses of History of International Relations at the University of Florence.

Seppo Hentilä is Professor of Political History (Contemporary History) at the University of Helsinki since 1995 and chair of the research projects 'Finland in the Cold War' and 'Détente, Finland and European Security' at the Academy of Finland. He has published on Swedish and Finnish labour history and German contemporary history – especially the history of the GDR. Current field of research is Finland and divided Germany during the Cold War.

Klaus Larres is Professor in International Relations and Foreign Policy at the University of London. Previously he was the Kissinger Professor in Foreign Policy at the Library of Congress in Washington DC, and Jean Monnet Professor for European Foreign and Security Policy at the Queen's University of Belfast (Northern Ireland). He has published widely on the international history of the Cold War, UK and US foreign policy, the history of European Integration, German foreign and domestic policy, and Anglo-German and German–US relations.

Wilfried Loth is Professor of Modern and Contemporary History at the University of Duisburg-Essen (Germany) and chairman of the European Union Liaison Committee of Historians. Most recent publications include *Overcoming the Cold War: A History of Détente, 1950–1991* (2002).

Vojtech Mastny directs the Parallel History Project on NATO and the Warsaw

Pact, based at the Swiss Federal Institute of Technology in Zurich (Switzerland) and the National Security Archive in Washington.

Gottfried Niedhart is Professor of Modern History at the University of Mannheim (Germany). He has published on English and German history, and on the history of international relations.

Torsten Oppelland is Privatdozent at the Department of Political Science of the University of Jena (Germany). Main fields of research: history of political parties in Germany, German foreign policy, influence of political parties on foreign policy.

Silvio Pons teaches East European History at Rome University 'Tor Vergata' (Rome II). He is the Director of the Gramsci Institute Foundation, Rome. He is the author of *Stalin and the Inevitable War 1936–41* (2002).

Marie-Pierre Rey is Professor at the University of Paris I Panthéon Sorbonne and Director of the Centre de Recherches pour l'Histoire des Slaves. She has published many articles related to the foreign policy of Russia and the Soviet Union.

Klaus Schwabe is Professor Emeritus of contemporary history at the University of Technology at Aachen (Germany). He has published on German history, European Integration history and the history of the Cold War.

Georges-Henri Soutou is Professor of Contemporary History at the University Paris IV. He is the author of *La guerre de cinquante ans: Le conflit est–ouest 1943–1990* (2001).

Maurice Vaïsse is Professor of International Relations at the Institut d'études politiques de Paris and is the editor of the French Diplomatic Documents for the Sixties.

Antonio Varsori is full Professor of History of International Relations and Jean Monnet Chair Professor of History of European Integration at the Faculty of Political Sciences of the University of Florence (Italy). He is also in charge of the Jean Monnet European University Pool. He published extensively on issues such as: the early Cold War, the European Integration process, Italy's foreign policy, Britain's postwar foreign policy.

Irwin Wall is Professor Emeritus at the University of California, Riverside, and Visiting Scholar and Adjunct Professor at New York University. He is the author of many books and articles on French history and politics.

Abbreviations

ANF	Atlantic Nuclear Forces
BZ	*Berliner-Zeitung*
CBI	Confederation of British Industry
CDU	Christian Democratic Union
CND	Campaign for Nuclear Disarmament
CFSP	Common Foreign and Security Policy
CPSU	Communist Party of the Soviet Union
CSU	Christian Social Union
DDF	Documents Diplomatiques Français
ECSC	European Coal and Steel Community
EEC	European Economic Community
EDC	European Defence Community
EDI	European Defence Identity
EDP	European Defence Policy
EFTA	European Free Trade Association
ENDC	Eighteen-Nation Disarmament Committee
EPU	European Political Union
EURATOM	European Atomic Energy Community
ERP	European Recovery Programme
ESDI	European Security and Defence Identity
FAZ	*Frankfurter Allgemeine Zeitung*
FBI	Federation of BritishIndustry
FCMA	Friendship, cooperation and mutual assistance
FDP	Free Democratic Party
FLN	National Liberation Front
FRUS	*Foreign Relations of the United States*
FRG	Federal Republic of Germany
FTA	Free Trade Area
GDR	German Democratic Republic
GPRA	Algerian provisional government
ID	International Department
IRBMs	Intermediate Range Ballistic Missiles
KfA	Kammer für Aussenhandel
MAE	Ministère des Affaires étrangères
MLF	Multilateral Nuclear Force
MP	Member of Parliament

NADET	NATO deterrent force
NATO	North Atlantic Treaty Organization
NFZ	Nuclear-free zone
NNF	NATO nuclear force
NPA	National People's Army
PCF	French Communist Party
PCI	Italian Communist Party
POWs	Prisoners of war
PRO	Public Record Office
SAC	Standing Armaments Committee
SACEUR	Supreme Allied Commander, Europe
SED	Socialist Unionist Party, East Germany
SPD	Social Democratic Party
UN	United Nations
UNO	United Nations Organization
WEU	Western European Union
WU	Western Union

Introduction

This book is about the role of Europeans in the Cold War – the role of European governments and of European societies. The thesis with which we begin is that Europeans were not merely objects of the Cold War – not simply followers of the United States or of the Soviet Union – but exercised real influence, and oftentimes that influence was decisive. The contributions to this volume seek to answer the question of what the Europeans' role looked like in detail. Did they aggravate the conflict, or did they contain it? Were they able to maintain their independence and achieve security? Or did the Europeans become victims of the Cold War after all?

In using the term 'Europeans', we are not only referring to Western Europeans, as was long the case in the Western historiography of the Cold War. We have considered the neutral countries as well as the countries of the Soviet bloc in particular. We believe that the history of the Europeans in the Cold War can also be read as the prehistory of the present, that is, as a contribution to the history of overcoming the Cold War.

In this respect, the years from 1953 to 1965, which receive special consideration in this volume, can be seen as a crucial period in the history of the Cold War. Superficially, they can be regarded as the 'Khrushchev Era'. Beyond that, these years were particularly marked by the struggle for a regulated coexistence in a world of blocs. An initial effort to find a temporary arrangement failed due to German desires to overcome quickly the *status quo* on the German question. When, however, the crises over Berlin and over Cuba demonstrated the danger of an unintended nuclear war, then at least a tacit arrangement becomes possible. Of course, it was based on a system dominated by a nuclear arms race, a development which the actors of the late 1950s and early 1960s were unable to avoid.

That in itself already indicates the central role of Konrad Adenauer. This volume further elucidates that role in so far as it shows that the West German chancellor played at high risk and for a short time was willing to agree to the demilitarization of Central Europe (Wilfried Loth). However, he shied away from the risk of nuclear war; therefore, he was at worst (but only at worst) willing to agree to a Two-State-Arrangement on the German question and a United Nations (UN) status for Berlin (Klaus Schwabe).

This volume offers essential new information on the role of the European communists. The Western communist parties' strong financial and psychological dependence on the Moscow centre (Marie-Pierre Rey) did not keep its leaders from taking sides on controversial issues within the Soviet ruling circle. With new finds made in Eastern European archives, Vojtech Mastny gives greater emphasis to an impression earlier offered by Hope Harrison, namely, that Walter Ulbricht was the driving force behind the second Berlin crisis. The stabilization of the German Democratic Republic (GDR) thus has to be considered Khrushchev's real intention.

The observation that two Western European powers, the UK and France, in fact made considerable efforts to establish a peaceful order in Europe but for the most part failed is another important result of the studies presented in this volume. Their lack of success was partially due to Khrushchev's preference for coming to agreements with the USA and also with West Germany (Antonio Varsori, Georges-Henri Soutou). However, exaggerated notions of both UK and French hegemony in Europe also had a negative tinge. Irvin Wall highlights the late colonial notions of 'Eurafrica' that motivated France at the time of the Algerian war. Maurice Vaïsse shows that during the Berlin crisis, de Gaulle argued against negotiations with the Soviet Union in an attempt to tie the West Germans to France strongly and irrevocably.

The 'neue Ostpolitik' (new Eastern policy) of the Federal Republic appears from this perspective to be the closing of a gap left by the overly ambitious policy of the UK and especially of France. Gottfried Niedhart demonstrates that Willy Brandt developed his concept even before the shock about Western behaviour after the building of the Berlin Wall. Eckart Conze makes plain how Brandt prepared the foundations with confidence-building measures. Torsten Oppelland explains how Gerhard Schröder contributed to establishing the policy despite all the limitations of his approach. If at the beginning of the years under discussion the Germans had served as a stumbling bloc on the road to détente, they now grew into a more productive role. It first took effect when the West German government decided to sign the nuclear non-proliferation treaty (Marilena Gala).

In the period under investigation, contacts reaching beyond the blocs hardly played a part. The Finnish proposals for an understanding were highly productive (Seppo Hentilä), but little attention was paid to them. De Gaulle's appeals were mired in superficial rhetoric (Georges-Henri Soutou). It was the case that only economic interests persistently worked for the rapprochement of East and West over the long term. Until a later period, there would be no coordination of de-escalation efforts among the leaders of the US, the USSR or Europe.

This book is part of a major international research project on 'Europe, East and West, in the Cold War, 1943–1989'. It began in 1996 with an international conference in Florence entitled 'The Failure of Peace, 1943–1953', organized by Antonio Varsori.[1] In the second phase, Georges-Henri Soutou chaired a conference on 'The Times of the Cold War, 1949–1953', in Paris in 1998.[2] The contributions to this volume, *Europe, Cold War and Coexistence, 1953–1965*, were initially discussed at a third conference which took place in

October of 2001 in Essen. Further conferences to cover the Brezhnev era and the end of the Cold War will follow.

The editor would like to thank all those who have contributed to the success of this third phase of the enterprise. The Steering Committee, comprised of Vojtech Mastny, Klaus Schwabe, Georges-Henri Soutou and Antonio Varsori, provided valuable advice and important contributions. Jost Dülffer, Gustav Schmidt, Odd Arne Westad, Kathryn Weathersby and Natalia Yegorova served as section leaders and commentators and contributed to focusing the discussion. Christian Müller and Corinna Steinert supported me in the organization of the conference in Essen. Michaela Bachem-Rehm, Robert F. Hogg and Henning Türk carried out the copyediting of the contributions to this volume.

The conference in Essen was made possible by generous support from the Volkswagen Foundation and the Deutsche Forschungsgemeinschaft. Without their assistance, the international cooperation of historians from both East and West would not have been possible – and such cooperation is the prerequisite for an objective understanding of the Cold War.

NOTES

1 The contributions were published in Antonio Varsori and Elena Calandri (eds), *The Failure of Peace in Europe, 1943–48*, Basingstoke/New York: Palgrave, 2002.
2 The contributions were published in Saki Dockrill, Robert Frank, Georges-Henri Soutou and Antonio Varson (eds), *L'Europe de l'Est et de l'Ouest dans la Guerre froide, 1948–1953*, Paris: Presses de l'Université de Paris-Sorbonne, 2003.

PART I:
EUROPE IN THE 'FIRST DÉTENTE', 1953–58

1

Britain as a Bridge between East and West

Antonio Varsori

In late July of 1955, in the aftermath of the Geneva summit conference, British Prime Minister Anthony Eden had a talk with Evelyn Shuckburgh, at that time a senior Foreign Office official. The Conservative leader spoke about his experience at Geneva, saying that in his opinion, 'the Russians were looking ahead, and saw in ten or twenty years a very strong China to the east of them and perhaps a very strong Germany to the West, and were looking for someone to hold their hands a little. They could not expect anything from the USA, and they saw that the French were no use, so they were looking for us.'[1] This statement is representative of the attitudes, feelings, hopes, and misperceptions which characterized Britain's policy toward the Eastern bloc and especially the Soviet Union during the early détente period. Furthermore, it may be argued that Britain played a leading part in favouring the end of the Cold War in Europe, although it would be difficult to claim that British decision makers gained much for their efforts.[2]

It would in fact be partially misleading to focus our attention only on the period from 1953 to 1956, that is, the two-and-a-half years from the death of Stalin to the crises over the Suez and Budapest. In order to understand the UK's policy during those crucial years, it would be of some help to go back to an earlier period. In the immediate postwar years, the Labour Cabinet did its best to create a new world order which could be based on some form of agreement not only with the USA and France but also with the Soviet Union.[3] It was especially on the European continent that the UK was confronted with a frightening power vacuum which could easily be filled only by the Soviet Union, British decision makers could not be sure of the USA's intentions, and a return to the isolationist tradition could not be excluded. In spite of Churchill's efforts in the late stages of the war, France was perceived as a defeated nation whose restoration as a great power would be an almost impossible task. Only the UK could counter Soviet ambitions to achieve hegemony over the whole European continent. At the same time, British decision makers were well aware of their nation's plight, which weakened their power despite the fact that the UK was still the centre of a great empire.[4] The Attlee government could not oppose both Soviet military strength and Stalin's political prestige, a consequence of the 'great patriotic war' and of the victory over Nazi Germany; from an ideological viewpoint, Labour's peaceful 'revolution' was no match for the almost religious appeal of the communist faith with its millions of loyal militants. Last but not least, wide sectors of British public opinion saw the Soviet Union as the gallant ally which had greatly contributed to the final victory rather than as a powerful and unfriendly competitor.[5]

So diplomacy and compromise were the tools through which London tried to create a lasting peace – especially on the European continent – which would safeguard Britain's imperial interests and allow the Labour Party to achieve its domestic goals.[6] In fact, the British leaders desperately needed time to implement the Labour social and political programme, to prompt the nation's economic recovery, and to reform the Empire; a stable settlement on the European scene would offer such a chance. In this regard, Britain tried to deal with the Soviet Union on the basis of traditional power politics – in Whitehall, it was hoped that the war had transformed the USSR into Russia and Stalin into a sort of Red Tsar.[7] Very early, however, British leaders realized that it would be quite difficult to achieve a lasting settlement with the Soviet Union. They thought that Stalin's policy was largely shaped by ideological bias which led Moscow toward an aggressive strategy, that is, toward conflict with the West. This interpretation was nothing new but rather the rediscovery of deeply rooted fears and beliefs which had their origins in the 1920s.[8] But only the USA had the power and means to counter effectively Stalin's imperial ambitions, and in 1947 the British Foreign Office and its head, Ernest Bevin, did their best in order to pave the way for the USA's involvement on the European scene.[9] On the other hand, the Truman administration were already working out a 'revolution' of the USA's international role, dramatically marked by developments such as the 'Truman Doctrine', the Marshall Plan, and later the creation of the North Atlantic Alliance.[10] Britain played a significant role in this process: the 'Truman Doctrine' was prompted by London's appeal concerning the deteriorating situation in Greece[11]; the British favoured the launching of the Marshall Plan, and the UK was the most important recipient of that ERP (European Recovery Programme) aid.[12] Bevin also launched the plan for a Western Union and concurred in shaping the main characteristics of the Atlantic alliance.[13] That was the beginning of the 'special relationship'. In 1948, Churchill, although at that time in the opposition, skilfully sketched out the priorities of the UK's foreign policy when he spoke of the three interlocking 'circles' (that is, the 'special relationship', the Commonwealth and Western Europe).[14] The 'special relationship' and the Cold War were in fact closely linked, and both elements became almost vital factors of Britain's foreign policy, as the Cold War was at the root of the 'special relationship', and the Anglo-American alliance, supported by the Commonwealth, gave new life to London's role as a great power with worldwide responsibilities and interests. In late 1949, the USA and Britain appeared to be the two pillars of a powerful transatlantic partnership, of an 'Atlantic community'.[15]

But Britain's 'special' position rapidly eroded. The Korean War marked a turning point in the Cold War, as the USA on the one hand were directly involved in the Far East and on the other they were very mindful of the communist threat to Central Europe, that is, to West Germany. In the latter case, the Truman administration singled out as their main goals West Germany's rearmament and closer economic, political and military integration among the nations of Western Europe. French fears and ambitions led the Fourth Republic's decision-makers to support Jean Monnet's 'functionalist' projects, and the French government launched both the Schuman Plan and the Pleven Plan.[16] So from the middle of 1950, West Germany's role became the main concern of the Truman administration, and France became the most important factor in US policy on Western Europe.[17] For their part, British leaders rejected London's involvement in both the Schuman Plan and the Pleven Plan, not only as a consequence of their dislike of vague 'federalist' projects but also on the ground that such a commitment would jeopardize Britain's world role.[18] That may be partially true, but for some time the creation of an effective Western European system appeared to be in the hands of French and West German decision makers as well as the US administration.

In the Far East, the British supported the political and military initiatives developed by Washington, but by late 1950, the Labour Cabinet began to be worried about General McArthur's aggressive strategy which could lead to a major nuclear war.[19] Furthermore, they could not forget the 'Commonwealth circle' and, in this regard, it was often difficult to reconcile the Anglo-American 'special relationship' with the close ties developed with some Asian members of the Commonwealth, especially Nehru's India, which had serious doubts about the USA's tough policy toward Communist China.[20] Last but not least, a serious illness led to Bevin's resignation; his substitute, Herbert Morrison, lacked experience, making the Foreign Office appear less effective.

In the autumn of 1951, the Conservatives won the general elections: Churchill was appointed prime minister and Eden was once again his foreign secretary.[21] Churchill was obviously interested in foreign policy, but his relationship with Eden was less smooth than in the war years, as the former was becoming an old man who clung to power and the latter was not happy at his being the prime minister's 'heir apparent', an heir who was waiting for a position which that old man had no intention of giving up.[22] In spite of those personal difficulties, both Churchill and Eden had a common goal: the confirmation of Britain as a world power which could stand with both the USA and the USSR. They were aware of their nation's weaknesses, but they still hoped to have some chance of achieving such an ambitious goal. In fact, Churchill and Eden developed different strategies. The prime minister seemed to nurture a sort of dream: to be remembered by posterity as a man of peace through his ending of the Cold War; dialogue with Moscow was the main goal of his 'last campaign'.[23] In case of a successful outcome of his strategy, Britain would impose itself at the centre of the international stage. He hoped that he could win Washington's support for his policy. Eden did not share Churchill's enthusiasms and was more concerned about the numerous problems which London had to face in various areas, from the Middle East, where Britain's relations with Egypt were more and more strained, to South East Asia, where the British were facing a communist guerrilla movement in Malaya. Additionally, the Foreign Office's evaluations confirmed the widespread opinion that Stalin was not interested in starting any dialogue with the West, and it is not surprising that the famous Stalin Note of March 1952 was rejected by Whitehall as a mere propaganda move.[24] On the other hand, creation of an effective Western European defence system was still perceived as the only instrument for constructing a strong bulwark against Moscow's aggressive policies. So, at least for the time being, Whitehall decided to be faithful to the close alliance with the USA and to cooperate with Washington on the European scene. The British cabinet gave growing support to the project for a European Defence Community (EDC), but the launching of the so-called Eden Plan for the revival of the Council of Europe, although doomed to failure, showed that the foreign secretary did not consider the 'functionalist' approach the only way toward European cooperation and that Britain wished to play some role in any future Western European political structure.[25]

In fact, the Republican victory at the US presidential elections in late 1952 and the death of Stalin in early 1953 prompted a dramatic development in Britain's policy toward the Eastern bloc. At first, Churchill hoped that it would be possible to renew close contacts with Eisenhower and to influence the new US administration's position toward the USSR, but he quickly discovered that the Republican administration was committed to a militant anti-communist policy which openly clashed with the prime minister's aspirations.[26] In Washington's opinion, the Western European allies had to show a more forthcoming attitude in their support of the 'Cold War' strategy under the firm leadership of the USA.[27] But the death of Stalin and the early statements by the new Soviet leaders seemed to mark a significant change in Moscow's position; it was the opportunity that the prime minister had been waiting for, and he focused his attention and hopes more and more on starting a dialogue with the Soviet Union.[28] As Eden was seriously ill and out of office, Churchill felt himself free to launch an ambitious foreign policy initiative. In May of 1953, he gave an important speech in the House of Commons in which he put forward the suggestion for a summit conference on the model of the wartime big three meetings in order to resolve the major international problems of the time. The Cabinet had doubts about the wisdom of the prime minister's proposal and Eden's reaction was negative as he thought that the project was premature and ill-conceived.[29] On the other hand, the US administration disagreed with Churchill's position as both Eisenhower and John Foster Dulles argued that the long-term goal of the new Soviet leadership was still the communist domination of the world and that the Kremlin had only changed its tactics.[30] Nevertheless, Western European public opinion warmly welcomed Churchill's move, which had raised great expectations. The prime minister's initiative did not, however, have any immediate consequences: the USA stated that before starting any talks with Moscow, the Western powers would have to work out a common policy. France wanted to be involved in any future Western initiative; Churchill's and Eisenhower's illnesses led to a delay in the Western decision-making process. Also, everyone in Washington, London and Paris thought it better to wait for the outcome of West Germany's elections, due to be held in September 1953, which would influence the fate of the EDC treaty.

During the second half of 1953, there appeared to be a rapprochement between Churchill and Eden: 'détente' with Moscow was not a goal 'per se', at least in Eden's opinion; it was nevertheless a fundamental step in a wider strategy, the vital aim of which was the defence of Britain's role as a world power. Beyond Churchill's belief in the almost thaumaturgical role of a summit conference, numerous factors seemed to confirm the British view-point. In Whitehall, it was hoped that Soviet leaders would be more interested in devoloping contacts with the British Cabinet rather than with a US admin-istration, which was still committed to the 'New Look' and appeared to be influenced by the right wing of the Republican Party.[31] On the basis of a realistic approach, however, the British thought that any future negotiation with the Soviet Union would be a hard bargain and, as a sort of prerequisite, the Western powers had to achieve a 'position of strength', which meant the implementation of an effective Western European defence system.[32] In 1953, such a goal was closely tied to the ratification of the EDC treaty, although most British decision-makers were more interested in West Germany's rearmament and in the expansion of North Atlantic Treaty Organization (NATO) than in the creation of a European army, not to speak of a European Political Community.[33] Although not a very clear-cut aspect of British foreign policy in 1953, Eden and the Foreign Office did realize that the West had to make some concessions to the Soviets, but it was thought that the recognition of the Soviet Union as a decent international actor could be enough. Numerous Western decision makers opined that the new Soviet leadership was weak in comparison to Stalin and that it was also in Moscow's interest to ease inter-national tensions. In Whitehall's view, the Kremlin was mainly concerned about Europe, especially Germany. Some form of joint agreement about Germany's future could be the major subject of talks between the USSR and the three Western powers, and some sort of European security system would be the almost obvious consequence of a rapprochement between East and West. Last but not least, if there were a successful outcome of Britain's policy, London would have more resources at its disposal in order to solve the numerous problems it was facing outside Europe in the 'imperial' context. Such a 'realistic' approach was based on the assumption that Moscow's foreign policy would be shaped less by ideology and more by 'realpolitik'. In light of that, it may be of some interest to stress the cautious British reaction to the Soviet supression of the uprising in East Berlin in June of 1953; on this occasion, Churchill's words seemed to show his understanding of the Soviet Union's 'responsibilities' as an occupying power and the need to maintain 'law and order'.[34]

Until the middle of 1954, in fact, the Soviets' achievement of a position of strength was regarded as an unavoidable prerequisite, and it was still very difficult to understand what would be the outcome of the struggle for power taking place in Moscow. At the Bermuda three-power conference in December of 1953, Churchill and Eden put strong pressure on Laniel and Bidault in order to get France to ratify the EDC treaty. The British leaders' position did not differ very much from Eisenhower's and Dulles' attitude.[35] At the Berlin foreign ministers' conference on the German question (January–February 1954), Eden consistently stuck to the plan which had been worked out by the three Western powers; this was based on the hypothesis of free elections in the whole German territory and was rejected by the Soviet delegation.[36] In that same period, however, it was decided that in a few months a conference would be convened on the Korean and Indochina crises. That meeting opened in April 1954 in Geneva, and all the parties involved in both questions – including the major communist powers, the USSR and Communist China – took part in the conference. Discussions on the Korean question almost immediately ended in failure, but it must not be forgotten that in 1953, despite the 'New Look' rhetoric, an armistice had been agreed with the consent of the United States. So the attention of the conference was focused on the Indochina crisis; for their part, the French had hoped that the meeting would offer them the chance for a diplomatic solution to an endless war which was becoming more and more unpopular and burdensome. Military developments, that is, the siege of the French garrison at Dien Bien Phu, highlighted the weakness of France's position, however. The Laniel government put strong pressure on the Eisenhower administration for US military intervention to relieve the besieged garrison. But US officials had no intention of becoming directly involved in the Indochina crisis, and they asked the British for political and military support, while warning the French that they could not give up their military responsibilities in South East Asia. Furthermore, the US delegation's position at the Geneva conference hardened due to fears that the French would accept a diplomatic solution, which would threaten the Western position in Asia to the advantage of both the Soviet Union and Communist China.[37] Both Churchill and Eden were irritated by the US attitude; the British thought that Western military intervention in Indochina would be a mistake, but, in their opinion, the Eisenhower administration's rigid position at Geneva was useless and only diplomacy could offer a way out for the West.[38] It was especially the case that Eden, who was playing a leading part in the negotiations, hoped that the outcome of the conference could be successful: a lessening of the tensions in the Far East would have positive consequences for Britain's position in those areas where it still had significant interests, from Hong Kong to

Singapore to Malaya, not to speak of the still important partnership with India.[39]

The fall of Dien Bien Phu led to Laniel's resignation and to the appointment of Pierre Mendès France, whose first task was resolution of both the Indochina crisis and the 'querelle de la CED'. A 'peace with honour' was quickly achieved in Indochina, but the Geneva agreements were perceived in Washigton as 'treason'. Dulles suspected that Mendès France had agreed to a 'global trade-off' with both the Soviet Union and Communist China in the form of Moscow's and Peking's forthcoming attitude on the Indochina question and France's abandonment of its commitment to ratifying the EDC. In London, however, the Geneva agreements were regarded as a positive compromise solution; Eden was proud of his diplomatic skill, which enhanced both his domestic and international position. In his opinion, the Soviet delegation had behaved sensibly; moreover, Britain and the Soviet Union would be the co-guarantors of the implementation of the Geneva agreements. Although there were some suspicions about the French leader's entourage, the British thought that the new French government's attitude could have positive consequences for Britain's international interests. Mendès France favoured the setting-up of close ties with London, and he had scant confidence in functionalist integration. In Whitehall, it was also thought that Britain and France as imperial powers shared some common interests – from the Middle East to the Far East – which, in their opinion, did not coincide with those pursued by the US administration.[40] So both nations were interested in promoting détente; such a development would confirm the two powers' independent role in the Western alliance, and they could move their scant resources from the European scene to the 'colonial' world. Those hopes were based on the assumptions that (a) Moscow was still focusing its attention on Europe, (b) the new Soviet leadership was weaker than Stalin had been, (c) a multi-polar international system where the USA would not be the only Western power would be in the Kremlin's interest. In two years' time, all those assumptions would be proven wrong.

Nevertheless, in late August 1954, when the French National Assembly rejected the EDC treaty – thus creating the worst crisis in the Western alliance before de Gaulle's decision to leave NATO – British leaders and especially Eden felt that this could become a precious opportunity for Britain and that Whitehall could play a leading role in shaping the Western system.[41] At first, the foreign secretary convinced Dulles to refrain from any retaliatory action against France. Then he launched a project based on West Germany's rearmament through Bonn's involvement in NATO and the creation of the Western European Union (WEU), which would include both the Federal Republic and Italy. Eden's plan was successful, and in late October 1954, the Paris agreement sealed West Germany's rearmament, the restoration of its sovereignty as well, its membership in both NATO and the WEU. The United States could be happy with the creation of an effective Western defence system; Germany had recovered the status of an independent nation; and France had saved its 'armée'. Moreover, because Adenauer's government had stated that it would give up its right to produce nuclear weapons, Paris could hope to maintain some form of military superiority over Germany. But Britain was the real winner. Whitehall had achieved all its goals: (a) the USA would maintain their commitment to Europe's defence, but Britain had confirmed its special role as a bridge between Washington and its European allies; (b) West Germany would be rearmed but with no independent nuclear weapons and would be under the double control of NATO and the WEU; (c) the functionalist 'approach' to European integration which isolated Britain from Western Europe had been defeated; (d) a close Anglo-French 'entente cordiale' had been restored. In this same period, Britain and Egypt had also signed a treaty which seemed to solve the Suez Canal question, and Eden played a role in the resolution of the Trieste problem, thus confirming both his international prestige and growing role in the Tory government.[42] In the British cabinet's opinion, the next step would be the exploitation of the 'position of strength' achieved in Europe as well as Britain's diplomatic prestige in order to start a dialogue with Moscow and create a stable European settlement acceptable to the Soviets. All those goals were obviously tied to the ratification of the Paris agreements, and it is not surprising that until the final decision by the French parliament in the spring of 1955, London's attitude was a cautious one; when in early 1955, Mendès France put pressure on the USA and Britain in order to launch an initiative toward the USSR, both Churchill and Eden disagreed with the French prime minister's move, regarding it as premature.[43]

But it was the Soviet Union which seized the initiative in March 1955: The Soviet government summoned to Moscow the Austrian leaders in order to find a solution to the problem of Austria. The Soviets were now eager to accept an end to the four-power occupation, but Austria would become a neutral state, a compromise which was also in Austria's interest. The Kremlin's move led to four-power negotations whose outcome was the signature of the Austrian state treaty by the four foreign ministers, which took place in Vienna in mid May.[44] In the meantime, Churchill had at last decided to resign. Eden became prime minister in April, and his position was then strengthened by a general election which confirmed his leadership.[45] In Eden's view, Moscow's political activism, which was further demonstrated by Khrushchev's visit to Belgrade, meant that the Soviet interest in détente was not only a propaganda move; furthermore, Whitehall thought that as a consequence of Malenkov's resignation, Khrushchev was emerging as the leading personality and that this development would give more substance to Moscow's foreign policy.[46] So Eden proposed to the Eisenhower administration and the French government that the Western powers seize the initiative to convene the summit conference which Churchill had dreamt of. Although the new French cabinet led by Edgar Faure obviously welcomed Eden's proposal, as Paris hoped that such an initiative could delay West Germany's rearmament, the US authorities showed scant enthusiasm, bowing to the European allies' will only because they knew that Western public opinion strongly hoped that a new peaceful era would dawn in East–West relations and realized that the USA could not reject such an important initiative that could lead to détente.[47]

It is not possible here to examine in detail the diplomatic process which led to the Geneva conference nor to explore its proceedings. As far as Britain is concerned, Eden was the driving force in the Western camp.[48] Of course, the British would not act alone and instead carefully looked for a common Western position – more precisely, a common Anglo-American position – but they were eager to shape the Western powers' strategy. In Whitehall's opinion, the summit could deal with all the major international problems, but the British were convinced that Soviet leaders would focus their interest on Europe and, to that end, Britain worked out a plan which, if accepted by the Soviets, could lead to Germany's reunification. The project was based on free elections on the whole German territory as well as on the creation of a de-militarized belt in Central Europe, comprising former East Germany as well as some parts of Czechoslovakia and Poland. To this could be added some guarantees about the stationing of NATO troops in Europe, as well as recognition of Soviet interests.[49] We may wonder whether Eden really believed that the Soviet leaders could comply with a project which would end Soviet control over East Germany. Perhaps Eden was influenced by some West German intelligence estimates that stressed alleged Soviet economic and political weakness. Morevover, it is likely that the British prime minister overrated the Kremlin's interest in achieving détente with the West at all costs. It was also the case that some British diplomats such as the ambassador in Moscow, Sir Willian Hayter, had a far less optimist view of Soviet aims.[50] Nevertheless, most British decision makers seemed to believe that the Soviet leaders were interested in starting serious talks with the West, especially as far as Europe was concerned; Whitehall thought that Moscow wanted to be recognized as a reliable international partner and that Soviet leaders were eager to achieve a stable European settlement. Consequences of this evaluation included not only the Eden Plan but also British willingness to recognize a role for the USSR on the European continent and, in the long term, negotiate a European security system which would include the Soviet Union.

As is well known, the summit conference – despite the so-called 'Geneva spirit' – led to no practical consequences. Furthermore, the Soviet Union showed no interest in the Eden Plan, and on their coming back to Moscow, Khrushchev and Bulganin paid a visit to East Berlin, where they openly stated the Kremlin's support for the German Democratic Republic, a confirmation of how Germany's division suited Soviet interests.[51] This was underscored on the occasion of Adenauer's visit to Moscow in September of 1955. Eden was only partially disappointed by the political outcome of the Geneva conference, but he did appear to resent the reaction of Western public opinion, which had singled out the USA and the USSR as the two main actors. On the contrary,

Eden still hoped that the USSR needed Britain and that a fruitful bilateral relationship could be worked out. He based this on the talks he had had with both Khrushchev and Bulganin.[52] The British cabinet invited the Soviet leaders to pay an official visit to Britain in early 1956. Khrushchev and Bulganin welcomed Eden's invitation, and, in London, it was often stressed that this would be the first visit by Soviet leaders to a great Western power. This decision appeared to confirm in British eyes the Soviet interest in Britain's international role.

Some episodes dampened Eden's optimism, however. In the autumn of 1955, Khrushchev and Bulganin paid a successful and much-publicized visit to Asia, during which their speeches harshly criticized British imperialism; furthermore, they voiced Moscow's support for the process of decolonization.[53] A few months earlier, in late April, numerous Asian and African leaders had met in Bandung and had given birth to the movement of the non-aligned countries. A communist leader, Chou En-lai, had played a significant role at the Bandung Conference, stressing that the communist bloc regarded the 'Third World' countries, although ruled mostly by 'bourgeois' leaders, as reliable and valuable allies. Last but not least, 'non-alignment' and the fight against colonialism were becoming two important goals for Yugoslavia, with which the Conservative government had hoped to renew close ties.[54]

Some Foreign Office officials began to realise that Soviet foreign policy was radically changing: in the eyes of the Kremlin's leaders, the achievement of 'détente' in Europe was an instrument which gave them more room for manoeuvre in the 'Third World', where Khrushchev was eager to develop close alliances with newly independent nations. The Soviets showed a confident attitude that 'peaceful coexistence' would favour Soviet goals. Worse still, they appeared to single out the colonial role of Britain and France as the weak link in the Western chain, and, to that end, they thought it useful to exploit the nationalist, anti-colonialist feelings which were shaping the attitudes of Asian and African peoples.[55] Britain's reaction was slow and largely ineffective. Some diplomats warned Eden about the dangerous developments in Soviet foreign policy, and someone in Whitehall thought it perhaps better to cancel Khrushchev's visit to Britain, but this idea was quickly shelved.[56] For his part, Eden thought it possible to have a frank conversation with Khrushchev. It is of some interest to note that the outcome of the twentieth congress of the Communist Party of the Soviet Union (CPSU) and Khrushchev's 'secret report' appeared to have a minor impact on Britain's decision-making.[57] The British cabinet now focused their attention on the Soviet attitude toward the 'Third World', especially the growing interest Moscow showed in the Middle East, where London's position was becoming weaker as a consequence of a rising tide of Arab nationalism, whose main standard-bearer was Nasser's Egypt. Soviet leaders openly criticized the Baghdad Pact, which London had joined in 1955.

In late April 1956, Khrushchev and Bulganin paid their official visit to Britain; in spite of a few minor incidents, the visit appeared to be successful.[58]

There were numerous bi-lateral conversations, and Eden explained Britain's position frankly. He highlighted the positive aspects of Britain's colonial experience and stated that Middle East oil was vital for the British economy, so much so that the British 'were prepared to fight for it'. But Khrushchev did not back down from his position and, as a Foreign Office official wrote, 'He was quick to reach agreement on matters which he did not regard as important: but on "questions of principle" ... he proved to be intransigent'.[59] It seemed to be the case that disruption of the British Empire was one of those 'questions of principle'. But Eden was under the illusion that he had convinced Khrushchev of Britain's determination and capacity to defend its vital interests.[60]

A few weeks later, Nasser made a speech announcing his decision to nationalize the Suez Canal Company, a move which generated waves of popular enthusiasm in the whole Arab world. As is well known, his decision was the beginning of a crisis which would seal the end of Britain's leading role in the Middle East and would be a serious blow to London's prestige as a world power.[61] It is not surprising that, as the British were too involved in the Suez crisis, they appeared to show little interest in the Budapest uprising, which was perceived mainly as a development that would favour the British and French intervention against Nasser.[62] Although the Soviet Union loudly supported Egypt's position, the main reason for Britain's surrender to the will of the United Nations was the negative reaction of the US administration. In spite of that, the relationship between London and Moscow had radically changed. In late November, a Foreign Office official had a talk with the Soviet ambassador in London, Malik, who was critical of Britain's decision to freeze cultural and trade relations with the USSR in retaliation for the Soviet intervention against Hungary. The British diplomat got the impression that Malik's words could be easily translated into 'we are proud and we are strong; if you do not wish to have cultural exchanges or trade with us, so much the worse for you'.[63] Eden's policy toward the Soviet Union had ended in failure, and the new prime minister's early goal was now the restoration of the 'special relationship': détente was too serious a business to be left in the hands of the British or the French and from 1956 on, the East–West confrontation – and dialogue – appeared to be mainly a bi-polar affair.

In conclusion, it can be stated that between 1953 and 1956, Britain consistently tried to develop an autonomous policy toward the Soviet Union, a policy which, however, had its roots in previous experiences. If Churchill often appeared to be influenced by personal motives and by a kind of dream, Eden's policy was more coherent and seemed to be based on rational factors. Both leaders believed that their main goal was the confirmation of Britain's role as a great world power; this meant that London had to have a leading position in the international arena, that is, in the East–West conflict. Yet in the opinion of British decision makers, the Cold War, which in the late 1940s had strengthened London's international role, above all through the 'special relationship', was now weakening that position, in particular because they felt that it was becoming less and less easy to influence US authorities. In some areas of the world, moreover, British interests and opinions began to differ from those of Washington. The British leaders thought that once the Western system had been able to achieve a position of strength (that is, via West Germany's rearmament and the strengthening of NATO), the Western powers could begin some form of dialogue with the USSR. In London's interpretation, the new Soviet leaders were eager to establish some 'modus vivendi' with the West and to that end were focusing their attention on the European scene. This development in the Kremlin's attitude was perceived as the consequence of a lessening of the ideological characters which had shaped Stalin's foreign policy. It is difficult to know whether Whitehall had a clearcut view of the main features of the agreement which could be achieved; the hope for Germany's reunification quickly vanished in the summer of 1955 in the face of the Kremlin's lack of interest; also, the hypothesis of a European security system was always very vague. It may be stated, however, that the British plans implied the Western recognition of Moscow's continued rule over most of East–Central Europe, as well as the existence of definite Soviet interests on the European continent. In fact, London's evaluation of Moscow's position was partly right – détente in Europe was in the Soviet leaders' interest, but, especially from 1955 onwards, Khrushchev hoped that a stable European settlement would offer him more room for manoeuvre in the 'Third World'. Furthermore, Soviet leaders were now convinced that their position had become stronger and that the real enemy – with which, however, it would be possible to negotiate – was the US administration, while Britain and France were only minor actors experiencing an unavoidable decline.

If Britain's aspiration to become a bridge between East and West – that is, to confirm its role as an autonomous international actor – was doomed to failure, and London reverted to the more modest role of significant pillar in the Western alliance, Britain's belief in its being able to develop some autonomous contact with the USSR did survive for a long while. As evidence of this, we may cite Macmillan's visit to Moscow, Harold Wilson's initiatives on finding a diplomatic solution to the Vietnam War through contacts with the Moscow leadership, and, last but not least, Thatcher's early interest in Gorbachev's policy. We may wonder, however, whether, from the mid-1950s, Moscow regarded Britain as a partner of any relevance.

NOTES

1 E. Shuckburgh, *Descent to Suez Diaries 1951–56*, London: Weidenfeld & Nicolson, 1986, p. 274.
2 For an overall view, see B.P. White, 'The British Contribution to East–West Détente 1953–63', and A. Varsori, 'Britain and Early Détente 1953–56', in G. Schmidt (ed.),

Ost-West-Beziehungen: Konfrontation und Détente, Bochum: Brockmeyer, 1993, pp. 99–116, 175–97.

3 See our remarks in A. Varsori, 'Reflections on the Origins of the Cold War', in O. Westad (ed.), *Reviewing the Cold War: Approaches, Interpretations, Theory*, London: Frank Cass, 2000, pp. 281–302.

4 On Britain and the origins of the 'Cold War' in Europe, see D. Reynolds, 'Great Britain', in D. Reynolds (ed.), *The Origins of the Cold War in Europe: International Perspectives*, New Haven/London: Yale University Press, 1994, pp. 77–95; V. Rothwell, *Britain and the Cold War 1941–47*, London: Jonathan Cape, 1982; see also the contributions by J. Kent and A. Lane, in A. Varsori and E. Calandri (eds), *The Failure of Peace in Europe 1943–48*, London: Palgrave, 2001. For an analysis which covers a longer period, see M. Trachtenberg, *A Constructed Peace: The Making of the European Settlement 1945–1963*, Princeton, NJ: Princeton University Press, 1999.

5 For a general view of Britain's attitude toward Soviet Communism, see F.S. Northedge and A. Wells, *Britain and Soviet Communism*, London: Macmillan, 1982; on the relations between the USSR and Britain, see Sir C. Keeble, *Britain and the Soviet Union, 1917–1989*, London: Macmillan, 1990.

6 On the Labour Government's experience, see K.O. Morgan, *Labour in Power 1945–51*, Oxford: Clarendon Press, 1984; on the Labour government foreign policy, see R. Ovendale (ed.), *The Foreign Policy of the British Labour Government (1945–51)*, Leicester: Leicester University Press, 1984.

7 On the development in Britain's policy, for example Whitehall's attitude toward the process of sovietization in Eastern Europe, see B. Arcidiacono, *Alle origini della guerra fredda: Armistizi e Commissioni di controllo alleate in Europa orientale 1944–1946*, Florence: Ponte alle Grazie, 1993. See Rothwell, *Britain and the Cold War 1941–1947*.

8 On Britain's changing attitude, see G. Warner, 'From Ally to Enemy: Britain's Relations with the Soviet Union, 1941–48', in F. Gori and S. Pons (eds), *The Soviet Union and Europe in the Cold War, 1943–53*, London: Macmillan, 1996, pp. 293–310; on Britain's attitude toward Communist Russia from the Bolshevik Revolution to the 1920s, see, for example, R.H. Ullman, *Anglo-Soviet Relations 1917–1921*, 3 vols, Princeton, NJ: Princeton University Press, 1968/1972.

9 On Bevin's foreign policy, see A. Bullock, *Ernest Bevin Foreign Secretary 1945–51*, London: Heinemann, 1983.

10 On the development of US foreign policy, see, for example, J.L. Gaddis, *The US and the Origins of the Cold War 1941–1947*, New York: Columbia University Press, 1972 and M. Leffler, *A Preponderance of Power: National Security, the Truman Administration and the Cold War*, Stanford, CA: Stanford University Press, 1992.

11 R. Frazier, 'Did Britain Start the Cold War? Bevin and the Truman Doctrine', *Historical Journal*, 27 (1984), 715–27; Rothwell, *Britain and the Cold War*, pp. 433–43.

12 M. Hogan, *The Marshall Plan, America, Britain, and the Reconstruction of Western Europe, 1945–1952*, Cambridge: Cambridge University Press, 1987.

13 A. Varsori, *Il Patto di Bruxelles (1948): tra integrazione europea e alleanza atlantica*, Rome: Bonacci, 1988.

14 A. Deighton, 'Britain and the Three Interlocking Circles', in A. Varsori (ed.), *Europe 1945–1990s: The End of An Era?*, London: Macmillan, 1995, pp. 155–69.

15 R. Edmonds, *Setting the Mould: The United States and Britain (1945–1950)*, Oxford: Clarendon Press, 1986.

16 G. Bossuat, *L'Europe des Français, 1943–1959: La IVème République aux sources de l'Europe communautaire*, Paris: Publications de la Sorbonne, 1996.

17 P. Melandri, *Les Etats-Unis face à l'unification de l'Europe*, Paris: Pedone, 1980; I. Wall, *L'influence américaine sur la politique française 1945–54*, Paris: Balland, 1989.

18 E. Dell, *The Schuman Plan and the Abdication of British Leadership in Europe*, Oxford: Oxford University Press, 1996.

19 P. Lowe, 'The Significance of the Korean War in Anglo-American Relations, 1950–53', in M. Dockrill and J.W. Young (eds), *British Foreign Policy, 1945–56*, London: Macmillan, 1989, pp. 126–48.

20 See, for example, A. Inder Singh, *The Limits of British Influence: South Asia and Anglo-American Relations 1947–56*, London: Pinter, 1993, especially chapter 3.

21 On Churchill, see M. Gilbert, *'Never Despair': Winston S. Churchill 1945–1965*, London: Heinemann, 1988; on Eden, see D. Carlton, *Anthony Eden: A Biography*, London: Allen & Lane, 1981; R. Rhodes Janes, *Anthony Eden*, London: Weidenfeld & Nicolson, 1986; D. Dutton, *Anthony Eden: A Life and Reputation*, London: Arnold, 1997.

22 On this difficult relationship, see, for example, Shuckburgh, *Descent to Suez Diaries*, *passim*.

23 J.W. Young, *Winston Churchill's Last Campaign: Britain and the Cold War 1951–1955*, Oxford: Clarendon Press, 1996.

24 On the Stalin Note, see R. Steininger, *The German Question: The Stalin Notes of 1952 and the Problem of Reunification*, New York: Columbia University Press, 1990.

25 On the Eden Plan, see Dutton, *Anthony Eden*, pp. 290–300.

26 See the outcome of the early contacts between Churchill and Eisenhower in P.G. Boyle, *The Churchill–Eisenhower Correspondence, 1953–1955*, Chapel Hill/London: The University of North Carolina Press, 1990.

27 For an overall analysis, see S. Dockrill, *Eisenhower's New Look National Security Policy, 1953–1961*, London: Macmillan, 1996.

28 A. Varsori, 'Britain and Stalin's Death', in Gori and Pons (eds), *The Soviet Union*, pp. 334–55.

29 On Churchill's speech, see Gilbert, *Never Despair*, pp. 827–45; on the Cabinet's attitude, see, for example, Public Record Office (hereafter PRO), CAB 129/61, C(53)194, memorandum 'Policy toward the Soviet Union' by Lord Salisbury, 7 July 1953, top secret; on Eden's reaction, see Dutton, *Anthony Eden*, pp. 337–8.

30 *Foreign Relations of the United States 1952–1954*, vol. VIII, *Eastern Europe; Soviet Union; Eastern Mediterranean*, Washington: US Government Printing Office, 1988, see especially pp. 1099 ff.

31 PRO, CAB 129/61, memorandum C(53)187, 'Foreign Ministers' Meeting in Washington – Policy toward the Soviet Union and Germany', by Lord Salisbury, 3 July 1953, secret.

32 Britain appeared to support the EDC; see, for example, PRO, FO 800/778, memorandum ZP 12/27 G, 'Meetings with Mr. Dulles and Mr. Stassen – Meeting in the Foreign Office at 11 a.m. on 4th February, 1953', secret.

33 On Britain's attitude toward the EDC, see, for example, PRO, CAB 129/60 memorandum C(53)108, 'The European Defence Community and European Unity', by H. Macmillan, 19 March 1953, secret. Macmillan hinted that a future European political and defence community could be under the hegemony of Germany and such a perspective was feared by the British politician.

34 Young, *Winston Churchill's Last Campaign*, pp. 176–9.

35 On Britain's position at the Bermuda conference, see J.W. Young, 'Churchill, the Russians and the Western Alliance: The Three-Power Conference at Bermuda, December 1953', *English Historical Review*, 101 (1986), 889–912.

36 On Britain's position at the Berlin conference, see, for example, Young, *Winston Churchill's Last Campaign*, pp. 238–47.

37 On the relations between France and the US in this period, see the interesting evaluations in J. De Folin, *Indochine 1940–1955: La fin d'un rêve*, Paris: Perrin, 1993, pp. 233–72; see also Wall, *L'influence américaine*, pp. 328–81.

38 Gilbert, *Never Dispair*, pp. 972–4; Dutton, *Anthony Eden*, pp. 343–4; Young, *Winston Churchill's Last Campaign*, pp. 260–5.
39 Inder Singh, *The Limits of British Influence*, pp. 157–76.
40 On Mendès France's attitude toward Britain, see M. Vaïsse, 'La Grande Bretagne, une partenaire privilégiée?', in F. Bédarida and J.-P. Rioux (eds), *Pierre Mendès France et le mendesisme*, Paris: Fayard, 1985, pp. 279–86; see also E. du Réau, 'Pierre Mendès France, la création de l'Union européenne occidentale (UEO) et son devenir', in R. Girault (ed.), *Pierre Mendès France et le role de la France dans le monde*, Grenoble: PUG, 1991, pp. 25–38.
41 S. Dockrill, 'Britain and the Settlement of the West German Rearmament Question in 1954', in M. Dockrill and J.W. Young (eds), *British Foreign Policy 1945–56*, London: Macmillan, 1989, pp. 149–72; A. Deighton, 'Britain and the Creation of Western European Union 1954', in M. Dumoulin (ed.), *La Communauté Européenne de Défense: Leçons pour demain?*, Bern: Peter Lang, 2000, pp. 283–308.
42 Dutton, *Anthony Eden*, p. 352; the author regards 1954 as Eden's 'annus mirabilis'.
43 G.-H. Soutou, 'Pierre Mendès France et l'URSS 1954–1955', in Girault (ed.), *Pierre Mendès France*, pp. 177–206; A. Varsori, 'Alle origini della prima distensione: la Francia di Pierre Mendès France e la ripresa del dialogo con Mosca', *Storia delle relazioni internazionali*, 8, 1–2 (1992), 63–97.
44 On the Austrian question, see G. Bischof, *Austria in the First Cold War, 1944–55: The Leverage of the Weak*, London: Macmillan, 1999.
45 For an overall view of the Eden Government's experience, see R. Lamb, *The Failure of the Eden Government*, London: Sidgwick & Jackson, 1987.
46 At any rate Britain's early views about Khrushchev were pessimistic, especially that of the British Ambassador, who appeared worried about such a development; see PRO, FO 371, NS 107/29, despatch No. 23, Sir W. Hayter (Moscow) to A. Eden (FO), 10 February 1955, confidential.
47 For an overall view of the Geneva summit conference, see G. Bischof and S. Dockrill (eds), *Cold War Respite: The Geneva Summit of 1955*, Baton Rouge: Louisiana State University Press, 2000.
48 See A. Varsori, 'British Policy Aims at Geneva', and S. Dockrill, 'The Eden Plan and European Security', in Bischof and Dockrill (eds), *Cold War Respite*, pp. 75–96, 161–89.
49 S. Dockrill, 'The Eden Plan'.
50 The weakness of the Soviet ecomomy was stressed by Adenauer, see PRO, PREM 11/893, tel. No. 76, Sir C. Steel (NATO-Paris) to FO, 8 May 1955, confidential. On Hayter's cautiousness, see, for example, his early reaction to the Soviet proposal for a visit to Moscow by the West German Chancellor, PRO, PREM 11/894, tel. No. 555, Sir W. Hayter (Moscow) to FO, 8 June1955, priority confidential.
51 V.M. Zubok, 'Soviet Policy Aims at the Geneva Conference, 1955', in Bischof and Dockrill (eds), *Cold War Respite*, pp. 55–74. For a wider view of Khrushchev's positions in the mid-1950s, see V. Zubok and C. Pleshakov, *Inside the Kremlin's Cold War: From Stalin to Khrushchev*, Cambridge, MA: Harvard University Press, 1996, pp. 174–94; see, moreover, W.J. Tompson, *Khrushchev: A Political Life*, London: Macmillan, 1997, pp. 147–52.
52 On Britain's goals, see, for example, PRO, FO 371, NS 10512/10, minute 'Proposed visit of Mr. Bulganin and Mr. Khrushchev to the United Kingdom', H.A.F. Hohler to the Secretary of State, 12 August 1955, confidential.
53 See the early British reactions in PRO, FO 371, NS 10512/94, minute 'Bulganin/ Khrushchev visit', H.A.F. Hohler to the Permanent Under-Secretary, 30 November 1955, confidential.
54 On Bandung and on British reactions, see Inder Singh, *The Limits of British Influence*,

pp. 180–5; on the development in Anglo-Yugoslav relations, see A. Varsori, 'La politica estera britannica e la Jugoslavia', in M. Galeazzi (ed.), *Roma-Belgrado gli anni della guerra fredda*, Ravenna: Longo, 1995, pp. 63–84.

55 See Sir William Hayter's opinions in PRO, FO 371, NS 1021/15, despatch No. 16, Sir W. Hayter (Moscow) to S. Lloyd, 18 January 1956, confidential.

56 PRO, FO 371, NS 10512/109, minute 'The Russian Antics in the Far East', Sir I. Kirkpatrick to the Secretary of State, 6 December 1955; see also PRO, CAB 128/129, CM(55)45th Conclusions, 6 December 1955, secret, and CM (56)3rd Conclusions, 11 January 1956, secret.

57 PRO, FO 371, NS 1015/65, despatch No. 75, Sir W. Hayter (Moscow) to S. Lloyd (FO), 23 March 1956, confidential; Hayter played down the importance of Khrushchev's secret report 'little happened at the Congress that was surprising or new'. See also NS 105/60, memorandum '20th Congress of the Communist Party of the Soviet Union Moscow, February 14–25' by the Northern Department, 24 March 1956, confidential.

58 On the visit, see the numerous files kept at the PRO.

59 PRO, FO 371, NS 1052/656, Note 'Bulganin and Khrushchev' by T. Brimelow and W. Barker, annex to memorandum No. 19771, 'Visit by Mr N.A. Bulganin and Mr N.S. Khrushchev to the United Kingdom – April 18–27, 1956', secret.

60 PRO, CAB 128/30, CM(56)31st Conclusions, 26 March 1956, secret. See also FO 371, NS1052/52, tel. No. 2354, FO to Washington, 1 May 1956, top secret.

61 On Suez, see, for example, Wm. R. Louis and R. Owen (eds), *Suez 1956: The Crisis and Its Consequences*, Oxford: Clarendon Press, 1991; W. Scott Lucas, *Divided We Stand: Britain, the US and the Suez Crisis*, London: Hodder & Stoughton, 1991; K. Kyle, *Suez*, London: Weidenfeld & Nicolson, 1991.

62 See the records in PRO, FO 371, piece Nos. 122373 to 122385, dealing with the Hungarian crisis. Such records seem to confirm the scant attention that Whitehall paid to the Hungarian question, with the exception of its consequences on ONU affairs.

63 PRO, FO 371, NS 1051/101, minute 'Conversation with Soviet Ambassador' by D.P. Reilly, 29 November 1956, confidential.

2

Adenauer's Final Western Choice, 1955–58

Wilfried Loth

The tendency toward an understanding on the basis of mutual respect between the blocs, as seen in the 'spirit of Geneva', was opposed above all by Konrad Adenauer. This is understandable given that such a *modus vivendi* between East and West implied that the division of Germany would continue for an indefinite period, provided that one did not suppoᵢ the neutralization of Germany or believe that the Soviet system would be liberalized. That in itself was unacceptable to Adenauer because his policy of Western integration could be increasingly called into question. He therefore had to use every means at his disposal to prevent official recognition of the German Democratic Republic (GDR) and avoid having interest in reunification retreat into the shadows in favour of tendencies toward de-escalation.[1]

I

By demonstrating Western strength and promoting internal difficulties for the Soviets, Adenauer's policies for Germany aimed at convincing the Soviet leadership to retreat from German affairs and to dispense with repressive methods in pursuing its interests in general. As he explained in March 1952, 'when the West is stronger than Soviet Russia, then the day for negotiation with Soviet Russia has come'. And 'then we have to make Soviet Russia understand that it cannot possibly keep half of Europe in slavery, and that by means of a confrontation the conditions in East Europe have to be rearranged'.[2] Four years later, he insisted 'we [can] only secure peace if we contribute to [making] the peace-loving part of the world stronger than the Soviet Union, not in order to suppress it, but actually to come to promising negotiations this way'.[3] In order to get there, he did everything in his power to strengthen the solidarity of the West and its military power; it is an oft-neglected fact that he also rejected all Soviet initiatives to intensify trade relations, which could have helped the Soviet Union in dealing with its economic difficulties.

Adenauer did not consider for one minute that such policies of strength might also be counterproductive, meaning that they might further harden the

Soviet position. He also did not have a precise definition of how to measure Western superiority; it did not matter to him that this superiority had long since been achieved in the economic arena and still obtained in nuclear affairs as well. Furthermore, he did not dwell on the question of whether strength alone would suffice to convince the Soviet leadership to give in. Occasional thoughts about having to pay a price for giving up the GDR were regularly overruled by the fear that a withdrawal of American troops from the Federal Republic would lead to the expansion of Soviet hegemony on the European continent. Thus, he did not dare accept more than a NATO disclaimer regarding the GDR's territory; and even this concession he himself did not offer to the Soviet Union. In practice, his Eastern policies were limited to keeping some sort of connection with Moscow in order to forestall an understanding between the USA and the Soviet Union based on the recognition of the status quo.

The sterility and problematic internal nature of Adenauer's reunification policy led many opponents to accuse him of not really wanting the reunification of Germany – particularly dramatic examples are the Bundestag speeches of Thomas Dehler and Gustav Heinemann on 23 and 24 January 1958. Such claims, however, are not accurate, especially when we consider Adenauer's belief that in order to keep the Germans with the West permanently, he needed to show successes on questions of reunification. 'If the question of reunification is not resolved in an appropriate period of time', he instructed his NATO ambassador Herbert Blankenhorn in February 1958, 'we will be running the risk that the unscrupulous agitation of our opposition will lead the majority of the people gradually to become muddled ... and that the question of loosening the ties to the West and the neutralisation of Germany will become a serious question, which it isn't yet.'[4] Further, his insistence on the Federal Republic's claim that it alone represented the German people, his opposition to widespread hopes for détente, his aim of putting strong pressure on the Soviet Union and, finally, his hard-line stance against the growing resistance within his own ranks clearly speak for themselves. However, with the claim to sole representation, Adenauer not only stubbornly opposed any establishment of the status quo in questions of policies for Germany, but he also prevented as long as he possibly could all attempts to foster a détente, which would rest on a reciprocal balance of Eastern and Western interests.[5]

II

In advocating his policies for reunification, Adenauer found himself from the very beginning on the defensive, although it might not have seemed so at first. In the run-up to the Geneva Summit of 18–23 July 1955, he managed to get the Western powers set to make Soviet concessions on the German question a prerequisite for movement on disarmament and détente in general.

Khrushchev's demand for the recognition of the GDR was denied; Adenauer was also successful in getting the Western powers to modify the plan for a zone of limited armament and reciprocal inspection of arms production on both sides of the line of demarcation in Germany, which Anthony Eden presented in Geneva. This plan was now to provide for the reduction of troops in Central Europe after the reunification of Germany, and rather than focusing on the Elbe–Werra line it now was to focus on the Oder–Neisse line. This form of the plan aimed at the elimination of Soviet influence in Germany and in the eastern part of Central Europe without any concession in return. Of course, it did not meet with any approval on the Soviet side; accordingly, the Geneva Conference of Foreign Ministers, which debated the modified Eden Plan in late October and early November of 1955, ended in failure.

The worry of being disadvantaged by the looming Soviet–US dialogue – and even more so the fear of not demonstrating enough initiative on the German question to his own public – led Adenauer as early as September 1955 to disavow his claim of sole representation. When in early June of that year, the Soviet leadership invited him to visit Moscow to begin talks on taking up regular diplomatic relations between the Soviet Union and the Federal Republic, he likely foresaw that this would involve efforts to gain indirect recognition of the GDR. In the process of replacing its occupational authority, the Soviet Union had gradually developed diplomatic relations with East Germany; the establishment of diplomatic relations between West Germany and the Soviet Union therefore threatened to become equated with an implicit recognition of East Germany. Adenauer was well aware of this danger and soon came to see the invitation to Moscow as quite a problematic gift.

Nevertheless, in order to avoid accusations of doing nothing for German unity, he did accept the invitation. As he and a large delegation negotiated with the Soviets in Moscow from 9 to 13 September, he also recognized that he could no longer content himself with merely establishing a bilateral negotiating commission as his foreign-policy experts had advised him. Adenauer had already ordered aircraft to be readied for an early departure from Moscow when Bulganin and Khrushchev promised him the release of the last ten thousand German POWs (prisoners of war) condemned to forced labour in Soviet camps. This made an agreement to establish diplomatic relations unavoidable but also tolerable: if he were to persist in his position, he would run the risk of being held responsible for the continued lot of the prisoners, whereas conceding in the question of recognition could be portrayed as the necessary price for a great humanitarian success.

The damage that Adenauer did to his conception by his inconsistency was in fact significant. Hardly had the West German delegation left for Bonn when a delegation from East Berlin arrived in Moscow. The Soviets and East Germans signed a 'Treaty on Relations between the GDR and the USSR' in September 1955. This document declared East Germany to be sovereign (except in regard to controlling Allied travel to West Berlin) and established the continued presence of Soviet troops on East German soil on the basis of an agreement between states. The way was now clear to end the secrecy surrounding the armament of the GDR in the form of barracked units of People's Police: On 18 January 1956, the Volkskammer approved a law on the formation of the 'National People's Army' (NPA). Ten days later, the political committee of the Warsaw Pact states approved the incorporation of the NPA into the armed forces of the alliance. Militarily, the GDR was now fully integrated into the Eastern bloc.

The US ambassador in Moscow, Charles E. Bohlen, was furious. Adenauer's staff members Heinrich von Brentano and Foreign Office State Secretary Walter Hallstein had earnestly warned the chancellor not to take such a step. In order to preserve as much as possible of the Federal Republic's claim that it alone represented all Germans, Wilhelm Grewe, head of the political department of the foreign office, drafted a policy during the return flight from Moscow. In 1956, this became known in the press as the Hallstein Doctrine after Grewe's superior. This policy explained away the Soviet Union's diplomatic relations with the GDR by reference to the Soviets' special status as victorious power and occupier. In contrast, the Federal Republic would not establish diplomatic relations with any other state that recognized the GDR, that is, with the other Eastern bloc states. Any state that sought to establish diplomatic relations with the GDR was threatened with 'serious consequences' up to and including the severing of ties with the Federal Republic.

These principles were strengthened at a conference of ambassadors in late 1955 and were presented to the Bundestag by Foreign Minister Heinrich von Brentano in mid-1956. This Hallstein Doctrine did actually help the Federal Republic keep the GDR isolated from the international community for a long time. It also made the West Germans somewhat vulnerable to extortion and above all prevented them from becoming active in the Eastern European nations and thereby contributing to the loosening of the Eastern bloc. When in October 1957 Josef Tito recognized the GDR as part of his compromise with the Moscow leadership, Adenauer decided to sever relations with the Yugoslav state. Also, the doctrine halted the Federal Republic's cautious approach to Poland after that nation's transition to the reform communist regime of Vladyslav Gomulka in October 1956.

III

Moreover, the Hallstein Doctrine could not prevent the Western powers from becoming less and less eager to prioritize West German desires for unification over a process of de-escalation. In the spring of 1956, the new French government under the Socialist Guy Mollet demanded that disarmament be given priority and, as part of this, that German armaments be drastically restricted. George Kennan produced a memo that built on his earlier neutrality conceptions by calling for the incorporation of a reunified Germany into a belt of neutral states running through Central Europe. Harold Stassen, Eisenhower's representative for disarmament and negotiator on the UN Disarmament Commission, sounded out Moscow on the disarmament question without taking into account the package deal involving disarmament and reunification as established by Dulles and Adenauer. The British government came out in favour of the plan to limit conventional weapons which the Soviets had presented in May of 1955.

In so far as these activities were still aiming at reunification through neutralization, Adenauer was able to mobilize the Western containment syndrome successfully. After severe reproaches from France's allies, Mollet saw himself compelled to reject any intention of neutralizing Germany. The joint document presented to the Disarmament Commission by the three Western powers and Canada in early May 1956 called only for the establishment of a control system in an initial phase, and postponed substantial steps on disarmament until an agreement had been reached on reunification.[6] The theme of disarmament remained on the agenda and even became more urgent when the Soviet Union announced on 14 May that it would unilaterally reduce its conventional forces by 1.2 million men.

On 13 July 1956, the *New York Times* reported that Arthur W. Radford, chairman of the Joint Chiefs of Staff, wanted to reduce US forces in Europe by 800,000 by 1960 as part of implementing the 'New Look' policy. This was all the more disquieting for Western Europeans and especially for the Adenauer government as the signs were multiplying that the two superpowers would come to an understanding at the cost of the European NATO members. When the revolt broke out in Hungary on 23 October, Dulles hurried to assure the world that the USA did not regard Soviet satellite states 'as potential military allies'.[7] When Soviet troops began to put down the revolt on 1 November by very violent means, the Eisenhower administration contented itself with protest resolutions before the UN General Assembly. The US president urged Britain and France not to intervene militarily in the conflict over the Suez Canal, which Egypt's president Nasser had declared national property in July. When the two powers did so anyway after an Israeli attack against Egyptian positions on the Sinai Peninsula on 29 October, the US government was able to push through an armistice on 6 November by means of UN votes as well as currency and trade sanctions. Despite the tragedy in Hungary, the US found itself in agreement with the Soviets, who had on the previous day made at least indirect threats to the two colonial powers that they would use nuclear weapons if the attack on Egypt were not halted.

In light of continued rumours about US plans for disengagement and the visible difficulties the Soviets were having in maintaining control over Eastern Europe, Adenauer in late 1956 and early 1957 considered whether he should take the bull by the horns – by taking the initiative to present a peace plan himself that would combine reunification with the withdrawal of all foreign troops from European nations. In accordance with conceptions developed by his press secretary Felix von Eckardt in the fall of 1956, Adenauer envisioned that US land forces would leave the Federal Republic by 1959 while Soviet troops would pull back from all Eastern European nations; the size of Eastern European armies and the West German Bundeswehr would be limited, and compliance would be monitored by a UN commission. In a second phase, elections to a German national assembly would then be held while the Soviet air force was withdrawn to the USSR and NATO air forces to the Western European periphery. Dissolution of the two alliance systems was not foreseen for the time being, but those nations on the Continent out of which superpower troops had been withdrawn were not to possess nuclear weapons.[8]

Adenauer's plan, which was contained in the draft of a letter to Eisenhower in early January 1957, notably put the West German chancellor on the same track as British opposition leader Hugh Gaitskell, who at the time was publicly calling for withdrawal of all foreign troops from both parts of Germany, Poland, Hungary and Czechoslovakia, and proposing that those areas be put under international oversight. Polish Foreign Minister Adam Rapacki was thinking along the same lines in that he envisioned the arms limits for Central Europe suggested by Eden at the Geneva summit extending to the East Central European states as well. There was even agreement from Ulbricht in so far as his proposal for a 'confederation' of the two German states officially proclaimed by the party in late January 1957 implied the withdrawal of all occupation forces from German soil. Given the fact that this plan confined itself to Germany and also required that Germany withdraw from both alliance systems as a first step, it did stand more clearly in the tradition of the neutralization proposals which Adenauer had always rejected. Nevertheless, there was some common ground for serious negotiations.

On the other side, Adenauer hesitated for some weeks to send the letter to Eisenhower out of concern for the destabilizing effect that support for the withdrawal of US troops could have. And since the Americans took into consideration the danger of losing the confidence of their European allies, the Eisenhower administration limited itself merely to thinning out its forces on the Continent; this meant that there was no longer any necessity to give up the existing structure of NATO. From the end of January 1957 onward, Adenauer instead began to plan for the Bundeswehr to be equipped with miniature battlefield nuclear weapons, a measure which Eisenhower envisioned as compensating for the reduction of US manpower in Europe.

IV

Adenauer saw the equipping of the Bundeswehr with 'tactical' nuclear weapons as a necessity if only because other important NATO allies including Britain, France, the Netherlands and Turkey also wanted them. In his view, there should not be any discrimination that could serve to draw an Eastern bloc attack on to those NATO forces not equipped with nuclear weapons. In the long term, all the larger NATO partners – including the British, French and also the West Germans – sought their own nuclear weapons. These would possibly be placed under the control of a European consortium in order to reduce costs and to escape from one-sided dependency on the US nuclear umbrella. As an optimal goal, he envisioned the power to use German-owned nuclear weapons. Only these could guarantee the Federal Republic's equality of rank within the Western alliance and compensate for the weakening of the US guarantee. He hoped that the European Atomic Energy Community (EURATOM) would help him bypass the renunciation of atomic, biological and chemical weapons agreed upon in the Treaty for Germany.[9]

As long as this goal could not be realized, however, he did not mind having the Bundeswehr equipped with nuclear weapons whose right of deployment rested with the Americans: this at least would avoid a scenario in which the German forces, being the only ones without nuclear arms, would be slaughtered as cannon fodder. And now, he also regarded it as indispensable that US forces in the Federal Republic be equipped with nuclear weapons. Since this obviously was the prerequisite for them to remain, he needed to push through approval in the Federal Republic. According to this view, US nuclear weapons should be supplied 'as low as the division level',[10] at the very least for the sake of treating all NATO troops equally in the framework of the 'New Look', which due to the then-growing nuclear retaliatory potential of the Soviet Union envisaged dispersing the threat of deterrence as well as arming troops for the limited use of such weapons in combat.

Although the public reception of a transition to nuclear armament remained somewhat unclear at first, it caused many worried critics to voice their concerns. A British announcement in early April 1957 that they too would begin nuclear armament forced Adenauer to allow his change of position on nuclear questions to be released to the public. This unleashed a storm of indignation. On 12 April, 18 renowned German physicists including Carl Friedrich von Weizsäcker as well as the Nobel Prize winners Max von Laue, Otto Hahn, Werner Heisenberg and Max Born presented the Göttinger Erklärung, in which they warned of the devastating effect of even so-called 'tactical atomic weapons' and stated that a 'small country like the Federal Republic ... today can best protect itself and is most likely to advance world peace, if it explicitly and voluntarily renounces the possession of nuclear weapons in all forms'.[11] Albert Schweitzer followed with an appeal to abolish all nuclear tests. The Social Democratic opposition was able to initiate a broad movement called 'Kampf dem Atomtod' ('Fight against Nuclear Death') that subordinated reunification to rapid and comprehensive disarmament. Various 'disengagement' plans strengthened this movement: the British opposition leader Hugh Gaitskell pleaded for the withdrawal of all foreign troops from the Federal Republic, the GDR, Poland, Czechoslovakia and Hungary, and called for an international system of control for the Central European region. The Polish Foreign Minister Adam Rapacki suggested grouping the Federal Republic, Poland and Czechoslovakia in a nuclear-free zone while maintaining these countries' memberships in their respective alliances. In the Reith Lectures on British radio in December 1957, Kennan also came to consider the creation of a nuclear-free zone the most urgent goal of Western peace policy.

Adenauer, who had just decided upon strengthening the Western alliance by means of nuclear weapons, could only see the Rapacki Plan as 'a Russian trap'. It was not only that this would imply more or less open recognition of the GDR and would relegate the Federal Republic to a subordinate rank in the defence of the West but also that it would endanger the carefully preserved presence of US troops in West Germany. After the Eisenhower administration had decided upon reducing the manpower of its European divisions by equipping them with nuclear arms, a ban on such weapons as envisioned in the Rapacki Plan could provoke a further withdrawal of US forces. Adenauer warned that implementation of the plan would 'lead to the dissolution of NATO'.[12]

Given that neither Dulles nor the French government wanted to endanger the NATO compromise, the alliance initially stayed with its existing position. At the NATO summit of 16–19 December 1957, it was decided that nuclear warheads would be stockpiled in the European territory of the alliance subject to the approval of the nations directly affected and that the commander of NATO's European forces would have medium-range missiles placed at his disposal. The Federal Republic, the Netherlands, Greece and Turkey all agreed to accept warheads on their territory. Only Italy and Turkey would take medium-range missiles, whereas West Germany refused them due to fears of becoming a high-priority target of a Soviet missile attack and of promoting disengagement from the strategic nuclear umbrella of the USA – an argument that, by the way, was used by the peace movement later during the Euromissile crisis.

Against this plan, the Soviets once again sought to mobilize public opinion. In early January 1958, they proposed a general summit of members of both blocs as well as neutral nations to discuss Rapacki's plan. The West German government received hints that it would be possible to withdraw all foreign troops from Europe in stages. In mid-February, the Polish government supplemented this suggestion to the effect that Czechoslovakia also be brought into this nuclear-free zone. In order to allay Bonn's concerns about recognition of the GDR, they proposed that each state sign a separate treaty of entry into the nuclear-free zone, documents that would not have the character of a multilateral treaty.

This intensified lobbying for the Rapacki Plan was not completely without success. On 31 March 1958, the governments of the US, Britain and France agreed in principle to a summit. Eisenhower perceived that he did not have much more time before the end of his second term to reach an agreement on disarmament. In June 1957, Khrushchev successfully repulsed a putsch attempt by the 'Anti-Party Group' around Molotov and Malenkov.[13] This made it clear to the US president with whom he had to reach such an agreement if he wanted it to be a lasting one.

Even Adenauer no longer offered any opposition to a disarmament summit. Just the opposite was the case – he came out strongly in favour of such a meeting, as Dulles learned with irritation. In order to keep issues involving the German question as open as possible given the spreading pressure for de-escalation, the chancellor raised the possibility of an 'Austrian solution' with Soviet Ambassador Andrei Smirnov on 19 March. How would it sound, he asked, if the Soviet leadership would agree to free elections in the GDR and allow it a neutral status patterned after the Austrian model? Under these circumstances the Federal Republic (FRG) would be able to renounce the demand for reunification and thus would pave the way for a settlement on disarmament.

Adenauer's course change on the disarmament question certainly did not mean that he was now prepared to let himself be won over by attempts for general disengagement in Europe. Rather, he saw it as necessary to demonstrate an openness to negotiation in order to win domestic approval for the nuclear armament of the FRG (against the lure of the Rapacki Plan) by demanding global negotiations on disarmament himself. He hoped that the Soviets would reveal themselves to such a degree that he would be able to push through the stationing of nuclear weapons in the Federal Republic. At the same time, he tried to undermine the Soviet initiative by offering a temporary renunciation of the demand for reunification. Mustering all rhetorical means, he managed to get a Bundestag majority to agree to a resolution calling for equipping the West German Army with the 'most modern weapons' should negotiations on controlled disarmament fail.[14] In great secrecy on 8 April, the defence ministers of the Federal Republic, France and Italy signed an agreement on the joint production of nuclear weapons.

The Soviets were in actuality unable to persuade the Western powers to put negotiations over a peace treaty with Germany on the agenda of the summit. The Soviets sought to increase public pressure on their negotiating partners by breaking off preliminary diplomatic talks and releasing material from them that was to demonstrate the West's lack of will to negotiate. This move proved counterproductive. Once again, it was the Soviet side that did not seem to be ready for genuine disarmament, and the partisans of nuclear armament in the West were able to strengthen their position. The summit project evaporated while preparations for the deployment of the new weapons continued apace. The conditions were set for the second Berlin crisis. As far as Adenauer was concerned, he had won a battle, but this victory over détente paved the way for serious new problems for German policy.

V

The 'politics of strength' was that particular variant of reunification policies bearing the least risk for Western security. It was contradictory inasmuch as it was supposed to maintain the Western status quo while revising that of the East. The outcome was uncertain – first, because it was unclear how to compel the Soviet Union to 'give in' and, second, because the Western powers' engagement for reunification had to decrease to the same degree to which the West Germans made themselves at home within the West. Correspondingly, they ran a major risk of reinforcing the building of blocs, which would be contrary to their intentions. And indeed this is what happened after 1955: in a laborious fight against the recognition of the status quo in the policies on Germany, Adenauer ruined all chances of evading the transition to reciprocal nuclear deterrence. The alternative to accepting the disengagement plans – as the opposition demanded – was, like the alternative of 1952, connected to greater risks for the immediate security of the Federal Republic. By the same token, it opened up the perspective of a real détente to a much greater degree, which would help the people in the Soviet sphere of influence gain more freedom and would make peace in Europe more secure overall. In the final analysis, it is due to the domination of a pessimistic view of the world that this alternative was not given a chance: the majority of the political forces in the Federal Republic once again did not want to acknowledge that the expansion of the Western system presupposed a certain willingness to take risks.

NOTES

1 For the general context, see my history of détente: Wilfried Loth, *Overcoming the Cold War: A History of Détente, 1950–1991*, Basingstoke/New York: Palgrave, 2002.
2 Address at a rally of the Christian Democratic Union (CDU) on 1 March.1952, in Heidelberg, in Bulletin des Presse- und Informationsamtes der Bundesregierung, Nr. 26, 4 March 1952, pp. 251–4, here p. 254.
3 Meeting of the parliamentary party on 18 March 1958, translated from Hans-Peter Schwarz, *Adenauer, Der Staatsmann: 1952–1967*, Stuttgart: Deutsche Verlagsanstalt, 1991, p. 424.
4 Adenauer to Blankenhorn, 14 February 1958, Personal Papers of Globke, citation according to Schwarz, *Adenauer, Der Staatsmann*, p. 143.
5 Historians still have a difficult time making an objective evaluation of Adenauer's reunification policies. From Adenauer's opposition to reunification without Western integration, see Rolf Steininger (most recently), 'Deutsche Frage und Berliner Konferenz 1954', in Wolfgang Venohr (ed.), *Ein Deutschland wird es sein*, Erlangen: Straube, 1990, pp. 35–88, and Josef Foschepoth, 'Westintegration statt Wiedervereinigung: Adenauers Deutschlandpolitik 1949–1955', in Josef Foschepoth (ed.), *Adenauer und die deutsche Frage*, Göttingen: Vandenhoeck & Ruprecht, 1988, pp. 29–69, who draw the inadmissible conclusion that he opposed any form of reunification. From Adenauer's commitment to 'global détente' as a prerequisite for reunification, on the

other hand, see Peter Siebenmorgen, *Gezeitenwechsel: Aufbruch zur Entspannungs-politik*, Bonn: Bouvier, 1990, who constructed an image of a pioneer of Western détente based on balance. Facts and sources that contradict such a stylized interpretation are plainly ignored; and the authors who have reached different conclusions are – and this is especially annoying in such proceedings – accused of a bias out of touch with the sources. Hans-Peter Schwarz more carefully speaks of 'inner contradictions of Adenauer-style détente' (*Adenauer, Der Staatsmann, 1952–1967*, p. 179); however, he abstains from detailing its consequences. For the interpretation presented here, see also Wilfried Loth, 'Adenauers Ort in der deutschen Geschichte', in Wilfried Loth, *Ost–West-Konflikt und Deutsche Frage*, Munich: dtv, 1989, pp. 141–58.

6 See Pierre Guillen, 'Le problème allemand dans les rapports Est–Ouest de 1955 à 1957', in *Relations Internationales*, 71 (Autumn 1992), pp. 299–309, here p. 303.

7 In a speech in Dallas on 27 October 1956, FRUS 1955–57, vol. 25, pp. 317ff.

8 Investigated by Schwarz, *Adenauer, Der Staatsmann*, pp. 321–7.

9 As shown in Schwarz, *Adenauer, Der Staatsmann, II*, pp. 299ff.

10 According to Defence Minister Franz-Josef Strauss at the NATO Council meeting from 11 to 14 December 1956, cited according to Schwarz, *Adenauer, Der Staatsmann*, p. 331.

11 *Archiv der Gegenwart*, 27 (1957), p. 6385.

12 Adenauer to von Brentano, 17 February 1958, citation according to Schwarz, *Adenauer, Der Staatsmann*, p. 383.

13 See Oleg Grinevskij, *Tauwetter: Entspannung, Krisen und neue Eiszeit*, Berlin: Siedler, 1996, pp. 58–73.

14 *Verhandlungen des Deutschen Bundestages*, 1958, vol. 40, p. 1160.

PART II:
EUROPEAN REACTIONS TO THE
BERLIN AND CUBAN CRISES,
1958–62

3

Adenauer and Nuclear Deterrence

Klaus Schwabe

I

The so-called 'Khrushchev Ultimatum' of November 1958 triggering the second Berlin crisis heralded one of the tensest phases of the Cold War in Europe. For the first time, it raised the spectre of a nuclear showdown in which the West no longer enjoyed an unquestioned superiority over the Soviet Union. This Soviet challenge tested first of all the credibility of the policies the Western powers so far had adhered to on the German and the Berlin questions. It tested the Cold War policies of the West by confronting its governments with a number of awkward questions: Were the three former Western occupation powers really resolved to insist on their rights in Berlin? Were they prepared to defend the political independence of the city's population and its ties to the Federal Republic? Were they determined to uphold West Berlin's position as the decisive gap in the Iron Curtain – an opening that permitted East Germans to flee to West Germany – created a continuous brain drain that undermined the GDR and, as the Bonn government claimed, thus preserved the chances of reunification? Were the Western powers resolved to risk a military or even nuclear showdown in order to defend all these various interests?

The military option was a problem which the West German Chancellor Konrad Adenauer had to cope with as well. In reacting to the Berlin crisis, he appears from hindsight to have been an extreme type of cold warrior because he risked nuclear war rather than consider yielding an inch to Soviet pressure, refusing to make any concessions whatsoever to 'Russia' by sticking to what he called a 'policy of strength'. This course alone, he predicted, would ultimately lead to the collapse of the Soviet Union and would bring about realistic chances of German unification. A closer look, however, reveals that Adenauer was not quite the 'iron chancellor' that some admirers (and critics) wanted him to be. To demonstrate this we will cite two examples: the way he reacted to the Berlin crisis and, more generally, the attitude he adopted toward NATO's nuclear strategy in the Berlin crisis.

In fact, the evidence is contradictory. On the one hand, Adenauer did indeed take an unyielding position *vis-à-vis* the Soviet challenge, apparently accepting the ultimate possibility of a military confrontation or even a nuclear one. On the other hand, he disappointed his Western colleagues by trying to avoid having West Germany share the military responsibilities, especially when he refused to consider the ultimate necessity of using nuclear weapons. This ambivalence touched on the fundamental problem as to how reliable Adenauer was as a partner of the West. How can these contradictions be explained? Did Adenauer, the wily 'fox' that he seemed to be, harbour ulterior motives? Was he dominated by considerations of diplomatic tactics or domestic politics? Was he in the last analysis not serious in the defence of his stand on the German and Berlin questions? Did he for some reason distrust the United States, the most powerful protector of the Federal Republic and Berlin?

In order to find an answer to these questions, it will be necessary to proceed in two steps. First, we will need to examine Adenauer's general attitude toward the nuclear defence of the FRG and the West German role in it. Second and more specifically, we will have to analyse his possibly changing positions on the Berlin crisis and his ways to cope with it militarily. In our conclusion, it should then be possible to appraise Adenauer's nuclear policies in context, to see to what extent they were logically consistent – or contradictory – and to pin down the primary political and/or military motives guiding him.

II

In devising West Germany's role in the nuclear defence of the West, Adenauer had to take into account the limitations that had been imposed on the Federal Republic in 1954, that is, at the moment when it had been granted so-called 'sovereignty' and had been permitted to join NATO. One of the prerequisites of West Germany's enhanced international status had been Adenauer's pledge that the Bonn Republic would abstain from acquiring bacteriological, chemical or nuclear weapons. The Federal Republic thus remained totally dependent on the US nuclear umbrella. What seemed acceptable or even desirable in 1954 became questionable in West Germany when in the summer of 1956 news leaked out about the so-called Radford Plan. In order to save money, the Pentagon was reported to be considering withdrawal of a sizeable part of the US forces from Western Europe and, in order to make up for this force reduction and to deter the Soviet Union, to put more emphasis on strategic nuclear weapons, which were to be employed immediately in the case that the Soviets used force against NATO.[1]

This plan for a 'new look' in the USA's strategy created a crisis of confidence in Bonn. Confronted with the Radford Plan, Adenauer and his military advisers feared two situations: either that in reacting to a local conflict with the Red Army – perhaps around Berlin – the United States would resort to immediate 'massive retaliation' and thus engulf all of Europe in a nuclear holocaust, or, as an alternative, that the USA would totally refrain from meeting a Soviet local military challenge, so as not to trigger a Soviet nuclear counterstroke that would hit the USA itself. Moreover, there were concerns that after the projected withdrawal of American troops from Europe, the West would become too weak to meet Soviet aggression. If abandoned by the USA, West Germany and possibly even all of Western Europe would ultimately be lost to the Soviets. The US defensive umbrella extending over Europe seemed, therefore, to have become defective, and still worse, sharing the monopoly of nuclear power with the USSR, the USA might even be tempted to strike a deal with Soviet Russia at the expense of Western Europe and West Germany in particular. This was the most intense fear that haunted the West German chancellor.[2]

Whether such suspicions were actually justified is of no concern in the context of the present chapter. Suffice it to say that Adenauer arrived at three conclusions. First, West Germany was entitled to acquire a measure of influence on Western nuclear planning in light of the new US emphasis on strategic nuclear defence. Second, the new West German army should at the very least be supplied with launching systems (above all fighters) for carrying US-controlled tactical nuclear weapons. If a war broke out it had to be able to resort to such weapons in its own defence, as was the case with the US forces in Germany which had been equipped with nuclear warheads since autumn 1953. Third, and better still, West Germany itself would have to participate in the production of nuclear hardware.[3] One way or another, the Federal Republic, he felt, should become a power that participated in the nuclear defence of NATO. He tried out two methods that promised to attain this aim without violating his pledge of 1954. First, he hoped that Euratom would become a European agency for the development of nuclear weapons. As these hopes foundered, he attempted to reach the same goal by way of Franco-German-Italian cooperation. The Eisenhower administration was kept informed of the new approach and at least did not veto this attempt at a European nuclear defence force, which was to be established within the framework of NATO.[4]

To be sure, the chancellor was by no means trigger-happy. In hindsight, he claimed that it was for moral reasons that he did not find it easy to opt for participation of the Federal Republic in the nuclear defence and deterrence framework of NATO.[5] He also dismissed the idea of a West German national nuclear force as financially and politically unfeasible. In fact, he feared that any European national nuclear force was likely to disrupt NATO.[6] He also refused to envision an actual all-out nuclear war – an option he regarded as irresponsible. But he saw no alternative to a nuclear strategy devised as an instrument of Western Cold War policies – a strategy in which Bonn played a part.[7]

Adenauer aimed at creating a NATO-controlled European nuclear force for the defence of Western Europe for three major compelling reasons. First, he hoped that in conjunction with US nuclear defences, the European nuclear force would attain credibility *vis-à-vis* the Soviet Union and thus would effectively help deter the Soviets. Second, and equally important to Adenauer, there was the expectation that in sharing the control over nuclear weapons with NATO, West Germany would acquire a voice in the fateful decision to use them in the event of a military showdown.[8]

Having attained nuclear 'Mitsprache' – that is, the position to co-determine NATO nuclear strategy – in case of a crisis, Bonn could either try to slow down a possible military escalation or, if a real military confrontation occurred, Bonn could ensure that NATO would convincingly threaten nuclear retaliation and, in the unlikely event that worst came to worst, would remain faithful to the concept of forward defence.[9]

A third ulterior motive that guided Adenauer was his desire to be rid of the status of inequality that the Federal Republic was forced into due to its virtual exclusion from having a say in questions of nuclear defence. The chancellor wanted instead to attain the status of equality for the Federal Republic as a great power enjoying enough weight to commit the other Western powers to his version of a policy of strength, that is, a policy of relying on the military superiority of the West and using it to exercise political pressure to promote German unification. Thus, an equal German voice on questions of nuclear defence was in Adenauer's eyes based on the same rationale as had been West Germany's rearmament. In the final analysis, he saw this as a political rationale. The Bonn Republic needed a state-of-the-art military backbone including a part in Western nuclear defence if it wanted to influence NATO's political strategy on questions of potentially vital importance to the German people – located as it was in the heart of Europe and at the fulcrum of the Cold War.[10]

West Germany's future military status in Europe ranked highest among such questions. It was threatened by plans such as the one proposed by Polish Foreign Minister Adam Rapacki providing for a nuclear-free zone in and military disengagement from Central Europe. If West Germany attained strategic nuclear equality, Adenauer was sure that it could veto all discriminatory schemes of that sort. And, despite his tactical agility, this was the point to which he in fact clung with stubborn determination. He wanted by all means to avoid any form of military discrimination against the Bonn Republic, discrimination that would jeopardize West Germany's international status and smacked of neutralization, if not of Soviet–American hegemony, one that manoeuvred the Federal Republic into a special position within (or outside) NATO and thus endangered Germany's ties with the West, not to mention European and NATO integration and cohesion.[11]

Before any plans defining West Germany's nuclear status had come to fruition, Adenauer's concept suddenly was subjected to a severe test. In November 1958, the Soviet head of state and party chief Nikita Khrushchev unleashed the second Berlin crisis by demanding that within a period of six months all Western troops be withdrawn from West Berlin and that the control of access to the city be taken over by officials of the German Democratic

Republic (GDR), a task for which the Soviets had been responsible up to that time. With this ultimatum, Khrushchev wanted to see the Western occupation powers leave Berlin, the GDR internationally recognized as the second German state, and all West German pretensions for reunification along Western lines thwarted once and for all.

How was the West to respond to this challenge? Was it advisable to enter into negotiations in order to prevent a confrontation with the Soviet Union? Should the West then offer any concessions? If so, what kind? How should the West react if the Soviets did resort to military means in order to implement their new German policy? In such a case, would the West respond politically or militarily, would it ultimately threaten massive nuclear retaliation? And, most importantly to Adenauer, what would be Bonn's role in the impending political or military showdown? For the first time Adenauer was thus confronted with NATO's contingency planning and the meaning of deterrence.

III

As has already been mentioned, Adenauer's reaction to contingency planning had puzzled his Western partners soon after Khrushchev's ultimatum had been issued. On the one hand, the chancellor insisted on a strong Western stand in all political questions raised by the Soviet ultimatum. Ostentatiously he resisted any suggestion of even cosmetic concessions to the Soviets regarding the control of access to West Berlin, not to speak of the continued presence of Western garrisons in the city. Even less negotiable in his eyes were the military status of the Federal Republic and its claim to an equal nuclear status.[12] His unyielding attitude impaired his friendship with US Secretary of State John Foster Dulles and strained his relations first with President Eisenhower and even more so with President Kennedy. It deeply troubled his relations with the British government as well. This was one side of the coin.[13]

The other side was that the chancellor, uninformed about allied contingency planning, evidently hesitated to face the military and nuclear consequences to which his unyielding stand might lead.[14] During the memorable last meeting he had with the fatally ill Dulles on 8 February 1959, Adenauer insisted that, in defending Berlin, the USA avoid the use of nuclear weapons. Seeing US contingency planning challenged, Dulles asked with irritation whether the chancellor wanted to rely solely on conventional weapons and thus to conjure up a devastating defeat for the West, as the Soviet Union enjoyed a clear superiority over NATO in conventional forces. Adenauer thereupon retreated somewhat by stating that he had only been arguing against the use of nuclear weapons in the event that the GDR would make difficulties on its own.[15] Patently disappointed that the German leader did not favour a strong contingency policy, Dulles then explained the USA's tactics of a phased response which would lead to a nuclear strike only as a last resort – if the Soviets remained unimpressed by the West's conventional military countermeasures, necessitating a strike which would force the Soviets finally to retreat. Dulles urged Adenauer to acknowledge the need for the West to show a unity of purpose including, if worse came to worst, the willingness to share the risk of an all-out conventional or even nuclear war.

The Chancellor endorsed the process delineated by Dulles including the ultimate risk of war but still insisted somewhat evasively that such a war over access to Berlin would not be understood by the public of any of the major NATO members, including the USA, and that the unity of the three Western powers was more important than nuclear weapons.[16] In other words, he advocated something similar to what was later called 'flexible response', preferring political to military means and making the need for a final nuclear strike less likely. In order to defuse an acute crisis over Berlin, he tentatively proposed an interim solution for the former German capital. This would have to be conditional on the USSR's abandoning its ultimatum deadline and thus helping avert the exodus of the West Berliners acting under Soviet pressure.[17]

Despite Adenauer's assurances, Dulles feared a head-on collision among the Western powers over the Berlin crisis.[18] Doubts as to the German government's real intentions persisted: in August 1959, Adenauer reiterated to Eisenhower that the German problems were not ones over which a nuclear war could or should be fought.[19] Referring to what had not been so clear a year before, when Adenauer had had that memorable discussion with Dulles, the Chancellor did assure Eisenhower in March 1960 that the Federal Republic was prepared to do 'all that was necessary' in order to resist Soviet force.[20] On the face of it, this implied the promise to support US contingency planning up to the point when a nuclear war had to be risked. But this promise was not explicit, and apparently this had been intentional because, a week before his meeting with the president, Adenauer confided to his party's parliamentary floor leader Heinrich Krone that the US ambassador had sounded him out as to how far the German government was prepared to go in the military defence of Berlin, 'Including the use of nuclear weapons'. Krone noted, 'the chancellor recognizes that this question was a ruse. If he answered that he was not willing to consider the ultimate possibility, the road would be open to a compromise over Berlin. If he answered in the affirmative, one day the public would regard him as the warmonger responsible for the outbreak of a Third World War. Whatever he would decide to do, some indiscretion was sure to make it public.'[21] Adenauer was aware of the balancing act he was forced to engage in, combining rigidity in maintaining the Bonn political position in the Berlin controversy with timidity in considering the need to use nuclear weapons in defending that position militarily. He had to avoid the impression that he was wavering in his support of US contingency planning and still upholding his reservations against a military policy he would be unable to control in an emergency.

To the Americans, Adenauer's deliberate ambivalence must have seemed all the more puzzling as he continued to press for the supply of the West German army with launching facilities for tactical nuclear weapons and generally for a German part in NATO nuclear strategy and, if necessary, nuclear warfare. In a meeting with the US Ambassador Dowling in August 1960 at the end of the Eisenhower administration, he explained what he saw as the serious problem: NATO members depended exclusively on the US president's decision to use nuclear weapons, although every European states-man had a particular responsibility to his own people.[22] Was Adenauer at that point doubting, at least by implication, the US president's resolution to resort to the ultimate weapon? But had he not himself expressed his uneasiness on the matter? Regardless of the answer, it was the case that when in September 1960 the NATO commander General Norstad proposed a NATO-directed multinational nuclear force equipped with medium-range submarine-based ballistic missiles – in other words, the forerunner of the later Multilateral Nuclear Force (MLF) – the chancellor grasped at this opportunity as a means of securing German participation in NATO nuclear strategy.[23]

IV

Such hopes were dashed when John F. Kennedy became president and dis-carded the project of an MLF at least for the time being. Gradually, the new administration turned toward an alternative to Eisenhower's strategic doctrine of massive retaliation. This was the doctrine of flexible response. This new strategic concept, for the first time outlined in November 1960 by General Norstad and officially promulgated in December 1961,[24] had two purposes – first, to upgrade conventional forces at the expense of nuclear ones in order to enable the West to fend off a local Soviet attack by conventional means without being forced to resort to an immediate nuclear counterstrike. Second, and more importantly, it aimed at preserving the Anglo-American nuclear monopoly and avoiding the creation of other national nuclear forces, especially in France and, of course, in Germany as well.[25] At first glance, one might expect that Adenauer would welcome this new doctrine, to which he himself had originally subscribed (as he had demonstrated by expressing misgivings about Eisenhower's concept of 'massive retaliation') and for which he had opted by implication in his above-mentioned discussions of nuclear contingency planning.

This was not the case. To him, the new doctrine proved what he had already feared during the Eisenhower period, that is, that the USA would ultimately retaliate with nuclear weapons only if the USA's own existence were imperilled and would not dare to use nuclear weapons at all to defend the European continent and certainly not to endorse West German claims regarding German unification. He believed that flexible response meant that the West would disclose publicly and in advance that it would expose itself to the superior conventional power of the Red Army. In case of war, he predicted, this Soviet superiority would paralyse every effort to make a sustained conventional defence of Western Europe – unless the USSR felt encouraged to carry out the first nuclear strike, making any plans for a conventional defence of Berlin illusory. In the final analysis, he feared that the West would altogether forgo the use of nuclear weapons in order to meet a Soviet military challenge such as blocking the access roads to West Berlin. In that case, the Western alliance had no other choice but to give up the city.[26] This is why he called the new doctrine 'childish'.[27] His concerns were deepened as the new president repeatedly underlined the need for unilateral US control of nuclear warheads and thus seemed even to question the agreement to provide such weapons to German troops in the event of hostilities with the Soviets.[28]

The beginnings of this divergence over strategy had a practical implication, inasmuch as the new administration for the first time demanded that the FRG commit German troops to participate in conventional military countermeasures by the three Western powers in case of Soviet interferences with the status of West Berlin. The question came up during Adenauer's first meeting with President Kennedy on 13 April 1961. The chancellor responded to this new situation by repeating what he had said to Dulles two years before, that is, that Germany was prepared 'to do everything that appeared necessary in the interest of this joint cause'. He refused, however, to commit German forces to initial military steps taken by the Western allies, as West Germany's legal position in Berlin, which technically was still an Allied occupied territory, had to be clarified beforehand. His ambassador added that German participation in any 'probing action' against the Soviets would trigger an East German uprising and thus aggravate the situation. It was only a few weeks before the erection of the Wall that Adenauer had expressed doubts as to whether the technical questions connected with the Berlin problem (border control and so forth) would suffice to make it clear to the US people that a nuclear war had to be risked. No wonder that these rather evasive statements created not a little 'puzzlement' on the US side.[29]

This was the second crisis of confidence afflicting Adenauer's attitude toward the USA in reaction to the new US strategy. The minimum US concession he demanded was the admission of German deputies to Allied contingency planning.[30] The building of the Berlin Wall in August 1961, preceded as it was by Kennedy's restrictive interpretation of US vital interests solely to *West* Berlin, made this latent crisis public. Carefully nurtured by de Gaulle, Adenauer's own doubts as to the reliability of the USA's nuclear umbrella for Germany and Berlin grew and gave force to his repeated demands for a NATO nuclear 'fire brigade', one not exclusively US controlled. It would need to be able to hit the Soviet homeland and, as Adenauer implied, even be able to launch the first nuclear attack without the US president's explicit order in case the latter was disabled or beyond reach at the critical moment of a Soviet attack.[31]

Relations between the young president and the elder statesman henceforth were overshadowed by mutual suspicions. This despite the fact that on 21 July 1961 the Federal Republic was admitted to the ultra-secret discussions dealing with US contingency planning and despite the fact that NATO commander Norstad assured Adenauer four weeks after the building of the Berlin Wall that the military defence of the city's access to West Germany would not necessarily be limited to conventional means.[32] Apparently, at least in part, in reaction to these concessions and, of course, to the crisis following the building of the Berlin Wall, the German ambassador to the USA, Wilhelm Grewe, 'reaffirmed' in October 1961 that the Federal Republic had formally abandoned all previous reservations and that it was prepared 'to go to war' to defend the freedom of Berlin.[33] Still, the ambassador demanded that two conditions had to be met as a prerequisite. First, that it should be agreed that conventional military countermeasures against a Soviet attack should be followed by a 'pre-emptive nuclear strike' if necessary, and that, in the case of war, the West German army should be supplied with nuclear warheads, which in peacetime were to be kept in US custody.[34] His remarks demonstrated that even then the dispute about the strategy of flexible response had by no means subsided. Adenauer showed this during his visit to Washington in November 1961 and afterwards by pointing out that the only real element of Western strategic superiority *vis-à-vis* the Soviets was nuclear weapons and that those weapons, therefore, had to be used at the very beginning of a war with the Soviet Union.[35] What he advocated was thus a kind of 'mitigated' massive retaliation.[36]

At the same time, Adenauer hectored the Kennedy administration *ad nauseam* about the reliability of the USA's military guarantee to defend the freedom of West Berlin.[37] To the chancellor, this guarantee was only valid if two conditions were met: first, that the West committed itself to a 'preventive nuclear strike' in case hostilities broke out with the Soviets – a strike that would have to hit the Russian homeland – and,[38] second, that the Soviets be aware of that commitment.[39]

In light of these conditions, he regarded talk about a flexible response as liable to undercut the efforts aimed at intimidating and deterring the Soviet leadership.[40] The chancellor himself saw to it that Moscow got the message about the Western resolution to use nuclear weapons if the Soviets intervened militarily against West Berlin.[41]

Once again, he was not trigger-happy. He repeatedly urged that as a first step a blockade be implemented rather than more severe military measures if the Soviets interrupted the traffic between West Berlin and the Federal Republic. A blockade, he explained, would do considerable damage to the Soviet Union and would provide a cooling off period; it would make the Soviets think twice about the dangers of a nuclear war; and, unlike actual hostilities, it could be called off at will and could possibly initiate negotiations about an interim solution for Berlin, which Adenauer had considered before.[42] A blockade would allow the West to avoid initiating an unpopular nuclear war over the complicated issue of Allied rights in West Berlin.[43] Briefly put, Adenauer believed that as a reaction to suspension of traffic to West Berlin by the Soviets or the threat of a Soviet military attack, a blockade combined with the threat of immediate nuclear retaliation would effectively deter the Soviets and thus preserve peace.[44]

The Kennedy administration did not accept this reasoning. It rightly surmised that Adenauer had lent no more than a qualified endorsement to Western contingency planning, and its spokesmen told the president that the German pleadings for a blockade amounted to an attempt to replace nuclear deterrence by economic measures. This demand, they stressed, seemed to reveal a lack of resolution on the German side to help defend the West and to assume responsibility for an ultimate nuclear counterstrike. Adenauer's politically motivated hesitance to increase West Germany's combat-ready conventional forces in the wake of the building of the Wall heightened such suspicions.[45] He experienced difficulties in trying to dispel those suspicions even more when he refused to consider any automatic military move to launch a nuclear war, but insisted that the civil governments, including his own, make the ultimate decision to use nuclear weapons. On this vital question of ultimate national control over the use of nuclear weapons in a military crisis, he adopted the same view that Great Britain and France had had all along.[46]

Adenauer's reticence to commit West Germany fully to the new US strategy was rooted in a basic suspicion as to the new administration's motives: why, he asked, did it heighten the threshold that demanded resort to nuclear instead of conventional weapons? Could one be sure that the US president would always be available to order the use of nuclear weapons in an emergency when hours counted?[47] Why did the Americans insist on an increase in West Germany's conventional forces but hesitate to commit tactical nuclear weapons to be turned over to the Germans in a critical military situation following a Soviet attack? Why had they so long postponed a decision to deploy medium-range nuclear missiles on the European continent? In the months between the building of the Wall and the Cuban missile crisis, Adenauer associated these US ambivalences with the pressure the Kennedy administration continued to exercise to elicit German support for various propositions for an interim solution of the Berlin problem – concessions that in Adenauer's eyes jeopardized the freedom of West Berlin and would demoralize the East German population. The anxious questions arose: was the USA ready to reach an understanding with the Soviet Union at the expense of Germany or was it truly committed to the pledge it had given in the Paris treaty of 1954 to lend full support to German unification?[48]

It was only in the autumn of 1962, after the Kennedy administration had demonstrated a tough stand against the Soviet Union during the Cuban missile crisis and simultaneously had deferred all efforts to approach the Soviet Union for a solution of the Berlin problem, that the chancellor dropped some of his distrust and assured Kennedy that German troops would be the first to defend Berlin. At the same time and despite Kennedy's grave fears that crossing the nuclear threshold even by using only tactical nuclear devices meant an all-out nuclear war, Adenauer insisted that tactical nuclear weapons would have to be employed at the outset of hostilities if there was to be a chance of prevailing against a Soviet onslaught.[49] There thus remained a clear divergence as to the military tactics to be chosen in an emergency.

The fundamental issue that underlay these controversies over contingency planning was obviously the question of where the final authority to decide on nuclear war would rest. The Nassau Agreement concluded between Great Britain and the USA on 21 December 1962 assigned British submarine-based nuclear warheads to NATO unless a supreme national interest was at stake – in other words, the ultimate British decision to participate in the operations of the NATO nuclear force was left to the British government. To Adenauer, this arrangement, and an expected similar agreement with France, discriminated against the Germans, to whom Kennedy had failed to offer a similar opportunity. A three-nation 'club' of nuclear powers seemed to have been established, from which West Germany had been excluded. Apparently in deference to Soviet wishes, Kennedy had relegated the FRG to the position of a third-rate power.[50]

As French President de Gaulle refused to participate in the US-sponsored nuclear NATO force and at the same time seemed to draw the Federal Republic away from NATO, the US government in mid-January 1963 formally proposed a NATO-controlled, sea-based Multilateral Nuclear Force (MLF) to Adenauer. This was a way to solve the problem of multinational control of nuclear strategy, even though ultimate control over the decision to use nuclear weapons would remain with the US president. Despite some doubts as to the MLF's capability of immediately responding to a Soviet nuclear attack from its positions at sea, Adenauer promised German participation in principle, as the MLF guaranteed that the US would decide to make use of nuclear weapons 'at the correct moment from the right place'. He did not fail, however, to point to the provision of the Nassau Agreement that reserved ultimate control of the British nuclear arsenal to Britain and thus undermined the principle of ultimate US control of the future MLF.[51] In general, the US MLF proposal did not fully lay to rest the controversy about the role of conventional versus nuclear weapons in a military emergency.

V

This is not the occasion to assess the validity of the arguments put forward by Adenauer in discussing the pros and cons of NATO nuclear deterrence.

Instead, it is appropriate to ask what ultimate rationale, what ultimate motivation underlay Adenauer's shifting and seemingly contradictory positions on that question. Where is it possible to make out a degree of consistency in the chancellor's equivocations? To repeat with some simplification what we stated earlier, at a time when the USA espoused the doctrine of massive retaliation, the chancellor came out for what in effect was a strategy of a flexible response. When under Kennedy, the USA came around to this very doctrine, Adenauer insisted on massive retaliation. In both cases, he took a rigid stand on the German question – an attitude which, much to the dismay of the British and US governments, seemed to make any arrangement with the Soviets less likely and thus increased the danger of a military confrontation.

There are different answers to these questions.[52] Wilhelm Grewe, Adenauer's own ambassador in Washington, criticized his boss for listening too much to his military advisers.[53] Furthermore, there can be no doubt that Adenauer himself harboured ambivalent feelings about so technical and at the same time so deadly an issue. There was certainly a tactical aspect that explains his shifting attitudes. It appears that he was more inclined to consider both the employment of West German troops in a military showdown over Berlin as well as to accept the ultimate use of nuclear weapons in a worst-case scenario once the Germans had been admitted to the NATO group responsible for contingency plans in the summer of 1961. The building of the Berlin Wall and the seemingly weak Western reaction to it also contributed to convincing him of the need for an effective Western nuclear deterrence strategy.[54] To some US critics, Kennedy included, Adenauer's ulterior motives amounted simply to bluffing in order to avoid being blamed in Germany for concessions the West might have to offer regarding Berlin during a severe crisis.[55] There is more than a grain of truth in this assertion, as Adenauer himself at least at one point admitted that some bluffing was inevitable in the Berlin confrontation.[56]

Still, these tactical aspects do not seem to reach to the real core of his political–military strategic thinking. There can be no doubt that he wanted by all means to avoid a nuclear war, not least because he was not sure whether it could be won by the West.[57] He also loathed a war which once more would originate in Germany.[58] Adenauer did not want to rush to the use of nuclear weapons if West Berlin alone was acutely threatened by the Soviets. Instead, as we have seen, he wanted to defuse any crisis over Berlin by resorting to less belligerent means such as a blockade.[59]

In his eyes, however, the most effective way to prevent a supreme crisis and a nuclear conflagration over Berlin consisted in a credible form of deterrence accompanied by an ultimate degree of flexibility in negotiations with the Soviets.[60] Such credibility was assured only if the Soviets were convinced of the Western resolution to resort to nuclear warfare rather than surrendering to Soviet military pressure. To Adenauer, this was the tactical essential of the Western contingency policy. As he saw it, public discussions regarding a nuclear threshold to be observed in an extremely critical situation undermined the credibility of Western deterrence. Still, nuclear credibility did not exclude the possibility of concessions in an extreme emergency. According to Adenauer, they would encompass the acceptance by Germany of the Oder–Neisse border, and acquiescence in a continued division of Germany, provided political freedom was granted to the GDR population; agreement on an interim solution for all of Berlin that would include a preliminary recognition of the GDR, a demilitarization of the city and an independent status granting democratic freedoms to all Berliners and guaranteed by the United Nations (the so-called Globke Plan of January 1959); and also discussions on a globally controlled disarmament.[61] Such sacrifices, however, would not encompass concessions at the expense of what Adenauer regarded as fundamental West German interests: the establishment of any regime of regional disarmament or regional détente in Central Europe leading to a special military status for the Federal Republic within NATO or its neutralization or to any permanent renunciation by West Germany of nuclear weapons to be employed within the framework of NATO. The essential work of Western contingency policy was, in Adenauer's view, the avoidance of such schemes.[62]

Under Cold War conditions, the doctrines of massive retaliation as well as flexible response, the latter more than the former, were both open to misinterpretation and misuse as Adenauer saw it. Both could undermine the credibility of Western deterrence. Both could lead to a renunciation of the USA's key responsibility for the nuclear defence of Europe – massive retaliation by exclusively relying on a kind of suicidal nuclear warfare, flexible response by substituting conventional warfare for nuclear deterrence. The results could be a Soviet attack, defeat of the West, and the USA's withdrawal from Europe.

In his politico-military thinking, Adenauer thus clearly revealed some of his unchanging priorities. These revealed a certain rationale behind his seemingly contradictory positions in reacting to the Berlin crisis and to contingency planning. Not least in order to win the German public over for his security policy, the chancellor insisted on a firm Western position backed up by a credible deterrence posture *vis-à-vis* the Soviet Union in all controversial issues arising from the Berlin crisis. When the chips were down, however, he was prepared for some concessions but not any on the military or international status of the Federal Republic within NATO. When that issue came up, he was determined to dig in his heels, still banking on deterrence but ultimately risking war, even nuclear war if it were unavoidable.[63] The chancellor not only wanted to deter the Soviets, he also wanted to deter the West from any plans that froze the Federal Republic into the discriminated position of a third-rank power. Such plans would create the impression that the USA as the military protector of West Germany was no longer needed and therefore could afford to withdraw from Europe. This is why he rejected all projects for a 'disengagement' from Central Europe or for preventing nuclear proliferation in exchange for Soviet concessions on Berlin.[64]

Non-discrimination was in part a military question for him – German soldiers should be as well armed as the troops of West Germany's allies.[65] But the whole discussion about contingencies appeared to him to involve the issue of civil control over the military, to involve above all a political question of supreme importance. It consisted of four essentials:

- the security-related standing of the Federal Republic,
- its fundamental equality as a NATO ally,
- its participation in nuclear contingency planning and, if the contingency actually occurred,
- German consent to the use of nuclear weapons in Germany.

In other words, West Germany's unquestioned integration into NATO as an equal partner and a great power on the one hand and the unquestioned cohesion of the Western alliance on the other were more important to the chancellor than the short-term Berlin problem or the long-term issue of German unification.[66]

There remains a big question mark: implicitly, Adenauer took it for granted that this justification for committing NATO to nuclear deterrence would be more convincing to the public in the West as a whole and in West Germany in particular than the defence of the specifically German interests in Berlin. It remains highly doubtful whether this analysis was correct.

NOTES

1 Norbert Wiggershaus, 'Adenauer und die amerikanische Sicherheitspolitik in Europa', in Klaus Schwabe (ed.), *Adenauer und die USA* (Rhöndorfer Gespräche, vol. 14), Bonn: Bouvier, 1994, pp. 26ff. Fearing damaging effects on Adenauer's prestige, Eisenhower actually hesitated to implement the 'new look' (Saki Dockrill, *Eisenhower's New-Look National Security Policy, 1953–1961*, Houndmills: Macmillan, 1996, pp. 203f.). I gratefully acknowledge the kind help Dr Michael Krekel and Dr Hans Peter Mensing extended to me during my work with the Adenauer Papers, located at the Stiftung Bundeskanzler-Adenauer-Haus (hereafter cited as NL Adenauer).
2 Marc Trachtenberg, *A Constructed Peace: The Making of the European Settlement 1945–1963*, Princeton, NJ: Princeton University Press, 1999, p. 235; Hans-Peter Schwarz, 'Adenauer und die Kernwaffen', *Vierteljahrshefte für Zeitgeschichte*, 37 (1989), 580; Johannes Steinhoff and Reiner Pommerin, *Strategiewechsel: Bundesrepublik und Nuklearstrategie in der Ära Adenauer–Kennedy*, Baden-Baden: Nomos Verlag, 1992, p. 60.
3 Wiggershaus, 'Adenauer und die amerikanische Sicherheitspolitik in Europa', p. 29; Steinhoff and Pommerin, *Strategiewechsel*, p. 22. Adenauer and his military advisers regarded an effective defence against a Soviet attack as impossible as long as there existed parts of the defensive line that had no access to tactical nuclear weapons and others that did. German troops then would be no more than 'cannon fodder' (Hans-Peter Schwarz, *Adenauer: Der Staatsmann, 1952–1967*, Stuttgart: Deutsche Verlagsanstalt, 1991, p. 331). As early as December 1954, NATO strategic planning

included the introduction of nuclear weapons and West German participation in Western defence (NATO document MC 48). In December 1957, NATO had agreed that in a military emergency, West Germany would have to gain access to nuclear war heads under a 'two keys system' (Kori N. Schake, 'NATO-Strategie und deutsch-amerikanisches Verhältnis', in Detlef Junker (ed.), *Die USA und Deutschland im Zeitalter des Kalten Krieges, vol. I, 1945–1968*, Stuttgart: Deutsche Verlagsanstalt, 2001, p. 368; Hanns Jürgen Küsters, *Adenauers Deutschland- und Nuklearpolitik in der Berlin-Krise 1958–1962*, in Guido Müller (ed.), *Deutschland und der Westen: Festschrift für Klaus Schwabe zum 65. Geburtstag*, HMRG Beihefte, vol. 29, Stuttgart: Steiner Verlag, 1998, p. 277).

4 Georges-Henri Soutou, *L'alliance incertaine: Les rapports politico-stratégiques franco-allemands, 1954–1996*, Paris: Fayard, 1996, pp. 83ff., 93, 102ff.

5 Konrad Adenauer, *Erinnerungen 1955–1959*, Frankfurt: Fischer, 1969, pp. 299ff., 302.

6 Adenauer, *Erinnerungen 1955–1959*, pp. 294, 297; Schwarz, 'Adenauer und die Kernwaffen', p. 579; Wolfgang Krieger, 'Sicherheit durch Abschreckung: Die deutsch–amerikanischen Sicherheitsbeziehungen 1945–1968', in Junker (ed.), *Die USA und Deutschland, vol. I*, p. 298; Hans Peter Mensing (ed.), *Adenauer Teegespräche 1961–1963* (Adenauer Rhöndorfer Ausgabe, vol. 8), Berlin: Siedler Verlag, 1992, p. 215.

7 Adenauer, *Erinnerungen 1955–1959*, p. 299; Schwarz, 'Adenauer und die Kernwaffen', pp. 302, 580.

8 Aufzeichnung 6 August 1960, Conversation Adenauer–Dowling, NL Adenauer III, 58. (Whenever possible the 'Aufzeichnungen' are dated according to the day of the copy's completion, not according to the date of the conversation; in the few cases where the date of the copy's completion is missing, the date of the conversation follows the identification of the speakers.) Aufzeichnung, date missing, Conversation Adenauer–Stikker, of 27 June 1961, NL Adenauer III, 87. In December 1957, NATO had adopted a NATO-controlled pool system for the stationing of nuclear warheads without defining the role NATO members were to play in developing the strategic plans for the use of them (Krieger, 'Sicherheit durch Abschreckung', p. 299).

9 Aufzeichnung, 10 October 1961, Conversation Adenauer–Javits, Nachl. Adenauer III, 60; Küsters, 'Adenauers Deutschland- und Nuklearpolitik', p. 277.

10 Küsters, 'Adenauers Deutschland- und Nuklearpolitik', p. 277; Schwarz, *Adenauer*, p. 330.

11 Aufzeichnung, 26 March 1959, Conversation Adenauer–Bruce, NL Adenauer III, 88; Wiggershaus, 'Adenauer und die amerikanische Sicherheitspolitik in Europa', pp. 34ff.; Schwarz, *Adenauer*, p. 383.

12 Aufzeichnung, 15 August 1961, Conversation Adenauer–Rusk, NL Adenauer III, 88; Aufzeichnung 12 October 1961, Conversation Adenauer–Dowling, NL Adenauer III, 60; Küsters, 'Adenauers Deutschland- und Nuklearpolitik', p. 272; Adenauer saw to it that a reference to an interim solution of the Berlin question was deleted from the copy of the memorandum, which reproduced his conversation with John F. Dulles on 8 February 1959, and was transmitted to the US government (Aufzeichnung, 11 February 1959, Conversation Adenauer–Dulles of 8 February 1959, NL Adenauer III, 88).

13 Christian Bremen, *Die Eisenhower-Administration und die zweite Berlin-Krise 1958–1961*, Berlin: de Gruyter, 1998, pp. 157ff.

14 In this context, one of his biographers – somewhat overstating his case – refers to Adenauer's 'nuclear pacifism' (Henning Köhler, *Adenauer: Eine politische Biographie*, Frankfurt: Propyläen, 1994, p. 1060).

15 Aufzeichnung, 11 February 1959, Conversation Adenauer–Dulles of 8 February 1959, 10.30, NL Adenauer III, 88. The US version of this conversation, according to which Adenauer had said that 'his nuclear point was addressed to the avoidance of using

non-conventional weapons against the GDR alone', seems to have been based on a misunderstanding (Memorandum of Conversation, 8 February 1959, in *Foreign Relations of the United States* (FRUS) 1958–1960, vol. 8: Berlin Crisis, Washington: US Government Printing Office, 1993, p. 346).

16 Küsters, 'Adenauers Deutschland- und Nuklearpolitik', pp. 271f., 274; Memorandum of Conversation, 8 February 1959, in FRUS 1958–1960, vol. 8, pp. 347 (this remark is missing in the German record).

17 Aufzeichnung, 11 February 1959, Conversation Adenauer–Dulles of 8 February 1959, 10.30, NL Adenauer III, 88. Compare Memorandum of Conversation, 8 February 1959, in FRUS 1958–1960, vol. 8, pp. 345ff.

18 Memorandum of Conversation between President Eisenhower and Secretary of State Dulles, 9 February 1959, in FRUS 1958–1960, vol. 8, p. 355.

19 Memorandum of Conversation, 27 August 1959, in FRUS 1958–1960, vol. 9, p. 19.

20 Aufzeichnung, date missing, Conversation Adenauer–Eisenhower of 15 March 1960, NL Adenauer III, 25. See also the English version in FRUS 1958–1960, vol. 9, p. 660ff.

21 Schwarz, *Adenauer*, pp. 556f. The US record of the meeting to which Adenauer was referring did not explicitly raise the question of the inclusion of nuclear weapons in the defence of Berlin, Adenauer himself pointing to the assurances he had given Dulles in February 1959, as he did four days afterwards in his conversation with Eisenhower (Dowling to Herter, 11 March 1959, FRUS 1958–1960, vol. 9, p. 216). See also Aufzeichnung 26 March 1959, Conversation Adenauer–Bruce, 26 March 1959, NL Adenauer III, 88.

22 Küsters, 'Adenauers Deutschland- und Nuklearpolitik', pp. 277ff.; Aufzeichnung, 6 August 1960, Conversation Adenauer–Dowling, NL Adenauer III, 58.

23 Küsters, 'Adenauers Deutschland- und Nuklearpolitik', pp. 280f.; Wiggershaus, 'Adenauer und die amerikanische Sicherheitspolitik in Europa', p. 39.

24 Steinhoff and Pommerin, *Strategiewechsel*, pp. 62ff.

25 Trachtenberg, *A Constructed Peace*, pp. 284ff.

26 Aufzeichnung, 8 September 1961, Conversation Adenauer–Norstad, NL Adenauer III, 89 I; Aufzeichnung, 20 February 1962, Conversation Adenauer–Kissinger, NL Adenauer III, 60; Memorandum of Conversation Adenauer–Kennedy, 20 November 1961, FRUS 1961–1963, vol. 14, p. 595 footnote. In background information, Adenauer even informed the press about his concerns: Mensing (ed.), *Adenauer Teegespräche 1961–1963*, p. 314; Steinhoff and Pommerin, *Strategiewechsel*, pp. 91ff. Franz-Josef Strauss, Adenauer's minister of defence, was aware that the Federal Republic had always basically tended towards the doctrine of flexible response. He regarded it, however, as harmful to the Western interest in deterrence to discuss such issues in public (Wilhelm Grewe, *Rückblenden 1976–1951*, Frankfurt: Propyläen, 1979, p. 481).

27 Aufzeichnung, 5 January 1962, Conversation Adenauer–McCloy, NL Adenauer III, 89 – 'Träumereien': Aufzeichnung 20 February 1962, Conversation Adenauer–Kissinger, NL Adenauer III, 60.

28 Köhler, *Adenauer*, pp. 1138f.

29 Memorandum of Conversation, W. Grewe–Dean Rusk–M. Hillenbrand, 15 April 1961, FRUS 1961–1963, vol. 14, Washington 1993, pp. 51ff., 54; Memorandum of Conversation Kennedy–Adenauer, 13 April 1961, FRUS 1961–1963, vol. 14, pp. 45ff.; Aufzeichnung, no date, Conversation Adenauer–Stikker, 27 June 1961, NL Adenauer III, 87; also Köhler, *Adenauer*, p. 1096; Grewe, *Rückblenden*, p. 465; Rolf Steininger, *Der Mauerbau: Die Westmächte und Adenauer in der Berlinkrise 1958–1963*, Munich: Olzog, 2001, pp. 186f.

30 Steinhoff and Pommerin, *Strategiewechsel*, pp. 88f.; Schwarz, *Adenauer 1952–1967*, p. 637.

31 Aufzeichnung, date missing, Conversation Adenauer–Stikker of 27 June 1961, NL

Adenauer III, 87; Conversation Adenauer–Kennedy, 20 November 1961, FRUS 1961–1963, vol. 14, pp. 617f.; Aufzeichnung, 20 February 1962, Conversation Adenauer–Kissinger, NL Adenauer III, 60. Küsters, 'Adenauers Deutschland- und Nuklearpolitik', p. 285; Steininger, *Mauerbau*, p. 301. See note 44.

32 Küsters, 'Adenauers Deutschland- und Nuklearpolitik', p. 284.

33 Schwarz, *Adenauer 1952–1967*, p. 706; Küsters, 'Adenauers Deutschland- und Nuklearpolitik', p. 285; Steininger, *Mauerbau*, p. 300.

34 Memorandum of Conversation, Grewe–Kennedy, 24 October 1961, FRUS 1961–1963, vol. 14, p. 527; Grewe, *Rückblenden*, p. 509.

35 Memorandum of Conversation Adenauer–Kennedy, 20 November 1961, FRUS 1961–1963, vol. 14, p. 595, fn; German version: Aufzeichnung, 20 November 1961, Conversation Adenauer–Kennedy, NL Adenauer III, 89. In this talk Adenauer somewhat enigmatically told Kennedy that the US President would need 'strong nerves' to 'push the atomic button' once the Red Army had occupied West German cities like Frankfurt or Hamburg. Did Adenauer have the 'Live Oak' contingency plan in his mind when he endorsed the strategy of a first strike which was to intimidate the USSR to such an extent that the Soviets would renounce the idea of a nuclear war? (Steininger, *Mauerbau*, p. 223). See also Aufzeichnung, 9 January 1962, Adenauer–Macmillan, NL Adenauer III, 89, and note 44.

36 Aufzeichnung, 19 November 1962, Conversation Adenauer–Kennedy, NL Adenauer III, 61; Aufzeichnung, 4 January 1961, Conversation Adenauer–McCloy, NL Adenauer III, 89; Aufzeichnung, 26 February 1962, Conversation Adenauer–Kennedy, NL Adenauer, III, 89.

37 For example, Aufzeichnung, 26 February 1962, Conversation Adenauer–Kennedy, NL Adenauer III, 89.

38 Aufzeichnung, 5 January 1962, Conversation Adenauer–McCloy, NL Adenauer III, 89.

39 Memorandum of Conversation Grewe–Kennedy, 24 October 1961, FRUS 1961–1963, vol. 14, p. 527, Aufzeichnung, date missing, Conversation Adenauer–Strauss–Stikker of 27 June 1961, NL Adenauer III, 87; Aufzeichnung, Conversation Adenauer–Nitze of 13 April 1962, NL Adenauer III, 60.

40 Aufzeichnung, date missing, Conversation Adenauer–Strauss–Stikker of 27 June 1961, NL Adenauer III, 87; Aufzeichnung, 16 January 1963, Conversation Adenauer–Ball, NL Adenauer III, 45; Aufzeichnung, date missing, Conversation Adenauer–Nitze, of 13 April 1962, NL Adenauer III, 60.

41 Aufzeichnung, 5 December 1961, Conversation Adenauer–Smirnow, NL Adenauer III, 89, I.

42 Apparently, the idea of economic sanctions came up first after the building of the Wall (Grewe, *Rückblenden*, p. 496). Franz-Josef Strauss, then minister of defence, claims the authorship of this idea (Franz-Josef Strauss, *Die Erinnerungen*, Berlin: Siedler, 1989, p. 387); Aufzeichnungen, 12 and 20 October 1961 and 23 February 1962, Conversation Adenauer–Dowling, NL Adenauer III, 60, III, 89, I and III, 60; also Aufzeichnung, 11 October 1961, Conversation, Adenauer–Senator Humphrey, NL Adenauer III, 89. Mensing (ed.), *Adenauer Teegespräche 1961–1963*, p. 98.

43 Aufzeichnung, date missing, Conversation Adenauer–Stikker, 3 July 1961, NL Adenauer III, 87; Aufzeichnung, 20 February 1962, Conversation Adenauer–Kissinger, NL Adenauer III, 60.

44 Aufzeichnung, 12 October 1961, Conversation Adenauer–Dowling, NL Adenauer III, 60. From early on, Adenauer was convinced that the demonstration of Western resolution to repel Soviet aggressive moves by all available means would prevent the Soviet leadership from risking a war (see, for example, Aufzeichnung, 18 March 1959, Conversation Adenauer–Macmillan, NL Adenauer III, 88). See note 35.

45 As a reaction to such measures of military preparedness Adenauer said he feared the

rise of 'feelings of anxiety' among the German population and, implicitly, losses at the impending federal elections (Schwarz, *Adenauer 1952–1967*, pp. 655f.; Strauss, *Die Erinnerungen*, p. 361); Aufzeichnung, 20 February 1962, Conversation Adenauer–Kissinger, NL Adenauer III, 60. According to this memorandum, Kissinger mentioned US concerns that, by insisting on a blockade, the Germans had shown that they did not want to defend Berlin, but wanted others to do this for them. See also, Aufzeichnung, 20 October 1961, Conversation Adenauer–Dowling, NL Adenauer III, 89; Tel. Dowling to Rusk, 17 February 1962, FRUS 1961–1963, vol. 14, pp. 826ff.

46 Schwarz, *Adenauer 1952–1967*, pp. 706, 775; Bremen, *Die Eisenhower-Administration und die zweite Berlin-Krise*, pp. 313f., 523.

47 Mensing (ed.), *Adenauer Teegespräche*, pp. 34, 143.

48 Schwarz, *Adenauer 1952–1967*, pp. 742f.; Steinhoff and Pommerin, *Strategiewechsel*, p. 81; Aufzeichnung, 12 October 1961, Conversation Adenauer–Dowling, NL Adenauer III, 60.

49 Aufzeichnung, 19 November 1962, Conversation Kennedy–Adenauer, NL Adenauer, III, 61; Schwarz, *Adenauer 1952–1967*, pp. 685, 774.

50 Aufzeichnung Adenauer, date missing, 'Der Brief des Präsidenten Kennedy an mich enthält viele Lücken …', NL Adenauer, III, 61.

51 Aufzeichnung, 16 January 1963, Conversation Adenauer–Ball NL Adenauer III, 45; Mensing (ed.), *Adenauer Teegespräche 1961–1963*, p. 378. The West German government officially decided that it would participate in the MLF on 24 April 1963 (Steinhoff and Pommerin, *Strategiewechsel*, p. 129).

52 An eyewitness, the former general Ulrich de Maizière, offers the somewhat simplified explanation that Adenauer insisted on a balanced nuclear-conventional defence posture for the West and thus was opposed to new US strategic plans that seemed to upset that balance (Schwabe (ed.), *Adenauer und die USA*, p. 57).

53 Memorandum of Conversation Grewe–Kennedy, 19 February 1962, FRUS 1961–1963, vol. 14, pp. 617, 831.

54 Wiggershaus, 'Adenauer und die amerikanische Sicherheitspolitik in Europa', pp. 40f.; Aufzeichnung, 24 February 1962, Conversation Adenauer–Kennedy, NL Adenauer III, 89.

55 Trachtenberg, *A Constructed Peace*, pp. 276, 337, 342f.; Steininger, *Mauerbau*, p. 346.

56 Memorandum of Conversation Kennedy–Adenauer, 22 November 1961, FRUS 1961–1963, vol. 14, p. 629; for an earlier example see Bremen, *Die Eisenhower-Administration und die zweite Berlin-Krise*, p. 414. Bremen thinks that Adenauer, once he was directly exposed to Soviet military pressure, was prepared to offer concessions in the Berlin question, but no sooner than that.

57 Aufzeichnung, 20 February 1962, Conversation Adenauer–Kissinger, NL Adenauer III, 60; Aufzeichnung, 24 February 1961, Conversation Adenauer–Joseph Kennedy, NL Adenauer III, 89.

58 Aufzeichnung, 8 September 1961, Conversation Adenauer–Norstad, NL Adenauer III, 89, I.

59 Aufzeichnung, date missing, Conversation Adenauer–Stikker of 27 June 1961, NL Adenauer III, 87; Aufzeichnung, 12 October 1961, Conversation Adenauer–Dowling, NL Adenauer III, 60.

60 Aufzeichnung, date missing, Conversation Adenauer–Stikker of 27 June 1961, NL Adenauer III, 87 (Strauss). For this and the following see Klaus Schwabe, 'Adenauer und das Militärische', in Wolfgang Krieger (ed.), *Adenauer und die Wiederbewaffnung* (Rhöndorfer Gespräche, vol. 18), Bonn: Bouvier, 2000, pp. 71ff.

61 Schwarz, *Adenauer 1952–1967*, pp. 478f.

62 Memorandum of Conversation Kennedy–Adenauer, 22 November 1961, FRUS 1961–1963, vol. 14 , pp. 624ff., 627f., 629, 630. I agree on this with Trachtenberg, *A Constructed*

Peace, p. 280, although he fails to mention the NATO context which was an integral part of Adenauer's views on West German nuclear armament.

63 Franz-Josef Strauss, his minister of defence, shared this priority: Steinhoff and Pommerin, *Strategiewechsel*, p. 90; Schwarz, 'Adenauer und die Kernwaffen', p. 585. For a different interpretation, see Trachtenberg, *A Constructed Peace*, pp. 329ff., who claims that Adenauer was totally unwilling to risk war. In the fundamental security question, it seems he did risk it, however, and he did not deviate from this line later on.

64 Schwarz, 'Adenauer und die Kernwaffen', pp. 583f.

65 Küsters, 'Adenauers Deutschland- und Nuklearpolitik', p. 285.

66 Adenauer, Aufzeichnung, date missing, 'Der Brief des Präsidenten Kennedy an mich enthält viele Lücken ...', NL Adenauer, III, 61, referring to a letter by Kennedy re MLF, date missing (January 1963), NL Adenauer III, 45 (see note 50).

4

France, NATO and the Algerian War

Irwin M. Wall

The historical literature dealing with US nuclear strategy, NATO and the challenge of Gaullism from 1958 to 1962, with few exceptions, generally ignores the Algerian War, in full swing during that time.[1] Similarly, the historical treatments of the Algerian War tend to treat that subject in isolation, as if it were a purely internal French affair. This is in one sense not surprising. The French regarded Algeria as part of France proper; it was administered by the Ministry of the Interior, early in the war as three, later as 13 departments of France. Maurice Couve de Murville, in his memoir of his period as Minister of Foreign Affairs for General de Gaulle, declines to consider Algeria altogether in his 'Une Politique étrangère'. Not his department, says Couve de Murville.[2]

But the conflict in Algeria could not fail to have the most profound effect on French relations with NATO and the USA. How could it be otherwise with 500,000 French troops engaged there? Two obvious things resulted from NATO's standpoint. First, Algeria was formally part of France and therefore covered by the Alliance; the US National Security Council reluctantly recognized in October 1960 that from the moment documentary proof was provided of Russian involvement on the side of the rebels, the USA through NATO would be obliged to come to the assistance of France.[3] Second, the involvement of the bulk of French forces in Algeria meant France was largely absent from its designated role as part of NATO's 'shield' in Germany. By the terms of the Lisbon agreement of 1952, France was eventually to provide 12 divisions for the defence of Western Europe. At no time in the history of the alliance in fact did France provide more than four, and those were usually understrength.

The war, pitting France against Algeria and the Arab states who were sympathetic to it, was an embarrassment to the USA and NATO, conscious of the emerging African–Asian bloc in the United Nations and its growing importance in world affairs. France had embarrassed NATO and the USA by dragging Israel into its joint operation in 1956 with Great Britain at Suez, to seize the canal and topple Nasser. The French motive for Suez was not so much the canal as Nasser, whose demise the French leaders saw as the key to the end of the rebellion in Algeria. A furious President Eisenhower lashed out at France and England, forcing their withdrawal. The British learned their lesson and thereafter aligned their foreign policy with that of the USA. The French, in their fury against the Americans, embarked on a path of independence, going ahead with their programme to build an atomic bomb, and pursuing European unity as a potential 'third force' independent of both East and West. These policies were subsequently carried to an extreme by de Gaulle.

But France's maverick policy in Algeria could not be left in isolation. In February 1958 the French military, apparently uncontrolled by civilian politicians, bombarded the Tunisian village of Sakiet, accused of being a 'sanctuary' for the rebels. Seventy innocent people were killed; the United States was dragged into the ensuing international crisis between France and Tunisia, offering its 'good offices' to settle the resulting dispute lest Tunisia bring the issue to the UN, with the USA forced to vote against France, and the disruption of NATO as a result. Faced with an apparently insoluble dilemma as a consequence of the Algerian War, the Americans resolved to force an end to it by imposing on Paris an agreement reflecting Tunisian terms and strongly hinting that France must negotiate with the Algerian rebels.[4] The ensuing political crisis in Paris led to the fall of the Fourth Republic in May 1958 and the coming of Charles de Gaulle. The Americans cautiously welcomed the coming of de Gaulle, hoping that he would be capable of ending the Algerian War, and he had hinted strongly to them his intention of doing so.

A parallel problem resulted from the vexing question raised by changing US nuclear strategy for NATO. Although Eisenhower himself was resigned to the inevitability of independent nuclear deterrents for England, which already had one, and France, on the way to becoming a nuclear power, both the State Department and the Atomic Energy Commission were adamantly opposed to nuclear proliferation, and Congress forbade the sharing of weapons information in the McMahon Act. Moreover, as the Soviet Union achieved nuclear parity with the USA, the allies began to speculate about whether the USA itself would really risk nuclear conflagration to rescue Europe from Soviet aggression. This concern, openly expressed by de Gaulle, was in fact shared by the British, whose nuclear cooperation with the United States was designed to assure their independent deterrent, not sacrifice it.[5]

Great Britain was granted an exemption from the McMahon act in 1958 on the ground that it had made 'substantial' progress in its nuclear programme; by 1959 the USA and the UK together were exercising a kind of hegemony in NATO, and the emerging British–US nuclear partnership was becoming a serious irritant in their relations with France.[6] US doctrine during the Eisenhower administration insisted that nuclear weapons existed to be used like conventional arms, but the Americans nevertheless sought a means of avoiding their inevitable use in case of war, moving toward 'flexible response', the origins of which appeared during the Eisenhower administration but which became official doctrine under Kennedy.[7] These considerations came together in the US proposals both to stockpile nuclear weapons in Europe and to 'share' the decision-making process into their eventual use with the USA's allies. In February 1958 US Thor missiles were installed in Great Britain under the 'dual key' arrangement, each power locked into consultation and agreement of the other before they could be launched, under an arrangement that was meant to be a model for other NATO countries, and a means of dampening the desire in France and Germany for independent nuclear deterrents.[8]

France, even under a Fourth Republic adamantly intent upon its own nuclear deterrent, refused to stockpile US weapons unless it was guaranteed absolute control over their use. But even shared control emerged as a problem for the Americans in France so long as France's government remained unstable and its army and colonial bureaucracy escaped central control, making their own policy in Algeria. Algeria meant that the Fourth Republic was a deeply problematic, even dangerous ally for NATO, and the role of France was a constant pre-occupation of the Americans and the British in their concerns for the elaboration of a NATO strategy.

The Americans, then, helped by the British, played a role in facilitating the transition in France from the Fourth Republic to de Gaulle. They were fully prepared for the fact that de Gaulle came to power with the intention of changing the nature of French participation in NATO, securing an enhanced role for France in the alliance, and reforming the operations of the alliance itself. These intentions were clear in de Gaulle's September 1958 memorandum to Prime Minister Macmillan and President Eisenhower in which he proposed a three-power 'Directorate', made up of England, France and the United States, to run not only NATO but the policies and politics of the entire 'free world'. The memorandum has been variously interpreted. According to the prevailing view it marks the beginning of independent French policies that culminated in the French withdrawal from NATO's integrated command in March 1966. De Gaulle himself is reported to have said that he 'asked for the moon' in proposing French equality with the 'Anglo-Saxons' in NATO, knowing he would be refused, but providing the ultimate rationalization for the realization later of his policy of French 'independence'.[9] But this view does not on the surface appear to make sense. De Gaulle was not proposing French independence in September 1958, but rather a radical form of inter-dependence, in which each of the big three would accept responsibility for backing the other two where their worldwide interests were concerned, and all three would jointly decide when and where the use of nuclear weapons might be called for. De Gaulle's claim that he did not mean his proposal seriously appears as *ex post facto* rationalization for the fact that his proposals were ultimately rejected.

The point to be understood here is that preserving Algeria, and North Africa in general, for France was central to the purpose of the September memorandum, and the Algerian war, detested by France's purported partners, was one of the central reasons, if not the single most important reason, for the very cool reception the initiative received from the British and the Americans.

This point would appear to have been missed by most of the literature dealing with de Gaulle's foreign policy.[10] De Gaulle when he came to power fully
intended to keep Algeria French. He was indeed the spokesman of military
insurrection in Algiers that brought him to power.[11] It is of little use to go into
all his statements on the subject before he came to power; they vary widely
according to whom they were made and provide little guidance as to his
ultimate intentions. It is enough to look closely at his acts once he came to
power. The Challe plan, which greatly intensified the war, and the plan of
Constantine, which was designed to industrialize Algeria, both with their
consequent increased expenditure in Algeria of both French blood and money
in 1959 and 1960, defy explanation in terms other than the aim of keeping the
territory French. It was only as both plans gradually revealed themselves
as unable to achieve their goals in 1960 that de Gaulle began to consider
independence for Algeria as an option. General Challe did win a kind of
military victory in Algeria. The Morice line held rebel incursions from Tunisia
to a minimum, while the interior was 'pacified'. But pacification could only
be defined in terms of numbers of terrorist incidents per month: what number
was tolerable? De Gaulle once ventured the figure of 200 per month, as
opposed to over 1,500 that were occurring during the war's apogee. But whatever the figure, in no respect did it ever appear that society in Algeria would
return to the halcyon days of what was once considered normal. Nor could the
plan of Constantine be implemented in the time-frame intended: much of the
private capital on which its broader aims were based was not forthcoming.
Private investors were more prescient than the state in anticipating that nothing
the French might do after 1958 was likely to prevent Algerian independence.
By 1961, despite over 7 billion new francs, or $2 billion of investment, most
projects were far from completion.[12] The evidence seems clear that for at least
two and a half years, from May 1958 until the end of 1960, de Gaulle tried,
while winning the confidence of the Muslim community through social
reforms and investment, to destroy by military means the entire infrastructure
of the nationalist rebellion.[13] Even in 1961, after he had begun talks with the
Algerian 'Provisional Government', de Gaulle instructed his Delegate
General in Algeria, Jean Morin, to seek alternative Muslim leadership to the
FLN from among elected Muslim moderates within Algeria who were willing to work with the French toward 'association'. His aim was to circumvent
the FLN and undermine its claim to be the sole legitimate representative of
the Algerian people. And he entertained seriously the idea of partitioning
Algeria between its European and Muslim populations should negotiations
fail.[14] Only when it was clear that he had failed did he entertain the idea of
granting independence to Algeria.

The National Liberation Front, at about the same time as de Gaulle dictated the September memorandum, declared itself a Provisional Government
of the future Algerian Republic and opened a campaign for recognition as
such. On 20 September 1958, in consequence, Couve de Murville instructed

all French diplomatic representatives to warn their host governments that recognition of the newly formed so-called 'Algerian provisional government' (GPRA) in Cairo would be construed as an unfriendly act to France and interference in French internal affairs.[15] The isolation of the putative rebel government in Cairo and then in Tunis thereafter became a major preoccupation of French diplomacy. The de Gaulle government from its inception protested angrily against the tolerant attitude Washington took toward Algerian rebel activities conducted on US soil. France also angrily rejected suggestions transmitted by the Tunisian leader Habib Bourguiba through Washington that Bizerte be turned over to NATO rather than continuing as a French base, and it remained furious that the Americans and British had begun a policy of giving small arms to Tunisia as a way of keeping it tied to the West rather than risking that it drift off toward the Soviet bloc.

Understood against the background of these issues the 18 September memorandum appears as part of a broader ensemble, an effort to enlist the USA, Great Britain, and France's allies in NATO in support of the French effort to retain hegemony in Algeria. This is most apparent in the French explanations of how the proposed Directorate was to work in the non-European world. Each of the three Great Powers, in consultation with and with the support of the other two, would exercise hegemony in its own area of concern. The three-power organism would in effect adopt the policy of 'la puissance la plus impliquée dans telle question ou telle zone. Au Maroc ou en Tunisie par exemple, une telle position commune "devrait être la position de la France".'[16] The USA would speak for the big three in Pacific affairs, and Britain in matters pertaining to the Commonwealth. The Anglo-Saxon powers similarly were to follow French policy in North and sub-Saharan Africa; and it followed that they must particularly do so in the case of Algeria.

Eisenhower and Macmillan could not refuse the French proposals for three-power talks despite their distaste for the Directorate idea, and discussions began in Washington in December 1958. One can see clearly the purpose of these discussions for the French in the instructions from Couve de Murville to the French Ambassador in Washington, Hervé Alphand, who became the French representative in these talks. Alphand was initially to 'educate' the British and Americans about French concerns. France wanted a unified world strategy of the three Western powers, as opposed to the NATO strategy, which was presently narrowly limited to European concerns and devised by the Americans alone.[17] But as was the case in NATO, the world strategy of the big three was to include military planning. As its first order of business, France needed a reorganization of NATO's military command in the Mediterranean to take into account of French interests in communications with and the defence of North Africa. Here de Gaulle made a rather extraordinary argument. France, he said, needed a national as opposed to an integrated defence for internal political reasons; French problems with the military, he said, stemmed in part from the army's insufficient consciousness of its role in the defence of France due to the subordination of its operations to an international organization in the abstract, that is to say, NATO. In other words, NATO was responsible for the French military's abandonment of its patriotic duty in the recent insurrection in Algeria. Alphand thus put the allies on notice that France intended to withdraw its Mediterranean fleet from the integrated NATO command, which it did in March 1959.

The tripartite talks convened on 3 December 1958. In the interval, on 27 November, the Soviets issued their famous note demanding the internationalization and demilitarization of Berlin under the control of the German Democratic Republic. This would necessitate recognition of the GDR if the Western powers were to continue to enjoy access to West Berlin. The Berlin crisis played directly into de Gaulle's hands as a device for demonstrating how his idea of a big-three directorate must work. De Gaulle took a firm anti-Soviet line, in his mind representing the European interest by his rigidity in support of Adenauer against the two Anglo-Saxon powers who preferred, particularly the British, a more supple approach to Moscow based on negotiations and some concessions.[18] Almost equally significant, in November 1958 British–French talks aimed at resolving the crisis between the Common Market and the British plan for a Free Trade Association broke down over French demands that the British accept a common agricultural policy and a joint external tariff, which London flatly refused to do. West Europe, it appeared, was now to split along the lines that Macmillan feared; according to Couve de Murville, 'Nous allons arriver au stade le plus critique des relations franco-britanniques depuis juin 1940.'[19]

It was against the background of these two crises that Alphand explained to the Anglo-Americans the meaning of de Gaulle's memo in a few basic points. NATO was no longer adequate to meet the needs of France, which was a nuclear power with worldwide interests. The three nuclear powers with world interests, the US, UK and France, must meet periodically to take common decisions on policy all over the world, France having equal rights of consultation as the other two. This was what they were currently doing with regard to Berlin. But NATO military planning in the Mediterranean must be revised to take into account the primary French role in the defence of North Africa.[20] What Alphand perforce left unsaid was against whom the reorganized Mediterranean command was to be directed. For London and Washington the enemy was Communist, and perhaps Nasserist subversion of the type that had led to the intervention in Lebanon in July 1958, an intervention in which Paris had been told, despite its historic interest in Lebanon, that its participation was unwelcome. For Paris, the enemy was Communism, Nasser and the National Liberation Front in Algeria, which it persisted in regarding as their puppet.

In 1959 the tripartite talks got down to serious business. The Far East was discussed first, on 5 February, then Africa on 16 April, continuing through 21 April. In the interval France withdrew its Mediterranean fleet from NATO. Couve de Murville laid out the reasoning Alphand was to use in explaining this move to the Americans. The USA, which had lost its atomic weapons monopoly, could no longer unilaterally make decisions about the use of such weapons; it must consult the other NATO powers with world interests, Great Britain and France. Only these three NATO countries, moreover, had the 'vocation, means, and tradition' of a veritable national defence. Of those three, France alone had up to now integrated its fleet with NATO; the Americans and the British did not do so. NATO had two main sectors of defence, Central Europe and the Mediterranean, the latter being the primary area of French concern. But NATO failed to protect French interests in the Mediterranean: its preoccupation was with the threat from the East, while the French concern was North–South, that is, communications with Algeria. Hence France would withdraw its fleet from the integrated Mediterranean command. Moreover, the question of the return of French ground forces to NATO's integrated command in Central Europe once the Algerian war was over remained to be addressed. Here was the first hint that France might not 'return' its divisions to NATO (they had never been there in significant strength) when the Algerian war ended. The task of the French fleet was the defence of France's North African shores and to guarantee transit between them and the metropole. 'Il n'est pas admissible que cette tâche soit une responsabilité partie britannique, partie américaine, alors que d'ailleurs que bien des problèmes politiques sont en cause et que la politique de nos alliés, à l'égard par exemple de l'Algérie, ne se confond nullement avec la nôtre.' In other words French cooperation in an integrated NATO command made no sense in Paris so long as NATO did not share in French aims with regard to Algeria. French demands could be reduced to three basic issues, according to Couve de Murville: tripartite cooperation on world strategy, tripartite decisions on the use of nuclear weapons and the remaking of naval organization in the Mediterranean, implying a joint defence of Algeria as part of France.[21] Couve de Murville gave no indication that these were separable, or that any one or two were more fundamental or basic than the others. The implication, it seems to me, was clear that, if France's demands in NATO were met, France's forces would return to be integrated with NATO's central command.

France's overall goals were once again spelled out in the Quai's 'Directives du Département pour ses conversations de Washington' of 25 March 1959, in preparation for the tripartite discussion of Africa scheduled for April. First, there must be a formal mechanism of consultation between the US, the UK and France on world problems: France could not permit itself to be dragged into an atomic war, in the decisions for which it would have no part. Second, there must be a Eurafrican zone of defence organized by the big three and centred around the Mediterranean and North Africa; NATO was insufficient to meet this challenge. North Africa and the Mediterranean were of particular importance to France, and NATO had no strategy for dealing with this part of the world. In general the same principles should apply in North Africa as elsewhere; one of the Great Powers must be responsible for security in the name of the others, with which it consulted regularly. 'Mais le gouvernement tient surtout à ce qu'ils [les principes] soient appliqués à une région du monde dans laquelle les responsabilités de la France sont prédominantes. Le rôle directeur de la France en Mediterranée occidentale, dans le Maghreb et dans l'Afrique noire doit être reconnu par nos alliés. De même, les commandements militaires à organiser dans ses régions doivent être confiés à des autorités françaises.'[22]

The long-coveted tripartite talks on Africa finally began on 16 April 1959, France being represented by Secretary General of the Quai d'Orsay Louis Joxe. Joxe raised three central points. Algeria was one of the 'pièces maîtresses' of the French presence in Africa, and no bilateral negotiations were possible there since it was directly under French sovereignty as part of metropolitan France; France recognized the independence of Tunisia and Morocco but must be responsible for their defence and maintain bases in both countries, in particular Bizerte; and the Sahara, the bulk of which lay in Algeria, was a 'French creation' where France would exercise primary responsibility. There must in fact be a united military approach by the West to Africa, a solid structure of defence stretching from the Western Mediterranean to the Congo in which the primary responsibility would be that of France. This would require the reorganization of NATO and the construction of new forms of military cooperation among the big three and France's NATO allies.[23]

The USA and Great Britain would not commit themselves to the support of a Mediterranean policy dictated by France so long as France continued a North African policy of which they disapproved. Eisenhower decided the issue for the moment by stating that 'we cannot support colonialism ... we will not gain strength for the west by letting the French and the Germans walk on us'.[24] Moreover, the Eisenhower administration was unable to accommodate de Gaulle by helping in the construction of the French nuclear programme, and the British, who enjoyed an exemption from the McMahon act, were still forced by its terms to keep from cooperation with Paris.

So long as the Eisenhower administration endured, the hope remained alive that French demands with regard to the big three could be satisfied and Algeria could be drawn into a lasting, meaningful association with France that would preserve French interests there, particularly the extensive oil reserves in the Sahara, also the site of French nuclear testing. De Gaulle's offer of self-determination to Algeria appeared, in September 1959, to be a welcome shift in French policy, and was greeted as such by the British and Americans, who had followed a policy of patiently waiting for him to carry out his promise to settle the Algerian crisis since May 1958. But de Gaulle's offer of either integration, the radical demand of the settlers, 'association', in which the basic interests of France would be preserved, and 'separation', painted in stark and despairing terms, left it clearly understood that independence was not a serious option. As the war dragged on during 1960 US patience wore out, and the June 1960 negotiations with the rebels at Melun revealed the totally unacceptable nature of the general's terms: he would carry out a cease-fire with the rebels of the National Liberation Front but would under no terms recognize their claims to represent the Algerian people in future negotiations, which must be conducted with an authority emanating from elections in Algeria carried out under French control. The rebels had ample experience demonstrating that elections that were free and simultaneously carried out under the auspices of the French army were quite impossible, and the Melun talks quickly collapsed.

By October 1960 the Eisenhower administration, in frustration over the failure of the Algerian crisis to come to a resolution, turned again to the policy of February 1958: active intervention, with implied severe pressure on France to bring an end to the war on terms acceptable to the rebels, that is, independence.[25] At the same time, France faced the election of President John F. Kennedy, who as a Senator had gone on record as early as 1957 as a firm opponent of the war in Algeria. Kennedy, who had been silent on the Algerian question since then, had nevertheless advocated an active policy of US intervention to force an end to the war on the basis of Algerian independence. De Gaulle was now between the proverbial rock and hard place. He agreed for the first time to recognize the National Liberation Front as the representative of the Algerian people and opened secret negotiations with it through Swiss intermediaries, leading to the Evian talks. But Kennedy's election also set the US administration on a firm and lasting policy of opposition to the existence of a French nuclear deterrent, or even a British one for that matter. With Algeria gone and France obliged to go it alone in its pursuit of a nuclear deterrent against US opposition, the bankruptcy of NATO as a means for preserving French interests was clear.

De Gaulle also failed in what stands as a triptych of policies that accompanied his pursuit of victory in Algeria. He sought to build a 'Europe of States' as opposed to a federal Europe, believing that in negotiations among 'equals' the views of France would prevail in the councils of a concerted Europe; and he tried to construct a federal Africa under French hegemony that would tie itself permanently to Europe through France, completing the construction of Eurafrique, the vast ensemble that France would then represent to the Anglo-Saxons in the councils of the big three. For contrasting reasons he failed in both of these aims, revealing by 1962 the total collapse of his policies. This was most apparent in Algeria, where continued delay in negotiating peace while France pursued unrealizable goals – joint citizenship for the Europeans in Algeria and the detachment of the Sahara – led to the worst exit imaginable, the flight or mass exodus of the settler population amid an uncontrollable outburst of terror and counter-terror that spread to the metropole and appeared to presage the simultaneous collapse of France and Algeria both. It is against the backdrop of these failed policies that the putative policy, or perhaps posture would be a better word, of French 'independence' from Washington and NATO must be understood.

NOTES

1 The exception is Douglas Stuart and William Tow, *The Limits of Alliance: NATO Out-of-Area Problems since 1949*, Baltimore, MD: Johns Hopkins University Press, 1990. Stuart and Tow take the position that de Gaulle tried to use NATO to help with his strategy to disengage from Algeria, which contrasts with the argument that follows here.

2 Maurice Couve de Murville, *Une Politique étrangère, 1958–1969*, Paris: Plon, 1971.

3 NSC 466, 7 November 1960, *Foreign Relations of the United States* (FRUS) 1958–1960, 13, Algeria, p. 707.

4 Irwin Wall, *France, the United States, and the Algerian War*, Berkeley, CA:University of California Press, 2001, especially chapters 4 and 5.

5 Ian Clark, *Nuclear Diplomacy and the Special Relationship: Britain's Deterrent and America, 1957–62*, Oxford: Clarendon Press, 1994.

6 Constantine Pagedas, *Anglo-American Strategic Relations and the French Problem, 1960–63: A Troubled Partnership*, London: Frank Cass, 2000.

7 Jane E. Stromseth, *The Origins of Flexible Response: NATO'S Debate over Strategy in the 1960s*, foreword by Denis Healey, New York: St Martin's Press, 1988. Also Andreas Wenger, *Living With Peril: Eisenhower, Kennedy, and Nuclear Weapons*, Lanham, MD: Rowman & Littlefield, 1997.

8 Pagedas, *Anglo-American Strategic Relations and the French Problem*; Marc Trachtenberg, *A Constructed Peace: The Making of the European Settlement 1945–1963*, Princeton, NJ: Princeton University Press, 1999.

9 Alain Peyrefitte, *C' était de Gaulle*, Paris: Fayard, 1994, p. 352.

10 With the notable exception of Edward Kolodziej, *French International Policy Under de Gaulle and Pompidou*, Ithaca, NY: Cornell University Press, 1974, pp. 75–6.

11 Pierre Miquel, *La Guerre d'Algérie*, Paris: Fayard, 1993, is particularly good on this point.

12 Daniel Lefeuvre, *Chère Algérie: Comptes et mécomptes de la tutelle coloniale*, Paris: Société Française d'Histoire d'Outre-Mer, 1997, pp. 310–17.

13 See Constantin Melnik, *Mille Jours à Matignon: Raisons d'Etat sous de Gaulle, Guerre d'Algérie 1959–1962*, Paris: Bernard Grasset, 1988, p. 211. Melnik, who worked closely for Debré, says that 'La thèse de l'abandon volontaire de l'Algérie par le général de Gaulle ne résiste pas à l'examen.'

14 Jean Morin, *De Gaulle et l'Algérie: Mon témoignage, 1960–62*, Paris: Albin Michel, 1999, pp. 185–93. Michel Debré reported a conversation with General de Gaulle on 23 March 1961 in which the general told him that if a part of Algeria no longer wanted France in Algeria, there would be a regrouping of populations and a partition. Michel Debré, *Entretiens avec le Général de Gaulle*, Paris: Albin Michel, 1993, p. 30. Morin believes, however, that de Gaulle intended regrouping of the population only as a preparation for its embarkation.

15 Couve de Murville to all French diplomatic representatives abroad, 20 October 1958, Documents Diplomatiques Français (DDF), 1958, II, pp. 396–7.

16 Quoted in Frédéric Bozo, *Deux Stratégies pour l'Europe: De Gaulle, les Etats-Unis, et l'alliance atlantique*, Paris: Plon, 1996, p. 39. The text of de Gaulle's memorandum is in Président de Gaulle au Premier Ministre Macmillan (et le Président Eisenhower), 17 September 1958, DDF, 1958, II, p. 377.

17 Couve de Murville to Alphand, 3 November 1958, DDF, 1958, II, pp. 620–1.

18 Bozo, *Deux stratégies*, pp. 46–9.

19 Couve de Murville, *Une Politique etrangère*, p. 43.

20 Alphand to Couve de Murville, 4 December 1958, DDF, 1958, II, pp. 802–8.

21 Couve de Murville to Alphand, 18 January 1959, DDF, 1959, I, 1–30 January 1959, 33, p. 68.

22 Directives du Département pour les conversations de Washington, 2 April 1959, DDF, 1959, I, 198, pp. 439–3.
23 Comptes rendus des conversations sur l'Afrique, 16–21 April 1959, DDF, 1959, I, 235, pp. 534–5.
24 Merchant to Herter, 10 July 1959; Satterthwaite to Herter, 13 August 1959; Memorandum by President Eisenhower, 21 August 1959, FRUS, 1958–1960, XIII, Algeria, pp. 664–8.
25 This point and what follows are developed more fully in Wall, *France, the United States, and the Algerian War.*

5

De Gaulle's Handling of the Berlin and Cuban Crises

Maurice Vaïsse

How did de Gaulle react towards the Berlin and Cuban crises?[1] Although both of these Cold War crises concerned France in different ways, the historical literature has left an image of great firmness from the General towards the Soviet Union during both. Why was this so? Did the firmness exist only in words?

The crises occurred in very different periods. The Berlin crisis took place soon after de Gaulle's return to office and coincided with the later years of the Algerian war. France's freedom of action and even its means were limited at the time. Whereas the Berlin crisis persisted from 1958 to 1962, the Cuban missile crisis was short – limited to the month of October 1962. Furthermore, the Cuban crisis occurred just as de Gaulle's diplomacy, freed by the ending of the Algerian war, came up to speed, giving France an increased freedom of action to insist upon its independence, especially within NATO and in relation to the USA. Was it the time to take advantage of the new diplomatic environment?

The geographical locations of both crises seem to militate in favour of this hypothesis, since Berlin is only a few hundred kilometres from Paris, whereas Cuba lies some 4,000 km from French coasts in an area of low priority for France. France's status as a victor over Germany in 1945 and as a great power was directly threatened by the Berlin crisis. It was thus predictable that de Gaulle would perceive the two crises differently, given that the Berlin case was not only close by but also directly implicated France, whereas the Cuban crisis was first and foremost a US–Soviet confrontation in the Caribbean with the European powers in the background.[2] De Gaulle's firmness in both affairs was the same. The why and how can only be explained by describing and analysing de Gaulle's attitudes before, during and after each crisis.

De Gaulle's Attitude towards the Second Berlin Crisis (November 1958)[3]

Before the Crisis

Following the Yalta and Potsdam agreements, the capital of the Reich was enclosed within the Soviet occupation zone in Germany and was itself split into four districts, each administered by one occupying power. Berlin's quadripartite status became the main area of confrontation of the Cold War in Europe. The West had managed to defeat the blockade of West Berlin that the Soviets had imposed in 1948. Continued Western presence in the city was regarded as calling into question the Soviet sphere of influence as well as the existence of a communist Germany, the German Democratic Republic (GDR), which remained unrecognized by the Western powers. Thus, the Berlin question was renewed in 1958, with the Soviet government stating in a memo of 27 November that the status of the city was outdated and ought to be replaced by a formal peace treaty, turning West Berlin into a demilitarized free city, with allied troops withdrawing within six months. Otherwise, the USSR would sign a peace treaty with the GDR, granting it control over all Western military traffic between West Germany and Berlin. It was apparently Khrushchev's main goal to force the West to change its position towards the GDR.

On 26 November, the day before the Soviet memo appeared, de Gaulle and Adenauer had held their second meeting at Bad-Kreuznach.[4] The Berlin crisis was to deepen their basic understanding and their agreement to prevent any modification of Berlin's status, since de Gaulle felt that concessions would endanger both France and Europe. De Gaulle agreed with Adenauer that changing the status quo would lead to a change in the political majority in the Federal Republic in favour of the Social Democrats, eventually leading to a neutralization of the whole of Germany. In the first half of 1959, French diplomacy unfolded its position, with a firm and fatalistic warning from de Gaulle to Soviet Ambassador Vinogradov on 2 March,[5] then firm support for the Federal Republic and a criticism of the British attitude and of Macmillan's visit to Moscow in February. De Gaulle, in his press conference of 25 March, declared that he was considering favourably a German reunification within current borders, that is, the Oder–Neisse line, and made reference to a 'Europe from the Atlantic to the Urals'.[6] Writing to Khrushchev in September 1959, de Gaulle encouraged the Russians to embrace international détente and to cease regarding the Federal Republic as a threat. He reminded Khrushchev that the Germans remained a great people necessary to the progress and equilibrium of Europe.

Prior to a Paris summit conference in May of 1960, a détente had been developing from the summer of 1959 to the spring of 1960[7] while heads of state undertook numerous visits to each other.[8] In preparation for the summit, Eisenhower, de Gaulle and Adenauer again demonstrated their firm intentions towards the Berlin question, while Macmillan remained silent, de Gaulle suggesting the crisis was essentially a Soviet bluff,[9] repeating this even to Khrushchev during the latter's visit to France (23 March–2 April 1960).[10] De Gaulle knew that the West could not keep the Soviets from signing a peace treaty with the GDR, but disapproved of the Pankow Republic and refused to recognize it or to withdraw Western troops from Berlin. He suggested to

Khrushchev that the German problem would be better resolved in the future when tensions had abated thanks to détente, and that, in the future, an un-threatened Western Europe might be able to better relate to Eastern Europe without the US intermediary. The collapse of the conference renewed East–West tensions.[11]

In the short term, Western ties were reinforced, with de Gaulle giving the impression of great support for the Atlantic alliance, and for Eisenhower in the face of Khrushchev's sly criticism, while a nervous Macmillan was will-ing to explore all options. France's firmness over Berlin vividly contrasted with that of other Western countries, notably Britain's. Macmillan desired to be rid of this stumbling block through the idea of 'discreet talks with the Russians',[12] and a change in the legal status of the occupation regime put forward by Lord Home.[13] With the election of John F. Kennedy, a new era of US policy began. Following a first meeting with Khrushchev in Vienna, de Gaulle advised the US President on 31 May 1961 'not to go towards small concessions, leading to greater ones later on'.[14] Following a tense dialogue between Maurice Couve de Murville and Andrei Gromyko on 16 June 1961,[15] Jean Laloy, returning from a visit to Washington,[16] reported that the Americans distrusted the pacifist British as much as the French. British energy consisted in words rather than deeds. Even the Germans were suspected of buckling under threats, which would give the disastrous impression of Western disunity, with the British stating their willingness to recognize the GDR while accusing the French of 'silliness and stoking the fire'. All these divergences were clear to see at a meeting between the three foreign ministers, Lord Home, Dean Rusk and Couve de Murville in Paris on 4–6 July,[17] with France refusing the Anglo–US suggestion to call a quadripartite conference. In an exchange of letters, de Gaulle and Kennedy outlined their respective measures to reinforce their defence networks: increasing of the US military budget with an eventual six extra US divisions sent to Europe, increasing the readiness of strategic aviation and civil defence, as well as recalling of two French divisions from Algeria. Although both men agreed on the necessity of firmness, the idea was to find an agreement without resorting to force.

The general's determination to keep the status quo in Berlin is coherent with his firmness towards the Soviet Union and his policy of Franco-German cooperation. Heeding Adenauer's and Brentano's pleas not to give up, de Gaulle had thus earned their trust,[18] for which Macmillan bitterly reproached him.[19] De Gaulle could thus obtain concessions from the chancellor on other points so as to consolidate the Franco-German partnership.[20] Writing to Khrushchev on 10 September 1959, de Gaulle directly entreated the Russians to embrace international détente and cooperation among the European states and to cease regarding the Federal Republic as a threat. He reminded his correspondent that the Germans 'remain a great people necessary to the progress and equilibrium of a united Europe' and that the free access to Berlin could not be questioned.[21]

The open crisis

The construction of the Wall on Sunday, 13 August 1961 apparently surprised the Westerners, who did not oppose it despite the urgings of Mayor Willy Brandt.[22] Since 1959, a tripartite allied commission had prepared emergency plans and exercises, but on this occasion French firmness turned into reticence.[23] The plan included diplomatic, administrative, economic and military measures, aimed at deterring the Soviet government without risking war,[24] and when the British and Americans suggested that a division made up of one-third of Frenchmen was necessary to reopen access to Berlin, the French Army was hesitant because it was still engaged in Algeria and suffering from an acute moral crisis.[25] The British thus concluded that, 'French firmness over Berlin was more verbal than real.' The French attitude is still an unsolved mystery. Unlike those of the UK and the USA, the French garrison was not reinforced, much to the grief of General Lacomme, who noted that France was 'lagging behind'.[26] Despite this, little known measures were taken such as the 17 August Defence Council called by de Gaulle which decided to recall army units and air squadrons from Algeria for redeployment in France and in Germany.[27] Even less well known was a decision taken by de Gaulle while at Colombey to crush the East German barbed wire.[28] But no one among the Allies was willing to die for Berlin,[29] and Plan Live Oak called only upon conventional means, thus reinforcing de Gaulle's conviction that the US were unwilling to defend Europe with nuclear weaponry.

The aftermath of the crisis

The Berlin affair engendered a deep mistrust between France and the USA, with the Western allies divided over tactics and unable to phrase a tripartite declaration.[30] When Kennedy and Macmillan suggested a joint note to the Soviets to begin negotiations without giving the appearance of weakness, Paris immediately had reservations as to the timing.[31] De Gaulle, writing on 18 and 25 August,[32] felt that discussions could only take place in a peaceful climate and that to negotiate at that time would begin a progressive abandonment of Berlin and would be a serious blow to NATO. To Ambassador Gavin on 2 September, de Gaulle solemnly promised that France would follow the USA in all circumstances.[33] Nevertheless, France would not join the initiative of the US Ambassador to Moscow, Thompson.[34] In Washington, Ambassador Hervé Alphand was asked to explain France's refusal to take part in negotiations while the USSR acted unilaterally.[35]

There were several reasons for French intransigence. The general feared most of all a reversal of alliances and a German–Soviet entente, a possibility explained by Couve de Murville to Fanfani on 26 November.[36] Germany would be better tied to the West if support was given to Adenauer and Berlin sternly defended,[37] but de Gaulle also wished to demonstrate to the Germans that they could not rely on the British and the Americans. A final preoccupation was to avoid having European problems resolved by a Soviet–American tête-à-tête. To the General, Berlin was a secondary question, Germany was the essential one. One almost sees a military man's judgment that it would be impossible to avoid the crumbling of the Western position in Berlin, it being too far within the Soviet zone. Instead, de Gaulle advocated a global approach to East–West relations, the only one capable of maintaining such a precarious position.[38] The German problem would only be solved in a relaxed atmosphere, and it was vain to try to tackle it in a tense environment. The Berlin problem would naturally resolve itself when Europeans from the Atlantic to the Urals would agree to end their quarrels. De Gaulle also refused to recognize the GDR, both as a calculated move to support Adenauer and through conviction that it was a purely Soviet creation.

In fact, de Gaulle's positions evolved with time; at the height of the crisis he found himself opposed both to the Soviets[39] and to the Anglo-Saxon powers. He even found himself out of touch with German opinion, whose confusion probably resulted in Adenauer's narrow success at the election of 17 September. The chancellor even visited Washington on 19–23 November before coming to Paris on 9 December, and German policy became in fact more open to negotiation,[40] with the Soviets baiting the German Ambassador to Moscow, Hans Kroll. De Gaulle was left alone with his inflexibility.

De Gaulle and the Cuban Missile Crisis[41]

From the French point of view, the Cuban crisis had two characters: first, it was a US–Soviet crisis in which the other countries, including European states, held no part. Paradoxically, however, France was supposed to have played a significant role in the crisis, because in a context of misunderstandings and rows, it was a proof of de Gaulle's solidarity with the Atlantic Alliance.[42]

Unlike Macmillan, de Gaulle had presented himself as firm in the Berlin crises and disarmament negotiations. By 1962, freed from the obstacle of the Algerian war and having survived the attempt on his life at Petit-Clamart, the general was busy reinforcing presidential authority through a referendum set for 28 October, which would introduce the election of the President of the Republic through universal suffrage. What explains this paradoxical attitude on General de Gaulle's part, so much in contrast to that of other allies and especially Macmillan?[43]

Before the crisis

Before the crisis, Cuba was the subject of information exchanges between France and the USA. The Secretary of State himself asked whether French services could communicate any information regarding the activities of

Castro's regime,[44] and French–US cooperation in this domain proved remarkable. It occurred via two channels. The first was the French Ambassador to Havana, du Gardier, a keen follower of events with good information on the anti-Castro movement for which he acknowledged much sympathy.[45] His valuable information was conveyed in difficult conditions.[46] On 10 August, du Gardier had reported on night-time landings in Cuban ports of obviously Slavic-looking Russian troops in Cuban uniform,[47] as well as sightings of Chinese and Algerians.[48] Most of all, he pointed to the arrival of missile-launching equipment and to the increasingly important role of the Soviet army in Cuban military dispositions.[49] All of this information was diligently passed on to the Americans.[50] The second source was General de Rancourt,[51] French military attaché to Washington. He learnt of the missile installations in Cuba through contacts with the anti-Castro faction, and informed the US Air Force which then sent reconnaissance flights.

Without denying the information collected by the CIA, it is important to note the frequency and quality of the information given by the French to the Americans, which they themselves acknowledged.

The crisis

When Dean Acheson came to the Elysée on 22 October at 5 p.m.,[52] de Gaulle replied that France approved of the defence of the USA, which was being directly threatened for the first time, noting that the Soviets might then retaliate at Berlin and that a tripartite consultation would then be necessary. The general, however, did not question any of the actions undertaken by the USA. In the event of a war breaking out, France would side with its US ally, although the general himself saw hard times ahead but not an actual armed conflict. Despite the fact that this had merely been a notification rather than a consultation, de Gaulle appreciated Kennedy's message.

The French context was not indifferent and the crisis had a strong impact on French public opinion, all the more because of the proximity of the referendum.[53] The French press had characteristic reactions, worried by the grave nature of the crisis.[54] Kennedy was suspected of bellicosity, of electioneering over the crisis, trying to prove that the Democrats could be firm against the Soviets, exaggerating the threat of Soviet missiles near the USA. Some columnists even doubted the authenticity of US documents, but for once, de Gaulle loudly proclaimed his support for the Americans. The French government also refused to allow Cuban-bound Soviet aircraft stopping in France.[55] Dean Acheson noted de Gaulle's acceptance of facts before seeing proofs, unlike Macmillan who wanted the photographs published in the press.[56] In London, Geoffroy de Courcel observed the reservations of British public opinion against the risky US decision, then its opposition to the blockade, since many Britons considered the freedom of the seas essential to trade. They would have preferred a negotiated solution.[57]

Following the council of ministers on 24 October, a communiqué stated France's 'understanding' of Washington's worries over the installation of missiles in Cuba[58] and reaffirmed that 'the reciprocal engagements of the Atlantic Alliance are and remain the basis of French policy'. At the UN Security Council meetings of 23–24 October, the French representative, Roger Seydoux, supported the US resolution proposal,[59] insisting on the threat represented by an accumulation of Soviet offensive weaponry in Cuba. Doing so, France did not fear placing itself against the Third World group led by Algeria, which countered the US position, and despite strong governmental and public reactions in Phnom Penh, Santiago de Chile, Dakar, Libreville, Jakarta and Rabat. French action took place both at the UN level, because of the need to pass the resolution, and in the African capitals from which the USSR was soliciting permission for its aircraft to land or fly over to try to break the US maritime blockade.

Although de Gaulle, who would later on strongly criticize the US grip over Latin America and the intervention in the Dominican Republic, could have been expected to disagree more strongly with the aggressive stance towards Cuba, it was the case that the surprise effect, the context and the area determined him to be supportive of Washington. The uncertainty of Khrushchev's aims startled French analysts.[60] In relation to the Berlin crisis, then at the centre of European preoccupations, the Cuban crisis seemed to confirm Soviet belligerence, and firmness over Cuba seemed to de Gaulle the natural continuation of his firmness over Berlin. The general was also impressed with the quick and determined response of the Kennedy administration, in contrast to his earlier suspicions of US weakness.[61]

The aftermath of the crisis

After the dénouement of the Cuban missile crisis, French–US contacts did not loosen[62] although France distanced itself. De Gaulle stated his admiration for the lucid and firm way the USA had handled the crisis.[63] Nevertheless, de Gaulle and Couve de Murville took note that the Americans had only bothered to inform them but had not asked anything of them.[64] Their main reservation came from a possible linking of the Cuban affair to Berlin's,[65] and de Gaulle took pains to separate Cuba from 'other subjects or areas in the world' in his letter to Kennedy on 1 December. The reason for this is simple – French support given to the Americans was not a blank cheque.[66]

De Gaulle's pessimistic feelings about relations between the blocs were also confirmed by the crisis, since in a matter of vital interest the USA and the Soviet Union had preferred direct discussion to find a face-saving compromise. In a way, the Cuban crisis brought water to de Gaulle's mill and arguments that would support his major efforts. It was an occasion to reaffirm the necessity for close contacts between France and Britain,[67] France and Germany,[68] and, in the absence of US consultation,[69] for a framework of cooperation between Paris, London and Washington,[70] especially if a purely US crisis were to affect Europe.

In East–West relations, General de Gaulle observed a significant change.[71] The Americans 'were able to see that Khrushchev backed away when told no' and as an important consequence, if neither the Russians nor the Americans wanted war, 'there will thus be no war, at least not for a certain time'.[72] Within the modified context of the Nassau agreements and the multilateral nuclear force project, de Gaulle made use of the Cuban crisis to support his argument for an autonomous European defence and for his own nuclear deterrent. At the NATO ministerial meeting of 13–15 December, Rusk and Robert McNamara declared that the Cuban crisis had proven the efficiency of a flexible response and went on to defend a reinforcement of conventional means, since a multilateral nuclear deterrent would render national forces useless.[73] The French position, however, was diametrically opposite to this. For de Gaulle the lesson of the Cuban affair was clear, the Americans would not be willing to risk nuclear war to defend Europe, and this was the best justification for a policy of independence and for a necessity of a French nuclear force as well as refusal of any integration as proposed by the multilateral force.[74]

Finally, General de Gaulle found in the Cuban crisis a reason to leave the military organization of NATO at a later stage.[75] The crisis was used as an argument for ending the presence of US troops in France.[76]

That French officials highlighted France's loyalty to the Atlantic Alliance did not change anything in the reality of the situation.[77] France's attitude in the Cuban crisis lay more in 'understanding' the US initiative rather than approving of it and more in firmness towards the Soviet Union than in following the US lead.

NOTES

1 Please forgive me for quoting first Maurice Vaïsse, *La Grandeur, politique étrangère du Général de Gaulle 1958–1969*, Paris: Fayard, 1998; Maurice Vaïsse (ed.), *L'Europe et la crise de Cuba*, Paris: A. Colin, 1993. Additionally, basic documentation is available through the publication of the Documents Diplomatiques Français (DDF) which have all been published for the period studied here.
2 Gabriel Robin, 'La crise de Cuba', *Espoir*, 69, p. 12.
3 On the Berlin crisis, see Geneviève Humbert, 'Le général de Gaulle et le mur de Berlin', *Études gaulliennes*, July–December 1978; Bernard Ledwige, 'The Berlin Crisis', in Cyril Buffet, 'La politique nucléaire de la France et la seconde crise de Berlin', *Relations Internationales*, 59, pp. 347–58; Cyril Schwoebel, *Les 2 K, Berlin et la paix*, Paris: Julliard, 1963; Robert M. Slusser, *The Berlin Crisis of 1961*, Baltimore, MD: Johns Hopkins University Press, 1973; Anne-Marie Le Gloannec, *Un mur à Berlin*, Brussels: Complexe, 1985; Charles Zorgbibe, *La question de Berlin*, Paris: A. Colin, 1970. Regarding memoirs, see François Seydoux, *Mémoires d'outre-Rhin*, Paris: Grasset, 1975; Pierre Maillard, *De Gaulle et l'Allemagne*, Paris: Plon, 1990.
4 DDF, 1958, II, 370, 372, 375, 377 and 378.

5 De Gaulle–Vinogradov conversation, 2 March 1959, DDF 1959, I, 120.

6 Discours et Messages (DM) 1958–1962, pp. 82–94. It must be noted that the Polish Ambassador Gajewski had asked de Gaulle to explain the French position towards Poland's borders (in CM 7, FNSP).

7 From 1958, when the summit was first planned, France sought to buy time, and de Gaulle insisted to Khrushchev that a 'preparatory discussion' implying a 'serene and objective' atmosphere should take place. In two letters dated the same day, 20 October, the one short to Macmillan and the other a lengthy brief to Eisenhower ('I am struck in noticing to what degree is your pressing desire for an East–West entente'), de Gaulle dismissed the idea of a quick summons of the conference which would result, in this context, in highlighting the fundamental disagreement between East and West. He suggested it should be postponed to May or June 1960. Less than a week later, while agreeing to an invitation for the Soviet Prime Minister to come to France, he renewed this argument by suggesting a meeting of the Western Powers in Paris in December, and this says much of de Gaulle's delaying tactics regarding 'this very important meeting', Letter to Khrushchev, 30 June 1958, Lettres, Notes et Carnets (LNC) 1958–1960, pp. 39–41 and 21 July, pp. 50–1; Letter to Macmillan, 20 October, LNC 1958–1960, pp. 269–70, to Eisenhower, 20 October, LNC 1958–1960, pp. 270–93; Letter to Eisenhower, 26 October 1959, LNC 1958–1960, pp. 275–7.

8 These delaying tactics had several reasons. France wanted serious preparation; de Gaulle felt that negotiation gave Khrushchev a chance 'to manoeuvre between the Western Powers and to divide them'. First cool towards a summit conference, he admitted its importance, provided a Western meeting preceded it 'in order to agree in a precise manner our common stance': de Gaulle to Macmillan, 25 April 1959, LNC 1958–1960, pp. 217–18, 270–3. De Gaulle also wished to have direct contact with Khrushchev after the latter had received Macmillan in Moscow and visited Eisenhower: Press Conference, 10 November 1959, DM 1958–1960, pp. 129–44. The essential reason for this was that France was to test its atomic bomb at the beginning of 1960 and it mattered to de Gaulle to bring France into the atomic club before the conference, which might decide to ban all tests; Maurice Vaïsse, 'La France et le traité de Moscou', in Maurice Vaisse (ed.), La France et l'atome, Brussels: Bruylant, 1999.

9 Western summit conference, 19–21 December, DDF, 1959, I, 295.

10 It was the turn for a Soviet leader to come to France, since Guy Mollet, as premier, had travelled to Moscow in 1956. Khrushchev was delighted and de Gaulle wished to meet him personally before the summit conference. Dejean–Khrushchev conversation, 16 October 1959, DDF, 1959, II, 186.

11 Telegram 1760, 4 May 1961, Dejean/MAE, DDF 1960, I, 198. De Gaulle–Khrushchev conversation, 15 May, DDF, 1960, 221. Meeting of the four Western leaders, 15 May 1960, DDF, 1960, I, 221, pp. 648–59.

12 Macmillan–Debré conversation, 19 May 1960, DDF, 1960, I, 235.

13 French–Italian conversations, 26 November 1960, DDF, 1960, II, 232 ; NATO meeting, 8–10 May 1961, DDF, 1961, I, 234 and 239.

14 Minutes of NATO Council, 5 June 1961, DDF, 1961, I, 269.

15 Gromyko–Couve de Murville conversation, Geneva, 16 June 1961, DDF, 1961, I, 269.

16 Report of Jean Laloy, 25 June 1961, DDF, 1961, I, 304.

17 Conversations of the three Western ministers, 4–6 July 1961, AD, EM, 1961.

18 According to Seydoux, Mémoires d'outre-Rhin, p. 250, 'Adenauer's gratitude to de Gaulle reached its zenith'.

19 Harold Macmillan, Pointing the Way 1959–1961, London: Macmillan, 1972, pp. 64, 394, 426.

20 Maillard, De Gaulle et l' Allemagne, p. 199.

21 Letter to Nikita Khrushchev, 10 September 1959, LNC 1958–1960, pp. 255–6.

22 Le Gloannec, *Un mur à Berlin*, p. 105. It is known that the spy Georges Pâques had given the Soviets NATO's plans regarding the defence of Berlin (letter by Georges Pâques published in *Le Monde*, 8 January 1994).

23 DDF, 1959, I, 101; DDF, 1959, II, 13; DDF, 1960, I, 102; DDF 1960, II, 6, 111, 121, 188. There were in fact three groups of experts: a political one on East–West relations sitting in Washington; a military group in Paris, Live Oak, supervised by General Norstad and studying Soviet intentions and the rules of engagement in case terrestrial access was blocked; and a third in Bonn planning how to prevent the GDR authorities from obstructing traffic between Berlin and the Federal Republic.

24 DDF, 1961, 25 April 1961, I, 215.

25 DDF, 1961, 1 June 1961, I, 263. The putsch of the generals had taken place a few weeks earlier.

26 According to General Lacomme, head of the French Military government in Berlin, to François Seydoux, telegrams 1555, 1560, 28 August 1961, DDF, 1961, II, 88.

27 Maillard, *De Gaulle et l'Allemagne*, p. 179.

28 'From Colombey-les-Deux-Églises, my father gave the order for French troops to use tanks to crush the barbed wire and barriers as they were being erected before them. But they were each time outflanked by East German militiamen who were let through the neighbouring American sectors without hindrance. After a few days, the French, isolated, were forced to give up on this tit-for-tat. There, as elsewhere, Soviet enforcers stood close behind.' Philippe de Gaulle, *Mémoires accessoires*, Paris: Plon, 2000, p. 111.

29 DDF, 1961, II, 71 and 73.

30 Letter from Kennedy to de Gaulle, 24 August 1961, JFK, NSF, Box 73.

31 The instructions sent by Couve de Murville to Alphand before the 18 August meeting of the quadripartite group are clear: it was out of the question to consider talks, it would be a 'new Munich'; the Allies should be encouraged to treat problems of substance before those of procedure. DDF, 1961, II, 75 and 78.

32 DDF, 1961, II, 77, 84.

33 Telegram 1200, Gavin to the Secretary of State, 2 September 1961, JFK, NSF, France, Box 70.

34 DDF, 1961, II, 137.

35 Ibid., 139.

36 French–Italian talks, 26 November 1960, DDF, 1960, II, 232.

37 In his conversation with Macmillan at Birch Grove, on the afternoon of 24 November, de Gaulle explained that 'if the Americans decide to dump the Germans, they must not blame us French for it, they must not say that even the French did not want to build up Europe and turn to the Russians for business'. DDF, 1961, II, 192.

38 De Gaulle did not travel to Berlin during his visits to Germany. Regarding this matter, see Cyril Buffet, *La politique nucléaire*. It was Kennedy, and not de Gaulle, who came to Berlin and proclaimed, 'Ich bin ein Berliner'; also, Letter, Chauvel to Couve de Murville, 29 November 1961, DDF, 1961, II, 196.

39 During his press conference of 5 September 1961, de Gaulle spoke of 'Soviet demonstrations' and he accused the Soviets of using the Berlin affair 'to allay their suspicions or someone else's'. He concluded that this was an arbitrary and artificial case, either the fruit of a premeditated coup, or of frenetic ambition or a derivative, in the face of great difficulties. Confronted with this, the Westerners would not reply with nuclear war ('because what good is there to rule over the dead?') but they had the means to retaliate. The Soviets ought thus to cease their threats. For its part, France would not back down. At the end of September, during a tour in the Massif Central, de Gaulle renewed his insistance, 'France should in no way retreat or bow down ... Confronted with threats, one relinquishes one's hat, then one's jacket, then one's shirt, then one's skin, and finally one loses one's soul', in DM 1958–1962, pp. 335–8.

40 Seydoux, *Mémoires d'outre-Rhin*, p. 283: 'Caught between the fear of sacrifice and that of losing touch with the United States, the Bonn government, its bases uncomfortable, gestured in confusion.'

41 The bibliography on the Cuban crisis is immense: James Blight and David A. Welch, *On the Brink: Americans and Soviets Reexamine the Cuban Missile Crisis*, New York: Hill & Wang, 1989; Marc Trachtenberg, 'The influence of nuclear weapons in the Cuban missile crisis', *International Security*, summer 1985; McGeorge Bundy's chapter in *Danger and Survival*, New York: Vintage, 1990; Aleksandr Fursenko and Timothy Naftali, *One Hell of a Gamble: Khrushchev, Castro and Kennedy 1958–1962*, New York: Norton, 1997. In French, see the thesis by Alain Joxe, *Socialisme et crise nucléaire*, Paris: L'Herne, 1973; Manuela Semidei, *Kennedy et la révolution cubaine*, Julliard, Coll. 'Archives', Paris, 1972; Gabriel Robin, *La crise de Cuba*, Paris: Economica, 1972; Gabriel Rubin, 'La crise de Cuba', *Espoir*, 69; Hervé Savon, 'Cuba 1962, les interprétations possibles d'une crise nucléaire', *Revue de défense nationale*, July 1971; and the memoirs by Charles de Gaulle, *Mémoires d'espoir*, Paris: Plon, 1970; Maurice Couve de Murville, *Une politique étrangère 1958–1969*, Paris: Plon, 1971; Étienne Burin des Roziers, *1962, l'année décisive*, Paris: Plon, 1985.

42 The support given by de Gaulle is especially highlighted in Étienne Burin des Roziers' recollections, *1962: l'année décisive*, p. 136. Noting that de Gaulle had taken it upon himself to bring France's unequivocal support to the USA although 'the case was not clearly located within the framework of the Atlantic Pact', Burin des Roziers adds that 'France's immediate and resolute assistance produced immediately great effects in Washington. She had been an exemplary ally.'

43 All following references come from the collections of the Archives diplomatiques.

44 Telegrams 1452–1455, 28 February 1962, Alphand to MAE.

45 Telegram 455, 3 September 1962, du Gardier to MAE. The intermediaries are still unknown. In any case, it was not the military attaché, Colonel Pépin Le Halleur, who was residing in Mexico City and completely 'out of the loop'.

46 Telegram 428, 25 August 1962, du Gardier to MAE.

47 Telegram 399, 10 August 1962, du Gardier to MAE.

48 Telegram 410, 18 August 1962, du Gardier to MAE.

49 Telegram 410, 18 August. 'Auxiliary employees from the Embassy have come across at night some military convoys driving eastwards and heavy tractors hauling platforms with rocket launch pads a dozen metres long on them.'

50 Telegram 4555, 20 August 1962, Lebel to MAE.

51 General de Rancourt's interview in *L'entourage du Général de Gaulle*, Paris: Plon, 1979, pp. 312–15. Interview 100 by the oral history section of the Service historique de l'armée de l'Air.

52 The diplomat Claude Lebel, who acted as interpreter in this meeting, confirmed to us the spirit and letter of the account given by Dean Acheson, who was chosen for this mission because, as part of the crisis management team set up by Kennedy, he had opposed the principle of a military blockade of Cuba. He was thus sent to Europe to meet with de Gaulle and Adenauer. In the letter delivered to de Gaulle by Acheson, Kennedy explained that the Americans 'now have an undisputed proof that the Soviets ... have installed bases for offensive nuclear missiles in Cuba' and he added that 'I do not need to call your attention to the possible effects which this dangerous Soviet initiative ... could have over the situation in Berlin.'

53 *L'Année politique*, 1962, pp. 117–18.

54 *Le Monde*, 24 October 1962, editorial.

55 Circular telegram, 19 October 1962.

56 'General de Gaulle didn't care whether anyone believed it or not; he did, this was enough for him.

57 Telegram 4009, 23 October, Telegram 4025, 24 October, de Courcel (London) to MAE.
58 De Gaulle, Lettres, Notes et Carnets, 1961–1963, p. 270.
59 Circular Telegram 89, 23 October 1962, MAE to all diplomatic stations.
60 Circular Telegram, signed Laloy, 28 October 1962, and de Gaulle/Macmillan conversation, Rambouillet, 15 December 1962.
61 Letter, de Gaulle to Adenauer, 26 October 1962, LNC, p. 270, and de Gaulle to Macmillan, 6 November, LNC, p. 272. In his letter to Adenauer, de Gaulle repeated his idea that 'The Cuban crisis has been for the Americans ... certainly salutary.' Writing on 30 November upon returning from a visit to the USA, Adenauer confirmed this impression to de Gaulle.
62 Letter, Kennedy to de Gaulle, 28 October 1962; Kennedy to de Gaulle, 20 and 22 November 1962.
63 Letter, de Gaulle to Kennedy, 1 December 1962, LNC, p. 278. However, according to Bernard Ledwidge, de Gaulle privately criticized Kennedy for not taking advantage of his success (ibid., p. 295): 'According to General de Gaulle, Kennedy should have demanded Castro's departure and refused to withdraw his missiles from Turkey.' But was de Gaulle aware of the bargain struck by the Americans and the Soviets over Turkey? And did this 'bargain' even exist? The idea of a withdrawal, suggested during a private conversation between Ambassador Dobrynin and Robert Kennedy, was used as a face-saving alibi for Khrushchev, despite the fact that their withdrawal had already been decided owing to their obsolescence.
64 Letter, de Gaulle to Kennedy, 2 November 1962; Couve–Ikeda conversation, 8 November 1962.
65 Letter, Kennedy to de Gaulle, 24 October 1962: 'a particular test in Berlin'.
66 According to the recollection of Léo Hamon, de Gaulle's words to other visitors on 22 October showed a very different state of mind. With General Gambiez, de Gaulle wondered aloud about ways in which France might be automatically linked to the USA and involved through the fait accompli of French–American relations. See L'entourage et Général de Gaulle, pp. 312–15. It was not possible to verify this allegation. M. Léo Hamon confirms it. General Gambiez's memoirs are unfortunately inaccessible.
67 Letter, de Gaulle to Harold Macmillan, 22 October 1962, LNC, p. 269. The same idea was discussed in an answer to Macmillan's own letter of 25 October in which the British Prime Minister asked de Gaulle: 'How can it be insured that Europe's interests will be better defended?'
68 Letter, de Gaulle to Konrad Adenauer, 26 October 1962, LNC, p. 270. De Gaulle's correspondence with the German Chancellor is both more more verbose and cordial in tone than that with the British Prime Minister. This was an idyllic period in Franco-German relations leading up to the Treaty of the Élysée.
69 Letter, de Gaulle to Macmillan, 6 November 1962, LNC, p. 272: 'It is true that neither you, nor we ... were consulted with.'
70 Maurice Vaïsse, 'Aux origines du mémorandum de septembre 1958', Relations Internationales, 58.
71 According to M. Burin des Roziers, 'It was from this crisis that the eastern wind began to bring a new melody to the General's ears.' De Gaulle's letter to President Kennedy seems to contradict this interpretation at least in the short term.
72 Minutes of the de Gaulle–Macmillan conversation, 15 December 1962.
73 Circular telegram 115, 19 December 1962.
74 'For us, in its kind, integration is not something that we can conceive', press conference of 14 January 1963, DM, vol. 4, p. 73.
75 Speech of Georges Pompidou to the National Assembly, 20 April 1966: 'We approved President Kennedy, but before we had even made our position known, whereas NATO forces were meant to be outside the conflict ... US forces in Europe, including those in

France, had been put on alert ... Does this give you cause for reflection? If there really should come a day on which a conflict should occur between the United States and the USSR regarding interests foreign to France and to our obligations within the alliance, who can argue that the fact of harbouring on our territory the American headquarters in Europe would not constitute for us an obvious and serious risk?'

76 Joxe, *Socialisme*, p. 548.
77 As witnessed in a declaration by Georges Pompidou to the National Assembly (13 December 1962, JO, 14 December, pp. 41–2): 'This crisis allowed, I believe, our powerful and old American allies to take this into account, and I have reason to believe that having recognized that in trying times the most self-assured allies are neither the less robust nor the less visionary, they will reach a few conclusions as to the very functioning of the Alliance.'

6

Cold War Crises and Public Opinion: West European Public Opinion and the Berlin Wall, 1961

Eckart Conze

The headlines of the *Bild-Zeitung* on 16 August 1961 are well known. Framed with drawings of barbed wire, Axel Springer's German mass tabloid declared in bold letters: 'Der Osten handelt – was tut der Westen? Der Westen tut NICHTS! Präsident Kennedy schweigt ... Macmillan geht auf die Jagd ... und Adenauer schimpft auf Willy Brandt' (The East Is Acting – What Is the West Doing? The West Is Doing NOTHING! President Kennedy Keeps Silent ... Macmillan Goes Hunting ... and Adenauer Complains about Willy Brandt).[1] The newspaper seemed to be expressing only what millions of Germans and above all Berliners were thinking in the days immediately after the building of the Berlin Wall on 13 August 1961. Rage and fury but also disappointment and bitterness were the prevailing emotions: rage and fury over the Ulbricht regime's measures, disappointment and bitterness over the obvious passivity of the West German government, but even more over that of the Western powers and especially the USA under President Kennedy. Two years later, however, the tide had turned. On 16 July 1963, the *Bild-Zeitung* looked back at the events of 1961 in another light: 'If there is one city where Kennedy – even if he wanted – cannot be a foreign conqueror, this city is Berlin. This city is alive because of America. ... On 13 August 1961 Kennedy was indeed afraid of conflict – of nuclear conflict. Perhaps this fear was unjustified. But someone who cares about mankind's survival does not deserve defamation.'[2]

This change of judgment characterizing not only the *Bild-Zeitung* is indeed remarkable. And it needs to be explained. This leads us to an important question, important in particular for the Federal Republic of Germany. Why, after August 1961, was it the case that neither did defeatist tendencies spread over West Germany nor did an extreme, German-centred, reunification nationalism gain ground? When the West Germans went to the polls on 17 September 1961, only one month after the events in Berlin, their political preferences changed only to a very limited extent. It is true that the Christian Democratic Union (CDU) and Christian Social Union (CSU) under Chancellor Adenauer lost the absolute majority which they had won in 1957. But the Social

Democratic Party (SPD), and its top candidate Willy Brandt, gained votes not because they were advocating, for example, a political course of national neutralism in order to bring about German reunification; indeed, exactly the opposite was the case. Brandt's SPD in 1961 stood for a clear Western orientation, and no one represented this Western orientation and, above all, the West German alliance with the USA better than did Berlin's governing mayor Willy Brandt. Perhaps, we could refer to an increased German nationalism as one factor, among others, for the electoral success of Germany's liberal third party, the Free Democrats (FDP). Under its chairman Erich Mende, a bearer of the Knight's Cross (Ritterkreuz), the liberal party achieved its best electoral results since 1949, some 12.8 per cent of the vote. We must, however, interpret this result not only as a consequence of the voters' opposition to a continued one-party government of the CDU/CSU and instead as support for a new government coalition of the CDU/CSU and FDP, and a strong desire to see the end of the Adenauer chancellorship as part of a CDU/CSU–FDP coalition agreement. However, it is important to note that the emotionalization of West German public opinion and public mood did not have direct and immediate repercussions for West Germany's political landscape.

We cannot simply apply these questions, developed with regard to West Germany and West Berlin, to other West European countries such as France or Britain on which, together with Germany, this analysis will focus.[3] The questions which this contribution will address are, first, whether public opinion in those countries had effects on the policies of London and Paris *vis-à-vis* Germany and Berlin and whether it actually did influence these policies. Second, we must ask whether and how the policies of the two governments affected public opinion. These questions are all the more important and interesting as they refer to two very different sets of policies. While the British government demonstrated its willingness to negotiate on the questions of Berlin and Germany and while Prime Minister Harold Macmillan declared, in the middle of a golf party, that the Wall crisis had been 'got up by the press',[4] the French government's, and particularly the French president's, public positions were extremely tough. General de Gaulle categorically ruled out negotiations – especially under the pressure of the ongoing crisis.[5] While during the summer of 1961 the French press was referring quite often to the experience with 'appeasement' and warning against a 'second Munich', the British press did not share this tendency to cite historical lessons.

A few brief remarks regarding the term 'public opinion' are important. To define 'public opinion' is an extremely difficult if not impossible task. Therefore, this chapter will not try to define or theoretically clarify the term. Political scientists, for example, have been arguing for quite some time about a so-called elite concept of public opinion as opposed to an integrationist concept. The elite concept, on the one hand, excludes the majority of the population from the formation and articulation of public opinion, due above all to a lack of knowledge and competence. Following this concept, public opinion is based on rationality and formed in a discourse of the educated and the competent aiming at political judgments and pursuing the idea of a common public interest. According to the elite concept, public opinion is a process of rational public discourse. The integrationist concept, on the other hand, includes every member of the society. Here, public opinion serves as a means of social control exercising the pressure of conformity, thus guaranteeing social cohesion and integration. Following this understanding, public opinion is based much less on rationality and much more on emotion, regulated by 'unwritten laws'. It is not rational arguments and positions that are of central importance, but rather morally charged values and emotions.[6] Of course, one could argue endlessly about these concepts and approaches. For our purposes, however, it is not necessary to choose between the analytical connection of political events and political action, on the one hand, and public opinion, on the other. Instead, this chapter will follow Vladimir O. Key's more pragmatic definition. Key was interested primarily in finding an 'applicable' understanding of 'public opinion'. Based on his empirical studies, Key developed a view that regards 'public opinion' *not* as a reality or a personified entity taking the initiative and working as a mechanism to transform its specific purposes into government action. Rather, Key sees 'public opinion' as 'a system of dikes, which channel public action or which fix a range of discretion within which debate at official levels may proceed. This conception avoids the error of personifying "public opinion" as an entity that exercises initiative and in some way functions as an operating organism to translate its purposes into governmental action.'[7] Elements of such a dyke system are the media (representing 'published opinion'), opinion polls, and also the voices of individual protagonists (politicians, journalists, intellectuals), the so-called 'opinion leaders'.

This chapter will first address the situation in West Berlin and West Germany in the aftermath of 13 August 1961. In the second and third parts, it will turn to the developments in Britain and France before finishing with a few concluding thoughts concerning the effects of the Berlin Wall in the 1960s on Western European public opinion *vis-à-vis* the Berlin problem and the German question and the East–West conflict in general.[8] It will concentrate on an analysis of national press and of opinion polls, two main pillars of public opinion. The article does not explicitly include radio and television coverage of the events, although the effects of televised images in particular on the formation of public opinion and public mood should not be underestimated. It is, however, difficult to describe exactly the way TV coverage of a certain event was received by the public and how TV images therefore influenced public opinion. Those dramatic images from Berlin – from the building of the Wall to the desperate attempts of East Germans to reach the West to the October 1961 tank confrontation at Checkpoint Charlie – must have left their marks on public opinion in both Germany and Western Europe. In 1960, some three million private households in the Federal Republic were equipped with a TV set, and, additionally, numerous pubs owned televisions and attracted a considerable number of viewers. The situation in France and Britain was similar.[9]

I

The federal election campaign in West Germany was approaching its final month when on Sunday, 13 August 1961, East German military and police units began a systematic closure of the border between Berlin's Eastern and Western sectors – first with barbed wire, later with a wall of bricks and concrete. That this occurred during the election campaign is important in and of itself for the simple reason that the two top candidates were at the same time holding the two most important political positions with regard to the Berlin crisis in West Germany: Konrad Adenauer as federal chancellor and Willy Brandt as governing mayor of West Berlin. Without a doubt, these two politicians' behaviour in the first days after the building of the Wall, their reactions to the events in Berlin, were strongly influenced by the campaign situation. Willy Brandt, travelling in a night train from an SPD national meeting (Deutschlandtreffen) in Nuremberg to a campaign stop in Kiel, was informed about the events in Berlin in the middle of the night; he interrupted his journey immediately and flew from Hanover back to his city, where he received an initial briefing in front of the Brandenburg gate before chairing a Sunday meeting of the Berlin Senate. A continuation of his campaign was ruled out; instead, the developments in Berlin determined Brandt's actions during the following days. In a public communiqué of 13 August, the mayor accused East Germany and the Soviet Union of 'illegal and inhumane measures'.[10] At the same time, however, he asked the West Berliners 'to remain calm despite their outrage'.[11] Brandt also publicly addressed the population in East Berlin and the GDR, urging them 'not to let themselves be carried away' however 'strong and legitimate the embitterment may be'.[12] The communiqué reflects Brandt's public course during these first days: condemning the East German measures and pressuring the Western powers to do something against them, on the one hand, and asking the populace to remain calm and to act wisely, on the other. In the weeks before 13 August, Berlin and the German question had only been marginal themes in Brandt's campaign. The increasing tensions over the city, owing to Kennedy's and Khrushchev's Vienna summit meeting in June as well as the daily growth in the number of East German refugees, did not play a significant role in the campaign. Brandt, the 'German Kennedy', consistently followed a campaign strategy based on the assumption that German voters were tired of the party-political quarrels of the 1950s and were also tired of an SPD opposition permanently saying 'no'; instead, the campaign strategy assumed a broad interest in material improvements and thus in economic and social stability. This situation changed after the building of the Wall: the questions of Berlin and of German reunification suddenly dominated the campaign agenda of all the parties, and the governing mayor of the divided city was the last person who could possibly avoid them.

Konrad Adenauer, at Rhöndorf when informed of the situation in Berlin, embarked on a very similar course – at least on 13 August. On that day the chancellor stressed in a public broadcast: 'Together with our allies, the necessary counter measures have been implemented.'[13] Apart from this statement, however, the chancellor too tried to calm the people and avoid both a war panic and uncontrollable, possibly violent, protests in Berlin. The crisis in Berlin must not turn into a 'second Hungary'; it must not be allowed to escalate or explode. 'There is no reason to panic', Adenauer stressed in a TV address that first day.[14] Adenauer did lose votes, perhaps even the absolute majority, because he did not fly to Berlin immediately in order to articulate his protest on the spot and show political presence and solidarity with the people of Berlin. We know that for a brief moment, the chancellor did indeed consider such a trip, but then refrained from it so as to avoid further 'heating up' the public mood, thereby making the dynamics of the situation even more incalculable. Politically, this decision may have been wise and statesmanlike. The public echo, however, in both Berlin and West Germany was devastating, and it had an effect on the elections of 17 September. That effect was further exacerbated by the fact that Adenauer not only continued to do 'business as usual', downplaying events as a 'pre-crisis', presenting them as one part of a 'war of nerves', but also that he even went ahead with his election campaign – without obvious irritation and without major changes. In order to demonstrate 'business as usual', he not only refused to cancel a campaign rally in Regensburg (Bavaria) on 14 August, but attacked Willy Brandt both politically and personally during this rally, calling him 'Brandt alias Frahm', a low blow directed against both his opponent's birth out of wedlock and his emigration from Germany during the Nazi years.[15] It was not only the *Bild Zeitung* (*BZ*) tabloid which regarded the 'Brandt alias Frahm' remark as an extremely unfair attack, politically and personally. More or less in unison, the German press from Axel Springer's *Welt* and the *Frankfurter Allgemeine Zeitung* (*FAZ*) to the more liberal *Süddeutsche Zeitung* condemned Adenauer's behaviour. It was during these days that an image took shape of a chancellor who in the middle of a dangerous international crisis continued his election campaign and party rivalry on the lowest level while, at the same time, Willy Brandt in a bipartisan way had interrupted his campaign in order to fulfil his duty at the scene of the crisis. In Germany, this image had effects even beyond 17 September, and it caused considerable political damage to Adenauer and the CDU/CSU. Opinion polls confirm these developments: while in July 1961, these polls saw the CDU and CSU still winning around 49 per cent of the votes, by mid-August, these numbers had fallen to 35 per cent. At the same time, the SPD percentage increased correspondingly. The degree of preference for Adenauer as a *person* ('Who – personally – is the better Chancellor, Adenauer or Brandt?') was still at 45 per cent at the end of August; the number of those disagreeing with Adenauer had, however, climbed between the end of July and the end of August from 18 per cent to 26 per cent.[16]

The reasons behind this negative trend for Adenauer were the chancellor's perceived passivity, his decision not to visit Berlin at an early date and his personal attacks on Brandt. Moreover, we must also include the perceived Western passivity after 13 August, for which Adenauer was also blamed. The chancellor's remarks about the 'pre-crisis' and the ongoing 'war of nerves' were indeed not the kind of arguments which could have motivated the Western powers to implement concrete countermeasures. Not only for the *BZ* was it the case that Adenauer, Kennedy and Macmillan were in the same boat, interestingly, de Gaulle was not mentioned when it came to blaming the West for inaction. The 'doing nothing' argument nevertheless dominated the German press commentaries and the headlines in the days immediately after 13 August. We must distinguish several patterns of argumentation. Liberal papers and those closer to the SPD explained the passivity of the West and above all of the USA with reference to Adenauer's policy during the 1950s – his political course of unconditional Western integration and his alleged lack of interest in the fate of the East Germans or East Berliners and on the question of German reunification in general. Marion Countess Dönhoff of the German weekly *Die Zeit* voiced this view when she declared that the building of the Wall and the passivity of the Western powers were 'the receipt for the long sleep'.[17] Papers on the right of the political arena, among them the Springer press published in Berlin (*BZ* and *Die Welt*) and also the *FAZ*, condemned primarily the passivity of the West implicitly or explicitly; even the accusation of 'treason' appeared in these papers.[18] In general, the papers on the right agreed, considering the situation a severe crisis of confidence between the Federal Republic and the West. Words with a very clear connotation, such as 'appeasement' and 'Munich,' appeared in headlines and articles. Against this background it was absolutely logical that the Bonn students who sent an umbrella to President Kennedy on 16 August had a close connection to the CDU: 'With your reluctant reaction to the events in Berlin', the students wrote in an open letter, 'you, Mr President, have proved to be today the most dignified bearer of this symbol of a failed policy.'[19] Since the 1938 Munich Agreement and the policy of 'appeasement' which belonged to the collective experience of a whole generation of Europeans – not only the British or Germans – the effect of these references can hardly be overestimated, although they do not lend themselves to precise measurement.

Together with the strong criticism in the media of Western passivity, public gestures like the umbrella for Kennedy were decisive in changing the policy in Washington, which took place approximately one week after the building of the Wall. Basically, the USA continued their policy of de-escalation and did not extend their political and military guarantees beyond West Berlin (as defined by Kennedy in his 'Three Essentials' on 25 July 1961).[20] But the danger of a crisis of confidence within the West and, therefore, of a crisis within NATO with unknown repercussions, the danger of alienating Germany from the West was the main motivation for Washington's countermeasures, its new policy of symbolical commitment. As a result of this, the USA sent a battle group – militarily meaningless – over the Autobahn from West Germany to West Berlin, where on 20 August the soldiers were welcomed by US Vice President Lyndon Johnson and, almost more important, by General Lucius Clay, the hero of the Berlin airlift. 'The West Berliners are cheering again' – 'Die Westberliner jubeln wieder' – ran the headline of the *Süddeutsche Zeitung* the day after, and that was a good description of the changing mood.[21] The dispatch of a US battalion may have been a merely symbolic act. But it was exactly the right measure given a collective conviction, deeply rooted in West Berlin especially, that the communists could only be driven back with the threat of force.

It is an ironic development, however, that the US measures took place at a time when in West Berlin and West Germany the media pressure against passivity and for strong Western countermeasures had started to decrease. This seems to have been the result of a growing awareness by these media of an imminent crisis of confidence between West Berliners and West Germans, on the one hand, and the Western allies, on the other. Obviously, the danger of a crisis of confidence, taken seriously on both sides, led to this double change of course.

Of equally decisive importance for US behaviour was a letter which Willy Brandt, in his role as mayor of West Berlin, had sent to Kennedy on 18 August, urging the president to do something.[22] And even this letter became part of the German election campaign. The office of the chancellor in Bonn, with which the letter had not been discussed in advance, leaked the letter to the press in order to be able to present Brandt as an inexperienced, boastful and, above all, unsuccessful politician, as somebody without any weight and voice outside Germany and especially in the USA. At the beginning, Washington's course seemed to confirm this argument, but, when the US changed its policy in order to avoid a crisis of confidence and so embarked upon its policy of symbolic measures, the chancellor and his staff had lost the game. Johnson's visit to West Berlin and the military dispatch provided an ideal opportunity for Brandt to present himself publicly as the man whose efforts had motivated a hesitant USA to act forcefully in Berlin. Adenauer had been duped, and his situation got even worse when Johnson refused to take the Old Man in his plane to Berlin – saying that he did not want to intervene in the German election campaign. Brandt had the opportunity to present himself for six hours in the eyes of the media together with the US vice president. Not only did the mayor take over the 'emotional crisis management' (Ch. Klessmann), but the visible harmony between Brandt and the US government had consequences as part of a process reaching beyond the year 1961 and beyond the city of Berlin. As late as 1960, Adenauer had told French Prime Minister Michel Debré that his close relations with the USA, which would make the West German population feel secure, had already helped him to win three elections.[23] If we take this statement as a basic principle of West German political life and electoral behaviour after 1949 – and there are many reasons to do so – it is no surprise that Brandt profited politically from events in the summer of 1961. After 1959–60, the SPD became more and more the USA's party in Germany, while, at the same time, the CDU/CSU seemed to lose touch with the USA. When Adenauer finally visited Berlin, a few days after Johnson, his reception there was cool and reserved: too little, too late. The Old Man had lost an important battle.

In view of his experience in Berlin, but even more in view of miserable opinion polls, Adenauer tried to regain lost ground during the last weeks before the election by presenting himself to the German public as the 'Chancellor of Peace' (Friedenskanzler), as a 'statesman of firm prudence'.[24] He intensified his contacts with Kennedy and Macmillan, stressing the West's common interests and the Western governments' responsibility for world peace. Adenauer kept emphasizing at campaign rallies that everything should be done to prevent Berlin from triggering a third world war. With these statements, the chancellor even earned written praise from Harold Macmillan, which had been unthinkable before 1961; he addressed Adenauer in a letter, immediately published by the German government, as 'My dear friend'.[25] The *Guardian* considered the letter 'probably the most welcome communication that the Federal Chancellor has ever received from a British Prime Minister'.[26] Together with the CDU/CSU's extreme campaign efforts, Adenauer's states-manlike appearances achieved the aim of reversing the trend against the chancellor and his party. Between mid-August and the eve of the election, the CDU/CSU increased their percentage in the opinion polls from 35 per cent to 46 per cent; on the election day, the Union parties received 45.3 per cent of the vote (48 per cent of the Bundestag seats); Brandt's SPD increased its results from 31.8 per cent in 1957 to 36.2 per cent. The liberal FDP won 12.8 per cent and once again became the coalition partner of the CDU/CSU.

What is remarkable about this election result and the general political mood in West Germany in 1961 is that the events in Berlin did not lead to a larger growth of right-wing nationalist tendencies. Nor was it the case that more left-wing national–neutralist forces were able to profit from the situation. The Deutsche Reichspartei (DRP), to mention just one example, had won 1 per cent of the vote in 1957; four years later, it only gained 0.8 per cent.[27] Voices like that of the nationalist and monarchist association Kaiser und Reich, criticizing the Federal Republic's alliance with the West and blaming the Bonn parties for selling out German interests, remained a tiny minority and did not enter or influence the mainstream of political discourse in West Germany.[28] What is important in this regard, however, is the overlapping of these right-wing positions with those expressed by the SPD's extreme left wing and beyond. Those voices spoke of a failure in Bonn's foreign policy, a failure caused by the policy's 'logical and moral contradictions'. Bonn's foreign policy had merely pursued the 'left-Elbian objective' of Western integration; it had 'provided no answer to the question of how to re-establish German unity'.[29] Of course, this argumentation had a core of truth: not only Adenauer's critics and opponents, but also the chancellor himself and his party were aware that the simple calculation of the 1950s – Western integration plus policy of strength equals German reunification – had, at least in the short run, not worked out, that the division of Germany had deepened and that it would be difficult in the foreseeable future to overcome it.

Without a doubt, the SPD would have been the political home and the main force of these neutralist positions only a few years earlier. But with its Godesberg party programme (1959) and with Herbert Wehner's Bundestag speech in June of 1960 in which he firmly committed his party to Western integration, the SPD had started to change. Willy Brandt's rise within the party was the most obvious sign of this change. The Social Democrats' new chancellor candidate, and party chairman a few years later, represented the SPD's new Western – that is, US – orientation. Nominating Brandt as its top candidate in 1960, the SPD publicly left its neutralism behind. And, with the building of the Wall, this political course had become irreversible. To change this policy in a time of crisis was unthinkable. It would have meant to stab Willy Brandt in the back, to damage him publicly and thus to commit political suicide. In the summer of 1961, there was no relevant political force in West Germany advocating national–neutralist positions. There was no force which would have been able – in view of the temporary lability of public opinion – to develop and pursue an alternative political course. We can hardly over-estimate this development for the history of the SPD, not only for its German and foreign policy positions. The *de facto* consensus between West Germany's important parties, above all between the SPD and the CDU/CSU, prevented the rise of extreme political positions in the realm of foreign affairs on the right as well as on the left. The role played by the SPD on the left was played by the CDU/CSU and the FDP on the right. The CDU/CSU and the SPD met in the centre – despite an ongoing election campaign. These last observations should warn us not to construct too direct a link between public opinion, on the one hand, and the behaviour of parties, politicians and governments, on the other. Public opinion, moods and tendencies require parties and political institutions with a corresponding disposition in order to have an effect.

II

The following opinion of a British reader of the *New York Times*, taken from a letter to the editor, was not an exception:

> Your correspondent … is probably right in his opinion that the British population as a whole does not hate the Germans in the present situation. But he is completely wrong if he thinks that there is unanimous support for NATO's obligations *vis-à-vis* Berlin. I have not met one of my fellow country-men who would be willing to risk annihilation in a nuclear war for Herr Willy Brandt and his Berliners, among which there are without any doubt many members of former Nazi youth organisations. Memories are deep, and our cities still show the scars caused by the brutal air raids carried out by a nation which to defend we are now obliged. It is no surprise that in this country the enthusiasm for a reunified Germany is so low.[30]

Of course, British attitudes toward Berlin and the German question varied considerably, but we can nevertheless clearly identify a general tendency. Much more often than was the case in the USA or France or West Germany, British politicians, journalists and others in public life argued for a moderate, softer course with regard to Berlin and Germany, advocating talks and negotiations. They were more prepared to accept the 'reality' of Germany's division. As was articulated not only in that letter to the editor, this division had been caused by Germany's 'historical guilt'.[31] This is reflected in the opinion polls: especially during the summer and autumn of 1961, more than 50 per cent of the British surveyed were willing to accept recognition of the GDR; less than 20 per cent were against it.[32] And while in the USA, 71 per cent of the people asked said that they were willing to accept the risk of war over Berlin, this quota was only 41 per cent in Britain.[33] 'Among the many aims for which I prefer not to die, I would give German reunification the first rank', declared the leading editor of the *New Statesman* a few days before 13 August 1961.[34] The atmosphere of tension following the building of the Wall may have increased the articulation of such positions and tendencies. They did not, however, come out of the blue but had been part of British public opinion in the 1950s. To mention just two examples, this had become clear in regard to the idea of 'disengagement' – during the discussion of the Rapacki plan or in George F. Kennan's BBC Reith lectures – or, later, in the aftermath of Khrushchev's Berlin ultimatum in November of 1958 and during the Geneva Foreign Ministers' Conference in 1959. Macmillan's 'Voyage of Discovery' to Moscow, which Konrad Adenauer considered treasonous, met with broad approval in Britain; this political trip improved Macmillan's public standing and his popularity considerably; and unlike Eisenhower, de Gaulle or Adenauer, Macmillan's 'valiant effort' to bring Western determination home to the USSR garnered praise from the British press.[35] There can be no doubt that his trip and his East–West policy in general further strengthened his image – at least at home – as a 'world statesman' and certainly helped him win the general election in October of 1959. His victory was a considerable personal triumph, securing a vast 107 seat Conservative majority over the Labour Party.[36]

British public opinion before and after 13 August 1961 was characterized – both by the overwhelming number of political or journalistic opinion leaders and by the man on the famous Clapham omnibus – by a willingness, though not any pressure, to negotiate on Berlin and the German problem. After 13 August, this did not prevent British countermeasures and signals of determination in Berlin, for example a reinforcement of British troops in the city and in West Germany. What the West Germans and, even more, the West Berliners welcomed enthusiastically in the US case, however, they hardly seemed to realize in that of the British. The image of Britain and its attitude was not one of firm determination or even willingness to go to war. What are the reasons? What are the roots of the British course and the broad public support it received in the UK?

As already mentioned, we must not underestimate the weight of history, the weight of the past, the significance of collective generational experiences related above all to Nazism and the Second World War, which around 1960 was not a very distant past. The Federal Republic had become a NATO ally during the 1950s. But had Germany and the Germans really changed? Very rarely did British politicians ask this question loudly or publicly; it would have been against the *'raison d'alliance'*. But there can be no doubt that scepticism or even hostility toward Germany was not limited to Lord Beaverbrook and his press such as the *Daily Express*, which wrote in August of 1961: 'Adenauer or Brandt? For us that doesn't make a difference. Both are Germans. And the Germans never change.'[37] Or when referring to West German demands to impose an economic embargo against the GDR or the whole Eastern bloc: 'As we know the West Germans, they will talk a lot about an embargo, but they will never stop the flood of their exports to East Germany. They bring too much money.'[38] Letters to the editor, published in all major newspapers and journals, allow conclusions about deeply rooted images, their continued strength and effect long after 1945 and their connection with current German affairs such as the Berlin crisis. One reader mentions a poster, displayed at one of the mass demonstrations in West Berlin after 13 August, showing a map of Germany with the borders of 1937: 'Does Britain support this position?' the letter asked.[39] Another reader referred to the TV coverage of the same event: 'Is there anyone above 40 who saw the televised picture of Wednesday's Berlin rally who could fail to be reminded of the days of Hitler? The same intonation of the German orator; the same well driven cheers at the proper causes; even the same appeal to the hatred of communism. Are we really going to allow these people to drag us into a third and last world war?'[40] These resentments and prejudices *vis-à-vis* Germany and the Germans were linked – especially on the left side of the political spectrum – with a remainder of good will toward the Soviet Union and the other Eastern European states as 'victims of fascism'.[41] Of course, collective memories are highly selective. Unlike the case in Germany or France, 'Munich 1938' did not, or only very rarely, come up as an issue or a catch-phrase in Britain. While the German and the French press were confronting the West with the 'lessons of 1938', the British government was not reminded publicly of the events of two decades earlier. 'Herr Brandt fears second Munich', was the title of a news article in the *Guardian*.[42] But in its commentaries addressing the London government, the danger of 'appeasement' was not mentioned. Not only the left and the liberal press were arguing for negotiations and, very often, for a solution to the German question and to the international tensions related to it through German neutralization and military disengagement; in their party conference resolutions in 1961, Labour and the British Liberals followed the same line. A Berlin resolution of the annual Labour Party conference in Blackpool asked for recognition of the current German–Polish border, official recognition of the GDR and for an arms control agreement in Central Europe.[43] The Liberals' Berlin resolution declared the party's commitment to the defence of West Berlin and, at the same time, the will to make concessions on the question of German reunification.[44]

Also deeply rooted in British elite thinking – and unlike that in the USA, for example – was the tradition of political realism, especially with regard to foreign affairs. This was a realism with sensitivity for the feasible and the achievable together with a pragmatic foreign policy influenced by an at least general preparedness to accept political facts – perhaps not for a distant future, but for the foreseeable future. 'A limited arrangement', the *Guardian* wrote in a commentary on 25 August, 'a limited agreement need not prejudice the future for all time. If attempts at it could be coupled with negotiations on nuclear-free zones in Germany … it might even, given skilful bargaining, be made to yield positive advantages.'[45]

It seems to me that an even more important factor influencing public opinion in the UK was the fact that an ideological, social and socio-cultural anti-communism was not as well developed as it was especially in the USA and the Federal Republic. To relate this general point to the Berlin question: unlike in West Germany or the USA, in Britain the defence of Berlin or of West Berlin was not regarded so much as part of a greater battle against the global communist threat to the so-called 'free world'. In the 1950s, this kind of thinking had not only united Konrad Adenauer and John Foster Dulles, in the years of the Truman and Eisenhower administrations, it had stabilized German–US relations politically on the elite level but also on a broader social level. The role of the British Communist Party in this context was marginal; McCarthy-style witch hunts had no chance in Britain. It was the Labour Party which represented an ideology of class struggle, and the Labour Party's existence and legitimacy were never questioned in British politics. And Labour was also the bridge over which – in a complex network of relations – the foreign and security policy thinking of the British peace movement (for example, of the Campaign for Nuclear Disarmament – CND) entered into and influenced party-political discourse.[46]

III

Asked in 1962 which Western politician had done the most for Berlin, the clear winner in both West Berlin and West Germany was John F. Kennedy: 61 per cent of the West Berliners and 44 per cent of the West Germans regarded Kennedy's behaviour as 'very good' or 'good'. Only 12 per cent and 10 per cent respectively considered Macmillan's Berlin policy as 'very good' or 'good'; 25 per cent of the West Germans called the British prime minister's behaviour 'poor' or 'insufficient'. Only one Western politician received equally bad grades from an even greater number of West Germans: French President Charles de Gaulle. Some 28 per cent of the West Germans saw his Berlin policy as 'poor' or 'insufficient'; only 12 per cent praised it as 'very good' or 'good'.[47]

These results may be surprising. Was not the French President the single Western politician who argued forcefully and without compromise for the maintenance of the status of Berlin, who was not willing to negotiate with the Soviets under pressure? The famous headlines of the *Bild-Zeitung*, quoted at the beginning of this chapter, blamed Adenauer and Brandt, Kennedy and Macmillan, but not de Gaulle for the Western passivity. We know the differences between the French and the 'Anglo-Saxon' policies on Berlin and Germany in the summer of 1961, and we know the political reasons for the French position: de Gaulle's endeavour to maintain France's status as a victorious power of the Second World War (after 1955, it was only in Berlin where this status was reflected *de facto* and *de jure*). We know about his strategy to build a closer alliance with the German chancellor so as to gain his support for the French European initiatives, with the objective also of winning general West German support for a French policy directed against US hegemony in Western Europe.[48] These reasons and motivations dominating de Gaulle's Berlin policy but not substantially related to it were not known to the broader French public, however. French opinion polls in 1961 did not reflect or support de Gaulle's tough attitude and uncompromising rhetoric. In the autumn of 1961, only 30 per cent of the French surveyed shared the opinion that their president was more able than Kennedy to deal with Khrushchev; 23 per cent thought exactly the opposite; and the largest number (47 per cent) were unsure. In August of 1961, 80 per cent of the people asked were against risking war over Berlin; 62 per cent thought that negotiations were possible. At the same time, however, 44 per cent wanted French troops to remain in the city; only 31 per cent supported a withdrawal. Forty-three per cent were of the opinion that the more the Western world conceded to the Soviet Union, the more the latter would demand; only 25 per cent did not share this position.[49]

Apart from these positions and data, it is important to note how de Gaulle's policy and his rhetoric were obviously developing relatively independently from the positions, preferences and tendencies of French public opinion.

Again, we are confronted with a situation that warns us not to draw too direct a causal link between amorphous public opinion and the actions of governments or political elites. The picture is more complicated. 'Munich' is one argument in this regard. Fears of war could not be ignored in France. 'Mourir pour Berlin?' was the question discussed in the French press. De Gaulle countered this question by pointing to 1938, which for the French too was not distant pre-history but still part of the present, a living generational experience. Had not de Gaulle in 1938 been an opponent of the Western policy, that of the British and the French, which had led to Munich? 'Un second Munich?' – De Gaulle's rhetorical worry was the headline on the front page of *Le Monde* on 30 August 1961, a paper that normally did not dramatize the events in Berlin: 'La crise actuelle n'est pas encore la grande crise qui menacerait Berlin-Ouest et les droits des alliés dans les secteurs occidenteaux de l'ancienne capitale.'[50]

If General de Gaulle was able to develop his policy toward Berlin and Germany relatively independently of French public opinion, it was because the Berlin crisis represented by no means the only and probably not even the most burning issue preoccupying the French during those months. For only a few days after 13 August did Berlin dominate the national headlines. And, despite an extensive series entitled 'Pourquoi fuient-ils?' published by *Le Figaro* over several days and on entire pages,[51] the main issue of the summer 1961 was not Berlin but rather Algeria.[52] Despite the increasing tensions around the German city, approximately 70 per cent of the French in the summer of 1961 considered Algeria to be the 'most important problem facing France today'.[53] Only a few months before, the generals had organized their putsch in Algiers, the activities of the Organisation de l'Armée Secrète (OAS) had preoccupied the French, and on 20 May 1961, in Evian, negotiations with the Front de Libération Nationale (FLN) over Algerian independence had begun. Additionally, the series of assassinations announced in the spring of 1961 by the OAS had obviously begun. On 15 July, the organization's attempt to kill the archbishop of Algiers had failed; and on 8 September 1961, the assassins reached France. In Pont-sur-Seine, General de Gaulle narrowly escaped an attempt on his life. These events overshadowed the Berlin crisis. They probably even created a space for action which de Gaulle needed for his independent political course on Berlin.

To be sure, de Gaulle's tough stance and his uncompromising rhetoric were not followed by corresponding actions. France did reinforce its troops in West Germany but, unlike the USA and Britain, not its garrison in Berlin. The highest-ranking French official to visit Berlin after 13 August was the French ambassador in Bonn, Seydoux. General de Gaulle himself never visited the divided city: would it have been too much of an honour for the capital of the 'Reich', or – at least in 1961 – was he making a deliberate attempt to de-escalate the situation? Only in 1963 when President Kennedy celebrated the greatest triumph of his German and European policies in Berlin – 'Ich bin ein Berliner!' – did de Gaulle briefly consider visiting Berlin during his next trip to Germany.[54]

What the opinion polls reflect in France and Germany – and in a comparable way in Britain too – is a clear assessment of power relations on the international scene but above all the power relations and power hierarchies within the West itself. Press and people may not have agreed with the US policy under Kennedy, regarding it as either too soft or wrong for wrong reasons. Nevertheless, in the eyes of the public, Kennedy was the West's foremost politician. The West's leading nation with regard to Berlin, politically and militarily, was the USA. Without the USA, any Western policy would have been condemned to failure; the USA were the ultimate protector not only of West Berlin and West Germany but of the entire West. No specific political competence was necessary in order to arrive at this conclusion. In Western public opinion, de Gaulle would never have been able to become the 'hero' that Kennedy so clearly was.

IV

What were the effects of the Berlin crisis and the building of the Wall on Western European public opinion? The answer to this question has several dimensions. On the one hand, the events of August 1961 provided the Western public once again, this time perhaps more drastically and more clearly related to the division of Germany, an insight into the 'true character' of communism, the Soviet Union and the East German regime. What had happened in Berlin that August and what continued to happen there (so-called 'border incidents' and 'Wall murders') confronted neutralists, supporters of disengagement, and also peace groups with considerable problems. 'Let them come to Berlin' became a standard argument after 1961. This is especially true for West Germany and West Berlin. But, even in the British case, we should not underestimate the relation between the Wall and the slow decline of the disengagement debate. Against the dominant public image of an aggressive East, whose regimes did not shrink from violence to achieve their aims and stabilize their rule, one could hardly argue for the East's 'desire for peace'. In this sense, August 1961 fell into the same category as June 1953 or October 1956.

On the other hand, and this is the second dimension of our answer, not only for the Western governments, but visibly also for the broader public, the Wall quite literally cemented the post-1945 status quo of the division of Berlin, of Germany, of Europe and even of the world. The building of the Wall made it more difficult to argue for a rapid change in this status quo. The events in Berlin clearly demonstrated that East *and* West accepted – or had to accept – this division, at least *de facto*, and also the Cold War's geopolitical spheres of power. Additionally, it became clear that every attempt to change this status quo unilaterally carried the risk of war – of nuclear war. In 1961, the USA no longer possessed the nuclear supremacy of the 1950s. The Sputnik shock, the intercontinental vulnerability of the USA and the emerging nuclear stalemate and the idea of 'mutual assured destruction' made simple nuclear threats – 'massive retaliation' – increasingly impossible. The dangers and risks of nuclear war were perceived by the public. This awareness contributed, above all in Germany, to the weakening, if not the elimination, of an aggressive or even militant nationalism of reunification (*Wiedervereinigungsnationalismus*). Instead, the events in Berlin made it clear that in this situation of an obviously unchangeable status quo, an easing of East–West tensions was thinkable only on the basis of this status quo. Détente against this background meant a pragmatic approach, not an ideological one, between East and West. On the contrary, the détente of the 1960s was only possible because the basic ideological conflict seemed to be and indeed was insurmountable.

We should not underestimate the social consequences of this new situation. In the East as well as in the West, and especially in both East and West Germany, the 1950s had been dominated by the conflict between the blocs, not only politically but also socially. In the West, a broad anti-communist consensus stabilized the political and social status quo including more right-wing, conservative governments. The gradual acceptance of the status quo and the renunciation of a policy of permanent attempts to change it created new spaces and possibilities for social and political developments. To a certain degree, the East–West conflict lost its role as the most important constitutive factor not only in the international order but in domestic socio-political and socio-cultural developments as well. Without question, this is one reason for the far-reaching political and social reforms and transformations taking place in all Western countries during the 1960s and culminating in 1968, although by no means limited to that single year. Especially in West Germany, the political and social rise of the left can only be understood as a consequence of the end of the climate of the Adenauer era with its specific political and social conditions determined by the Cold War. After 1961, those conditions were no longer valid.

Against this background, further development regarding the Berlin Wall and public opinion followed two courses. On the one hand, almost all protagonists of this public opinion condemned – at least in their rhetoric – not only the Wall, but the SED regime, the GDR, the Soviet Union and communism in general; all were completely discredited. Opinion polls broadly reflected this attitude. On the other hand, however, public opinion – not just the political elites – began to accept the status quo and the beginnings of détente on the basis of it. In this context, it is remarkable that concrete détente measures began where the Cold War had led, at the most dangerous crises at the beginning of the 1960s. Like Brandt and his team, who after 1961 embarked on a policy of local détente in Berlin, the US government after the Cuban missile crisis – in which the USA for the first time had become a front-line theatre of the Cold War – began its policy of détente. Brandt was acting locally, Kennedy globally. The motives and approaches of their respective policies were, however, similar, if not exactly the same, and public opinion supported détente at both levels.

NOTES

1 *Bild-Zeitung*, 16 August 1961.
2 Ibid., 16 July 1963.
3 The main reason why I concentrate my efforts on these two countries is their specific status with rights and responsibilities toward Berlin.
4 Quoted in John P.S. Gearson, *Harold Macmillan and the Berlin Wall Crisis, 1958–62: The Limits of Interest and Force*, Houndsmills: Macmillan, 1998, p. 187. Gearson's book is also the best recent study of British Berlin policy under Prime Minister Harold Macmillan.
5 For a French study of France's Berlin policy, see Georges-Henri Soutou, *La guerre de Cinquante Ans: Les relations Est–Ouest 1943–1990*, Paris: Fayard, 2001, pp. 357–99.
6 For a short overview of the two concepts, see Alexander Gallus and Marion Lühe, *Öffentliche Meinung und Demoskopie*, Opladen: Leske & Budrich, 1998, pp. 10–12.
7 See Vladimir O. Key, *Public Opinion and American Democracy*, New York: Knopf, 1961, p. 552.
8 This article cannot offer a survey of post-1945 Berlin policies and Berlin crises. Over the decades, however, these issues have been treated by numerous authors. Some more recent studies include the works of Cyril Buffet, *Mourir pour Berlin: la France et l'Allemagne, 1945–1949*, Paris: A. Colin, 1991; Gearson, *Harold Macmillan*; and Thomas A. Schwartz, 'The Berlin Crisis and the Cold War', *Diplomatic History*, 21 (1997), 139–49, as well as Michael Lemke, *Die Berlinkrise 1958 bis 1963: Interessen und Handlungsspielräume der SED im Ost–West-Konflikt*, Berlin: Akademie, 1995, and Rolf Steininger, *Der Mauerbau: Die Westmächte und Adenauer in der Berlin-Krise 1958–1963*, Munich: Olzog, 2001. One of the first attempts to link, albeit on a very general level, an analysis of public opinion and the events in Berlin was Ernst Fraenkel, *Öffentliche Meinung und internationale Politik*, Tübingen: Mohr, 1962. For every analysis of public opinion questions in the context of the Berlin Wall, Kurt Shell's comprehensive study is still extremely valuable: Kurt L. Shell, *Bedrohung und Bewährung: Führung und Bevölkerung in der Berlin-Krise*, Cologne/Opladen; Westdeutscher Verlag, 1965. A more recent study, reaching beyond Berlin and beyond the year 1961, is Manuela Glaab, *Deutschlandpolitik in der öffentlichen Meinung: Einstellungen und Regierungspolitik in der Bundesrepublik Deutschland 1949–1990*, Opladen: Leske & Budrich, 1999.
9 See Axel Schildt, 'Der Beginn des Fernsehzeitalters. Ein neues Massenmedium setzt sich durch', in Axel Schildt and Arnold Sywottek (eds), *Modernisierung im Wiederaufbau: Die westdeutsche Gesellschaft der 50er Jahre*, Bonn: Dietz, 1993, pp. 477–92.
10 Quoted in Shell, *Bedrohung*, p. 35.
11 Ibid.
12 Ibid.
13 Quoted in ibid., p. 37.
14 Ibid.
15 See Hans-Peter Schwarz, *Adenauer: Der Staatsmann, 1952–1967*, Stuttgart: Deutsche Verlags-Anstalt (hereafter DVA), 1991, p. 662.
16 For the numbers, see *Jahrbuch der öffentlichen Meinung 1958–1964*, p. 303, and *Jahrbuch der öffentlichen Meinung 1965–1967*, pp. 198–9.

17 *Die Zeit*, 18 August 1961.
18 For example, in *Die Welt* and in *Berliner Zeitung*; for a detailed analysis, see Shell, *Bedrohung*, pp. 228–86.
19 Quoted in Shell, *Bedrohung*, p. 44.
20 The complete text of Kennedy's televised speech can be found in *Public Papers of the Presidents of the United States: John F. Kennedy, 1961*, Washington, DC: US GPO, 1962, pp. 533–40.
21 *Süddeutsche Zeitung*, 21 August 1961.
22 Brandt's confidential letter to Kennedy was leaked to the press and published by *Der Tagesspiegel*, 20 August 1961.
23 Konrad Adenauer, *Erinnerungen 1959–1963*, Stuttgart: DVA, 1968, p. 75.
24 Schwarz, *Adenauer*, p. 670.
25 See Harold Macmillan, *Pointing the Way, 1959–1961*, London: Macmillan, 1972, p. 394.
26 *Guardian*, 26 August 1961.
27 See *Parteienhandbuch: Die Parteien der Bundesrepublik Deutschland*, Richard Stöss (ed.), Opladen: Westdeutscher Verlag, 1986, vol. 2, p. 1171.
28 See Shell, *Bedrohung*, p. 236.
29 Quoted in ibid., p. 237.
30 *New York Times*, 24 August 1961.
31 See Shell, *Bedrohung*, pp. 87–8.
32 Ibid., p. 88.
33 Ibid.
34 *New Statesman*, 62, 4 August 1961, p. 146, quoted in Shell, *Bedrohung*, pp. 87–8.
35 See Gearson, *Harold Macmillan*, pp. 75–8.
36 See ibid., pp. 117–20.
37 *Daily Express*, 18 August 1961.
38 Ibid., 17 August 1961.
39 *Guardian*, Letter to the Editor, 19 August 1961.
40 Ibid.
41 See Shell, *Bedrohung*, p. 88.
42 *Guardian*, 17 August 1961.
43 See Shell, *Bedrohung*, p. 89.
44 See ibid., p. 90.
45 *Guardian*, 25 August 1961.
46 See Stephen Howe, 'Labour and International Affairs', in Duncan Tanner, Pat Thane and Nick Tiratsoo (eds), *Labour's First Century*, Cambridge: Cambridge University Press, 2000, pp. 119–50, and Richard Taylor, *Against the Bomb: The British Peace Movement, 1958–1965*, Oxford: Clarendon, 1988.
47 See Shell, *Bedrohung*, p. 96.
48 For a more detailed analysis of de Gaulle's policy in this context, see Maurice Vaïsse, *La grandeur: Politique étrangère du général de Gaulle 1958–1969*, Paris: Fayard, 1998, pp. 225–62, or Eckart Conze, *Die gaullistische Herausforderung: Deutsch-französische Beziehungen in der amerikanischen Europapolitik*, Munich: Oldenburg, 1995, pp. 202–26.
49 *The Gallup International Public Opinion Polls: France 1939, 1944–1975*, vol. I (1939, 1944–1967), New York: Random House, 1976, pp. 300–1, 304.
50 *Le Monde*, 15 and 30 August 1961.
51 *Le Figaro*, 23, 24, 25 August 1961.
52 See Irwin Wall's contribution to this volume; further, see Vaïsse, *Grandeur*, pp. 59–110.
53 *Gallup France*, p. 294.
54 See Conze, *Herausforderung*, p. 283.

7

The Italian Communist Party between East and West, 1960–64

Silvio Pons

As the 1960s began, the Italian Communist Party, the PCI, was Western Europe's leading communist party, and at the same time an organization with some features unique within the international communist movement. There were three major differences: the fact that it was a mass party (which made the PCI much more permeable to and rooted in society than any other European communist party); its link to the Italian Constitution (which reflected the Italian communists' contribution to developing the system); and the original mark left by Gramsci's thinking (which bestowed upon Italian communist culture a national and intellectual credibility decidedly superior to that enjoyed by other communist parties). Moreover, after Khrushchev denounced Stalin's crimes, Palmiro Togliatti was the only communist leader to speak (in June 1956) of 'degeneration' of the Soviet system. This criticism never went down well in Moscow and served to strengthen the idea of an 'Italian road' toward socialism, different from the Soviet model.[1]

This was, however, also the limit beyond which Togliatti did not push his differentiation from the USSR until his final years. The unique features of the PCI could exist in clear continuity with the international system led by Moscow. This was made clear in 1956, when Togliatti spearheaded a hard-line position against Imre Nagy on the eve of the Soviet intervention in Hungary. When the post-Stalin succession struggle in the USSR was over, the links between Moscow and the Italian communists seemed to have been renewed: the PCI was the main beneficiary of the funds that Moscow allocated to all the communist parties; its organizational networks with Eastern Europe were still in place (although the extra-legal structures were being dismantled); and political and diplomatic contacts were reaffirmed by the international communist conferences held in the Soviet capital in 1957 and through the mutual exchange of delegations.[2]

Stalin's successors persisted in perceiving the Cold War as a continuation of the policy of isolating and suffocating the Russian Revolution, a policy that had been pursued by the Western powers in the immediate aftermath of the First World War. The new leaders also conceived of Soviet expansion in Central and Eastern Europe as a legitimate defence justified by aggression against the USSR during the Second World War. As a consequence, the West's leading communist parties were seen as a strategic reserve and as a tool to influence opinions and policies in the nations of Western Europe. This vision was not contested by the Italian communists, who continued to present themselves as members of the 'socialist camp', convinced that the integral defence of the USSR was in their prime interest, an essential resource for the party's identity and cohesion. Although the Soviet invasion of Hungary had devastating effects among intellectuals and weakened the PCI's political influence due to the resultant break with the Italian Socialists, it did not compromise the party's mass electoral strength. In international politics, the Soviet leadership's orientation toward 'peaceful coexistence' appeared to open up new areas for the PCI to act and exercise influence. Although the communists' isolation in the national political system was even more marked after the rise of the centre-left alliance of Christian Democrats and Socialists, the tendency in Italian foreign policy toward building a new East–West relationship was sufficiently fertile terrain for engaging in combat.[3]

Maintaining the Soviet myth, highlighting communism's powerful expansion in the Third World, and touting the prospects opened up by the start of international détente processes were the inseparable elements feeding the PCI's international culture throughout the decade following Stalin's death. This inheritance was put to the test by international developments in the early 1960s. In light of the considerations cited thus far, it is no surprise that events within the international communist movement (the crisis between the USSR and China) more than international events in and beyond Europe (the U2 spy plane incident, the Berlin and Cuba crises) served to elicit meaningful reaction from the PCI. In other words, the organic link with the USSR prioritized the geopolitical position of Italian communists in the Western arena and marked the boundaries of their international perception. Therefore, the specific nature of their reaction to the changes and crises in these years is not to be exaggerated: Italian communists represented themselves as being on the forefront of politics and culture in the 'socialist camp' even though this status was rife with tensions.

The first moment of tension in the international communist movement emerged between the Soviets and the Chinese at the conference of 81 communist parties held in Moscow in November of 1960.[4] On this occasion, the Chinese presented themselves as the main defenders of an intransigent tendency which aspired to leadership of the international communist movement, re-launching a form of ideological orthodoxy and an open anti-imperialistic challenge. The Italian delegation led by Luigi Longo took a moderate stance in order to prevent opposing formations from developing. The Italian communists declared their opposition to any attempt to 'transform ideological and political dissent … into dissent regarding state relations between certain socialist countries'.[5] This methodology allowed them to reaffirm positions of principle at the political level which were diametrically opposed to the theses put forth by the Chinese. In particular, Longo held firm to a basic motif that had been embraced for some time by the PCI, solemnly declaring that 'the socialist revolution does not need to clear a path for itself using thermonuclear bombs and ruins and endless mourning', and that a nuclear war would destroy 'the very material bases of modern civilization'.[6] At the same time, he confirmed his party's autonomy and declared that he rejected 'any formulation that may lead us to think of parties that lead and parties that are led', and stated his belief that 'there cannot be a single world leadership of the entire communist movement'.[7] Both these positions were to be firmly held by the PCI in subsequent years, reflecting two of Togliatti's strategic suppositions.

First, Togliatti expected that the easing of tensions between the super-powers would allow for a process aimed at bringing an end to the Cold War (and therefore get the PCI back into the national political arena, from which it had been alienated since 1947). Second, Togliatti's strategy entrusted the PCI's fate to a simultaneous development both of the 'socialist camp' and of bi-polar coexistence (with the conviction – and illusion – that communism would have a more promising future than capitalism if it were freed of the old catastrophist prospects). In this dual perspective, the PCI's alignment with Soviet foreign policy was unwavering. To a certain extent, the very opening of the polemical conflict between the Soviets and the Chinese contributed toward this identification: defending the 'peaceful coexistence' principle against the extreme positions of the Chinese encouraged Italian communists even more strongly to uphold Soviet policy as the one most sensible for the whole communist movement.

This was the case even when Soviet policy led the Italian communists to set aside their hopes for relaxing the division of Europe. In August of 1961, the Italian party wholeheartedly fell into line with Moscow's justifications for the building of the Berlin Wall. In September, Togliatti publicly voiced his concern over the crisis in international relations, for which he held the Westerners entirely responsible. He defended the thesis of economic recognition of East Germany and presented the building of the Wall as a requirement imposed by the situation. In other words, Togliatti adhered uncritically to the Soviet position, showing no sensitivity to the Wall's symbolic significance in dividing Europe.[8] This clearly revealed a contradiction between the Italian communists' aspiration for international détente and the Soviets' rigid bi-polar conception, which left little room for a dynamic vision of détente.

Despite this, Togliatti appeared satisfied with the reaffirmation of 'peaceful coexistence' made by the Twenty-Second Congress of the Communist Party of the Soviet Union (CPSU) in October of 1961. In his report to the PCI's leadership and Central Committee, Togliatti even praised the Soviet slogan of 'building communism', sidestepping Khrushchev's new denunciation of Stalin's crimes. This attitude led to perplexity and criticism among many members of the PCI's leadership group, exciting intense internal debate. The most important speech was by Giorgio Amendola, who maintained that the PCI was making too great a sacrifice on the altar of communist unity; he urged that this 'fictitious unity' be broken and that the Italian communists take on a more active international role, which should include a contribution to de-Stalinization.[9] Togliatti's reply was completely negative and uncharacteristically argumentative, linking a conservative reticence on the issue of de-Stalinization to prioritizing the issue of the unity of the communist movement.[10] Shortly thereafter, in December of 1961, Longo reported his own conversation with Mikhail Suslov, in which the Soviet leader had expressed his displeasure over the 'anti-Soviet positions' of some PCI leaders, and regretted the fact that Togliatti had insisted, as in 1956, that there had been a 'degeneration' in the Soviet system. Suslov had at any rate supported the positions taken by Togliatti against Amendola and the other leaders who had been critical, and he had promised a reprisal if these leaders persisted in their 'anti-Soviet positions'. Togliatti concluded that a communiqué had to be sent to the CPSU to acknowledge that 'there have been erroneous, dangerous positions that we propose correcting'. In his view, this debate had done the PCI 'great damage in the international communist movement' because the Italians' prestige was based on the 'method of not wounding the sensibilities of brethren parties', particularly those of the Soviets, 'who are facing the great Chinese problem'.[11] Togliatti thus had no difficulty in defending his position of extreme diplomatic caution, reaffirming his leadership once again based on his privileged connections with Moscow.

Nevertheless, even Togliatti's circumspection was put to a severe test by developments on the Chinese question. While the issue had helped consolidate the Italian communists' alignment with Soviet policy in 1960–1961, it was now to create some friction between the PCI and Moscow, and Togliatti's efforts could scarcely alleviate Suslov's disappointment with the Italian communists. On 12 January 1962, Togliatti addressed a letter to the Soviets to express doubts concerning their proposal to call the Chinese back to order with a document signed by the communist parties that had endorsed the Moscow conference resolution. He feared that the Chinese would see this step as 'the start of a struggle against them' and that consequently 'the conflict with them, already quite serious', would be intensified. Togliatti preferred to stress his concerns over a break in the international communist movement and maintained that everything possible should be done 'to overcome all dissent and reinforce unity at all times'; but for this very reason, he thought it impossible at that time to call another conference of the communist parties.[12] The problems raised by Togliatti were likely to have helped induce the Soviets to abandon their proposal. In February of 1962, they sent their own letter to the Chinese, attacking the Albanians and appealing for the unity of the movement.[13]

In more general terms, it was in 1962 that the Italian communists began outlining a slight – although in the long run, important – distinction from the Soviet position on Europe, one which lay in their judgment of the European

Economic Community: with increasing insistence, such communist leaders as Giorgio Amendola maintained the need to acknowledge the Community's existence and also moderated their more ideological opinions of it. The positions of the Italian communists revolved around the general demand for a 'revision' of the Common European Market treaties, and an uncertain distinction between Europeanism and Atlanticism.[14] But, for the time being, these positions were of a non-official nature and, although they diverged from the Soviet stance, they were also quite remote from those of the leading parties of the Western left.[15]

On the other side, the Italian communists' identification with Soviet foreign policy was in fact fully confirmed at the time of the Cuban crisis of October 1962. Once the peak of that crisis had passed, Togliatti took a public stance in his report to the Tenth PCI Congress in early December, approving the USSR's conduct without reservation and condemning the USA's 'imperialism'. At the same time, he made reference to a 'turning point' in international relations and to a re-launching of 'peaceful coexistence'.[16] The Soviets expressed a positive opinion of the party congress.[17] The PCI's foreign section presented an optimistic report on the party's improved relations internationally and with the USSR.[18] Shortly thereafter, on 20 March 1963, Togliatti made a famous speech in which he focused on nuclear war as threatening the annihilation of all mankind and linked the party's future prospects even more closely to those of bi-polar détente.[19] International developments appeared to warrant moderate optimism when the crisis of late 1962 ended with the international non-proliferation agreement between the USA and the Soviet Union the following summer. Nevertheless, it was the Cuban crisis and the subsequent resumption of détente that aggravated the break with the Chinese, who had no difficulty accusing Khrushchev of 'adventurism' and 'capitulationism'. But they went further. In early 1963, after Togliatti had openly criticized China's attacks on 'peaceful coexistence', a press war broke out between Chinese and Italian communists. The former openly attacked Togliatti (thereby implicitly recognizing his calibre as a leader of international communism), and accused him of revisionism and of 'replacing, on a world scale, class struggle with class collaboration'. The Italian leader responded with a moderate but firm tone, yielding nothing to the Chinese position.[20] At this point, Togliatti realized that the PCI could no longer declare itself in principle against calling a conference of communist parties, and told his party's Directorate that the Soviets had to be assured 'that we want to join them but by debating without polemics'.[21]

In June and July of 1963, the crisis between the Soviets and the Chinese flared up with an exchange of accusations that left no room for mediation and in fact producing a full-blown break. In its 'open letter' of 17 July 1963 to the Chinese communists, the CPSU claimed for itself the leading role and listed all the reasons for friction, starting with 'peaceful coexistence'. Togliatti again expressed his concern to the PCI Directorate:

Concern for a Conference to be held now with the participation of the CCP and the Asian parties. This means deepening the rift. What do the Soviet comrades think of the relations between the two states? Grave consequences of the break for all the parties. Greater difficulties in combating anti-Soviet positions. I am not enthusiastic about how the Soviet comrades are conducting the debate. They kept quiet for too long about the Cuba issue as well. Now they are becoming exasperated. Problems are cropping up too forcefully in relations between the two countries, creating some perplexities. The foolishness of the Chinese does not change this impression. Raise with the Soviet comrades our concerns as to the appropriateness of the conference. We are one of the strongest parties in dealing with this problem because we have developed our policy in depth. But the worsening polemics will cause us difficulties.[22]

Soviet pressure to call a conference of international communism grew in September and October of 1963. The Italian party sent a delegation to Moscow with the purpose of repeating their reservations regarding an initiative of this kind, but it achieved no results. The Soviets declared that, although no decision had yet been made, 'many parties' had requested a conference and that it was also necessary for the purpose of 'a position-taking that reaches the Chinese masses'. They made it clear that the preparatory work was going ahead. The CPSU and PCI had clearly locked horns. Moreover, as an instrument of pressure, Moscow used the position of the French Communist Party (PCF), which was pushing for the convocation of the world conference while ruling out a European conference, which would have met with the approval of the PCI; the French had assumed a sharply polemical attitude *vis-à-vis* their Italian comrades.[23] Commenting on the delegation's report, Togliatti declared himself no less 'perplexed' than before on the issue of calling a conference of international communists: 'this can only end in a condemnation which will be translated into a break and spread'. But the main dilemma was of a political nature: 'the fundamental problems of interest to the workers' movement at present are those being argued between the Soviets and the Chinese, but they are being posed in a different, more advanced way. The problem is no longer whether or not we are for détente, but how we are to develop détente policy.'[24] In truth, this observation could imply a criticism aimed much more at the Soviets' conduct of foreign policy than at the ideological outbursts of the Chinese (which had already been largely subject to criticism), but Togliatti did not go that far. Nevertheless, the idea of the unity of the communist movement as defended by Togliatti did not seem to be in harmony with that defended by the Soviets.

On 13 February 1964, the CPSU sent all communist parties a letter denouncing the Chinese attempt to create a 'fractionist bloc' in the international communist movement.[25] This was followed by yet another exchange of invective between Moscow and Beijing. Even as the Italian communist press continued to uphold the Soviet position, considerable friction now emerged between Moscow and the PCI after Togliatti, upon returning from a trip to Yugoslavia, had defended the Yugoslav communists from Chinese criticism with the argument that the organization of the 'socialist world' could not be reduced to a single bloc and had cited Stalin's break with Tito as a negative precedent. These arguments irritated the Soviets, who clearly saw in them both a violation of the united front deemed necessary at such a delicate juncture and an insidious claim for autonomy. Referring to the results of a trip to the USSR, Longo noted to the Directorate that Suslov had explicitly expressed his displeasure over Togliatti's positions. At the same time, the Soviet position on the 'Chinese question' had further hardened. Although Longo had repeated the PCI's reservations, Suslov believed that a conference could not be put off any longer, and called upon the Italian communists to see the 'general interest' and not just their own. Togliatti repeated his concern that a conference would simply sanction the break, observing that 'on both sides, they attack those who don't take a clear position in their favour, and want to argue without reaching a split. The prestige of the parties, of the CPSU and of the Chinese CP, is damaged.' His speech explained the nexus between the PCI's stance on the 'Chinese question', the openings toward Yugoslavia, and the hidden expectations of international détente; with an obvious allusion to the PCI's prospects, Togliatti noted that the Yugoslavs had followed their own road 'without falling into the capitalist camp' and that 'there can be countries that start on the way of socialism without immediately entering the socialist camp'.[26]

The subsequent public stance by the French communists in favour of a world conference of the communist movement led Togliatti and Longo to write a letter to the CPSU in an attempt to block the issuing of a formal convocation, which would have been difficult to refuse.[27] The letter, dated 8 April 1964, stubbornly laid out the persistent reservations of the Italian communists. A conference would formalize the break then taking place, thereby causing a 'schism' and creating 'two organizational centres of the international communist movement in bitter struggle with one another'; another damaging development would thus be added – a 'return, in practice, to conceptions and forms of organization of the communist parties that have historically been overcome', which was to compromise 'the autonomy of the individual parties'; the two Italian communist leaders specified that they would never sign any formulation that spelled a step backward from the distinct 'national roads' to socialism.[28] Immediately thereafter, the PCI again sent a delegation to Moscow, but its achievements were no better than those of the previous one: the Soviets confirmed that they deemed the conference 'inevitable' and essentially refused to take notice of the reservations made by the Italian communists.[29] Togliatti then came to the conclusion that these reservations had to be expressed 'in a new way, which is to say that our proposal was intended to render the struggle against the Chinese positions more effective'. To avoid misunderstandings, he reminded the PCI's highest leadership that 'in the world, there is the camp of the communist parties, and only that. Our party cannot be imagined as not belonging to it. We are not in power, so our possibilities of movement are more limited.' Enrico Berlinguer interpreted Togliatti's thought clearly, noting that 'beyond our autonomy, we must safeguard the link with the CPSU. Dissent with the CPSU is one thing, a break with it is quite another thing – and inadmissible.'[30]

On 22 May, Togliatti and Longo wrote another letter to the CPSU: they remained firm on the positions they had already taken, specifying that the PCI would take part in the conference if it were called, but that the party considered it counterproductive to the movement's unity. This time, however, they expressed themselves polemically against the French communists, who at their recent congress had called for the convocation of the conference and stressed their closeness to the CPSU – and, plain as day, drew attention to their distance from the PCI.[31] According to the two Italian leaders, this French attitude constituted a 'manifestation of the spirit of intolerance that led our movement to commit serious errors in the past'.[32] The statement sounded like nothing less than criticism of Suslov, who had taken part in the congress of French communists and had heaped praise on them. The reply by the Soviets on 25 June was no less obstinate: they asked the PCI to support the initiative in the name of the movement's unity and to this end also to 'put an immediate stop to the divisive action'.[33] In the debate at the Directorate, Togliatti called for maximum flexibility of behaviour, to differ from the Soviets without rejecting participation in the conference *a priori*:

> Don't give the impression that we don't comprehend the general needs of the movement. There is a centrifugal process underway that must be brought under control. It is not in our interest that the Soviet leadership group's prestige be shaken in the international movement ... Avoid distancing our party from the CPSU, which would create a serious situation.[34]

On 7 July, the Italians responded that 'nothing has occurred that would lead us to think we have overcome our reservations and concerns about convoking the international conference at the present time'; the communist movement was facing new problems, which could not be dealt with merely by reaffirming the documents from the 1960 conference, which were in many ways outmoded.[35]

It is clear this was a dialogue in which neither side listened to the other, although it did not herald any traumatic event. On 30 July 1964, the CPSU sent a letter to all the parties which in fact started the process leading up to the conference, aiming to meet in Moscow in December of that year.[36] Shortly thereafter, Togliatti visited the USSR to speak directly with the Soviets, and it was there that he died in August 1964. The issue of the proposed conference of international communists remained on the agenda, but nothing was to come of it.

Some concluding remarks are in order. The crisis in Sino-Soviet relations dealt a harsh blow to the concept of a 'polycentric' evolution of the communist movement capable of adjusting to a new international system characterized by bi-polar détente, thereby leaving the PCI the prospect of a 'road to socialism' in Italy other than immediate membership in the 'socialist camp'. The position taken by the PCI was inspired by prudent diplomacy, which, on the one hand, adhered fully to Soviet foreign policy and, on the other, strayed subtly from the USSR's tendency to force a taking of sides within the communist movement. Togliatti drew a distinction between dissenting from the Chinese in their positions and excommunicating them, dodging Moscow's demand to call a new conference of communist parties for that purpose. The Italian communists thus sketched out a realistic acknowledgement of the extent of the Sino-Soviet conflict, a critique of Chinese extremism and a cautious positioning aimed at thwarting another fissure in the communist movement.

Nevertheless, this did not keep the break from becoming public and involving the PCI as well. In this circumstance too, Togliatti maintained a moderate and realistic tone in response to the dogmatic accusations of 'revisionism' hurled against him by the Chinese. All the same, the break between China and the USSR was inevitable and was also precipitated. From that moment on, Togliatti expressed increasing concern over the ideological and non-political nature of the discussion (which in his eyes boiled down to making a pronouncement for or against détente as opposed to furthering the development of that policy) and was quite pessimistic as to the possibility of preserving the unity of the communist movement. But he did not modify the view he had held up to that time against further exacerbating the issue and continued to resist Soviet pressure to excommunicate the Chinese.

However, the cautious stance taken by Togliatti during the crisis between Moscow and Beijing only partially represented a transition toward a new relationship between the PCI and the USSR. Togliatti's emphasis was mainly on the need to preserve the unity of the international communist movement as expressed in his renowned Yalta memoir – his political testament and the celebrated *Magna Carta* of the PCI's autonomy – written in the summer of 1964, shortly before his death. This document displayed Togliatti's realistic pessimism regarding relations between China and the USSR as much as it expressed his appeal to the relationship with the USSR as an element in the party's cohesion. His thesis of 'unity in diversity' still made reference to the USSR's constituent role, underestimating the Soviets' tendency to absorb the function of the communist movement into its own policy of power with the ambition of exercising undisputed leadership over the anti-imperialist forces. And it was with this less-than-clear inheritance that the post-Togliatti leadership had to contend with the Soviet invasion of Czechoslovakia.

NOTES

1 On the main features of the PCI after 1956, see D. Sassoon, *Togliatti e la via italiana al socialismo*, Turin: Einaudi, 1980. And, more recently, A. Agosti, *Palmiro Togliatti*, Turin: UTET, 1995, chs 9 and 10.

2 See S. Pons, *L'URSS e il PCI nel sistema internazionale della guerra fredda*, in R. Gualtieri (ed.), *Il PCI nell'Italia repubblicana*, Rome: Carocci, 2001.

3 On the first détente's impact on relations between the United States and Italy and also on the first openings of Italian foreign policy to the USSR, see L. Nuti, *Gli Stati Uniti e l'apertura a sinistra: Importanza e limiti della presenza americana in Italia*, Rome-Bari: Laterza, 1999.

4 For a reconstruction of the crisis in USSR/China relations based on archival documents, see. O.A. Westad (ed.), *Brothers in Arms: The Rise and Fall of the Sino-Soviet Alliance, 1945–1963*, Stanford, CA: Stanford University Press, 1998.

5 See L. Longo, *Opinione sulla Cina*, Milan: La Pietra, 1977, p. 27.

6 Ibid., p. 36.

7 Ibid., pp. 47–8.

8 Agosti, *Palmiro Togliatti*, p. 517.

9 On the debate within the ruling group of the PCI after the 22nd Congress of the CPSU, see Agosti, *Palmiro Togliatti*, pp. 518–23.

10 See R. Martinelli, 'Togliatti, lo stalinismo e il XXII Congresso del PCUS: Un discorso ritrovato', *Italia contemporanea*, 219, June 2000, 297–302.

11 APC, Direzione, Verbali, 7 December 1961.

12 APC, URSS, 1962, mf 0503, 481–82.

13 APC, URSS, 1962, mf 0503, 486–500.

14 APC, Direzione, Verbali, 1 and 13 January 1963.

15 See M. Maggiorani, *L'Europa degli altri: Comunisti italiani e integrazione europea (1957–1969)*, Rome: Carocci, 1998, pp. 165 ff.

16 Togliatti, *Opere scelte*, Rome: Editori Riuniti, 1974, pp. 1069–122.

17 APC, Direzione, Verbali, 1 February 1963.

18 APC, Esteri, 1963, mf 0489, 2720–9.

19 Togliatti, *Opere scelte*, pp. 1123–35.

20 'Rinascita', 12 January 1963.

21 APC, Direzione, Verbali, 1 February 1963.

22 APC, Direzione, Verbali, 12 September 1963.

23 APC, Direzione, Verbali, 11 October 1963.

24 Ibid.

25 APC, URSS, 1964, mf 0520, 2435–9.

26 APC, Direzione, Verbali, 26 February 1964.

27 APC, Direzione, Verbali, 2 April 1964.

28 APC, URSS, 1964, mf 0520, 2514–20.

29 APC, Direzione, Verbali, 12–13 May 1964.

30 Ibid.

31 APC, Direzione, Verbali, 27 May 1964.

32 APC, URSS, 1964, mf 0520, 2538–44.

33 APC, URSS, 1964, mf 0520, 2621–6.

34 APC, Direzione, Verbali, 2 July 1964.

35 APC, URSS, 1964, mf 0520, 2621–6.

36 APC, URSS, 1964, mf 0520, 2649–65.

PART III:
EUROPE IN SEARCH OF DÉTENTE, 1962–65

8

Britain, East Germany and Détente: British Policy toward the GDR and West Germany's 'Policy of Movement', 1955–65

Klaus Larres

During the Cold War, Britain's foreign policy was a very cautious one. In general, London conducted relations with the Soviet Union and its Eastern European satellite states in a much more circumspect way than did the USA. Both in the second half of the 1940s as well as in the 1950s and 1960s, British prime ministers from Attlee to Wilson pursued a policy which continued the close alignment with the USA and, on the whole, also successfully managed to avoid dangerous military entanglements. For instance, after the initial commitment of fighting the war in Korea, London could not be persuaded to contribute to General MacArthur's envisaged escalation of the conflict. Prime Minister Attlee even felt the need to travel to Washington in early December 1950 to persuade President Truman not to consider deploying atomic bombs in the Korean War.[1] The British also refused strong US pressure to provide military assistance to the desperate French position at their Indo-Chinese military base at Dien Bien Phu in 1954; a decade later, Britain rigorously ignored US requests to participate in the Vietnam War.[2] London also often managed to avoid being drawn into overly rigid and fundamentalist political–diplomatic positions toward that superpower and its allies beyond the Iron Curtain. During the first two decades of the Cold War, for example, the British recognized Mao's China while it took the USA until the early 1970s to accept the diplomatic existence of a communist China.[3]

On occasion and particularly during the early Cold War years when Britain still viewed itself as one of the world's leading great powers, London did not shrink from openly adhering to policies which were not favoured in Washington. Rather than pursuing a course which would not antagonize the USA, Prime Ministers Churchill, Eden and Macmillan did their utmost to bring about a summit conference with the Soviet Union, which they believed would be a major contribution to de-escalating the Cold War and defusing the tension surrounding the German question, including the situation in divided

Berlin. While Churchill merely talked about travelling to Moscow in the early to mid-1950s but did not dare to do so given the strong opposition of President Eisenhower, Macmillan chose to ignore US wishes and actually embarked on his controversial journey to the USSR in the summer of 1959.[4] A similar independence of mind can be seen in both the British government's policy toward the German Democratic Republic (GDR) during the 1950s and 1960s and London's strong support for West Germany's cautious and very slow policy of *rapprochement* with Eastern Europe toward the end of the Adenauer era.

This chapter deals with two distinct but closely connected issues. It first investigates Britain's perception of the GDR and London's policy toward the non-recognition of the second German state. Above all, we will examine the uneasy position the British found themselves in with respect to their Western allies. While in principle London fully agreed to the diplomatic non-recognition of the Ulbricht regime – it even had been one of the decisive initiators of this policy in late 1949 – by the mid-1950s the British were increasingly keen on trading with the GDR. This however, caused much anger in West Germany and also some in the USA. Britain was thus in the difficult position of having to balance its own economic interests with great efforts not to displease Bonn and Washington.

Second, the chapter explores the interconnection of recognition, trade relations and détente including Britain's perception of West German Foreign Minister Gerhard Schröder's 'Policy of Movement' in the early to mid-1960s. London strongly approved of Foreign Minister Schröder's cautiously initiated détente policy; Whitehall appreciated that Schröder was able to continue this policy while maintaining his post in the new Erhard government which took office after Adenauer's retirement on 15 October 1963. As early as the late 1950s, the Macmillan government had concluded that non-recognition of the GDR was an unwise and counterproductive policy. After all, it was obvious that the GDR did exist, continued to enjoy the unflagging support of the Soviet Union, was supported by a growing number of East Germans (as it seemed to the West) and also managed to expand its economic base. The British concluded that the East German state would undoubtedly remain in existence for a prolonged period of time. It seemed that for Britain to overcome the tension of the Cold War and arrive at a *rapprochement* with the USSR meant the acceptance of existing realities: this included the existence and *de facto* recognition of the GDR. Long before Willy Brandt's *Ostpolitik* of the early 1970s, it was already argued in London that the possibility of developing an enduring East–West détente and a de-escalation of Cold War tension surrounding the German question would only arise if Moscow's Eastern European sphere of influence was accepted by the West. The results achieved by both *Ostpolitik* and the 1975 Helsinki conference[5] were essentially the political aims which the British had cautiously begun to pursue in the late 1950s and early 1960s.

Prior to the official international recognition of the GDR in early 1973, British governments of all political persuasions, from Macmillan to Wilson, largely agreed on a very similar if not identical policy toward the GDR and on the need to support the development of a genuine East–West détente. It was also fully recognized in London that Britain's relations with the GDR ought to be conducted with a view to West Germany. In fact, London's relations with East Berlin were influenced significantly by British–West German political and economic competition as well as Bonn's reluctance to consider East–West détente and a more flexible policy in the German unification question.[6]

Britain and the 'Creeping Recognition' of the GDR, 1949–57

With the founding of the German Democratic Republic in October 1949, Britain and the other Western allies began to insist on the international non-recognition of the East German state.[7] The Foreign Office persistently argued that 'in the absence of a peace treaty with a unified Germany' and in view of the fact that the GDR could not be regarded as a normal state, there could be 'no question of recognising the German authorities there as a 'government'. London was convinced that 'the German authorities in East Germany … fail the test for recognition as a government, since they are not independent'; after all, the GDR was 'entirely dependent' on the military and economic support of the Soviet Union.[8] Britain adhered to its position that the West German government was 'the only truly constitutional and legitimate government in Germany'; it was 'the only government entitled to speak for Germany in internal affairs'.[9] Only after the Basic Treaty was concluded between Bonn and East Berlin in November/December 1972 did London establish diplomatic relations with the GDR in early 1973.[10]

During the early and mid-1950s in particular, British policy makers were convinced that any official or unofficial dealings with East Berlin would boost the prestige of the undemocratic regime in the Soviet occupation zone. It was also clear that any contacts with East Germany would be deeply resented by the West German government in Bonn.[11] Furthermore, it was apparent that once one of the allied powers recognized the GDR, many other governments, particularly in the developing world, would follow suit and thereby strengthen the Soviet Union's dictatorial client state. That would enable Moscow to lay claim to an important victory in the Cold War.[12]

Thus, political recognition – either *de jure* or *de facto* – was out of the question for decision makers in Britain. While London could not afford to endanger its friendly relations with Bonn and Washington, recognition would also have run counter to political-ethical principles held in Westminster. Particularly in the early part of the 1960s, East Germany's image remained badly tarnished by the Berlin Wall, erected in August 1961. Still, in the late 1950s and the 1960s, the British became increasingly doubtful about the value of adhering to the Western non-recognition doctrine. Largely due to the prolonged Berlin Crisis of 1958–63 and the fallout from the dangerous 1962 Cuban Missile Crisis, the Soviet Union had succeeded in dividing the united front of anti-communism and non-recognition in the Western alliance to a considerable extent. Indeed, throughout the 1960s, one could observe a certain 'creeping recognition' of the GDR in the Western hemisphere and notably in the developing and non-aligned world.[13]

As far as the British were concerned, the Ulbricht regime was particularly able to make progress toward *de facto* recognition of the GDR in the field of economic and trade relations. For instance, the first British–East German business deal, albeit a private one, was concluded less than four years after the establishment of the GDR during the Leipzig trade fair in the autumn of 1953 and thus only a few months after the uprising of 17 June.[14] Subsequently there were only muted objections in London to the exploitation of an increasing number of private business contacts between the independent Federation of British Industry (FBI) and its successor organization the Confederation of British Industry (CBI) and their East German counterparts. Although behind the scenes the British government became increasingly involved in the complex and gradually expanding trade deals with the GDR, London did its utmost to ensure that this would not become public knowledge.[15]

In the second half of the 1950s, the beginnings of an indirect and informal trading relationship with the GDR and a simultaneous mental weakening of the non-recognition doctrine could be clearly observed in Britain. Continuing Churchill's early Cold War summit diplomacy, both Prime Minister Anthony Eden and, during the Berlin Crisis, even more clearly his successor Harold Macmillan believed that it was becoming increasingly urgent to overcome the dangerous instability of the Cold War in Europe by achieving a *rapprochement* between East and West. Setting up neutral zones in the middle of Europe to disengage East and West from each other was seen as a way to reduce Cold War tension; it was also a solution viewed favourably by the Soviet Union. Such schemes which indirectly acknowledged the reality of a divided Germany were, however, strongly opposed by both Bonn and Washington.[16] Yet, Macmillan's ten-day visit to Moscow between 21 February and 3 March 1959 led to Foreign Secretary Selwyn Lloyd's tentative declaration to Khrushchev that Britain might be prepared to recognize the GDR. That caused a severe crisis in British–West German relations and to some degree also in Anglo-American relations.[17] Although for the time being this kind of thinking was buried and the policy of non-recognition was upheld, the 'creeping recognition' of the GDR did continue.

Both before and after the erection of the Wall, the British government continued to reject any official trade links with the GDR; it also remained very cautious about a *rapprochement* with East Berlin in the political and cultural spheres.[18] In the 1950s and 1960s, Britain's policy remained 'based on the general principle that contacts with East Germany should not be encouraged (except in certain circumstances, for trade contacts) and that all East Germans whose visits have a predominantly political character should be excluded' from the UK.[19] Yet, in view of increasing pressure by British industry and a number of MPs with close business links, the Macmillan government felt that it was imprudent to take West German protestations too much into consideration. Bonn claimed that its own trade with the East Germans isolated the GDR and drove a wedge between East Berlin and Moscow. It also facilitated the purchase of 'major political concessions' and substantially helped 'to humanise conditions in the Soviet zone by offers of economic benefits in exchange'. In contrast, it was argued that British and other Western trade contacts with East Berlin would only 'stabilise the regime'; it was therefore unacceptable to the Federal Republic (FRG).[20]

Neither the Macmillan government nor its successors had much sympathy for this not entirely convincing West German point of view. Not least due to Britain's increasingly difficult economic situation and its rising trade deficit with the outside world, West Germany's flourishing inter-zonal trade with the GDR was regarded with envy in Whitehall. For instance, a major steel export deal valued at £40 million was lost as the Board refused to give a credit guarantee which would have gone beyond the 1959 trade agreement between the East German Kammer für Aussenhandel (KfA) and the Federation of British Industry, and would thus have met with strong West German condemnation. There was much public criticism of this inflexibility and Britain's exaggerated willingness to take West Germany's wishes into consideration. By the mid-1960s, this and similar cases had made some sections of British business and industry develop the view that essentially Britain's policy toward the GDR was made in Bonn.[21]

By 1960, Western states including the FRG and Britain but not the USA had entered into private or even semi-official trade relations with the GDR. This appeared to be a cautious movement toward *de facto* recognition of the GDR. This dilution of the original non-recognition doctrine was closely observed in East Berlin. Accordingly, Ulbricht believed during the 1960s that the GDR's endeavours to overcome its international isolation were most likely to succeed with Britain, a country whose postwar economic situation was less than satisfactory.[22] This reflected the British government's belief that it was regarded as a soft target for East German propaganda. The GDR appeared to have embarked on increased propaganda activities in Britain in order to obtain 'popular recognition as a means of pressure for ultimate official recognition'.[23] The Foreign Office was convinced that Britain was a 'particularly favourable ground' for the effectiveness of East German propaganda due to 'a combination of circumstances'. These consisted of three important factors which the GDR skilfully attempted to exploit. First, there existed a 'deep-seated mistrust of a strong Germany in general and of the Federal Republic in particular'. Second, British industry was keen on trading with the GDR; there were also close contacts between some British MPs from both major parties and representatives of the East German regime. And last, it was widely believed in the Foreign Office without undue modesty that Britain's liberal laws and regulations 'regarding the admission of foreigners played into the hands of the GDR'.[24]

The East German leadership did indeed have reason to believe that it might be possible to exploit the resentment which existed in London against the booming West Germany and its economic miracle. After all, throughout the decade, a number of British parliamentarians of all political persuasions kept reminding the successive governments of the huge difference in trade volume with the GDR between West Germany and Britain. Even as late as 1971, for instance, after more than a decade and a half of more or less intensive British–East German trade relations, Britain's exports to the GDR had a value of only £17 million, while West Germany's exports to the GDR were worth almost 20 times this amount (approximately £250 million). It was therefore perhaps not too surprising that a number of British MPs tended to agree with the claims made by East German propaganda that only the recognition of the GDR would boost British–East German trade relations.[25]

Although the assumption that recognition would result in improved trade relations was always disputed by the Foreign Office,[26] East Berlin never grew tired of hoping that closer trade relations would eventually lead to that very result. In contrast, the Foreign Office was convinced, however, that closer trade relations and *de facto* recognition of the GDR would further a climate of détente and perhaps result in the possibility of overcoming the Cold War for good. Neither the GDR nor Britain believed that the policy of non-recognition, limited trade, the long-standing Western 'policy of strength' and the FRG's unification ambitions were advantageous for either side in the Cold War. Toward the end of the Eisenhower administration and during John F. Kennedy's tenure in office, this also became the view of the USA.[27]

The Interconnection of Recognition, Trade Relations, and Détente, 1958–64

The first real breakthrough regarding some degree of recognition of the GDR by the Western world occurred in the course of the Berlin Crisis of 1958–63 and under the impact of the 1962 Cuban missile crisis. It became clear that, under US leadership, the West was slowly moving away from wholeheartedly supporting West Germany's rigid non-recognition policy in favour of a new spirit of *rapprochement* with the Eastern bloc. By implication, this meant the acceptance of Khrushchev's 'two-state theory' and the definite removal of any serious consideration of German unification from the agenda of East–West negotiations. As early as in May and June 1959, delegations from both German states were given permission for the first time ever to attend the four-power foreign ministers' conference in Geneva as advisers, of which Britain strongly approved. This was interpreted by East Berlin and Moscow as the international *de facto* recognition of Ulbricht's state. The Foreign Office felt confirmed in its conviction that recognition and détente were closely related factors.[28]

Despite all the short-term anger expressed everywhere in the Western world, the building of the Berlin Wall on 13 August 1961 paradoxically led to a gradual worldwide acknowledgement that the GDR was indeed a separate state with its own distinct territory and political and cultural identity.[29] In London, in fact, the building of the Wall was seen as an opportunity to further a *rapprochement* in East–West relations on the basis of clear spheres of influence. Thus, the Wall not only helped the internal stabilization of the GDR, it also contributed to the development of East–West détente. Toward the end of 1961, the British government reinvigorated its attempts to push the Western alliance down the road toward recognizing the GDR, including the Oder–Neisse line. For example, at the Bermuda meeting with Kennedy in December 1961, Macmillan explained to the US president that non-recognition of the GDR was an unrealistic policy. He claimed that neither the Western alliance nor even the majority of West Germans were keen on German unification.[30] By late 1961, it was generally accepted within the British government that 'by no means all the consequences of the Wall have been negative'. Although 'formally' the West had to regret it, the Wall 'had removed a great deal of Berlin's sting from the Soviet point of view' and in fact it had 'made negotiations easier'.[31]

Yet, the West was not prepared to move too fast. Despite realizing the potential advantages for an improvement of East–West relations thanks to the Wall, it was also seen as a highly objectionable and despicable symbol of the 'evil empire'. When only a few months after the building of the Wall, East Berlin proposed setting up consular offices in West European capitals, the idea was angrily rejected.[32] But the GDR was not easily disheartened. In December 1961, the Volkskammer's interparliamentary group cheekily invited an international conference of parliamentarians to Weimar to outline the necessity of the 'security measures' taken in August 1961. In March of the following year, the GDR expressed a desire to explain its own distinctive disarmament concept to the UN disarmament conference in Geneva; yet the Western allies ensured that as an internationally unrecognized state the GDR did not receive an invitation to the conference.[33]

With the Berlin crisis continuing after the building of the Wall and the Soviets 'engaging in a sort of noisy inactivity *vis-à-vis* the West', Britain considered taking the initiative in early 1962. Once again, the Macmillan government began toying with disengagement schemes and other 'fall-back positions' including the recognition of the GDR as a sovereign state so as to de-escalate East–West tensions.[34] In a conversation with Soviet Foreign Minister Andrei Gromyko in Geneva on 21 March 1962, Foreign Secretary Lord Home referred to the GDR regime as a sovereign government and also to the possibility of *de facto* recognition. He told Gromyko: 'The Russians must not expect us to give *de jure* recognition to East Germany, but he could say that we did not want to upset the government of East Germany or infringe upon their sovereignty.'[35] Most politicians and officials in London were aware, however, that the prospects for the conversion of such views into practical politics were severely limited. Apart from firm West German resistance, it was also most questionable whether the Americans were 'prepared to go as far as we should consider acceptable in the direction of recognizing the sovereignty of the D.D.R.; accepting its frontiers; restricting nuclear weapons for German forces; and so on.'[36] This kind of thinking did not help reverse the rapid deterioration in British–West German relations which had begun with Macmillan's Moscow trip in 1959. It continued unabated; in late September 1962 the German ambassador was told about the undesirability of a visit by the Chancellor to London with the flimsy excuse that 'there was always the problem of our climate at this time of the year'.[37]

Although Lord Home's sentiments regarding the GDR's sovereignty were not repeated subsequently,[38] Macmillan's trusted Private Secretary Philip de Zulueta was still arguing in November 1962 that 'much the best solution would be a tacit acceptance by both sides of the *status quo*, that is Soviet acceptance of the Allied presence and rights in Berlin and Allied acceptance of the existence of the D.D.R.'. He was hopeful that 'President Kennedy might be ready to speak frankly to Dr Adenauer when the latter visits Washington'; he thought that Kennedy might tell the old chancellor 'that he must now swallow some form of recognition of the D.D.R.'.[39] Other officials shared his reasoning. Sir Christopher Steel at the Bonn Embassy, for example, wrote to the Foreign Office that he believed there was 'fundamentally only one direction in which a long-term *modus vivendi* over Berlin can be obtained. That is the exchange of some degree of recognition for the East German regime against new hard and fast arrangements for access, our troops of course remaining.'[40] Serious consideration of the British proposals was, however, prevented by continued West German and US opposition to the Macmillan government's readiness to give in over Berlin and to recognize the GDR as Khrushchev had requested. There were also accusations in the German press that Britain was attempting to appease the Soviet Union.[41] London was aware that it had to tread carefully. After all, the British wished to obtain West German support for its EEC applications; thus both in 1961–62 and in the years prior to 1967 (when London applied for the second time after French President de Gaulle had vetoed the first application in early 1963), the British were careful not to alienate Bonn too much by taking an overly forceful position on the West's new policy of détente toward the Soviet Union. The British therefore left it largely to the Kennedy and Johnson administrations to enlighten the West Germans about the alliance's new policy toward the Soviet Union and its satellite states.[42]

During both John F. Kennedy's presidency and Lyndon Johnson's subsequent administration, it became increasingly obvious that the West considered

NATO as an instrument for protecting West Berlin and West Germany rather than for bringing about German unification. It was also seen as a device for implementing East–West détente on the basis of a divided Europe. In May 1964, Johnson had spoken of the necessity of 'building bridges' between East and West; in October 1966, he proposed the idea of 'peaceful engagement' with the countries of the Eastern Bloc. Subsequently, the important Harmel Report, approved by the NATO Council in December 1967, and the NATO Council of Ministers' meeting in Reykjavik in June 1968 expressed the desire to make progress with East–West détente and commence negotiations for troop reductions in Europe.[43]

In West Germany, the developments in international politics were reflected in new Foreign Minister Gerhard Schröder's 'policy of movement' – a cautious, mostly economic opening to several Eastern European countries; the focus was no longer only on attempting to achieve an improvement of relations with the Soviet Union.[44] From the early 1960s, West Germany began to lean toward the elimination of the increasingly outdated Hallstein Doctrine. It was gradually realized in Bonn that the rigid political and legal aspects of Adenauer's traditional 'policy of strength' toward the East was self-defeating; it unnecessarily isolated West Germany both in Eastern Europe and in the developing world.[45] It also made the FRG's relations with its Western allies increasingly difficult. But Bonn was still a long way from embarking on the course advocated by a 1967 declaration of the Warsaw Pact countries which encouraged West Germany to recognize the GDR and to bring about an East–West *rapprochement*. Instead, Schröder, whom Adenauer had first appointed foreign minister in 1961, favoured undermining the GDR by continuing Bonn's long-standing policy of ignoring the state while simultaneously embarking on an improvement of relations between Bonn and most Eastern European countries. Schröder intended to encircle the GDR with a complex net of trade treaties, thereby hoping to isolate it in Eastern Europe and depict its non-recognized status as a highly anachronistic one. In 1963, Bonn concluded trade treaties with Poland, Rumania and Hungary; a year later, a treaty with Bulgaria followed; trade missions were established in each case. Only the Czech government was hesitant to embark on such a course as it resented the inclusion of West Berlin in the envisaged trade treaty.[46]

Although Schröder only modified and essentially continued West Germany's priority of obtaining unification, London regarded him as a progressive German politician who clearly favoured the further strengthening of the Atlantic alliance; he did not seem to sympathize too much with French President de Gaulle's rather independent and iconoclastic Cold War approach.[47] This contributed to the fact that Britain belatedly recognized in the early to mid-1960s that West Germany was not merely a major source of tension in the East–West conflict but had actually become one of the Cold War's major players. London began to treat West Germany's policy initiatives with greater respect and attention than heretofore; this soon led to a certain improvement in British–German relations. It was hoped that this would be useful in obtaining West German support for Britain's EEC ambitions.

Still, in view of West Germany's new treaty relationship with various Eastern European countries, London felt encouraged in late 1963 to upgrade the British trade missions in Bulgaria, Hungary and Romania to the status of full embassies. Behind the scenes, moreover, Britain continued its attempts to push the Western alliance toward Britain's preferred policy on the recognition question and away from Adenauer's long-standing policy of strength. As it appeared to be impossible to implement a wholesale policy of East–West détente after the failure of the disastrous four-power summit meeting in Paris in May 1960, British foreign policy attempted to prop up the stability and self-confidence of Eastern Europe. In the summer of 1962, London entered into a secret agreement with Poland regarding the Oder–Neisse line. This commitment essentially ran counter to British reassurances to West Germany, repeatedly uttered since 1949, that Britain fully supported West German ambitions to obtain reunification with East Germany. According to a recent insightful doctoral thesis, Macmillan's policy in this respect rested on three main considerations: (1) Bonn would eventually have to accept the Oder–Neisse Line in any case; (2) it would put Britain at a political and economic advantage when a *rapprochement* between West Germany and Eastern Europe would eventually occur; (3) there was little risk that the USA would oppose the British move if it found out about it as the Kennedy administration was not supportive of Adenauer's rigid, legalistic position in the unification question.[48] One should add that the British were also well aware that Germany had to be convinced to accept the Oder–Neisse line because otherwise Poland would continue to feel utterly dependent on a Soviet security guarantee, thus prolonging Moscow's hold on Poland.[49]

London had realized at an early stage in the Cold War that the widespread Eastern European perception of a continuing German threat and renewed German militarism – as emphasized by Moscow – was one of the Soviet Union's most potent weapons in its arsenal for continuing to subjugate Eastern Europe. Unless West Germany itself took some action to undermine these allegations, détente with Eastern Europe would prove very difficult if not impossible; the full international recognition of the Oder–Neisse line was the best reassurance West Germany could offer Poland and the other Eastern European countries about Bonn's peaceful and non-revanchist foreign policy. Although Britain's secret pledge to Poland constituted a violation of its commitments to help West Germany realize its political priorities, it was a very real effort to reduce tension in Europe and bring about an East–West détente. The secret nature of the deal was an attempt to overcome the stalemate in the Cold War as well as Western disenchantment with Bonn's slow movement toward a more flexible policy with respect to Eastern Europe – while at the same time avoiding alienation of West Germany. Britain always believed that it was better to reduce tension in Europe, including strengthening the stability of the GDR, rather than having to deal with an Eastern Europe and an East German state which were about to collapse for either political or economic reasons; it was believed that such developments would bring about a very serious crisis. Britain also had its economic advantages very much in mind. London never overlooked the fact that Eastern Europe was a huge potential export market for British products; establishing good relations with countries such as Poland therefore made good political as well as economic sense.

This new evolving attitude toward East–West relations and the GDR recognition question became apparent in connection with the initialling of the Nuclear (or Partial) Test Ban Treaty on 25 July 1963 by the USA, Britain and the Soviet Union; it had been negotiated in complex and difficult rounds of talks over the previous eight years. While Britain had been able to act as a generally respected mediator between the superpowers in the negotiations, the new 'policy of engagement' which Washington and Moscow were prepared to embark upon in the aftermath of the Cuban missile crisis had been decisive for the conclusion of the pact. The treaty was of unlimited duration and represented a major milestone on the road to an East–West *rapprochement*; it entered into force on 10 October 1963. The Test Ban Treaty forbade nuclear tests in the atmosphere, underwater and in space but not underground; despite this limited nature, the nuclear powers France and China refused to sign it.[50] It was therefore regarded as vitally important that as many other countries as possible, including non-nuclear powers, sign the treaty. West Germany, however, protested vehemently when the non-recognized GDR was allowed to accede to it.[51]

Both Kennedy and Macmillan were keen on de-escalating the international arms race and preventing further dangerous pollution of the environment by unlimited test explosions which had been proliferating since 1945. Given that negotiating the treaty with the Soviet Union had been difficult enough, both politicians were also keen on avoiding all unnecessary complications with the ratification of the Test Ban Treaty in the national parliaments. They therefore refused to give in to Bonn's desire to see East Germany excluded from signing it. London was convinced that the West Germans were vastly exaggerating the risk that the GDR's signing of the Test Ban Treaty would lead to an improved international standing for Ulbricht's regime. At the same time, the British wished to court favour with Bonn and were thus prepared to make great efforts to diminish any West German apprehensions. Yet, it was quickly recognized that the mere assurance that Britain would 'avoid any actions which might be construed as an act of recognition of the D.D.R.' was not sufficient to satisfy Bonn.[52] West German Foreign Minister Schröder even went so far as to ask Lord Home, his British counterpart, to make London's private reassurances public by writing in this vein 'to all states of the world not having diplomatic relations with the Soviet-occupied Zone'. Bonn expected that both Britain and the USA would make it 'unambiguously' clear that despite the Test Ban Treaty's having been signed by unrecognized states 'no treaty-like relations come into existence between them and territories they have not recognized as states'.[53] Although this was regarded as an unjustified and quite unreasonable fear, London and Washington agreed to Schröder's request. Only the Federal Republic's desire to see the GDR excluded from any conference convened under the Treaty was not accepted because Moscow was likely to object.[54]

While the new Erhard government in Bonn was grateful to the British for their readiness to make their views on the recognition question clear to the world, the West Germans did not cease 'making a fuss over East German accession to the Nuclear Test Ban Treaty'.[55] Above all, the FRG feared that 'a number of neutralist states' might soon begin talking about East Berlin's 'national sovereignty'.[56] However, there was not much else the British could reasonably be expected to do. The Federal Republic had to be content with the fact that the two Western powers would neither permit the East German signature on their copy of the treaty nor would they be prepared to receive the instruments of ratification or accession from the GDR. Instead, they would accept notification from the Soviet government that such instruments and the East German signature had been obtained in Moscow. London and Washington made it clear that they believed East Berlin had not entered into a treaty relationship with the West but was bound to observe the Test Ban Treaty due to its contractual relationship with the Soviet Union. It was generally concluded in London that Ulbricht was so keen on signing an international treaty that the East Berlin regime would behave in a reasonable way so as to 'appear as a responsible government'. In any case, it could be expected that subsequently the East Berlin regime would try to exploit the very fact of its signature; it would maintain that it signified the international recognition of the GDR 'irrespective of whether we accept it or not'.[57]

Bonn was also disappointed with the Western and particularly the British reaction to the building of the Wall. Despite strong Western condemnation of the construction of this horrendous barrier, London still appeared to be overly keen on re-establishing trade relations with the GDR after their brief inter-ruption due to the events of August 1961. As London did not recognize the GDR, there was naturally 'no question of official participation' in the Leipzig Spring Fair in March 1962, the first such event after the construction of the Berlin Wall. In British governmental circles, however, it was argued that the government ought not deter the FBI and British firms from attending the fair. After all, it did not appear as if the West Germans themselves were actively preventing or even discouraging their businessmen from attending.[58] Bonn was not even planning 'to reduce inter-zonal trade at all'.[59]

Most Foreign Office officials sympathized with the view of not advising against participation in the Leipzig trade fair; this approach was particularly forcefully defended by the Board of Trade. The Foreign Office also believed that it would be inadvisable for Britain to commence an economic warfare campaign against the GDR.[60] Officials were even prepared to ignore the wishes of NATO. While it would be disappointing 'if we were left in an isolated position in NATO', it was in Britain's interest to trade with East Germany and to do so in the most efficient way possible. 'We must ensure that our goods are known and a trade fair is one of the best ways of achieving this.'[61] Moreover, if respectable British firms were encouraged not to attend, the only British firms present would be those of a more dubious character and they would undoubtedly claim that they were representatives of British industry.[62] Yet, it was realized that the government faced a dilemma: 'Although it is in the United Kingdom's interest to trade with East Germany, it is contrary to our interest to take any action which will help the regime to bolster their prestige.'[63] The majority of officials at both the Foreign Office and the Board of Trade appeared to believe that trading with East Berlin was more important for Britain's health than running the risk of giving a degree of indirect recognition to the GDR; while the latter was not desirable, it had to be accepted. Above all, the government had no power to prevent British companies and indeed individuals from attending the Leipzig fair. It was concluded that companies should therefore merely be asked to review 'the scale of representation' and critically assess whether or not 'commercial considerations' required participation in Leipzig.[64]

This, however, ran counter to the advice of the British embassy in Bonn, which expected that such a course of action would lead to 'resentment and dismay' in both Bonn and Washington; London would again be accused of a 'weak attitude' toward the GDR.[65] In early February 1962, Foreign Secretary Lord Home decided that Britain could not afford to oppose its NATO allies on this question. In a long memorandum, he explained that in view of the government's allegedly weak attitude and controversial activities in the Berlin crisis, sometimes referred to as appeasement, Britain should avoid becoming isolated within the Political Committee of NATO. He therefore advised that the government demonstrate its solidarity with its NATO allies rather than oppose the NATO resolution which asked Western companies to boycott the Leipzig Fair. Home concluded that the political advantages of going along with the resolution 'will far outweigh any economic or commercial benefits we may hope to achieve'. Thus, the British government should 'take some positive step to discourage the participation of British firms at Leipzig' and the FBI 'should be asked to abandon the arrangements they are making' for a British pavilion at the fair which was to be partially financed by the British taxpayer. The Foreign Secretary pointed out that 'it would be most unfortunate if we were to find ourselves in a situation in which British businessmen and the F.B.I., alone of all the NATO allies, flock to the Leipzig Fair'.[66] Home emphasized in his memorandum that it was not governmental policy 'to give Ulbricht's regime any assistance in surmounting its difficulties, or in improving its image toward its people or the world at large'. He explained that Britain should avoid contributing to 'an impression in the Russians' minds that we think that the East Germans can stand on their own feet as an independent country and that a major Western power is willing to help them along this road'.[67] Britain decided to embrace the NATO resolution.

Thus, only very few Western companies attended the 1962 spring trade fair in Leipzig. Yet, this boycott of the fair did not last long. Two years later, Western firms once again began regularly attending and Britain became the second largest Western exhibitor after France. In view of the country's economic troubles, the Board of Trade had largely succeeded with its argument that 'the Zone represents a good potential market for British exports, and that the Leipzig Fair is one of the best leads into that market'.[68]

The British frequently found themselves in similar dilemmas throughout the 1960s. It seemed hardly ever possible to benefit from trading with the GDR without antagonizing Bonn or Washington. In early March 1963, for example, a Scottish company wished to sell a second-hand tanker to the GDR. The Foreign Office hesitated to grant the firm the required credit cover. Once again, 'fierce' reactions from both the Americans and the West Germans were anticipated which would 'outweigh the commercial advantages derived' from the sale. As this kind of tanker was not a forbidden item under the COCOM list, however, the Foreign Secretary eventually agreed to review the application for credit cover favourably. In this as in similar cases, moreover, it was decisive that the industrial situation in the north of the United Kingdom urgently needed financial support and that British shipyards were 'badly in need of all the orders they can get'. In addition, London never overlooked the competition for East German trade with other Western nations, in particular with France. The Foreign Office pointed out: 'We ought not to allow the French to steal a commercial march on us.'[69] For political reasons the Foreign Office, however, felt rather uneasy about the entire issue. Therefore, the officials were relieved when they realized that the international uncompetitiveness of Britain's shipyards meant that it was unlikely that many similar requests from the GDR would materialize. 'Fortunately, from the Foreign Office point of view, we seem likely to obtain few, if any orders, largely owing to the higher prices quoted by United Kingdom builders.'[70]

Détente, the Two Germanies and the Wilson Government, 1964–65

East Berlin had undoubtedly hoped, and the West German government had greatly feared, that the election victory of Harold Wilson's Labour Party in October 1964 would inaugurate a new phase in Britain's policy toward the GDR. During its party conference in 1961, the majority of Labour Party delegates had made clear their sympathy for *de facto* recognition of the GDR. In February 1963, when Wilson had been elected leader of the Labour opposition after the premature death of the popular Hugh Gaitskell, he declared that in return for a satisfactory solution of the Berlin problem, the

West should be prepared both to give *de facto* recognition to the GDR and to accept the Oder–Neisse line as the permanent German–Polish border. During a visit to Poland in June 1963, he also expressed sympathy for the Rapacki Plan which envisaged a ban on the deployment of nuclear missiles in both the FRG and the GDR as well as other Central European states. Throughout the 1950s, moreover, Wilson had been well-known for his patriotic anti-German statements as well as his great distrust of the German 'national character' and the FRG's capitalist orientation. By contrast, his ideological and emotional sympathy for the Russian peoples and his frequent journeys to Moscow and talks with Soviet leaders were also well known.[71] Although Shadow Foreign Secretary Patrick Gordon Walker was regarded as a strong supporter of the traditional policy of integrating the Federal Republic into the West, Wilson's declarations as leader of the opposition deeply worried Bonn.[72]

Once Wilson had been elected prime minister in October 1964, however, he did not repeat such sentiments; he instead adopted an increasingly pragmatic approach.[73] After all, like his predecessors Macmillan and Douglas Home, the new Labour prime minister also realized that he needed West German good-will and support to overcome de Gaulle's suspicions regarding London's aspiration to join the EEC. Moreover, Britain's increasingly precarious economic situation made it important to renegotiate the burden-sharing arrangements regarding the costs of the British Rhine Army; a West German government which was well-disposed toward the British government could certainly be helpful in the matter. On the Rhodesian question and the discussions over the future strategy for NATO, a sympathetic government in Bonn would also be helpful for London's positions. It made little sense to undermine support for some of Britain's vital interests for the sake of improving relations with the GDR a little or emphasizing the importance of the recognition of the GDR. Moreover, it was widely believed in Britain that in due course the latter would occur in any case. Thus, during a visit to West Berlin in early 1965, Wilson confirmed that he was convinced that the FRG was the only German government lawfully entitled to speak for the whole of the German nation. He skilfully avoided uttering an opinion on the necessity of recognizing the GDR and the Oder–Neisse line.[74] In late 1964, Patrick Gordon Walker, the new Labour foreign secretary, had considered raising with Schröder the touchy issue of British 'support for the Oder–Neisse line as the eventual frontier of Germany'. It was believed that this was something 'that many Germans already accept in their heart of hearts'. In the end, however, the Foreign Office decided that the British could not be quite as certain what went on in the hearts and minds of the West Germans as Britain's politicians frequently believed; the officials wisely advised postponing discussion of the matter with Schröder.[75]

Unlike Macmillan, Wilson and his foreign secretaries also refrained from attempting to make Britain a mediator between the Soviet Union and the Federal Republic or to negotiate with Moscow over the German question behind the back of the West Germans. While the prime minister pursued a very active policy toward Eastern Europe, it was not his intention to ignore the Federal Republic or negotiate over the heads of the politicians in Bonn on questions of vital importance to the Germans – as both Churchill and Macmillan had preferred. Moreover, Wilson also proceeded very cautiously with regard to expanding British trade links with Eastern Europe where West Germany had already built up a dominant position; the secret commitment to Poland, entered into by Macmillan in 1962, was not developed either. The Wilson government had no desire to antagonize the West German government unnecessarily; it was too important to be able to draw on Bonn's good offices if needed.[76] Wilson's foreign policy aimed at bringing the Federal Republic 'into the process of détente'; the prime minister did not intend to make the German question merely 'the object of its deliberations'.[77]

Wilson was also quite happy to leave it to the USA to impress upon the Erhard government the need for détente and greater flexibility on the German question. This would avoid the many difficult and damaging Anglo-German clashes of the recent past. It was, however, clear that Wilson expected the postponement of West German aspirations for reunification in favour of a more realistic policy of détente and *Ostpolitik*. Schröder and Erhard, however, essentially intended to continue pursuing Bonn's long-standing aim of obtaining a reunified Germany in the reasonably near future. In contrast, the Wilson government clearly hoped that Bonn would soon have no alternative but to subscribe to détente and bury its reunification dreams. It was expected that Bonn would have no other option given Erhard's and Schröder's suspicion of de Gaulle's anti-US course, the general's desire for a French-led policy of détente as well as the looming threat that the two superpowers would ignore their allies and agree on a common approach to the East–West conflict. Yet despite all increased flexibility and genuine attempts to embark on a new relationship with Eastern Europe, Erhard and Schröder were never fully able to overcome their strong dislike of recognizing the GDR and the Oder–Neisse line; they always remained caught in a mental framework which made it impossible for them to give up the notion of working for German unification as a short- to mid-term goal.

Such a policy would have to await the grand coalition formed on 1 December 1966 and led by Chancellor Kiesinger and Foreign Minister Brandt and above all the election of Willy Brandt's social-liberal coalition government in late October 1969. Wilson's cautious and cooperative policy toward the Erhard government in 1964–65 had laid the foundation for a constructive Anglo-German working relationship in the subsequent years. This contributed to the fact that after deep animosity, if not hostility, between Macmillan and Adenauer, Britain was trusted again in West Germany in the later 1960s and 1970s.[78] Compared with the strong suspicions which initially prevailed in Richard Nixon's White House about Brandt's Eastern policy and his personal reliability, Britain became a strong supporter of *Ostpolitik*. Brandt in turn convinced de Gaulle's successor Georges Pompidou to agree to admitting the British into the EEC in 1972.[79]

Issues such as the recognition of the GDR and the intensification of trade links with East Germany had burdened Anglo-German relations since 1949; they became a serious bone of contention between the two countries in the late 1950s and early 1960s during the tenures of Prime Ministers Macmillan and Douglas Home. It is not an exaggeration to claim that in the entire post-war era, Anglo-German relations were hardly ever as bad as they were between 1958 and 1963 when Macmillan and Adenauer seriously clashed on several occasions. Wilson had managed to learn from these developments; he began to treat the Federal Republic as a serious player on the world scene and to take seriously its concerns with regard to unification and the recognition of the GDR and the Oder–Neisse line. British policy under Wilson attempted to do away with the condescending superiority with which Macmillan tended to treat Britain's former enemy. Wilson must thus be credited with pursuing a more pragmatic and less arrogant policy than his Conservative predecessors; essentially, however, he hardly differed from traditional postwar British policy on the German question.

Both Macmillan and Wilson were convinced that the GDR and the Oder–Neisse line needed to be recognized so as to make Europe a more stable and less dangerous place. To the British, the recognition of the GDR appeared to be the precondition for successful East–West negotiations which might lead to a general détente and an easing of Cold War tensions. This was not only a superbly pragmatic but also an eminently successful position. The successful pursuit of *Ostpolitik* as well as the conclusion of the 1975 Helsinki Conference demonstrated that the recognition of the Soviet sphere of influence in Eastern Europe, including an internationally recognized GDR, was indeed necessary for the development of détente. Ultimately, it would even give the Eastern European nations a growing degree of security and confidence which would gradually enable them to begin questioning the Soviet Union's authoritarian hegemony in Eastern Europe. It is perhaps unlikely that German unification would have occurred if many years prior to this event, the GDR had not been fully recognized by the Western world as an independent state on the world stage. With recognition, the GDR was also regarded as having become responsible for its policies as well as its successes and economic failures. In order to be able to fail, the GDR needed to be allowed to demonstrate whether or not it had the potential to survive and to offer, as frequently promised, a better way of life to its citizens than the other German state. While the British were not aware of all the dimensions connected with recognition of the GDR, as early as the late 1950s and early 1960s London had a much clearer conception than Bonn of the potential long-term benefits for overcoming the Cold War which could accrue from recognition. It would take the West Germans until the late 1960s to arrive at similar insights.

NOTES

1 See C.A. MacDonald, *Britain and the Korean War*, Oxford, 1990; A. Farrar-Hockey, *The British Part in the Korean War*, 2 vols, London: HMSO, 1990 and 1995.

2 See K. Ruane, 'Refusing to Pay the Price: British Foreign Policy and the Pursuit of Victory in Vietnam, 1952–54', *English Historical Review*, 90, 435 (1995), 70–92; A. Short, *The Origins of the Vietnam War*, London, 1989, pp. 138–44; R.H. Immerman, 'Between the Unattainable and the Unacceptable: Eisenhower and Dienbienphu', in R.A. Melanson and D. Mayers (eds), *Reevaluating Eisenhower: American Foreign Policy in the 1950s*, Urbana, IL, 1987, pp. 120 ff.; also L.S. Kaplan, D. Artaud and M.R. Rubin (eds), *Dien Bien Phu and the Crisis of Franco-American Relations, 1954–55*, Wilmington, DE, 1990.

3 See Q. Zhai, *The Dragon, the Lion and the Eagle: Chinese–British–American Relations, 1949–1958*, Kent, OH, 1994; V.S. Kaufman, *Confronting Communism: US and British Policies toward China*, Columbia, MO, 2001; J.T. Tang, *Britain's Encounter with Revolutionary China, 1949–1954*, Basingstoke, 1995; E.W. Martin, *Divided Counsel: the Anglo-American Response to Communist Victory in China*, Lexington, KY, 1986.

4 See K. Larres, *Churchill's Cold War: The Politics of Personal Diplomacy*, New Haven, CT, and London, 2002; also K. Larres, 'Politik der Nachgiebigkeit; Harold Macmillan und die britische Strategie in der Berlinkrise 1958–1961', in H. Timmermann (ed.), *Der Bau der Berliner Mauer*, Berlin, 2002. For a good analysis of the international dimension of the entire Berlin crisis, see R. Steininger, *Der Mauerbau: Die Westmächte und Adenauer in der Berlinkrise 1958–1963*, Munich, 2001.

5 On Ostpolitik, see P. Bender, *Die 'Neue Ostpolitik' und ihre Folgen: Vom Mauerbau bis zur Vereinigung*, 3rd rev. edn, Munich, 1995. On the Helsinki conference: W. Loth, *Helsinki, 1 August 1975: Entspannung und Abrüstung*, Munich, 1998; V. Mastny, *Helsinki, Human Rights, and European Security: Analysis and Documentation*, Durham, NC, 1986; J.J. Maresca, *To Helsinki – the Conference on Security and Cooperation in Europe, 1973–1975*, Durham, NC, 1985.

6 I have analysed this in greater detail in my article 'Britain and the GDR in the 1960s: The Politics of Trade and Recognition by Stealth', in J. Noakes *et al.* (eds), *Britain and Germany in Europe, 1949–1999*, Oxford, 2002; for an overview, see also K. Larres, 'Britain and the GDR: Political and Economic Relations, 1949–1989', in K. Larres with E. Meehan (eds), *Uneasy Allies: British–German Relations and European Integration since 1949*, Oxford, 2000, pp. 63–98. See also Henning Hoff's Ph.D. thesis (University of Cologne, 2001) and Hoff's interesting article '"Largely the Prisoners of Dr Adenauer's Policy": Großbritannien und die DDR (1949–1973)', in U. Pfeil (ed.), *Die DDR und der Westen: Transnationale Beziehungen 1949–1989*, Berlin, 2001, pp. 185–206. For a comprehensive recent account of West German–British relations, see S. Lee, *Victory in Europe: Britain and Germany since 1945*, Harlow, 2001.

7 See *Foreign Relations of the United States* (hereafter FRUS) 1949, vol. 3, p. 532 (December 1949).

8 Public Record Office, London (PRO), FO 371/189 154/RG 1011/4, 17 February 1966; also FO 371/169 212/CD 1075/3, 6 August 1963.

9 PRO, FO 371/172 131/RG 1062/1, 13 September 1963; also PRO, FO 371/189 154/RG 1011/4, 17 February 1966.

10 See C. Munroe, 'The Acceptance of a Second German State', in A.M. Birke and G. Heydemann (eds), *Britain and East Germany since 1918*, Munich, 1992, pp. 121ff. At the same time France also entered into relations with the GDR.

11 At the allied nine-power conference in London in September/October 1954, the Western allies declared that the West German government was 'the only German Government

freely and legitimately constituted and therefore entitled to speak for Germany as the representative of the German people in international affairs'. PRO, FO 371/189 154/RG 1011/4, 17 February 1966.

12 See K. Larres, 'Zwischen allen Fronten: Großbritannien und der Konflikt um die Anerkennung der DDR in der "Dritten Welt" und bei Internationalen Organisationen', in A. Bauerkämper (ed.), *Britain and the GDR: Relations and Perceptions in a Divided World*, Bodenheim, 2002.

13 In the documents, the expression was above all used with reference to the developing world, such as Ceylon. See, for example, PRO, FO 371/177 933/RG 1062/10, 11, 20 and 19 February 1964; also FO 371/177 904/RG 1023/3, 19 March 1964.

14 See PRO, FO 371/103 857/CS 1111/13, 13 and 19 November 1953. The contract is in PRO, FO 371/103 857/CS 1111/11, 29 October 1953 and 2 September 1953. See also M. Bell, 'Britain and East Germany: The Politics of Non-Recognition', M.Phil. thesis, University of Nottingham, 1977, p. 136; B. Becker, *Die DDR und Großbritannien 1945/49 bis 1973: Politische, wirtschaftliche und kulturelle Kontakte im Zeichen der Nichtanerkennungspolitik*, Bochum, 1991, pp. 193–4.

15 See Larres, 'Britain and the GDR, 1949–1989', pp. 73–9, 88–90.

16 See, for example, J.P.S. Gearson, *Harold Macmillan and the Berlin Wall Crisis, 1958–62: The Limits of Interest and Force*, Basingstoke, 1998, pp. 26–30; J. van Oudenaren, *Détente in Europe: The Soviet Union and the West since 1953*, Durham, 1991, pp. 24ff., esp. 29, 46, 206, 226; also Michael Howard's classic *Disengagement in Europe*, Harmondsworth, 1958, and E. Hinterhoff, *Disengagement*, London, 1959.

17 See my article 'Politik der Nachgiebigkeit' referred to in note 4 above. For the discussions during the Moscow visit, see in detail PRO, CAB 133/293, including Top Secret annex; also PREM 11/2690, 11/2716; FO 371/143433–440 and 143686–688; CAB 21/3233; PRO, FO 371/143 439/NS 1053/179, 9 March 1959; FRUS 1958–1960, Vol. 7, Part 2, pp. 837–41. See also Harold Macmillan, *Riding the Storm, 1956–1959*, London, 1971, pp. 592–634; Gearson, *Harold Macmillan*, pp. 70–5.

18 For the relatively few but growing number of cultural links between Britain and the GDR, see PRO, FO 371/163 695/WG 1052/17, 17 November 1960; and Becker, *DDR und Großbritannien*, pp. 236ff.

19 PRO, FO 371/163 695/WG 1052/17, 17 November 1960.

20 PRO, FO 371/177 920, 16 October 1964. See also FO 371/189 250/RG 1154/10, 9 February 1966; FO 371/177 963/RG 1154/42, 29 December 1964.

21 See PRO, FO 371/183 049/RG 1054/21, 17 May 1965; also, for example, Becker, *DDR und Großbritannien*, p. 222; see also M. Howarth, 'KfA Ltd. and Berolina Travel Ltd.: Die DDR-Präsenz in Großbritannien vor und nach der diplomatischen Anerkennung', *Deutschland-Archiv* 4 (1999), 591–600.

22 For details, see Larres, 'Britain and the GDR, 1949–1989', pp. 64ff. France was also greatly interested in intensifying its trade relationship and – due to de Gaulle's striving for greater independence from Washington – its political relations with East Berlin. For a good overview, see Walter Schütze, 'Westeuropa: Frankreich', in H.A. Jacobson *et al.* (eds), *Drei Jahrzehnte Außenpolitik der DDR: Bestimmungsfaktoren, Instrumente, Aktionsfelder*, Munich, 1979, pp. 489–500.

23 PRO, FO 371/163 695/WG 1052/17, 17 November 1960.

24 Ibid. See also PRO, FO 371/183 049/RG 1054/8, 21, 23, 28 (February–May 1965).

25 See, for example, D. Childs, 'British Labour and Ulbricht's State: The Fight for Recognition', in Birke and Heydemann (eds), *Britain and East Germany since 1918*, pp. 95ff.

26 The FO's scepticism was largely confirmed in the course of the 1970s. See Larres, 'Britain and the GDR, 1949–1989', pp. 93–7.

27 For the USA and the GDR, see C.F. Ostermann, 'Im Schatten der Bundesrepublik: Die DDR im Kalkül der amerikanischen Deutschlandpolitik (1949–1989/90)', in K. Larres

and T. Oppelland (eds), *Deutschland und die USA im 20 Jahrhundert: Geschichte der politischen Beziehungen*, Darmstadt, 1997, pp. 230–55; for the years after recognition, see B.C. Gaida, *USA–DDR: Politische, kulturelle und wirtschaftliche Beziehungen seit 1974*, Bochum, 1989.

28 See also Becker, *DDR und Großbritannien*, pp. 133–4.

29 See for example A. James McAdams, *East Germany and Détente – Building Authority after the Wall*, Cambridge: Cambridge University Press, 1985, p. 10.

30 PRO, PREM 11/3782, Bermuda Conference, 20–23 December 1961.

31 PRO, FO 371/163 527/G 1011/1, Steel to FO, Annual Review of Events in the FRG for 1961, 2 January .1962.

32 See Becker, *DDR und Großbritannien*, p. 139.

33 See ibid., *DDR und Großbritannien*, pp. 139–40; also A. Dasbach-Malinckrodt, *Propaganda hinter der Mauer: Die Propaganda der Sowjetunion und der DDR als Werkzeug der Außenpolitik im Jahre 1961*, Stuttgart, 1971.

34 PRO, PREM 11/3805, Brief No.1 by E. Shuckburgh, 20 June 1962. British disappointment about Adenauer's failure to support Britain's first application to join the EEC may well have been a motivating factor. See Gearson, *Harold Macmillan*, p. 203.

35 PRO, PREM 11/3805/IAD 410/614, 29 March 1962.

36 PRO, PREM 11/3804, FO telegram No. 1692, 24 February 1962.

37 PRO, FO 371/163 559/CG 1051/17, 20 September 1962.

38 See, for example, PRO, PREM 3806/CG1071/233, 21 July 1962; CG 1071/240, 23 July 1962; WP 7/54, 28 September 1962; WP 7/55, 1 October 1962; also FO telegram No. 4155, 9 October 1962.

39 PRO, PREM 11/3806, Top Secret Minute Zulueta to Macmillan, 1 November 1962.

40 PRO, PREM 11/3806, Bonn telegram No. 898, 30 October 1962.

41 For an article about British 'appeasement' in the West German magazine *Spiegel*, see for example, PRO, PREM 11/3806, Bonn telegram No. 778, 13 September 1962.

42 See M. Camps, 'Britain, the Six and American Policy', *Foreign Affairs*, 39, 1 (1960), 112–22.

43 For NATO and Détente, see my article and the literature 'North Atlantic Treaty Organization', in A. DeConde *et al.* (eds), *Encyclopedia of American Foreign Relations: Studies of the Principal Movements and Ideas*, rev. and expanded 2nd edn, vol. II, New York, 2002, pp. 573–93; R.L. Garthoff, *Détente and Confrontation: American–Soviet Relations from Nixon to Reagan*, Washington, 1994, pp. 123–4, 127–8.

44 For a good account of Schröder's career, see F. Eibl, *Politik der Bewegung: Gerhard Schröder als Aussenminister 1961–1966*, Munich, 2001. See also the forthcoming biography by Torsten Oppelland and his brief but succinct portrait in T. Oppelland (ed.), *Deutsche Politiker, 1949–1969*, vol. II, Darmstadt, 1999, pp. 74–84.

45 See my article 'Zwischen allen Fronten' referred to in note 12 above. For the Hallstein-Doctrine, see W. Kilian, *Die Hallstein-Doktrin. Der diplomatische Krieg zwischen der BRD und der DDR 1955–1973*, Berlin, 2001; R. Booz, *Hallsteinzeit: Deutsche Aussenpolitik 1955–72*, Bonn, 1995. For the doctrine's origins, see W. Grewe, *Rückblenden 1951–1976*, Frankfurt/M., 1979, pp. 251–62.

46 See, for example, M. Görtemaker, *Geschichte der Bundesrepublik Deutschland: Von der Gründung bis zur Gegenwart*, Munich, 1999, pp. 398–400.

47 For Schröder as the 'German progressive', see R.G. Hughes, 'British Perspectives on the Ostpolitik, 1955–1967', unpubl. Ph.D. thesis, University of Wales at Aberystwyth, 2000, pp. 171–2. For de Gaulle's policies, see, for example, W. Loth and R. Picht (eds), *De Gaulle, Deutschland und Europa*, Opladen, 1991.

48 See Hughes, *British Perspectives*, pp. 132–3, also 159–64.

49 See, for example, PRO, PREM 111/3921, Zulueta to Samuel, FO, 19 October 1961; General Anders, Polish President-in-exile, to Macmillan, 23 February 1962.

50 For a good account, see O. Kendrick, *Kennedy, Macmillan, and the Nuclear Test-Ban Debate, 1961–63*, Basingstoke, 1998; M.M. Lepper, *Foreign Policy Formulation: A Case Study of the Nuclear Test Ban Treaty of 1963*, Columbus, OH, 1971; R.J. Terchek, *The Making of the Test Ban Treaty*, The Hague, 1970; see also the unpubl. N.J. Gurr, 'Arms Control and Middle Powers: The Role of the UK in the Partial Test Ban Treaty Negotiations, 1952–1963', Ph.D. thesis, University of Southampton, 1994.

51 PRO, FO 371/169 212/CG 1075/3, 26 July 1963. This account is based on the analysis in my article 'Britain and the GDR in the 1960s: The Politics of Trade and Recognition by Stealth', as referred to in note 6 above.

52 PRO, FO 371/169 212/CG 1075/3, 30 July 1963.

53 Ibid., CG 1075/8, letter Schröder to Home, c.5 August 1963, unofficial translation.

54 Ibid., CG 1075/3, 1 August 1963; /8, 6 August 1963; see also, for example, /3, FO telegrams Nos 194 and 195, 6 August 1963.

55 PRO, FO 371/172 132/RG 1071/8, 3 November 1963.

56 PRO, FO 371/169 212/CG 1075/15, 9 August 1963.

57 PRO, FO 371/183 058/RG 1075/2, 8 April 1965; also FO 371/169 212/CG 1075/3, 30 July 1963.

58 PRO, FO 371/163 702/CG 1861/1, 16 January 1962.

59 Ibid., 18.1.1962. Bonn did not think that the Federal Republic was legally entitled to breach the inter-zonal trade agreement; moreover, it was reasoned this would only result in the GDR making difficulties over access to West Berlin.

60 Ibid., 18 January 1962.

61 Ibid., 19 January 1962.

62 Ibid., 16 January 1962; also 18 January 1962.

63 Ibid., 19 January 1962.

64. Ibid., 3 January 1962.

65 Ibid., 19 January 1962.

66 Ibid., letter Home, 3 February 1962.

67 Ibid.

68 PRO, FO 371/189 308/RG 1861/9, 4 August 1966; also FO 371/189 308/RG 1861/5, letter to Gibbs, 23 February 1966.

69 PRO, FO 371/177 944/RG 1082/64, 9 July 1964; see also FO 371/103 857/CS 1111/7, 22 June 1953.

70 PRO, FO 371/169 263/CG 1154/5, 21 March 1963.

71 See Hughes, *British Perspectives on the Ostpolitik, 1955–1967*, pp. 213–14.

72 Ibid., pp. 214–16.

73 For a good overview, see Lee, *Victory in Europe*, pp. 97–123.

74 See Becker, *DDR und Großbritannien*, pp. 143–4; also P. Ziegler, *Wilson: The Authorised Life of Lord Wilson of Rievaulx*, London, 1993, pp. 149–50. Wilson's own account reveals very little, see his *The Labour Government, 1964–70: A Personal Record*, London, 1971, pp. 81–2.

75 See PRO, FO 371/177 843/RG 1081/15, 5/12/1964, 13 November 1964.

76 See PRO, CAB 129/122, C.(65)119: 'Policy toward Germany': memorandum by Foreign Secretary Michael Stewart, 9 August 1965; see also M. Stewart, *Life and Labour: An Autobiography*, London, 1980; also PRO, PREM 13/329, memorandum of talk between Erhard and Wilson, 8 March 1965.

77 Hughes, *British Perspectives on the Ostpolitik, 1955–1967*, p. 221.

78 For a good overview of the years 1969–1974, see Lee, *Victory in Europe*, pp. 124–47.

79 See K. Larres, 'Germany and the West: The Rapallo Factor in German Foreign Policy from the 1950s to the 1990s', in K. Larres and P. Panayi (eds), *The Federal Republic of Germany since 1949: Politics, Society and Economy before and after Unification*, London/New York, 1996, p. 305; see pp. 315–18 for Nixon's and Kissinger's deep suspicions of Brandt and his *Ostpolitik*.

9

'Sole Master of the Western Nuclear Strength'? The United States, Western Europe and the Elusiveness of a European Defence Identity, 1959–64

Ralph Dietl

When Chancellor Adenauer told Special Assistant for National Security Affairs McGeorge Bundy in October 1962 that the French and the British were quarrelling about leadership in Europe, Bundy remarked that for the next 15 years only one country would lead Europe, the United States of America.[1] This statement epitomizes the inseparable connection between the European quest for a European Defence Identity (EDI) and the search for a postwar European order. This chapter analyses the different national conceptions for the politico-military reconstruction of Europe and focuses on the clash between emancipation and control – the two concepts at the base of postwar European security architecture.

The European quest to create a Common Foreign and Security Policy (CFSP), a European Security and Defence Identity (ESDI) or a European Defence Policy (EDP) is not a phenomenon of post-Yalta Europe. The only recent aspect is the terminology utilized. Long before the Treaties of Maastricht, Amsterdam and Nice – long before the end of the Cold War – European nation states challenged the Cold War security architecture, attempted to create an ESDI within the Atlantic Alliance or even separate from it and also attempted to emancipate the Old World from US control and to replace the US reconstruction of Europe with a truly European order. Transatlantic tensions are as old as the transatlantic partnership, and even predate the signing of the Washington Treaty of 4 April 1949, the founding charter of the Atlantic Alliance.[2] These tensions led to numerous efforts to reform or revolutionize Western defence designs, mostly in times of détente. In such times, the reduced threat, or the perception thereof, and the simulta-neously emerging perspective on recreating Europe on an all-European basis, emboldened Europeans, on the one hand, to challenge the US reconstruction of Europe and to look for a new European order, while, on the other, it encouraged the Americans to extend existing European structures to the East, in order to smooth the way for a disengagement of US troops from Europe.

Thhis chapter will mainly examine attempts to create an EDI in the years 1959–1964, the period preceding the era of détente. To assume that emancipatory politics within the Western bloc were a simple function of East–West relations would be erroneous, however; they were at least as much a function of Anglo-American relations. The Anglo-American nuclear 'special relationship' always had a decisive impact on the formation of Western security. This chapter will thus argue that the Anglo-American 'special relationship' was utilized by Washington to secure US control of affairs in Europe and to safeguard NATO's supremacy. Western security architecture, therefore, is much more the result of an intense struggle among the allies than of US goodwill. The existing opportunities to create an ESDI during the Cold War surely were shattered by the preponderance of power of the USA but also – and above all – by European jealousies and rivalries.

Soon after Stalin's death in 1953, in the wake of the first *détente*,[3] Europeans started to mourn the loss of their own defence organization, the Western Union (WU). The military organization of the Brussels Pact of 1948, the WU had been scrapped in December 1950 in order to create a single command structure in Western Europe.[4] A streamlining of the Western defence structure would enhance the effectiveness of NATO and was deemed necessary after the outbreak of the Korean War. Just two years later, following Stalin's death and the settlement of the Korean War, politicians on both sides of the Channel started to rethink the decisions made between 1949 and 1951–52. These were the years in which the organizational structure of the NAT, namely NATO, was established.[5] As early as 1953, plans emerged in the British Foreign Office and at the French Quai d'Orsay to revive the Brussels Treaty Organization in order to re-establish a European Defence Identity.

Events in Asia not only led to structural reforms within the Western Defence architecture but also to plans to rearm West Germany so as to increase Europe's own defensive capability. Yet to forestall the envisaged re-establishment of German national forces, France developed a concept which combined rearmament and effective control – the Pleven plan for a supra-national European Defence Community (EDC). The French thereby invented a strategy to utilize European integration as an instrument of 'double containment'. French attempts to make the EDC a full-fledged European defence organization, however, foundered on US resistance, which demanded a clear (if not binding) definition of the relations between the prospective EDC and NATO at the NATO Council Meeting in Lisbon in February 1952. The result: the prospective EDC was integrated into NATO and the primacy of NATO safeguarded.

It was the lack of European control of the European Defence Forces in the Treaty establishing a European Defence Community of 27 May 1952 that triggered alternative planning in France and the UK, and which inspired the above-mentioned plans to revive the Brussels Treaty Organization. The EDC Treaty neither established a European command structure nor envisaged

European political control of the European defence forces. The European Army would have been commanded by the SACEUR of NATO, a US general, with political guidance given by the NATO Council.[6]

The EDC was not a manifestation of a European defence identity. The EDC Treaty, as signed in 1952, served mainly the US reconstruction of Europe. For the USA the supranational EDC was more than an instrument of 'double containment'; it was an instrument of 'triple containment' – to use an expression from Ronald Pruessen – a mechanism 'to tame difficult European behaviour'.[7] Washington in effect tried to replace the old European order with a new 'progressive' one; an order that would guarantee internal and external peace, and form the basis of overcoming the division of Europe in the Cold War. Only rearmament of Germany in a European context would leave the path open for an all-European settlement of the German question. A NATO solution to the issue of German rearmament would only stiffen the Cold War fronts and reduce the possibility of creating an all-European postwar order. The policy of 'triple containment' was not only aiming at a general pacification of Europe but implied the aim of controlling France, in addition to Germany. The stipulations of annex I and II to article 107 of the EDC Treaty, limiting the production of nuclear fuel to 500g per annum, made the EDC Treaty a perfect instrument of nuclear non-proliferation, by making the development of national nuclear deterrents impossible.[8] Nuclear non-proliferation was essential to ensure equality between France and the Federal Republic, one of the pillars of European integration, and also to guarantee US hegemony in Europe. It also enabled the USA to work out an all-European settlement based on an integrated and conventionally armed Europe, the security and territorial integrity of which would be guaranteed by the super-powers.[9] In order to avoid being contained by the EDC, however, France attempted to endow the EDC with a European command structure, European political control and a nuclear capability – the three keys to forming a European defence identity – as a precondition for ratification. The USA fore-stalled such a development in order to safeguard the integrity of NATO and US control of affairs in Europe. The USA also precluded Georges Bidault's plan to establish a directing council for NATO that was meant to save France from being contained by the EDC Treaty.[10] Left without any hope of revising the treaty, the French National Assembly rejected the project altogether. The renunciation of the EDC Treaty in 1954 was therefore nothing less than an act of emancipation, nothing less than an expression of revulsion against the US ordering of Europe. This 'rebellion' against the US integration of Europe led not only to the downfall of the EDC and the preservation of French sovereignty but also to a thinly concealed confrontation between France and Britain on the one hand and the United States on the other about control of European affairs.[11] Winston Churchill, who helped French Prime Minister Mendès France to end the 'EDC tomfoolery', warned the USA not to force an order on Europe: 'European federation may grow but it cannot be built. It must be a volunteer not a conscript'. An inevitable straining of Anglo-American relations was the result.[12]

Freed from the straitjacket of the EDC, French Prime Minister Mendès France pleaded for the creation of a 'little NATO'. The Brussels Treaty Organization had to be revived as 'une realité politique et militaire' to allow the Europeans to regain control of European affairs.[13] Mendès France was seeking an organization that would enable the Europeans to shape their own destiny. Like his successors, Mendès was striving for the three pillars of a European defence identity: a command structure, political control and nuclear capability. Facing the opposition of the USA, being dependent on the protective shield of NATO, and lacking the whole-hearted support of the British, France was obliged, however, to settle for the Paris Agreements of 23 October 1954. Now the question of German rearmament was separated from initiatives to foster European integration. The Federal Republic joined NATO, and a revamped Brussels Pact, the WEU, would serve as a control mechanism for German rearmament. The French attempt to return to a situation in which Europe was defended by Europeans subsequently failed. NATO remained the only Western defence organization in Europe. The revised WEU, although lacking a command structure and primarily concerned with controlling the arms of the Federal Republic, nevertheless constituted a suitable forum for the discussion of politico-military matters. The Standing Armaments Committee (SAC) of the WEU could even be considered as the nucleus of a European military organization. Furthermore, the SAC enhanced the military autonomy of Europeans by fostering defence cooperation among the seven member states of the WEU.[14] Most important of all, the Paris Agreements freed the signatories of the EDC Treaty from many of the restrictions of Article 107 of the EDC Treaty. Only the Federal Republic had to accept special regulations and was prohibited from producing nuclear, biological or chemical weapons, within her own territory. The Paris Agreements, therefore, did not hinder France from becoming a nuclear power or Western Europeans from embarking upon military and nuclear cooperation.[15]

It is neither astonishing that the Europeans attempted to utilize the machinery of the WEU to enhance European emancipation nor that the USA in defence of their European policy – aiming at a reconstructed Europe which would enable the USA to relax somewhat without losing control of the affairs in Europe – tried to hinder the Europeans from building upon the WEU. After the failure of the EDC project, the Eisenhower administration pleaded for a strict division of military affairs and European integration – a policy that had already left its first imprint on the Paris Agreements. While blocking development of the WEU, the USA promoted a 'relance européenne' based on the European Coal and Steel Community (ECSC).[16] Nevertheless, a European security identity did emerge among the Seven. In 1956 and 1957, even a European defence identity seemed within reach, for the UK – dismayed with 'American bullying' during the Suez crisis – threatened to embark on a policy of sharing nuclear technology. Steps were thus undertaken by the British to create a military organization within the WEU. British Foreign Secretary Selwyn Lloyd even pleaded for creation of a European nuclear arms pool based on the WEU. Thus, the US ordering of Europe was endangered.[17]

To face this challenge, the US succeeded in efforts to 'unhook the British from the French.'[18] And indeed, the challenge to the US reconstruction of Europe was stopped temporarily by the re-establishment of the Anglo-American special relationship in the autumn of 1957. The institutionalization of politico-military consultations at the Anglo-American summit meetings at Bermuda (21–23 March 1957) and Washington (23–24 October 1957) ended all chances of building a European defence identity based on the WEU. While Anglo-American relations improved, leading to a revision of the US Atomic Energy Act of 1954, favouring nuclear cooperation with the British, emancipatory politics suffered a major setback.[19] Yet the struggle to secure for the Europeans a voice in the defence of Western Europe continued in the early 1960s. The Continentals were forced to look for new ways to free themselves from the USA. Two main paths can be distinguished: First, there were attempts to create an EDI aimed at emancipation through independence, by the creation of a 'Third Force'. Second, efforts were undertaken to preserve, but reform, the Atlantic structure, which aimed at emancipation through co-determination.

Immediately after having gained power in France, Charles de Gaulle began looking for an adjustment of the new situation in Europe. The French President did not react to the re-establishment of the Anglo-American special relationship by creating a European defence identity based on the Six, however. He even contributed to the downfall of the FIG project, a French–Italian–German venture in advanced arms technology, sponsored by his predecessor to enhance the defence capability of the Continent.[20] Instead, de Gaulle focused on the emancipation of France, not Europe. He toyed with reviving the postwar meetings of the Big Three to secure France a status equalling that of the UK. He hoped that nuclear proficiency would enable France to rejoin this exclusive club and therefore he concentrated first and foremost on enhancing the French military nuclear programme.[21]

The threat of an understanding between the superpowers on nuclear non-proliferation – a prospect looming after the Geneva Conference on Methods to Identify Nuclear Explosions of July and August 1958 – forced de Gaulle to insist on a reform of NATO which would promote France instantly to a status of equality with the UK. France needed to act before the window of opportunity for her to join the exclusive club of nuclear powers was closed once and for all.[22] De Gaulle's famous September memorandum was the result: a plea to institute a trilateral British–French–US politico-military directing council of the West. France thereby was requesting a voice in the control of the Western deterrent.[23] In the event this were granted, there would be no need for France to build a national nuclear deterrent; should the 'Anglo-Saxons', however, block such a reform of NATO, de Gaulle would feel bound '*to denounce NATO*' and build up the Europe of the Six as the basis for the emancipation of France.[24]

The initial reaction to the September memorandum was extremely negative. The notion of giving France a voice in the control of the Western deterrent was 'just a little crazy', to use the words of President Eisenhower. The request challenged one of the pillars of the reconstruction of Europe, namely the equality of the Federal Republic and France. The US could not lend support to the institutionalization of a class structure within NATO – an attitude applauded by most Europeans.[25] The British reaction was far more cautious. Harold Macmillan feared that an outright rejection would lead de Gaulle to build a 'Continental' European bloc to challenge the 'Anglo-Saxons'. This would deliver a deathblow to the current FTA negotiations between the UK and the EEC countries and widen the already existing economic rift between the EEC and the rest of Western Europe. Interested in an association with the Continent, Britain seemed willing but – due to US pressure – was unable to accede to French wishes.[26]

In Paris, alternative planning began. However, France's EEC partners were interested neither in building up a Continental European power bloc nor in being represented by France in a 'Council of the West'. The Berlin Crisis, however, led to a drastic change. Adenauer, fearing an all-European settlement among the superpowers that would discriminate against the Federal Republic, now realized it might be in the interest of a more integrated Europe for a continental European power to have a voice in Western, if not global, political and strategic planning. This conviction was strengthened by Macmillan's journey to Moscow in February 1959. The German chancellor finally came to the conclusion that European structures must be improved, that France and the Federal Republic must be integrated to safeguard Germany from a lesser legal status. Integration would make discrimination against one into discrimination against all. Settlement of the German question should not be pursued before this integration was achieved, before a European power bloc had been constructed. Any precipitate settlement would only lead to discrimination against Germany and against the European Continent. Europe had to become a power factor, a nuclear power, in order not to be at the mercy of the superpowers, and then start to negotiate with the Soviet Union to achieve a just settlement. Furthermore, this schedule had to please de Gaulle. France would support the Federal Republic in blocking a discriminatory settlement of the German question, while the Federal Republic would support France in her drive to build up a European power bloc – economically, politically and militarily.[27]

Sensing a Franco-German alliance, President Gronchi of Italy took the initiative to propose to de Gaulle on 24 June 1959 a *rilancio europeo*. The Frenchman quickly responded and proposed a coordination of the foreign policies of the Six so as to emancipate Europe. This would create a strong and unified Europe able to work out an agreement with the Soviet Union in an all-European framework.[28] Most Europeans were puzzled by the Franco-Italian initiative. The UK was shocked. To build up Europe on the basis of the Six instead of utilizing the WEU was not only a deliberate attempt to exclude the UK, but would torpedo British foreign policy aims of reaching an all-European settlement based on the arms control regime of the WEU. The USA, however, supported a *rilancio europeo*; they might even have prompted the revival of European integration to block a cooperative arrangement. A supranational European Political Union (EPU) based on the Six would not only contain France and block discrimination against the Federal Republic, but also eradicate the danger of a revival of WEU arms cooperation, which had recently been transferred to NATO. The utilization of the WEU as a vehicle to create a European Political Union would threaten to revive defence cooperation between the UK and the Continentals and thereby endanger US control of European affairs.[29]

With the launching of the EPU negotiations, an intense battle began among the conflicting interests and visions of 'Europe' – those of the USA, France, the UK and Germany. De Gaulle's determination to build the EPU on a confederal basis, and US determination to rearrange its military commitment in Europe (to reduce the costs of its overseas forces), opened up new perspectives.[30] A confederate Europe would allow the UK to participate, while US force reductions would make the UK's participation attractive for the Continent. A historic opportunity thus emerged for the UK to refashion its ties to Europe. A revival of the Anglo-French *entente* of the years 1954–57 seemed achievable, if the UK would be willing to share its nuclear expertise and therefore European leadership with France. In case the UK should scrap its plans for an all-European settlement based on the WEU and embrace the institutions of the Six as a means to contain Germany, even the Federal Republic might prefer to support a Europe thus reconstructed instead of facing a discriminatory all-European settlement that would allow the USA to 'sit back a little and relax somewhat'.[31]

Whitehall did indeed grasp the opportunity, and began to align its policy with that of France to recreate the Anglo-French *entente* broken by the re-establishment of the Anglo-American special relationship in 1957. The change of heart did not pass unnoticed. The French Prime Minister Michel Debré declared after deliberations with Selwyn Lloyd on 12 November 1959, '[que] les objectifs fondamentaux de la politique européenne étant d'ailleurs, si je ne me trompe pas, les mêmes à Londres et à Paris.'[32] The scheme of the British and French to build Europe together did, however, fail to get the support of the Federal Republic. Chancellor Adenauer announced in Paris on 1–2 December 1959 that he would support an association of the UK with the Continent but not British membership in the Communities of the Six because European cooperation with British participation would probably offend the USA.[33] The Federal Republic would support enhanced military cooperation with France, but reject the idea floated by Debré that France, the UK and the Federal Republic should bear the responsibility for the security of Europe. West Germany would support the creation of a European deterrent, but would not participate in a visionary policy to replace the Atlantic Alliance with a European defence community. The creation of European forces capable of defending the European Continent independently of the USA was fictitious as long as no agreement on general nuclear disarmament was in sight. Even with a *force de frappe*, Europe would be utterly dependent on the US strategic deterrent. The policy of the Europeans, Adenauer argued, should limit itself to a reform of NATO that would guarantee Europe a voice in nuclear affairs. A Franco-German axis should form the nucleus of the future Europe of the Six. Franco-German integration would allow a restructuring of Europe that would rid its institutions of an excess of supranationalism. Adenauer thus envisaged a special relationship of his own between France and Germany. The trilateral agreement foreseen by Prime Minister Debré and President de Gaulle would not only challenge the USA, but also lead to a Anglo-French leadership in Europe and therefore threaten to discriminate against Germany.[34]

The USA now felt obliged to take precautions. The drive for emancipation had to be carefully redirected, if not controlled. The future Europe had to be a supranational one. For this, a multilateral nuclear NATO force might be created to control Europe's drive for greater autonomy. To secure French partnership, moreover, Eisenhower was even willing to accept trilateral deliberations 'on a clandestine basis'.[35] An institutionalization of such arrangements was, however, rejected. If the French chose not to participate in a NATO nuclear deterrent, France would be isolated. To prepare the ground for this scheme, the Europeans had to be cut off from the military means necessary to develop a European defence identity. The development of independent nuclear potentials among the allies would be blocked. Above all, the USA had to rethink their decision of December 1957 to provide assistance for the coordinated NATO development and production of Intermediate Range Ballistic Missiles (IRBMs). The pledge of assistance had led to the transfer of responsibility from the Standing Armaments Committee of the WEU to NATO, but this did not, however, block the development of indigenous European IRBM production. If the British would abandon their IRBM programme, the USA could make their assistance to the European production effort dependent on the adoption of US missile technology, for any other solution would involve unjustifiable costs and endanger the NATO IRBM requirements for 1963 defined by the Supreme Allied Commander, Europe (SACEUR). There were multiple advantages to furnishing NATO allies with the US Polaris missile. First, the NATO IRBM requirements could be met; second, the Americans could make their offer dependent on the creation of a NATO strategic deterrent under SACEUR, which would create a European deterrent but guarantee NATO control of strategic weaponry in Europe. Furthermore, the adoption of the Polaris missile by NATO would deprive

France of an independent deterrent. The warhead of the Polaris was techno-logically so difficult to produce that France, even after having become a nuclear power, would not be able to utilize Polaris as a delivery system for its national nuclear forces. France, therefore, would have to choose either full integration into NATO or the expensive development of an entirely new strategic deterrent – without the support of NATO allies. Last, but not least, NATO nuclear forces would be dislocated according to SACEUR's plans, thereby allowing NATO to avoid stationing IRBMs on German soil, render-ing an all-European agreement based on a denuclearized Central Europe possible.[36]

First and foremost, the USA had to come to terms with the UK. The ideal underlying the US reconstruction of Europe was a federal system that included the UK. For its part, however, the UK was traditionally sensitive to any abrogation of its national sovereignty and had always rejected submersion into a supranational Europe. This had forced Washington to gently pry British affairs away from the Continent and to recreate a special relationship, which would guarantee US control of affairs in Europe and ensure the integration of continental Europe. The *rilancio europeo*, the development of an EPU, questioned the isolation of the UK. The Europe of the Six would soon emerge as a power bloc with special relations to the USA as well. In case the UK would not participate in and thereby help reshape Europe, it would sooner or later feel constrained between two power blocs. It was therefore only too logical that Whitehall resume its courtship with the Continent. The USA, how-ever, would make their *placet* to an association of the UK with the Continent conditional on the UK's phasing out of the nuclear deterrent business and on the UK's participation in NATO nuclear forces. The first appropriate steps in this direction were undertaken in March and April 1960. Harold Macmillan agreed on 27 March to support the NATO IRBM programme based on Polaris. The UK would give up its Blue Streak project in its entirety and furnish the US with facilities for Polaris submarines in Scotland. The US would in return furnish the Royal Air Force with the Skybolt air-to-ground missile, giving the V-bomber force a new lease on life.[37] Thereafter, in the 1970s, the UK would phase out of the nuclear deterrent business. Washington envisaged a similar solution for the French Mirage strike aircraft to ensure de Gaulle's *placet* for the establishment of a NATO deterrent force. The F-104 'Starfighter' would ensure similar capabilities for the other NATO allies, who, in contrast to the British and French, would depend entirely upon warheads from the NATO nuclear stockpile.

Just four days after the UK's acquiescence, US Secretary of Defence Thomas S. Gates offered NATO an alternative to its armaments programme for the multilateral production of IRBMs – namely, procuring US-produced Polaris missiles. The proposal shocked the Europeans, especially after news reached European cabinets that the US would take a very dim view of European production. European control of IRBM forces thus seemed entirely out of reach. This appeared to be nothing more than the EDC transplanted to the nuclear field.[38] French opposition softened, however, after the USA hinted that the increased bloc tension resulting from the abortive summit meeting with Khrushchev of 16–18 May 1960 would justify more intensive trilateral talks. Eisenhower soon clarified that he did not propose to establish a directorate to run the world. Nevertheless, trilateralism was back on the agenda. Harold Macmillan even told French Prime Minister Debré on 19 May 1960 that the UK supported trilateralism, for such a mechanism 'pouvait transformer, en l'améliorant, le fonctionnement de l'Organisation atlantique, et également … rendre plus aisée la solution des problèmes européens.'[39]

France and the UK hoped the USA would finally agree to a special status for France, to the installation of a directing council, which would allow France to give attention to the creation of NATO nuclear forces. The firm establishment of a NATO deterrent would also allow the UK to join the European communities free from any US intervention. But the subsequent announcement to NATO that the US and UK would start trilateral deliberations with France was badly received by the other allies, who felt betrayed. The essential equality of NATO membership seemed threatened. Hence the outcry of other Europeans obliged the USA to soft-pedal the issue of trilateralism – once again.[40] The hesitation of the USA now convinced President de Gaulle that 'it was firm US policy to remain sole master of Western nuclear strength'.[41] The apparent US unwillingness to concede France special status at the cost of its own NATO leadership led de Gaulle to openly challenge a US policy based on integration. He not only threatened to denounce NATO but actively set the process in motion to form a Europe for the Europeans, an inter-governmental European Political Union of the Six – one of the prerequisites for an EDI. In short, France became willing to undermine NATO 'protection'. The USA and the UK had to be more forthcoming or face the consequences. De Gaulle was thereby pressuring the USA to agree to a trilateral leadership council.[42]

But this strategy also forced de Gaulle to come to terms with Adenauer. The chancellor, although hurt by utterances of the French Prime Minister Debré that the UK, France and the USA formed the pillars of the West, agreed at Rambouillet (29–30 July 1960) to plans for a thorough reform of NATO suggested by de Gaulle, plans that would end the US integration of Europe. Suffice it to say that de Gaulle's plea for a confederated Europe did not fall upon deaf ears. The Chancellor, however, rejected the role of the UK as outlined by the French president. Adenauer did agree to the inclusion of the UK, in case British participation in the deliberations was not intended, before the Six agreed on the principles governing the EPU. Finally, Adenauer insisted upon intensifying Franco-German cooperation. One thing needed affirmation, namely 'que la France et l'Allemagne sont les piliers de ce nouvel édifice'.[43] If this partnership were guaranteed, the support of the Federal Republic for an EPU of the Six, even an EPU with military competences, would be forthcoming. The relationship with London would be maintained with the help of the WEU.

The chancellor tried to win equal status for the Federal Republic, attempting to lure France away from trilateralism and draw her into a Europe of the Six. Furthermore, Adenauer thoroughly disliked Paris's preoccupation with the creation of a French *force de frappe*. Immediately following the deliberations at Rambouillet, the German chancellor warned US Ambassador Dowling that French filibustering in NATO would increase as long as France was denied a voice in the control of the Western deterrent. This was not necessarily a plea for special status – on the contrary. Dowling was warned that the Federal Republic's renunciation of ABC weapons on its territory was made *rebus sic stantibus*, that is, as long as an equality of status existed between France and the Federal Republic. The creation of a trilateral directing Council giving France but not the other allies a voice in the Western deterrent would force the Federal Republic to renounce the declaration of 1954. The German chancellor pleaded for a rapid realization of NATO nuclear forces under the control of the NATO Council, as envisaged by the SACEUR General Norstad. Expected control by the NATO Council would safeguard the principle of equality within the alliance.[44]

The Norstad Plan originated in 1959. It was a timely reply to the desire of the European allies to have a voice in nuclear defence. By responding to that legitimate quest, Norstad hoped to forestall a proliferation of strategic weapons, that is, the emergence of a European Political Union with a capacity for self-defence against the Warsaw Pact. The Eisenhower administration was slow to respond to the Norstad Plan, however. The outgoing administration was willing to furnish ballistic missiles to form a NATO nuclear force (NNF) but remained silent on control measures. Recommendations on sharing in the nuclear field were worked out but not implemented, for Eisenhower considered it appropriate that the final decision should be left to the incoming administration.[45] Norstad's own presentation of the plan to Adenauer, Dirk Stikker and Paul-Henri Spaak at Cadenabbia on 9 September 1960 nevertheless made France's EEC partners reluctant to rush matters among the Six. Adenauer was thoroughly impressed by the Norstad Plan, which would give the Europeans a voice in the control of the Western deterrent.[46] He therefore requested that French Prime Minister Debré accept the principle of the NNF, embrace Norstad's plan, which envisioned the utilization of nuclear weapons by NATO without previous consultation with the president of the USA. An implementation of the Norstad Plan would make it superfluous to furnish the EPU with military competences. The future EPU must be limited to its proper sphere, politics.[47] Lacking the support of the chancellor, de Gaulle decided not to insist on furnishing the EPU with a commission of defence. The now rather moderate French proposal, introduced at the Conference of the Foreign Ministers of the Six on 10–11 February 1961, was nevertheless rejected thanks to Dutch resistance to the inter-governmental character of the proposed EPU, which would necessitate British membership to counterbalance Franco-German 'domination'. The Six, however, decided to study the question further. For that purpose a Commission d'Etudes, the so-called Fouchet Commission, was established.[48]

Although he had inherited far-reaching recommendations on co-determination from the previous administration, the issue was still undecided when John F. Kennedy assumed the US presidency in January 1961. Among these was Robert Bowie's report on NATO in the 1960s. Bowie recommended a two-step approach to the creation of a NATO deterrent force (NADET). The US should immediately furnish NATO with Polaris missiles to meet the NATO requirements for 1963. A pre-delegation was advocated which would give the SACEUR the authority to utilize the NADET if an emergency precluded a decision by the NATO Council. The US would, however, retain the right to utilize the Polaris unilaterally. The second step would be the creation of an indigenous strike force of a multilateral, multinational character. The warheads of this multilateral strike force would remain under control of the Americans (who would, however, refrain from vetoing its utilization). Bowie even proposed that the US 'might consider allowing NADET to be organized under the European Community or WEU' if the Europeans so desired, once they met prescribed conditions and put the deterrent force at the disposal of NATO.[49] Yet he also recommended that the USA propose a package deal making its offer conditional on a previous decision by NATO partners to increase their conventional capabilities – which in turn would allow the USA to reduce their forces in Europe without weakening the shield forces of the alliance.[50] There were other preconditions. NADET had to be a multinational submarine missile force under common financing and ownership, and with mixed crews, to forestall the development of national potentials. To utilize NADET as a system of nuclear non-proliferation, the USA had not only to refrain from installing a directing council and from enhancing France's nuclear programme but had also to secure British abandonment of its national nuclear forces altogether and accept membership in the European Communities. Under this scheme, a transatlantic 'partnership of equals', a two-pillared structure of NATO, would evolve.[51]

Yet while Kennedy's new administration was formulating its European policy, the concept of NATO strategic forces suffered a major setback.[52] The UK and France voiced opposition to the arrangement since it challenged the independence of their national nuclear defences. In fact, Harold Watkinson, the UK's Minister of Defence, rejected the notion entirely: 'The British Government was quite clear that in their view NATO should not become a strategic nuclear power.'[53] Similar voices could be heard on the other side of the Channel. According to Pierre Messmer, Watkinson's French counterpart, 'France was utterly opposed to making NATO a fourth or fifth nuclear power.'[54] Paris and London expressed instead their interest in a revival of the WEU, trilateralism and nuclear 'cooperation'. Harold Macmillan even suggested that Kennedy might remodel NATO to safeguard joint tripartite political control of all nuclear weapons assigned to the alliance.[55] The

Franco-British flirtation and the perspective of NATO reform left its mark on the 'Bonner Erklärung' of the Six of 18 July 1961. De Gaulle, meanwhile, showed restraint. The French president even agreed to make the EPU compatible with the Atlantic alliance, that is, with a reformed alliance.[56] Taking advantage of the Anglo-French honeymoon, the UK on 31 July 1961 announced its decision to apply for membership in the EEC – a move encouraged by French Foreign Minister Couve de Murville. He had signalled that France would not block the UK's application, which was made on 9 August 1961. The Benelux countries heartily welcomed this. They strongly endorsed European emancipation but not a construction of Europe that would secure French hegemony, advancing de Gaulle's own policy of creating a class structure within NATO. As a result, hardly any resistance emerged to a co-operation among the Seven. Instead, there began a revival of arms-cooperation within the WEU. Emancipation, on the basis of an Anglo-French alliance, was in the making.[57]

Once again fearing the political exclusion of the Federal Republic in these deliberations, German Defence Minister Franz-Josef Strauss signalled to US Secretary of Defence Robert McNamara on 5 December 1961 that a decision on NNF be presented soon, otherwise the creation of such a force would be forthcoming within the WEU.[58] Strauss surely exaggerated the threat, not only to save West Germany from Anglo-French domination, but also to create a *fait accompli*. A NNF would save the Federal Republic from being discriminated against in a comprehensive, all-European, settlement of the pending Berlin question and therefore Bonn was determined to forestall any legal status different from the other non-nuclear NATO countries. The Germans now steadfastly refused requests by the allies to link Germany's renunciation of the manufacture of ABC weapons with the East–West negotiations. The Berlin question had to be dealt with in isolation. A linkage would only allow the Soviets to use Berlin to achieve other ends and would only invite the allies to discriminate against the Federal Republic.[59]

In Washington, meanwhile, the Kennedy administration began to fear that NATO nuclear forces not subject to a direct US veto would only allow the Europeans 'to drag the US into a general war'. The USA thus remained un-responsive. The USA even declared at the NATO Ministerial Council Meeting of December 1961 that Europe's security would be best served not by IRBMs but by a conventional arms build-up allowing a more flexible response to any aggression against Western Europe by the Warsaw Pact. The creation of a sea-based multilateral IRBM force controlled by a NATO Nuclear Committee remained a remote possibility. The conventional build up – already outlined in Bowie's report – was given priority. German hopes were shattered. The US plan breathed discrimination instead of emancipation. The very creation of a NATO deterrent force was questioned, and there loomed the threat of an all-European settlement based on a denuclearized Central Europe. Furthermore, 'flexible response' made European security even *more* dependent on US good will. Consequently, the German quest for a European Defence Identity received fresh impetus.[60]

Shortly afterwards, at the Anglo-American summit meeting in Bermuda (21–22 December 1961), Kennedy signalled to Macmillan his support for both British membership and leadership of the EEC – on the condition that 'the British would phase out of the nuclear deterrent business', refuse to furnish France with nuclear technology and ensure that the EEC would be tightly knit without the association of the British Commonwealth. Kennedy implemented Robert Bowie's recommendations. The United Kingdom must become a member of the EEC and the NNF. Stripped of its power and influence, Britain would be reinstated as the leader of Europe, to safeguard a liberal development of the European Communities and the establishment of the EEC as the European pillar of NATO.[61] Four weeks later, de Gaulle was informed by the USA that there was no prospect whatsoever that France would receive nuclear assistance from the USA for the build-up of its own, independent deterrent forces. Eisenhower's former restrictive policy on nuclear sharing was likewise adopted by Kennedy.[62]

The expected reform of NATO was not forthcoming. The French reacted instantly. Negotiations among the Six were reactivated. The Fouchet Plan of 19 October 1961, the French blueprint for a European Political Union, was redrafted to make the planned EPU an instrument of emancipation. The references to NATO were deleted, and a commission of defence reintroduced. Once again, President de Gaulle was challenging NATO supremacy.[63] His measures, however, lacked the support of the Europeans.[64] The fact that the USA seemed unwilling to grant France any special status might have even reinforced NATO solidarity. For Adenauer, US impertinence toward Europe generally was much easier to bear than impertinence toward the Federal Republic alone. The Chancellor therefore considered it unwise to challenge the USA. The Europeans should concentrate on a common foreign policy and not on an EDI. A commission for defence could be installed any time after the EPU had taken off.[65] The Netherlands and Belgium likewise opposed de Gaulle's plans and quickly insisted upon a 'package deal' between the EPU and the British EEC application negotiations. The blocking vote of the Low Countries guaranteed that there would be no EPU unless the UK was admitted to the Common Market.[66] The French hoped to achieve a lifting of the blocking vote, enabling France to form a European Defence Identity based on the Six. These hopes faded when Lord Privy Seal Sir Edward Heath used the WEU Council meeting on 10 April 1962 to declare that the United Kingdom 'quite accepts that the EPU will have a common concern for defence problems and that a European point of view of defence will emerge', which will change the balance within the Atlantic alliance.[67] The EPU negotiations stalled. Why should the EEC member states, which were ill prepared to defend themselves, risk a transatlantic rupture and face the danger of French hegemony in Europe when Europe's emancipation seemed achievable without risk? At the Foreign Ministers Conference of 17 April 1962, the French plan to lead Europe finally did not come off.[68]

De Gaulle was trapped. He must either accept British leadership in the EEC or choose a showdown, rejecting the UK's admission and thus hoping to regain the momentum to organize Europe politically. The USA feared that de Gaulle would make his decision dependent on British nuclear cooperation, placing the UK under pressure to build up the EEC militarily.[69] These concerns were well founded. Pierre Pflimlin, a member of the French Cabinet, left no doubt that de Gaulle would use the defence issue as the touchstone for forming his own opinion as to whether the British were sincere in their desire to take part in Europe. Consequently, what the prime minister could say to de Gaulle on this subject would determine the success or failure of the Brussels application negotiations.[70]

On 17 April 1962, the day the EPU negotiations stalled, Counsellor of the Department of State Walt Rostow advised the president that the USA must negotiate at an early stage a limited long-term role for Europe within a unified Atlantic plan and command structure to pre-empt any European scheme challenging trans-Atlantic supremacy.[71] And, indeed, Macmillan seemed not to have resisted the temptation, but seemed to have toyed with the idea of forming a European 'independent deterrent force' based on the EEC. This is revealed in minutes of a meeting of the British prime minister with Ambassador Chauvel on 19 April 1962.[72] Soon thereafter, during the prime minister's stay in Washington of 27–29 April 1962, Macmillan was told yet again that the USA would not tolerate any form of nuclear sharing – even if the French bargained for British nuclear technology as their price for admitting the UK into the Common Market. Dean Rusk made it crystal clear that despite speculations to the contrary, 'the US were determined not to help France in the nuclear field, either directly or indirectly through the United Kingdom'.[73] Having tested the UK's leeway, Macmillan changed his strategy. Facing an almost certain rejection of the UK's application to join the EEC, the British Prime Minister focused on isolating France. Sensing this in his encounter with Macmillan in Champs on 2 June 1962, de Gaulle instructed the French delegation in Brussels to maintain its position but avoid isolation.[74] The UK and France started to position themselves for the struggle following a rejection of the UK's application, instead of negotiating a settlement.

As de Gaulle remarked on 21 June 1962, 'l'Europe a manqué son heure'.[75] Days later, alternative planning set in and France now approached the Federal Republic. During the Franco-German Summit of 3–5 July 1962, the French President proposed a Franco-German accord along the lines of the Fouchet Plan in case the EPU, that is, the application negotiations, were to fail. The Franco-German Union would serve as the nucleus for a revival of the political cooperation among the Six. Adenauer acquiesced once de Gaulle assured him that the Franco-German Union would serve to form a common foreign policy towards the East. It would be a 'veritable osmosis' of the two countries.

Once the emergency efforts of Italy's Prime Minister Amintore Fanfani for an agreement on the basis of the Six had faltered (due to the fact that the proposals were entirely based on the US conception of Europe, that is, a supranational Europe within transatlantic bounds), Adenauer and de Gaulle reached agreement on Franco-German Union at a summit on 6 September 1962. Unimpressed by threats from the USA not to contemplate a Franco-German axis at the expense of NATO, de Gaulle presented two weeks later the outline of what would serve as a basis for the Elysée Treaty of January 1963.[76]

Britain meanwhile approached the USA for a common assessment of European attitudes toward the nuclear problem. The British initiative was well received in Washington. The Americans were keen to participate in a planning exercise on European defence. Clarity about the future structure of European defence had to be regained in order to safeguard NATO's centralized command and control. The 'Anglo-Saxons' agreed upon common planning. London, however, urged Washington not to force decisions until the question of the UK's admission to the EEC had been settled so as not to shatter the already minimal chances of its success. Kennedy seemed to acquiesce. Soon, initial results of the planning exercise were forthcoming. The UK Working Group on European Integration and Defence drafted a blueprint for a NATO Nuclear Force comprising parts of the US deterrent and all of the UK and French nuclear strike forces. This arrangement would have neither the dangerous international impact of a truly multilaterally owned and controlled NATO force, as foreseen by the Kennedy administration, nor that of an independent European deterrent as envisaged by de Gaulle. The British intended to create a flexible structure easily adaptable to all eventualities.[77]

When Harold Macmillan met de Gaulle at Rambouillet on 15 and 16 December 1962, the French president still seemed hopeful of constructing Europe *with* the UK. De Gaulle's indispensable prerequisite for further collaboration was that the UK showed itself determined not to relapse into greater dependence on the United States. The British too must preserve their independence in the defence field. Already committed to the alternative plan, the British prime minister, however, rebuffed de Gaulle's offer to build a truly independent Europe together.[78]

Days after Macmillan's talks with de Gaulle at Rambouillet, an increasingly anxious President Kennedy used the Skybolt cancellation to force the British to draft an agreement on European security to be presented to NATO partners before the final deliberations on the UK's EEC application. Thus the USA used the Nassau Summit of 19 and 20 December 1962 to secure an Atlantic framework for a future European defence community, irrespective of the impact of this on the UK's admittance to the EEC. The White House thereby made the UK's acquiescence in a transatlantic security architecture a *sine quo non* for US support for its EEC membership. US decision makers were fully aware that the cancellation of the Skybolt would force the USA to extend the Anglo-American relationship into the MRBM field of nuclear deterrence so as to forestall an adverse reaction by the British, thereby boosting the emergence of a European deterrent force. In the event that the Europeans did not strive for a separate EDI, the extension of the nuclear special relationship would not affect the British application negotiations. If the Europeans, on the other hand, did indeed aim at an independent EDI based on Anglo-French nuclear cooperation, the extension of the special relationship would halt such a development, discredit the UK among the Europeans, and 'damage the EEC-UK negotiations' – thereby making the UK entirely dependent on US goodwill. The Skybolt cancellation was both an insurance policy and a political litmus test.[79]

At Nassau the USA proposed to furnish the UK with POLARIS missiles in case the UK would participate in a truly multilateral NATO force. But Whitehall hesitated, insisting instead on a more flexible structure in line with British alternative strategic planning. To entangle the British as well as enmesh the French, the USA tactically compromised on the force structure. Finally, Kennedy agreed to the creation of para. 6 or inter-allied forces, combining the existing nuclear forces in NATO under a new command as a supplement to the para. 8 or multilateral forces; that is, multi-manned sea-based IRBM forces, operating within the NATO framework as originally envisaged.[80] The Americans, moreover, were determined to modify the formula to work their way back to a truly multilateral solution as soon as the UK entered the EEC. But Britain preferred to build on the inter-allied forces and create a European defence identity within NATO without being submerged into a multilateral force.[81] The Nassau Agreement made the creation of an independent EDI based on the EEC almost impossible. The UK sided with the USA, and opted for an Atlantic, instead of a European, framework for the future European defence structure.[82]

De Gaulle reacted by activating his plans to form a Franco-German Union. The recent Cuban missile crisis had convinced him that Warsaw Pact aggression was not imminent. The USSR, as well as the USA, was frightened at the prospect of a serious, open conflict. Neither one would use force unless its national existence was being threatened. This state of mind enabled the Europeans to challenge US supremacy without jeopardizing Europe's security.[83] Simultaneously, the UK tried to secure the support of the allies for the Nassau arrangement, which, thanks to its flexibility, formed a credible basis for the creation of a European defence organization within the Atlantic alliance. No attempt, however, was made to win over the French, for, as Sir Pierson Dixon stated: 'De Gaulle's hostility … gives us the possibility to out-manoeuvre him … and to bring about the situation in which the five would construct the political unity of Europe à Six with Britain instead of France.'[84] The UK's calculation seemed to work. De Gaulle's interview of 14 January 1963 and the collapse of the application negotiations in January 1963 left France in an untenable position.[85] Nevertheless, the strategy of isolating de Gaulle failed. Adenauer signed the Elysée Treaty on 21 January 1963 once de

Gaulle assured him that France would not categorically object to the Federal Republic's building its own nuclear weapons. The French president even discussed Franco-German collaboration on missile technology. The creation of an EDI within NATO was endangered yet again. Even worse, a European 'Third Force' was threatening to emerge – a Europe ready to sever trans-atlantic links in order to come to terms with the Soviet Union on German reunification and to create a new Europe stretching from the Atlantic to the Urals under Franco-German leadership. To forestall such a development, it was necessary to come to terms with Premier Khrushchev before de Gaulle did. Fanfani immediately urged the alliance 'to arrive in Moscow before de Gaulle' in order to isolate him. De Gaulle's policy forced the alliance into a policy of détente. The 'Anglo-Saxons' were furious.[86] While the USA pressured the Federal Republic to revise the Franco-German Treaty,[87] the British drafted a concept of Europe compatible with NATO and the Nassau agreement. A genuine alternative to Gaullist Europe was needed. By February 1963, the UK, the Benelux countries and Italy had agreed upon a Solemn Declaration to create an economic and political organization based on the WEU to be responsible for administrating the inter-allied forces of the Nassau Agreement.[88]

Chancellor Adenauer was not supportive. The inter-allied forces did not imply a deployment of IRBMs and would therefore neither add to the security of Europe nor guarantee the Federal Republic equality of status. The arms control regime of the WEU further decreased the attractiveness of the British plan.[89] To keep the Federal Republic from further drifting toward de Gaulle (who was pushing the idea of building Europe around the French *force de frappe*) and to secure centralized control, the USA felt compelled to build on the paragraph 8 forces of the Nassau Agreement, the so-called MLF (Multilateral Force). The question of control, however, remained problematic. Washington insisted on a veto; Bonn on a revision clause that would – after a transition period – allow majority voting, which would be indispensable in the formation of a European nuclear force.[90] European support for the MLF was meagre, however. Rome hesitated, but finally agreed to support it. A European clause was drafted that foresaw the withdrawal of the US contingent after the successful formation of a European Political Union. A truly European nuclear force would be the result. Yet, Italy insisted not only upon UK membership but that the UK furnish the nuclear warheads for an MLF.[91]

The perspective of a European-controlled MLF made the USA look for alternatives. Washington focused more and more on the inter-allied forces. This would allow the USA to drop the deployment of IRBMs altogether. Furthermore, discrimination against the Federal Republic would facilitate a settlement with France and clear the way for an important agreement with the Soviet Union on non-proliferation. Henry Kissinger therefore informed the British in May that the MLF proposal was 'utter nonsense'. The UK ought to establish a European deterrent within the Atlantic framework.[92] A few days later, Kennedy inquired whether France would furnish the Federal Republic with nuclear information, should the USA give up the MLF project. Couve de Murville reassured him France would never do so.[93] Now, the US president was ready for a change of policy. Washington approached Moscow on nuclear non-proliferation. McGeorge Bundy hinted to Sir Harold Caccia that the Harriman–Hailsham Mission to Moscow might affect the future of the MLF. The USA expected a breakthrough on non-proliferation and that the Russians would handle the Chinese, while the USA would look after the French. Caccia, however, was at a loss about what the USA had in mind for winning over the French. 'Bribes or threats or both?' Caccia remained sceptical.[94] But the policy of *détente* soon started to bear fruit. Khrushchev proposed on 2 July 1963 to sign a limited Test-Ban Treaty.[95] With this, Kennedy and Macmillan agreed to restart trilateral deliberations and to furnish the French with nuclear secrets enabling them to develop and manufacture nuclear weapons without further testing – if France would also sign and ratify a Test-Ban Treaty; agree not to furnish third parties with nuclear information; assign the *force de frappe* to an inter-allied force; and, finally, smooth the UK's accession to the EEC. But again the US proposal was rejected by de Gaulle with the remark that it was unacceptable for a country such as France, which valued its independence – unlike the UK. This, however, did not hinder the USA and the UK from signing such a Test-Ban Treaty with the Soviet Union in Moscow on 5 August 1963.[96]

Meanwhile, the MLF negotiations continued unabated so as not to alarm the Germans. Withstanding a French propaganda initiative to create an independent European deterrent, general agreement was reached that the foreseen transformation of the MLF into a European deterrent force would be gradual and *pari passu* with the advance of European integration. After the demise of Adenauer the Federal Republic was firmly set in favour of the MLF in order to *increase* the US commitment in Europe.[97] The whole project was finally questioned, however, when President Lyndon B. Johnson announced on 21 January 1964 that the USA, the USSR and their respective allies should agree to a controlled freeze on all nuclear weapons.[98] The declaration was coldly received by the European allies and especially by the Germans. The Americans were trying to please the Soviets and lock the door to the exclusive club of the nuclear powers. The Auswärtige Amt instantly announced that German adherence to an agreement on nuclear non-proliferation could only follow the realization of the MLF.[99] Ludwig Erhard, Adenauer's successor, was now determined to speed the process and to clear all obstacles endangering a quick realization of the MLF to assure a European voice in nuclear affairs. Only the MLF would secure a partial fulfilment of the IRBM requirements, enable the Europeans to create a European Defence Identity, and bind the Americans into the European security architecture. For Erhard, the MLF was an absolute necessity; if the MLF failed and US forces withdrew from Europe – following a settlement with the Soviet Union – de Gaulle would invariably assume guardianship of the Continent.[100] Just in case de Gaulle would agree to the formation of a genuine European nuclear force, the MLF could become super-fluous. The German Chancellor therefore asked de Gaulle point blank whether the truly independent Europe propagated by the French would have control over the *force-de frappe* or whether those forces would remain under French control. De Gaulle's answer that French control would be maintained had been expected. A *Europe des patries* and a European Nuclear Force were incompatible. For Germany there remained no alternative to the MLF.[101]

The MLF project, however, did not fare well. The MLF contradicted the Johnson proposal and countered the principle of non-proliferation, which prohibited the transfer of control of nuclear weapons to states which did not possess them. But the European clause in the MLF charter proscribed exactly such a transfer. In order not to endanger an agreement with the Soviet Union, either the MLF project itself or the European clause (and therefore European co-determination) had to be abandoned.[102] Now seemed the appropriate moment to present an alternative to the MLF. The long-awaited opportunity to get rid of the MLF and revive the British scheme of inter-allied forces arrived, a scheme perfectly compatible with the principle of nuclear non-proliferation.[103] Soon after the Labour government of Harold Wilson was installed, the UK presented an alternative scheme, based on paragraph 6 of the Nassau Agreement, which dealt the final blow to the MLF project. In December 1964, London proposed the creation of Atlantic Nuclear Forces (ANF). These would operate under a single authority. The UK, the United States, France and 'Europe' – that is, the powers participating in its mixed-manned element – would have a veto over the use of strategic weapons. The single authority would provide political guidance, approve targeting and operational plans, develop doctrine and cooperate with the US Strategic Air Command. In order to assure the new arrangement would not lead to the dis-semination of nuclear weapons, a clause was foreseen prohibiting the nuclear powers from giving over ownership or control to individual member countries or a group of such countries.[104] The ANF concept was tailored to foster détente. In contrast to the MLF, the ANF did not entail the deployment of an IRBM force. The ANF did not strengthen the offensive capability of the West but did prevent the creation of a future independent European nuclear force, and thus maintained the nuclear status quo, not to mention Anglo-American leadership within the Western Alliance.[105]

With the ANF, which was well received in the USA, the project to create a European Defence Identity finally fell prey to the policy of non-proliferation. The ANF can even be conceived as 'a non-proliferation treaty disguised as an offer for nuclear sharing'.[106] The ANF project foreshadowed the conclusion of the Nuclear Non-Proliferation Treaty of 1968 and the replacement of the project to form multilateral forces by a consultative arrangement, the *Nuclear Planning Group* of NATO.[107] The Americans had prevailed. They had come to terms with their Soviet antagonists on nuclear non-proliferation before the

Europeans even became a power factor. US control of an all-European settlement was thus guaranteed. The efforts of the French and Germans to construct
a Europe, their own Europe, before all-European negotiations would begin,
had failed.

It was less the preponderance of power of the USA which hindered the
development of a European Defence Identity than the utter incompatibility of
European and US conceptions of Europe. The leading Western European
powers, the UK and France, strove to reconstruct postwar Europe by enhancing
the power base of their nation states, in order to emancipate not necessarily
Europe as a whole but the UK and France from superpower dominance.
European unity was conceived as a tool enabling them to draw upon the
resources of the Continent to achieve purely national policy aims. The EDI
envisaged was a separate one. The USA, in contrast, deemed it necessary to
thoroughly reconstruct Europe in order to eliminate an order based on the
nation state that had traditionally bred rivalries and jealousies. The USA
advocated – as a long-term aim – a Europe that would check the self-serving
ambitions of its own constituency and safeguard the autonomous rights of
small powers to maintain peace and stability. The USA favoured a federal
Europe based on a supranational EPU, and *possibly* vested with a European
Nuclear Force. This conception of Europe would render the USA's disengagement from the European Continent possible without threatening the
USA's own national security. A reconstructed and prosperous Europe in which
democracy could flourish would free the USA from an enduring military
presence overseas, from commitments that threatened political liberty and free
enterprise at home.

The two models of 'Europe' were thoroughly incompatible. France and the
UK tried to overcome their present weakness. The USA, on the other hand, tried
to curtail their ambitions by insisting upon the very basis of the supranational
experiment: a balance of power. In order to create and maintain the balance
necessary for a progressive order to flourish, Washington felt compelled to
control affairs in Europe. This control was guaranteed as long as fundamental
NATO structures were left intact. It was assured as long as Western Europe's
ultimate security depended on US deterrent forces. To maintain this control,
the USA were obliged to retain their Western nuclear monopoly. Consequently,
the USA insisted on nuclear non-proliferation. The USA not only tried to
prevent any continental European country from acquiring a nuclear potential,
but kept the UK aloof from the Continent and forfeited possible Anglo-French
nuclear cooperation by offering the UK a special nuclear relationship. British
participation in Europe was made conditional on their willingness to accept a
supranational construction of Europe, while simultaneously phasing out of the
nuclear deterrent business, that is, to accept NNF. With these premises, the
USA offered the UK the leadership of the reconstructed Europe.

As opposed to being submerged into but rather aiming at leading Europe,
France and the UK rebelled against the US integration of Europe. To

safeguard the US reconstruction of Europe, the UK was granted the special relationship with the USA, thus being quieted and bound. France, however, not being offered such a special relationship with the USA and thus a status equal to the UK, continued to challenge the US reconstruction of Europe. To secure France a status of predominance within Europe, NATO would have to be reduced to a guarantee pact, integration abolished and a European architecture created which would either endow France with a special status or enable it to monitor Europe thanks to the political and military weight gained by its emerging nuclear potential. The former solution, entailing the establishment of a European directorate, was improbable; the latter required an inter-governmental European structure – as envisaged by the Fouchet Plan.

The aims and interests of the Federal Republic were entirely different. Bonn first and foremost needed to secure for the Federal Republic a place among the free nations, and felt compelled to rid the nation of its pariah status in the international community. Germany stood to gain the most from a supranational solution since it guaranteed Germany a status of equality in Europe. Bonn, therefore, keenly supported integration – European as well as Atlantic. Integration, however, was threatened by a premature all-European settlement. Such a settlement threatened to block Europe's – but especially West Germany's – path toward emancipation. It would freeze the status quo, that is, a still rather discriminatory order. Premature détente therefore frightened the Federal Republic as much as it did France, which tried to establish its own predominance in Western Europe before talks on an all-European settlement commenced in the hopes of enabling France to shape Europe's future order. The spectre of an all-European settlement based on the WEU, as advocated by the UK, made Adenauer support France's emancipatory politics and a Franco-German alliance. An EPU along the lines of the Fouchet Plan meant protecting Europe from a discriminatory all-European settlement, while a Franco-German union protected the Federal Republic from being discriminated against by France. Deprived of this due to the demise of the Elysée Treaty for Franco-German Union, the Federal Republic gave up its support for the creation of a separate European Defence Identity. Realizing then that the Gaullist *Europe des Patries* was incompatible with the creation of a truly collective European nuclear force, the Federal Republic turned to the supranational MLF concept envisaged by the Nassau Agreement.

As mentioned above, an EDI did not fail to emerge because the notion was opposed by the USA but because the Europeans were faced with two mutually exclusive concepts of Europe, two ways to achieve a European Defence Identity: within the Atlantic framework supranationally by integration, or outside NATO inter-governmentally by emancipation as a 'Third Force'. An EDI failed to emerge because the UK and France rejected the supranational concept. Yet the inter-governmental concept lacked the support of the USA and was hampered by the fact that the two powers capable of guiding Europe, namely the UK and France, competed for European leadership. Both tried to utilize their nuclear capabilities to achieve a dominant position in Europe. Such a potential was a precondition for offering Western Europe an alternative to the existing security architecture; nuclear proficiency was the basis of power and influence. France was therefore bound to insist on nuclear sharing as a prerequisite for the UK's admission to the EEC so as to secure France a status equalling that of the UK. If nuclear sharing were not forthcoming, French leadership in Europe could only be maintained through the exclusion of 'Anglo-Saxon' influence. The UK – whose nuclear forces were a wasted asset – needed US backing and therefore an Atlantic framework to guarantee the UK's predominance in Europe. Such a backing, however, could only be expected if the UK stuck to a policy of nuclear non-proliferation.

The nuclear technological expertise of the USA – and the utter necessity of the European nation states to command nuclear forces so as to be able to shape Europe – empowered Washington to an atomic diplomacy that paved the way to the US integration of Europe. It was the nuclear special relationship that enabled the USA to follow a classic policy of *divide et impera* to make integration work and to make the development of a separate EDI fail.

NOTES

This chapter presents aspects of the author's on-going 'Habilitationsprojekt' on 'Europe in Western Security, 1948–1963'. Further aspects of the project are published in: Ralph Dietl, 'Die Westeuropäische Union: Rüstungskooperation und Europäische Integration in den fünfziger Jahren', *Historische Mitteilungen*, 12, 1 (1999), 90–112; Ralph Dietl, 'Die Westeuropäische Union – "a return to the dark ages"?', in Ralph Dietl and Franz Knipping (eds), *Begegnung zweier Kontinente: Die Vereinigten Staaten und Europa seit dem Ersten Weltkrieg*, Trier: 1999, pp. 67–86; Ralph Dietl, '"Une déception amoureuse"? Great Britain, the Continent and European Nuclear Co-operation, 1954–1957', *Cold War History*, 3, 1 (2002), 29–66. I thank Professor Beatrice Heuser (King's College, London) and Dr Saki Dockrill (King's College) for their kind support and helpful suggestions. I am grateful to Howard J. Fuller (King's College) for his proof-reading.

1 Aufzeichnung Osterheld, vom 2 November 1962, footnote 22, Gespräch des Bundeskanzlers mit dem französischen Botschafter de Margerie, 11 June 1963, *Akten zur Auswärtigen Politik der Bundesrepublik Deutschland* (AAPD), 1963, II, Nr. 192; Eckart Conze, 'Hegemonie durch Integration? Die amerikanische Europapolitik und ihre Herausforderung durch de Gaulle', *Vierteljahrshefte für Zeitgeschichte*, 43 (1995), 297–340, here p. 331.

2 Cf. John W. Young, *Britain, France and the Unity of Europe*, Leicester: Leicester University Press, 1994; Richard Ovendale (ed.), *The Foreign Policy of the British Labour Governments 1945–1951*, Leicester, Leicester University Press, 1994; John Kent and John Young, 'British Policy Overseas: The "Third Force" and the Origins of NATO – in Search of a New Perspective', in Beatrice Heuser and Robert O'Neill, *Securing Peace in Europe, 1945–1962: Thoughts for the Post-Cold War Era*, London: Macmillan, 1992, pp. 41–61; John Baylis, 'British wartime thinking about a post-war European security group', *Review of International Studies*, 9 (1983), 265–81.

3 Antonio Varsori, 'Britain and Early Détente (1953–1956)', in Gustav Schmidt (ed.), *Ost–West Beziehungen: Konfrontation und Détente 1945–1989*, Bochum: Brockmeyer, 1995, pp. 175–200; John W. Young, *Churchill's Last Campaign: Britain and the Cold War 1951–1955*, Oxford: Clarendon, 1996; Klaus Larres, *Politik der Illusionen: Churchill, Eisenhower und die deutsche Frage 1945–1955*, Göttingen and Zürich: Vandenhoeck & Ruprecht, 1995. See also the contributions to the conference 'The First Détente, 1953–1958', organized by Seppo Hentilä in Helsinki in 1999.

4 Maurice Vaïsse, 'L'échec d'une Europe Franco-Britannique ou comment le Pacte de Bruxelles fut crée et délaissé', in Raymond Poidevin (ed.), *Histoire des débuts de la construction européenne mars 1948–mai 1950*, Brussels and Baden-Baden: NOMOS, 1985, pp. 369–89; Pierre Melandri, 'Le rôle de l'unification européenne dans la politique extérieure des Etats-Unis 1948–1960', in ibid., pp. 25–45; Ennio di Nolfo (ed.), *The Atlantic Pact Forty Years Later: A Historical Reappraisal*, Berlin and New York: de Gruyter, 1991; Antonio Varsori, *Il patto di Bruxelles (1948): tra integrazione europea e alleanza atlantica*, Rome: Bonacci, 1988; Beatrice Heuser, 'European Strategists and European Identity: The Quest for a European Nuclear Force 1954–1967', *Journal of European Integration History*, 1, 2 (1995), 61–80, here p. 63; Seventh Session of the Consultative Council, 7 November 1949, Relationship Between Brussels Pact and Atlantic Pact, Metric Doc No. 352, Public Record Office, London (PRO), DG 1/1/2; WU Defence Committee, Relationship Between the Brussels Treaty Defence Organization and Atlantic Pact Organisation, Report by the Western Union Chiefs of Staff, 17 November 1949, and Report by the Military Supply Board, 19 November 1949, PRO, DG 1/5/34; Resolution by the Consultative Council of the Brussels Treaty Organization of 20 December 1950 on the Future of the North Atlantic Treaty Organisation Military Structure, 20 December 1950, PRO, DG 1/11/56.

5 *Foreign Relations of the United States* (FRUS) 1950 III, pp. 548ff., 564ff., 582, 585ff., 595ff.; NATO Reorganization, 17 December 1951, NA RG 59 Lot 55 D 115 European Regional Affairs 1946–1953, J.G. Parsons Files, box 4, Top Secret 1951; National Security Council Progress Report by the Undersecretary of State on the Implementation of United States' Position Regarding Strengthening the Defense of Europe and the Nature of Germany's Contribution thereto (NSC 82), 3 April 1951, Harry S. Truman Library, Independence/MO, *Papers of Harry S. Truman*, President Secretary's File, B-File, The Integration of Western Europe, 10 of 13, box 1.

6 'Principles which should govern the relationship between the European Defense Community and the North Atlantic Treaty Organization', 7 December 1951, Ministerie van Buitenlandse Zaken, The Hague (B.Z.), EDG-Archief, Dossiers met betrekking tot de Europese Defensie Gemeenschap, 999.0. Algemeen, Verhouding EDG-NAVO 1951–1954, Inv. Nr. 14; Inter-allied Organisation, Report By Major General Sir Ian Jacob, 12 December 1951, PRO, FO 371/102482; Theodore Achilles to the Department of State, 11 December 1951, National Archives, Washington (NA) RG 59 Lot 36 D 38, Records of the Component Offices of the Bureau of European Affairs 1944–1962, box 31, EDC-NATO; NAT Council Preparations, Lisbon, Draft Report of a Working Group of the Council of Deputies on EDC-NATO Relations as of 9 February, 1952, Library of Congress, Manuscript Division (LC), Averell Harriman Papers, Special Files, Public Service, NATO-TCC Subject File, Meetings and Trips, NATO Lisbon, box FCL1; FRUS 1951 III, pp. 921ff., 947ff.; FRUS 1952–1954 V/1, pp. 230ff., 458ff., 461ff.; FRUS 1952–1954 V/2, pp. 799ff., 860ff., 863ff., 1774–86, here pp. 1779ff.; FRUS 1952–1954 VI/2, pp. 1197, 1287f.; Documents on British Policy Overseas (DBPO), Series II, Volume I, no. 29; Heads of Government Meeting, Mid-Ocean Club, 5 November 1953, Bermuda Hagerty Notes, box 1, International Series, Dwight D. Eisenhower Papers, Dwight D. Eisenhower Library, Abilene/KS (DDEL); Olaf Mager, 'Anthony Eden and the Framework of Security: Britain's Alternatives to the European

Defence Community, 1951–1954', in Heuser and O'Neill, *Securing Peace in Europe*, pp. 125–38; Wilfried Loth, 'De Gaulle und Europa: Eine Revision', *Historische Zeitschrift*, 253 (1991), 629–60, here pp. 643, 645.

7   Ronald W. Pruessen, 'Cold War Threats and America's Commitment to the European Defense Community: One Corner of a Triangle', *European Integration History*, 2, 1 (1996), 51–69; Klaus Larres, 'Die Welt des John Foster Dulles (1939–1953)', *Historische Mitteilungen*, 9, 2 (1996), 256–82.

8   Gesetz betreffend den Vertrag vom 27. Mai 1952 über die Gründung der Europäischen Verteidigungs gemeinschaft, 28 March 1954, BGBl. 1954 II, pp. 342ff, 371.

9   Cf. Jean Delmas, 'Naissance et développement d'une politique nucléaire militaire en France 1945–1956', in Klaus A. Maier and Norbert Wiggershaus, *Das Nordatlantische Bündnis 1949–1956*, Munich: Oldenburg, 1993, 263–72; Klaus A. Maier, 'Amerikanische Nuklearstrategie unter Truman und Eisenhower', in ibid., pp. 225–40; Dominique Mongin, 'Forces armées et genèse de l'armement nucléaire français', *Relations Internationales*, 59 (1989), 301–15; Georges-Henri Soutou, 'Die Nuklearpolitik der Vierten Republik', in *VfZ*, 37 (1989), 605–10; Georges-Henri Soutou, *L'alliance incertaine: Les rapports politico-stratégiques franco-allemands, 1954–1996*, Paris: Fayard, 1996.

10 See note 6; Brief for the Secretary of State's Talks with Mr Dulles in Washington: French Proposals for Tripartite Consultation (Annex A & B), 25 February 1953, PRO, FO 371/108041; FRUS 1952–1954 V/2, pp. 748ff.; Documents Diplomatiques Français (DDF) 1954 II, no. 25.

11 The Ambassador in France Dillon to the Department of State, 30 August 1954, FRUS 1952–1954 V, pp. 1091f.; Scott to Foreign Office, 27 August 1954, PRO, FO 371/113349; Klaus A. Maier, 'Die Auseinandersetzung um die EVG als europäischen Unterbündnis der NATO 1950–1954', in Hans-Erich Volkmann and Walter Schwengler (eds), *Die Europäische Verteidigungsgemeinschaft: Stand und Probleme der Forschung*, Boppard: Boldt, 1985, pp. 447–73; Donald Cameron Watt, 'Die konserv-ative Regierung und die EVG 1951–1954', in ibid., pp. 81–100, here 99; Brian Duchin, 'The "Agonizing Reappraisal": Eisenhower, Dulles and the European Defense Community', *Diplomatic History*, 16 (1992), 201–21; Dietl, *Dark Ages*, pp. 67–86.

12 Conversations at Chartwell with M. Mendès France, 23 August 1954, PRO, PREM 11/618; FRUS 1952–1954 V/2, pp. 1225f., 1227f.

13 Roberts to Kirkpatrick, 25 August 1954, PRO, FO 371/113350; Viscount Hood Minute, 1 September 1954, Mason to Roberts, 1 September 1954, PRO, FO 371/113351; DDF 1954 II, nos 125, 128, 193; 'Thursday de Margerie told me Brussels pact concept is for "window dressing", but I did not get this impression from Mendès because he appears deadly serious about Brussels' role. Once he said, "NATO will be superior organization but it will not exercise all functions. Some must be handled by Brussels Organization."' The Ambassador in France Dillon to the Department of State, 19 September 1954, FRUS 1952–1954 V/2, pp. 1228f.

14 FRUS 1952–1954 V/2, pp. 1170–7, 1189, 1198f., 1317, 1338f., 1380ff., 1414ff., 1429; Jebb to Foreign Office, 16 September 1954, PRO, FO 371/113357; Statements Made by Ministers Concerning the Production and Standardisation of Armaments, Nine Power Conference, NPC/PARIS-D/15, 22 October 1954, PRO, DG 1/47 or Proceedings of the Conference of Ministers held in Paris, 20–23 October 1954, PRO, FO 371/113377; Entschließung über Rüstungsproduktion und standardisierung, 21 October 1954, Politisches Archiv des Auswärtigen Amtes Bonn/Berlin (PA-AA), Referat 211, Bd. 69, p. 42 or Bundesarchiv-Militärarchiv Freiburg (BA-MA) BW9/4162, p. 21 – cf. 'In the execution of the Treaty the High Contracting Parties and any organs established by Them under the Treaty shall work in close co-operation with the North Atlantic Treaty Organization. Recognizing the undesirability of duplicating the Military Staff of

NATO, the Council and its agency will rely on the appropriate Military Authorities of NATO for information and advice on military matters', Article IV, Treaty between Belgium, France, Luxembourg, the Netherlands and the United Kingdom of Great Britain and Northern Ireland (Text of the Treaty as modified by the Protocol Modifying and Completing the Brussels Treaty, of 23 October, 1954), 23 October 1954, BGBl 1955 II, pp. 283ff.; Draft Decision of the Western European Union Council, WEU Interim Commission, Working Party on Production and Standardisation of Armaments, 19 April 1955 (PWG/0/1), PA-AA Referat 211, Bd. 95, pp. 47ff.

15 FRUS 1952–1954 V/2, pp. 1321ff., 1324ff., 1345ff.; Eighth Plenary Meeting, Nine Power Conference, London, 1 October 1954, PRO, FO 371/113285; Protocol No. III on the Control of Armaments, 23 October 1954, and Protocol No. IV on the Agency of Western European Union for the Control of Armaments, 23 October 1954, BGBl. 1955 II, pp. 266ff., 274ff.; Fritz Rademacher and Heinrich Rentmeister, *Rüstungskontroll- verifikation durch die Westeuropäische Union (WEU): Methoden, Erfahrungen und Schlußfolgerungen* (Stiftung Wissenschaft und Politik. Forschungsinstitut für Inter- nationale Politik und Sicherheit), Ebenhausen: Eggenberg, pp. 14ff.; Georges-Henri Soutou, 'La politique nucléaire de Pierre Mendès France', *Relations Internationales*, 59 (1989), 317–30.

16 Van Roijen (Washington) aan Min van Buitenlandse Zaken, 3 November 1954, B.Z., Archief WEU, Periode 1947–1954, Inv. Nr. 10, 999.0 Ratificatie Parijse Accorden, WEU 1954; Beyen/Luns aan Van Roijen, 8 November 1954, Van Roijen aan Min Buitenlandse Zaken, 24 November 1954, B.Z., DDI/BB 76/7 doos 29 GA 999 WEU Algemeen; DDF 1954 II, no. 311, 1955 I no. 23; Long Range Prospects for European Organizations, Mendès France Talks, Briefing Paper, 10 November 1954, NA RG 59 Executive Secretariat, Conference Files 1949–1963, box 61, Mendès France Talks; Mendès France Visit, The Economic Problem, 9 November 1954, France December 53–December 54 (6), OCB 091, box 32, OCB Central File Series, National Security Council Staff Papers 1948–1961, WHO, DDEL; Questions Involved in the Implementation of the Paris Agreements, including Relationship between NATO and WEU, NATO Council Meeting, 10 May 1955, C-R (55) 21, *NATO Archives Brussels*, PDN (96) 7; FRUS 1955–1957 IV, pp. 263–7, here 266.

17 FRUS 1955–1957 IV, pp. 367ff., 369, 369ff.; DDF 1956 I, nos 147, 161, 417, and 1956 II, nos 15, 71, 72; FRUS 1955–1957 XXVII, p. 73; Memorandum, The Pineau Visit, 21 June 1956, France January 55–January 56, OCB 091, box 32, OCB Central Files Series, National Security Council Staff Papers 1948–1961, WHO, DDEL; Aufzeichnung aus Anlaß des Staatsbesuches des Herrn Bundeskanzlers in Rom, 1–4 July 1956, Bundesarchiv, Koblenz (BA), *NL Brentano*, N 1351, Bd. 102; C.E.F. Gough, WEU Standing Armaments Committee, 26 July 1955, PRO, FO 371/118630; Hoyer Millar to Foreign Office, 23 July 1956, PRO, PREM 11/1269; Consultation on the Political Effect of the Strategic Planning for Western Defense, Minutes of the 56th Meeting of the Council of WEU, London, CR (56) 22, 25 July 1956, PRO, DG 1/55; Straub Aufzeichnung, über die Unterredung zwischen Bundeskanzler Adenauer und dem italienischen Verteidigungsminister Taviani, Rom, 5 July 1956, Stiftung Bundeskanzler Adenauer Haus Rhöndorf (StBKAH), III/4; Vortrag des Bundeskanzlers vor den Grandes Conférences Catholiques, Brussels, 25 Sepember 1956, BA NL *Blankenhorn*, N 1351, Bd. 67; FRUS 1955–1957 XVI, pp. 634ff.; Political Association of the United Kingdom with Europe, 25 October 1956, Political Association of the United Kingdom with Europe, Redraft, 13 November 1956, PRO, FO 371/124822; Bericht über die 69. Sitzung des Rates der WEU vom 19. Dezember 1956, 7 January 1957 CR (56) 35, BA-MA BW2/585; 69th Meeting of the Council of Western European Union, 19 December 1956, CR (56) 35, PRO, DG 1/57; Dr Halter, Aufzeichnung betr. Englisches Grand Design zur Harmonisierung der europäischen politischen

Organisationen, 8 February 1957, PA-AA Referat 201, Bd. 101; AmEmbassy London to Secretary of State, 7 February 1957, NA RG 59 Lot 61 D 179, Records of the Component Offices of the Bureau of European Affairs, 1944–1962, box 20, Grand Design II; Jebb to Hood, 9 February 1957, PRO, FO 371/130967; cf. Gustav Schmidt, 'Tying (West) Germany into the West – But to What? NATO? WEU? The European Community?', in Clemens Wurm (ed.), *Western Europe and Germany: The Beginning of European Integration 1945–1960*, Oxford/Washington: Berg, 1995, pp. 137–73; Anthony Adamthwaite, 'La France pendant la crise de Suez vue par la Grande-Bretagne', *Relations Internationales*, 58 (1989), 187–94; Paul M. Pitman, 'Un Général qui s'appelle Eisenhower: Atlantic Crisis and the Origins of the European Economic Community', *European Integration History*, 6, 2 (2000), 37–59.

18 Memorandum of a Conference with the President, White House, 20 October 1956, FRUS 1955–1957 XVI, pp. 833ff.

19 Dietl, *Déception amoureuse*, 47, 50f.; FRUS 1955–1957, XXVII, pp. 736ff., 766, 800f.; Memorandum of Conference with the President, 22 March 1957, Bermuda – Substantive Questions (1), box 3, International Trips and Meetings, Records of Paul T. Carroll, Office of the Staff Secretary, WHO, DDEL or Mandatory Review Executive Order no. 12958, Saturday 23 March 1957(1), Bermuda 957 – Chronology, box 2, Office of the Staff Secretary: Records, WHO, DDEL; United States Delegation of the Bermuda Meeting, 21–23 March 1957, Memorandum of Conversation, Atomic Energy Items, Mid-Ocean Club, March 23 1957, NA RG 59 Lot 68D 58, Deputy Assistant Secretary for Politico-Military Affairs, Subject Files of the Special Assistant for Atomic Energy and Aerospace 1950–1966, box 12, Nuclear Sharing, UK Consultation, Bermuda 1957; Report to the President and the Prime Minister from Lewis Strauss, Donald Quarles, Sir Edwin Plowden and Sir Richard Powell, 25 October 1957, PRO, PREM 11/2329 and Mandatory Review Executive Order no. 12958, Partial declassification, 26 October 2000: Memorandum of Understanding, 25 October 1957, 23–25 October, Macmillan, 1957 (4), box 23, International Series, Ann Whitman File, DDE, DDEL; Jan Melissen, 'The politics of US missile deployment in Britain, 1955–1959', *Storia delle Relazioni Internationali*, 13, 1 (1998), 151–85; Ian Clark and David Angell, 'Britain, the United States and the Control of Nuclear Weapons: The Diplomacy of the Thor Deployment 1956–1958', *Diplomacy and Statecraft*, 2, 3 (1991), 153–77; John Baylis, 'Exchanging Nuclear Secrets: Laying the Foundations of the Anglo-American Nuclear Relationship', *Diplomatic History*, 25, 1 (2001), 33–51.

20 DDF 1957 II, no. 380; Colette Barbier, 'Les négociations franco-germano-italiennes en vue de l'établissement d'une coopération militaire nucléaire au cours des années 1956–1958', *Revue d'Histoire Diplomatique*, 104 (1990), 55–89; Leopoldo Nuti, 'The F-I-G Story Revisited', *Storia delle Relazioni Internationali*, 13, 1 (1998), 69–100; Mervyn O'Driscoll, '"Les Anglo-Saxons", F-I-G and the Rival Conceptions of "Advanced" Armaments Research and Development Co-operation in Western Europe, 1956–1958', *European Integration History*, 4, 1 (1998), 105–30; Peter Fischer, 'Das Projekt einer Trilateralen Nuklearkooperation. Französisch-deutsch-italienische Geheimverhandlungen 1957/58', *Historisches Jahrbuch*, 112 (1992), 143–56.

21 FRUS 1958–1960 VII/2, pp. 36f.; Roberts to Hoyer-Millar, 18 June 1958, Roberts to Foreign Office, 24 June 1958, Roberts to Foreign Office, 26 June 1958, Roberts to Foreign Office, 4 July 1958, PRO, FO 371/137819; Georges-Henri Soutou, 'Le général de Gaulle et le plan Fouchet d'union politique européenne: un projet stratégique', *Revue d'Allemagne et des Pays de langue allemande*, 29, 2 (1997), 211–21, here p. 211.

22 DDF 1958 II, nos 16, 56, 125; FRUS 1958–1960 VII/2, p. 77; Macmillan to Eisenhower, 21 August 1958, Macmillan–President 6/1/1958 to 9/30/1958, box 24,

International Series, Ann Whiteman File, DDE, DDEL; Baylis, *Ambiguity and Deterrence*, p. 260.

23 DDF 1958 II, no. 15; FRUS 1958–1960 VII/2, pp. 81ff; General de Gaulle to Harold Macmillan, 17 Sepember 1958, PRO, FO 371/137820; Maurice Vaïsse, 'Aux origines du mémorandum de Septembre 1958', *Relations Internationales*, 58 (1989), 253–68.

24 DDF 1958 II, no. 234.

25 Representations of Ambassador Brosio to the President re de Gaulle letter, Clarke to Foreign Office, 2 October 1958, PRO, FO 371/137820; FRUS 1958–1960 VII/1, pp. 359, 362f., 366ff.; FRUS 1958–1960 VII/2, pp. 88ff., 145; Caccia to Foreign Office, 11 December 1958, PRO, FO 371/137826.

26 '[I]t was equally clear that he wanted to establish a position in which France would speak for Europe in the proposed Three Power Western world directorate. This was entirely unacceptable. If it were not so serious, this development would be quite ridiculous … It would, however, be the end of the Western alliance, so far as Germany and the European continental allies were concerned, if major issues affecting all its members were handled by a self-appointed directorate of the three Western Powers with world interests', Roberts to Foreign Office, 1 October 1958, PRO, FO 371/137820; General de Gaulle's Plan for Reorganizing the Western Alliance, Memorandum by Sir Gladwyn Jebb, 30 Sepember 1958, A Commentary on General de Gaulle's Plan for Reorganising the Western Alliance, 1 October 1958, Roberts to Rumbold, 2 October 1958, PRO, FO 371/137820; Caccia to Foreign Office, 9 October 1958, PRO, FO 371/137821; FRUS 1958–1960 VII/2, pp. 90ff.; Jebb to Foreign Office, 18 October 1958, PRO, FO 371/137822; Conze, 'Hegemonie', p. 314.

27 DDF 1958 II nos 370, 378, 1959 I nos 74, 131, 133; Roberts to Foreign Office, 27 November 1958, PRO, FO 371/137825; Adenauer to John Foster Dulles, 30 January 1959, Adenauer 1959(5), box 15, International Series, Ann Whitman File, DDE, DDEL; Memorandum of Conversation with Couve de Murville, 7 February 1959, Memos of Conversation A-D(4), box 1, General Correspondance and Memoranda Series, John Foster Dulles Papers, DDEL; Foreign Office to Washington, 20 January 1959, PRO, FO 371/143686; Foreign Office to Moskau, 23 January 1959 and 2 February 1959, PRO, FO 371/143433; European Security, Memorandum of Conversation, 21 March 1959, Macmillan 1/10/1958–20/3/1959 (1), box 24, International Series, DDE, DDEL; Tripartite-Quadripartite Meeting, Washington, 31 March–1 April 1959, Tri-/Quadripartite Meetings (1), box 19, Subject File Series, Executive Secretary's, Secretary Council Staff Papers, 1948–1961, National Security Council Staff, WHO, DDEL; Deutsche Botschaft Washington an AA, 24 March 1959, BA NL *Blankenhorn* N 1351, 98b.

28 DDF 1959 I, no. 371; Kommuniqué anlässlich der Besprechung zwischen den Staatspräsidenten Frankreichs und Italiens, 27 June 1959, PA-AA, Referat 201, Bd. 369; Jansen an Blankenhorn, 30 July 1959, BA NL *Blankenhorn* N 1351, Bd. 98b; Aufzeichnung des Gesprächs zwischen Bundeskanzler Adenauer und dem italienischen Botschafter Quaroni, Palais Schaumburg, 7 July 1959, StBKAH III/88; FRUS 1958–1960 VII/2, pp. 532ff.; Yves Stelandre, 'La Belgique et le Plan Fouchet', *Revue d'Allemagne et des Pays de langue allemande*, 29, 2 (1997), 221–30, here 223.

29 A.D.F. Pimberton Pigott Minute, 6 July 1959, Foreign Office to The Hague, 6 July 1959, Secretary of State to Jebb, 9 July 1959, Hoyer Millar Minute, 8 July 1959, Clarke to Foreign Office, 9 July 1959, PRO, FO 371/146265; Political Consultation Among the Six, F.C.D. Sargeant Minute, 21 July 1959, PRO, FO 371/146266; FRUS 1958–1960 VII/2, pp. 532ff.

30 Cf. Ralph Dietl, 'The Quest for a Global Pax Americana: Myths and Realities, a Reply', in Norbert Finzsch and Hermann Wellenreuther (ed.), *Visions of the Future in Germany and America*, Oxford: Berg, 2001, pp. 231–48, here pp. 244f.

31 Marc Trachtenberg, *A Constructed Peace: The Making of the European Settlement 1945–1963*, Princeton, NJ: Princeton University Press, 1999, p. 147; DDF 1959 II, nos 109, 112, 130; FRUS 1958–1960 VII/2, p. 546; Entretiens entre M. P. Wigny and M. Couve de Murville, 3 July 1959 et entretiens entre le Président de Gaulle et M. P. Wigny, 4 Sepember 1959, Ministère des Affaires Etrangères Bruxelles (A.E.-B.Z.), dossier 15661; Jebb to Foreign Office, 18 September 1959, Ellis-Rees to Foreign Office, 24 Sepember 1959, Rumbold Minute, 18 Sepember 1959, Jebb to Foreign Office, 24 Sepember 1959, Roberts to Foreign Office, 24 Sepember 1959 (No. 381), Roberts to E.E. Tomkins, 21 Sepember 1959, PRO, FO 371/146267; Ivan B. White to Secretary of State, 21 Sepember 1959, NA RG 59, Bureau of European Affairs, Office of Atlantic Political and Economic Affairs, Alpha Numerical Files 1948–1963, box 4, Political Consultation 1957–1962; Paul de Zulueta Memo, The Organisation of Europe, 21 October 1959, Planning Section Memorandum, United Kingdom Policy Towards Western Europe: the Six and the Seven, 27 October 1959, Planning Section Memorandum, United Kingdom Policy Towards Western Europe: the Six and the Seven, 27 October 1959, PRO, PREM 11/2985; Memorandum for the National Security Council, Issues of US Policy Regarding the Defense Posture of NATO, 5 November 1959, NATO April 1953–July 1960 (2), box 5, Subject Subseries, NSC-Series, Office of the Special Assistant for National Security Affairs, WHO, DDEL.

32 Conversations Franco-Britanniques de Paris, 11–12 November 1959, DDF 1959 II, no. 224.

33 'J'ai [Adenauer] ajouté que les Etats-Unis, à cause de l'état difficile de leur balance de paiements, avaient intérêt à ce que l'Europe soit en bonne santé économique, mais qu'ils craignaient cependant, et M. Dillon l'avait récemment dit, qu'une intégration européenne qui engloberait le Royaume-Uni pourrait être dangereuse pour l'Amérique.', Entretiens Franco-Allemand, 1–2 December 1959, DDF 1959 II, no. 263.

34 DDF 1959 II, nos 263, 270; Blankenhorn Tagebuch, 8 December 1959, BA NL *Blankenhorn*, N 1351, Bd. 97a.

35 Memorandum of Conversation, 21 December 1959, FRUS 1958–1960 VII/1, pp. 558f.; Memorandum for Brig. Gen. A.J. Goodpaster. Secret Tripartite Meetings, 26 January 1960, State MEPCO Cables (January–April 1960), box 5, State Department Subseries, Subject Series, Office of the Staff Secretary, WHO, DDEL; FRUS 1958–1960 VII/2, pp. 317ff.; DDF 1959 II, no. 295. Cf. 'C'est entre trois que nous devons parler de l'Alliance, de l'Afrique et de l'Allemagne. Le président Eisenhower suggère que soit créé un mécanisme clandestin c'est-à-dire un organisme permettant aux trois puissances d'étudier les problèmes qui leur sont communs sans pour autant susciter de susceptibilité … Le Président Eisenhower le met en garde contre le risque de heurter les susceptibilités de pays tels que l'Italie. Il faut, dit-il, ne pas prêter le flanc à l'accusation selon laquelle les grands pays envisageraient de créer un triumvirat', ibid., Réunion des Trois à Rambouillet, 20 December 1959; Record of Informal Meeting Between the Secretary of State and Mr Herter, 21 December 1959, PRO, PREM 11/2987.

36 FRUS 1958–1960 VII/1, pp. 525ff., 531; DDF 1959 II, no. 276; Memorandum for Brig. Gen A.J. Goodpaster, Secret Tripartite Meetings, 26 January 1960, State MEPCO Cables (January–April 1960), box 5, State Department Subseries, Subject Series, Office of the Staff Secretary, WHO, DDEL; D. Kohler to the Secretary of State, 19 February 1960, NA RG 59 Bureau of European Affairs, Office of European Regional Affairs, Records of the NATO Advisor 1957–1961, box 2, Production of IRBM in Europe, January–June 1960; The MRBM Program and a NATO Strategic Deterrent, [undated], NA RG 59, Bureau of European Affairs, Office of European Regional Affairs, Records of the NATO Advisor, box 1 (NATO Strategic Force). NATO MRBM Program – General Considerations, [undated], NA RG 59, Bureau of European Affairs,

Office of European Regional Affairs, Records of the NATO Advisor 1957–1961, box 2 (Production of IRBM in Europe June 1960–October 1960); Memorandum of Conversation, First Round US–UK Talks on Nuclear and Strategic Weapons in NATO, 11 March 1960, NA RG 59 Lot 71 D 163, Deputy Assistant Secretary for Politico-Military Affairs, Subject File of the Special Assistant for Atomic Energy and Aerospace 1950–1966, box 15 (Nuclear Sharing 1960–1962); Memorandum for the President, Discussion with Adenauer of Norstad Plan for European Inspection Zone, 12 March 1960, Germany vol. II of III (2), box 6, International Series, Records of Paul T. Carroll, Office of the Staff Secretary, WHO, DDEL.

37 Memorandum from the President to Prime Minister, 29 March 1960, Annex A: Memorandum of Understanding, SKYBOLT, United States Department of the Air Force and United Kingdom Ministry of Aviation Technical and Financial Agreement Concerning the SKYBOLT, 27 Sepember 1960, United Kingdom (4) [October, November 1960], box 13, International Series, Records of Paul T. Carroll, Office of the Staff Secretary, WHO, DDEL; Memorandum for the President, Macmillan Talks: UK Interest in SKYBOLT and POLARIS, 27 March 1960 & Memorandum for the President, The President's Talk with Prime Minister Macmillan, 26–30 March 1960, Macmillan vol. II of III(5 & 4), box 14, International Series, Records of Paul T. Carroll, Office of the Staff Secretary, WHO, DDEL; Draft Memorandum from Prime Minister to President, 29 May 1960 and US Position, SKYBOLT, POLARIS and MRBMs, 26–30 March 1960, Macmillan Visit 26–30 March 1960, box 25, International Series, DDE, DDEL; John A. Calhoun Memorandum for Brig. Gen. A.J. Goodpaster, British and US Public Statements on SKYBOLT and British Statement on POLARIS, 7 April 1960, John A. Calhoun, Memorandum for Brig. Gen. A.J. Goodpaster, SKYBOLT and POLARIS MRBMs, 9 April 1960, UK(2), box 13, International Series, Records of Paul T. Carroll, Office of the Staff Secretary, WHO, DDEL; FRUS 1958–1960 VII/2, pp. 860ff.; Caccia to FO, 30 March 1960, PRO, PREM 11/3261; De Ranitz aan Ministerie van Buitenlandse Zaken, 31 March 1960, B.Z., DDI/BB 76/7 doos 28, NATO 999.22.2, Raad van Plaatsverangers, Defense Production Board; Caccia to Foreign Office, 22 April 1960, PRO, PREM 11/3723.

38 Memorandum for the Record, Meeting between US and UK Defence Ministers, 30 March 1960, NA RG 59 Bureau of European Affairs, Office of European Regional Affairs, Records of the NATO Advisor, box 2, Production of IRBMs in Europe, January 1960–June 1960; Lieutenant-Général Cumont, Note pour M. le Ministre, Système d'engins balistiques à porté intermédiaire (MRBM) pour le Commandement Allié en Europe, 6 May 1960, Ministère de la Défense National Bruxelles, SGR/CDH-MDN/SAT – 1960 – CD 165.5; DDF 1960 I, no. 149 and 1960 II, no. 125; FRUS 1958–1960, VII/2, 336ff.; FRUS 1958–1960 VII/1, pp. 591ff.; Gerard C. Smith to Merchant, 8 June 1960, NA RG 59, Bureau of European Affairs, Office of European Regional Affairs, Records of the NATO Advisor 1957–1961, box 2, Production of IRBM in Europe, June 1960–October 1960.

39 Entretiens de M. Macmillan et du Premier ministre à l'Hôtel Matignon, 19 May 1960, 24 May 1960, DDF 1960 I, no. 235.

40 Brewster H. Morris to Robert N. Magill, 19 May 1960, NA RG 59, Bureau of European Affairs, Office of European Regional Affairs, Records of the NATO Advisor, box 1, NATO Strategic Force; Memorandum of Conversation, NATO Long Term Planning: Views of NATO Secretary-General Paul Henri Spaak, 13 June 1960, NATO (4), box 5, International Trips and Meetings, Office of the Staff Secretary, WHO, DDEL; FRUS 1958–1960 VII/2, pp. 386ff.; Secretary of State's Visit to the Hague including Record of the Ministerial Meeting of the Council of Western European Union, 15–17 June 1960, PRO, FO 371/154647.

41 Roberts to Foreign Office, 22 July 1960, PRO, FO 371/154576.

42 Roberts to Shuckburgh, 25 July 1960, PRO, FO 371/154576; M. J. van deer Meulen to M. P. Wigny, 28 July 1960, A.E.–B.Z. dossier 15661.

43 Réunion de clôture en présence de Messieurs les Ministres des Affaires étrangères et les ambassadeurs des deux pays, 30 July 1960, Entretiens franco-allemand de Rambouillet, 29–30 July, DDF 1960 II, no. 54; cf. Blankenhorn Tagebuch, 29 July 1960, BA NL *Blankenhorn* N 1351, Bd. 102; De Gaulle, Vermerk über die Organisation Europas, 30 July 1960, StBKAH III/58; DDF 1960 II, no. 54; A.J. Goodpaster, Memorandum of Conference with the President, 12 August 1960, State Department 1960 (August/September)(1), box 4, State Department Subseries, Subject Series, Office of the Staff Secretary, WHO, DDEL; M.R. Baert to M. Wigny, 5 August 1960, E. Champenois, Communication téléphonique du Prince de Mérode, 8 August 1960, Entrevue Adenauer–de Gaulle, Baron Jaspar à P. Wigny, 9 August 1960, A.E.–B.Z. dossier 15661; Jacques Bariéty, 'Les Entretiens de Gaulle–Adenauer de Juillet 1960 à Rambouillet. Prélude au plan Fouchet et au traité de l'Elysée', *Revue d'Allemagne et des Pays de langue allemande*, 29, 2 (1997), 167–75; Soutou, *Plan Fouchet*, pp. 213f.

44 Aufzeichnung: der Herr Bundeskanzler empfing am 4. August 1960 in Anwesenheit von Herrn Generalkonsul Dr Bach den amerikanischen Botschafter Herrn Dowling, 4 August 1960, StBKAH III/88.

45 FRUS 1958–1960 VII/1, pp. 628ff., 638ff., 648ff., 675ff.; Memorandum of Conversation, Multilateral Sharing of Nuclear Weapons, 13 September 1960, NA RG 59, Bureau of European Affairs, Office of European Regional Affairs, Records of the NATO Advisor 1957–1961, box 2, Production of IRBM in Europe, June 1960–October 1960; Memorandum of Conversation, NATO MRBM Force, 3 October 1960, NATO (6), box 5, International Trips and Meetings, Office of the Staff Secretary, WHO, DDEL; Houghton to Irwin, 15 October 1960, ATOM – Nuclear Policy 1960, box 85, Norstad Papers, DDEL.

46 Blankenhorn Tagebuch, 9 September 1960, BA NL *Blankenhorn*, N 1351, Bd. 103; Houghton to AmEmbassy Bonn, 10 Sepember 1960, Chancellor Adenauer 1960–1961(5), box 16, International Series, Ann Whiteman File, DDE, DDEL; Roberts to Foreign Office, 13 Sepember 1960, PRO, FO 371/154576; Roberts to Shuckburgh, 17 Sepember 1960, PRO, FO 371/154572; Douglas Dillon, Memorandum for the President, 4 October 1960, Germany vol. III of III (4), box 6, International Series, Records of Paul T. Carroll, Office of the Staff Secretary, WHO, DDEL; Eisenhower to Adenauer, 6 October 1960, StBKAH III/2; Adenauer to Dean Acheson, 13 February 1961, StBKAH II/1.

47 Blankenhorn an AA, 22 Sepember 1960, Blankenhorn Tagebuch, 24 Sepember 1960, Blankenhorn an AA, 28 Sepember 1960, BA NL *Blankenhorn*, N 1351, Bd. 103; Roberts to Foreign Office, 29 Sepember 1960, PRO, PREM 11/3334; Aufzeichnung über Gespräch des Bundeskanzlers mit dem ehemaligen französischen Ministerpräsidenten Paul Reynaud, 3 October 1960, StBKAH III/58; DDF 1960 II, no. 162; Aufzeichnung des Herrn Bundeskanzlers über Gespräch mit dem französischen Ministerpräsidenten Michel Debré, 7 October 1960, StBKAH III/88.

48 Adenauer an de Gaulle, 8 October 1960, *Archiv für Christlich-Demokratische Politik*, Sankt Augustin (ACDR), NL *Globke*, I-070-044/3; R. Baert à M. Wigny, 12 October 1960, télégramme par courrier no. 77, 12 October 1960, Note pour M. le Ministre des Affaires Étrangères, 13 October 1960, A.E.–B.Z. dossier 15661; Straten, télégramme par courrier no. 675, 7 December 1960, Note pour Monsieur le Premier Ministre, Réunion du 10 février, à Paris, des Chefs de gouvernement des Six, 3 February 1961, Jaspar, télégramme par courrier no. 400, 10 February 1961, A.E.-B.Z., dossier 18684 I; Russell Fessenden to W. Walt Butterworth, NA RG 59, Bureau of European Affairs, Office of Atlantic Political and Economic Affairs, Alpha-Numerical Files 1948–1963, box 4, Political Consultation 1957–1962; Aufzeichnung betr. Treffen der Staats-bzw.

Regierungschefs und der Außenminister der EWG-Staaten vom 10–11 February in Paris, 15 February 1961, PA-AA Referat 291, Bd. 372; Soutou, *Plan Fouchet*, p. 215; Hartmut Mayer, 'Germany's Role in the Fouchet Negotiations', *European Integration History*, 2, 2 (1996), 39–58, here p. 47.

49 Bowie Report (1), box 6, Alpha Subseries, Subject Series, OSS, WHO, DDEL; cf. Increased Nuclear Sharing with Allies, Briefing Note for NSC-Meeting 8/25/60, 24 August 1960, box 14, Nuclear Sharing With Allies, Briefing Notes Subseries, NSC-Series, Office of the Special Assistant for National Security Affairs, WHO, DDEL; FRUS 1958–1960 VII/1, pp. 615ff.; Marilena Gala, 'The Multilateral Force: A Brief History of the American Efforts to Maintain the Nuclear Satus Quo within the Atlantic Alliance', *Storia delle Relazioni Internationali*, 13, 1 (1998), 121–49, here pp. 134f.

50 Bowie Report (1), box 6, Alpha Subseries, Subject Series, OSS, WHO, DDEL.

51 Ibid.

52 Note for the Record, Watkinson–Joxe Talks, 17 December 1960, PRO, FO 371/154573; Paul-Henri Spaak to Adenauer, 4 January 1961, StBKAH III/6; Record of a Conversation between the Prime Minister and President de Gaulle, Rambouillet, 29 January 1961, PRO, PREM 11/3322; cf. Oliver Bange, *The EEC Crisis of 1963: Kennedy, Macmillan, de Gaulle and Adenauer in Conflict*, London: Macmillan, 2000, pp. 37ff.

53 Record of a Meeting Between the Rt Hon. Harold Watkinson, MP, United Kingdom Minister of Defence, and M. Messmer, French Minister of the Armed Forces, in Paris, 13 April 1961, PRO, FO 371/161231; Harold Watkinson–Robert McNamara Talks, Washington 21 March 1961, PRO, FO 371/161197.

54 Record of a Meeting Between the Rt Hon. Harold Watkinson, MP, United Kingdom Minister of Defence, and M. Messmer, French Minister of the Armed Forces, in Paris, 13 April 1961, PRO, FO 371/161231.

55 Sir Norman Brook Minute, 25 April 1961, PRO, PREM 11/3311; Macmillan to Kennedy, 28 April 1961, PRO, PREM 11/3319; Record of a Conversation between the Prime Minister and President de Gaulle, Rambouillet, 29 January 1961, 11 a.m., PRO, PREM 11/3322; '[Macmillan] For example, a joint Anglo-French policy in Europe would be of great advantage to the whole Free World. M. Debré said that he entirely agreed. He was in favour of the development of a common European policy, but this must include the United Kingdom. He wanted to see Britain brought into Europe even more. One of his main objects in pursuing a European policy was to find a way of limiting future German ambitions. He certainly did not wish to abandon NATO, but he felt that Anglo-French co-operation was of the highest importance.' Record of a Conversation between the Prime Minister and President de Gaulle, Rambouillet, 29 January 1961, 2.45. p.m., PRO, PREM 11/3322; Rumbold to Shuckburgh, 15 April 1961, PRO, FO 371/16231.

56 Meeting of the Six Heads of Government, Bonn, 18 July 1961, PRO, FO 371/161254; Jansen an Deutsche Botschaften Brüssel, Den Haag, Paris, Rome, London, Washington, 19 July 1961, BA NL *Blankenhorn* N 1351, Bd. 116; Déclaration des Chefs d'Etat ou de Gouvernement, 18 July 1961, Notes sur la conférence de Chefs d'Etats et de Gouvernement, Tenue à Bonn le 18 juillet, 20 July 1961, A.E.-B-Z. dossier 18684 I; Mayer, *Fouchet*, p. 50; Soutou, *Plan Fouchet*, pp. 216f.

57 Ministerial Meeting of the Council of Western European Union, 1 August 1961, PRO, FO 371/167114; Conseil des Ministres de l'U.E.O. réuni à Paris le 1er août 1961, A.E.-B.Z. 6643-2(a); Memorandum for the President, Certain Implications for American Policy of Prime Minister Macmillan's Statement on the EEC, 7 August 1961, *John F. Kennedy Library Boston/MA*, Papers of John F. Kennedy (JFK), National Security Files, box 170, UK General 8/2/61–9/5/1961; Draft Record of the 48th Meeting of the Standing Armaments Committee held on 21st September 1961, SAC

(61) R/48, 16 October 1961, B.Z., WEU-Archief, Periode 1955–1964, Inv. Nr. 124, 999.23 SAC records; Stelandre, *Fouchet*, pp. 226f; Loth, *De Gaulle*, pp. 652f.

58 'As I recall, you made the following points: (a) A solution to the MRBM problem is required urgently; (b) Your government proposes the creation of a NATO nuclear force, composed of national contingents, to be controlled by SACEUR. If such a proposal is unable to move forward reasonably soon in NATO you might subsequently recommend the creation of such a force within the framework of the Western European Union ... As for the creation of an MRBM under the framework of WEU, it is my opinion that this would have serious implications and might even signal the end of NATO as we know it', Robert S. McNamara to Franz J. Strauss, 5 December 1961, in Library of Congress, Declassified Documents Reference System, Microfiche 1255 (1997).

59 Memorandum of Conversation, Meeting Between the Secretary of State and the German Foreign Minister, 22 November 1961, JFK, National Security Files, box 75, Germany, general 2/62.

60 NATO Ministerial Meeting, Paris, 13–15 December 1961, Position Paper, MRBMs, 4 December 1961, JFK, National Security Files, Regional, Security, box 216, Multilateral Force, General 1/61–6/62; North Atlantic Council Ministerial Meeting, MRBMs, 13–15 December 1961, PRO, FO 371/161271; North Atlantic Council, Ministerial Meeting, 14 December, Item II: Military Questions. NATO Strategy and MRBMs, 14 December 1961, PRO, FO 371/161272.

61 'Mr Ball referred to the "non commercial aspects" of the Rome Treaty and explained that we attached great importance to these provisions ... Of equal importance, Mr. Ball stated were the Brussels institutions. Here the full acceptance of the existing institutions was important to show that Britain was accepting fully the implications and objectives of the Six', Memorandum of Conversation Between Under Secretary Ball and Lord Privy Seal Heath on Six–Seven Problem in London, 30 March 1961, JFK, National Security Files, box 174A, Countries, UK, Macmillan, Briefing Book 4/4/1961–4/9/1961; 'We envisage that the United Kingdom should take the leading role in the creation of a strong European entity, initially in the economic sphere and then in the political with progress on both fronts toward the creation of single powerful entity ... we expect that the UK will bring its liberal influences to bear within the enlarged community.' The Atlantic Community and European Integration, Bermuda Meeting with P.M. Macmillan, 21–22 December 1961, General Position Paper, 17 December 1961, NA RG 59 Lot 65D134, Deputy Assistant Secretary for Politico-Military Affairs, box 3, Macmillan Visit 1962; Bermuda Meeting with P.M. Macmillan, Position Paper, Assistance for Military Nuclear Programs, 16 December 1961, NA RG 59 Lot 65 D 14, Deputy Assistant Secretary for Politico-Military Affairs, Subject Files 1961–1968, box 3, Macmillan Visit 1962 – cf. Frank Costigliola, 'The Failed Design: Kennedy, de Gaulle, and the Struggle for Europe', *Diplomatic History*, 8 (1984), 227–51, here p. 234.

62 'I have come to the conclusion that it would be undesirable to assist France's efforts to create a nuclear weapons capability', Kennedy to Macmillan, 8 May 1961, PRO, PREM 11/3319; Rumbold to Shuckburgh, 18 January 1962, PRO, FO 371/166995; cf. Gala, *MLF*, pp. 121ff.

63 Fernschreiben Brüssel an Auswärtiges Amt, 23 January 1962, PA-AA, Referat 201, Bd. 374; Hensch Vermerk, betr. Überleitung eines Teiles der Aufgaben der Westeuropäischen Union nach deren möglicher Auflösung, 19 January 1962, PA-AA, Referat I A1, Bd. 396; Projet de Traité établissant une Union d'Etats et des Peuples Européens, texte établi par le groupe chargé de l'étude du statut européen, 1 February 1962, DDI/BB 76/7 doos 26, GA 996 EPG; Blankenhorn Tagebuch, 2 February 1962, NL *Blankenhorn* N 1351, Bd. 120b; cf. Daniel Kosthorst, 'Die "Unerwünschte Liaison": Thesen zur Vorgeschichte des deutsch-französischen Vertrages vom 22.

Januar 1963', *Revue d'Allemagne et des Pays de langue allemande*, 29, 2 (1997), 177–94, here pp. 179f.

64 Taking the decisions of John F. Kennedy into account, the motives of de Gaulle to change the Fouchet Plan might not be as complex as Georges-Henri Soutou asserts in his groundbreaking article 'Le général de Gaulle et le plan Fouchet d'union politique européenne: un projet stratégique' (Soutou, *Plan Fouchet*, pp. 217f.). The sudden revision into a more nationalistic plan seems to be strategically and not commercially motivated as Andrew Moravcsik argued in *Grain and Grandeur*. Andrew Moravcsik, 'De Gaulle between Grain and Grandeur: The Political Economy of French EC Policy, 1958–1970 (Part 1)', *Cold War Studies*, 2, 2 (2000), 3–43, here pp. 34ff.

65 'La référence à l'OTAN, en ce qui concerne la politique de défense commune est un problème fondamental. Pour le gouvernement belge, il n'y a pas de défense européenne indépendante de l'OTAN, l'Europe organisée ne peut être une troisième force, mais doit être un élément plus fort de l'OTAN.' Paul-Henri Spaak, in Stelandre, *Fouchet*, p. 229; Aufzeichnung über Gespräch des Herrn Bundeskanzler mit Präsident de Gaulle, Palais de l'Elysée, 9 February 1962, StBKAH III/59; Blankenhorn Tagebuch, 12 February 1962, BA NL *Blankenhorn*, N 1351, Bd. 128b.

66 Dixon to Foreign Office, 21 March 1962, PRO, FO 371/167008; Dixon, Europe, [n.d.], PRO, FO 371/167011.

67 Statement by the Lord Privy Seal to the Council of Western European Union, 10 April 1962, PRO, FO 371/167114.

68 Thier, Réunion ministérielle de l'U.E.O. du 10 avril 1962, 13 April 1962, A.E.-B.Z. 6643-2(a); Baron J. van der Elst à M. Spaak, Attitude de l'Italie en vue de la réunion des Ministres des Affaires Étrangères des Six le 17 avril 1962, 11 April 1962, A.E.-B.Z. dossier 15561; Blankenhorn Tagebuch, 18 April 1962, BA NL *Blankenhorn* N 1351, Bd. 130a.

69 'Today Soutou bitterly complained about the behaviour of the British in the EPU negotiations. For him there is not any doubt that the English wilfully torpedoed the conference of the Foreign Ministers of the Six *par personne interposée*, namely the Netherlands and Belgium … Now, it might happen that the General will delay the accession of Britain, or even that he will lose interest in an accession' [translation], Blankenhorn Tagebuch, 19 April 1962, BA NL *Blankenhorn* N, 1351, Bd. 130a; 'All my observations lead me to believe that the French government will create obstacles in order to hinder British accession to the Common Market and thereby as well to the EPU. This would clear the way for France to lead continental Europe – which is desired by de Gaulle' [translation], Blankenhorn Tagebuch, 23 May 1962, BA NL *Blankenhorn* N 1351, Bd. 132a; 'We use the occasion of the Macmillan visit not only to reject his plea for nuclear sharing with the French but also to open his eyes to the possibility of sharing with a multilateral European force which would absorb the POLARIS and the British capacity.' Walt Rostow, The Nuclear Role of Britain France and Germany, 17 April 1962, NA RG 59 Lot 67 D 496, Deputy Assistant Secretary for Politico-Military Affairs, Combined Policy Office, Subject Files 1961–1966, box 2, Nuclear Role of France, United Kingdom and Germany.

70 '[T]he success of the negotiations turned entirely on the question of defence and would be determined by what the Prime Minister could say or propose to de Gaulle at their forthcoming meeting … as matters of timing and method of taking decisions about the use of nuclear weapons in the defence of western Europe, de Gaulle would expect us to display a European as distinct if need be from an American outlook.' Pierre Pflimlin, 14 May 1962, in Richard Davis, '"Why did the General Do It?" De Gaulle, Polaris and the French Veto of Britain's Application to Join the Common Market', *European History Quarterly*, 28, 3 (1998), 373–97, here p. 380; cf. Wolfram Kaiser, 'The Bomb and Europe. Britain, France and the EEC Entry Negotiations 1961–1963', *European Integration History*, 1 (1995), 65–85.

71 'The further we permit the Continentals to go it alone … the higher degree of freedom of our veto they will be able to negotiate with us, and the less likely they are to develop their nuclear force within an Atlantic framework.' Walt Rostow, The Nuclear Role of Britain France and Germany, 17 April 1962, NA RG 59 Lot 67 D 496, Deputy Assistant Secretary for Politico-Military Affairs, Combined Policy Office, Subject Files 1961–1966, box 2, Nuclear Role of France, United Kingdom and Germany.

72 'This development of a European entity within the alliance would involve developments on the nuclear level. In saying this, the Prime Minister was not thinking of conditions of control but of the formation of an independent striking force.' Conversation between the Prime Minister and M. Chauvel, 19 April 1962, PRO, PREM 11/3793.

73 Record of a Conversation at Luncheon at the State Department, 28 April 1962, PRO, FO 371/166969; cf. Heuser, *John Bull*, p. 563.

74 'It is of the first importance to isolate General de Gaulle both in France and among the Six. To do this we must avoid having a row with him while progress is being made at Brussels. The only circumstances in which a row would be profitable would be towards the end of the negotiation if he were more or less alone in opposing reasonable solutions … But provided we can carry the other Five, especially the Germans, the French cannot carry obstruction beyond a certain point unless they are prepared to be seen to be the people who are making agreement impossible.' Brief for Discussion with the Prime Minister, 26 May 1962, PRO, FO 337/166973; Blankenhorn an Auswärtiges Amt, 4 June 1962, BA NL *Blankenhorn*, N 1351, Bd. 134b.

75 Blankenhorn an Auswärtiges Amt, 21 June 1962, BA NL *Blankenhorn* N 1351, Bd. 134a; Rumbold to Barnes, 12 October 1962, PRO, FO 371/167024.

76 Blankenhorn Tagebuch, 8 July 1962, BA NL *Blankenhorn* N 1351, Bd. 138; De Gaulle an Adenauer, 20 September 1962, StBKAH, III/3; Hermann Kusterer, 'Intention und Wirklichkeit: Von der Konzeption zur Ratifikation des Deutsch-Französischen Vertrages', *Revue d'Allemagne et des Pays de la langue allemande*, 29, 2 (1997), 195–200, here pp. 196f.; Cyril Schweizer, 'Le Gouvernement italien et le projet d'union politique de l'Europe 1961–1962', *Revue d'Allemagne et des Pays de la langue allemande*, 29, 2 (1997), 231–41, here pp. 238ff.; Kosthorst, *Unerwünschte Liaison*, pp. 183, 186.

77 Rumbold to Ramsbotham, 6 June 1962, PRO, FO 371/166973, Finletter to Secretary of State, 5 July 1962, France 1960–1962(1), box 48, Norstad Papers, DDEL; Working Group on European Integration in Defence Policy, EIDP (WG)/P (62) 3 & Annex: Problems of Nuclear Defence, 18 October 1962, Thomson to Barnes, 21 November 1962, DEFE 10/547; cf. 'The US Administration agree that decisions on the ultimate shape of nuclear defence in Europe should not be taken until the result [of] the current negotiations on British membership of the Community of Six is clear.' Working Group on European Integration in Defence Policy, EIDP(WG)/P(62) 8, 4 December 1962, PRO, DEFE 10/547.

78 Record of a Conversation at Rambouillet, 15 December 1962, Record of a Conversation at Château de Rambouillet, 16 December 1962, PRO, FO 371/1373297; cf. 'Turning to defence, the General said he had been impressed by the PM's determination to possess and keep an independent British atomic power. He was sure that it would be quite wrong to rely solely on the Americans. He was interested in the possibilities of Anglo-French co-operation in nuclear matters … In any case, he considered that the UK had taken the right road in trying to come closer to Europe.' Prime Minister's meeting with General de Gaulle at Rambouillet, 15/16 December 1962, PRO, PREM 11/4230; Davis, 'Why Did the General Do It?', pp. 383; Loth, *De Gaulle*, p. 653.

79 Henry Owen to Acting Secretary of State, 16 December 1962, JFK, National Security Files, Regional Security, box 227, NATO Weapons, SKYBOLT; Kennedy–Macmillan

Nassau Meeting, 19–20 December 1962, Background Paper, Current Political Scene in the United Kingdom, 13 December 1962, JFK National Security Files, Trips and Conferences, box 238, Presidential Trips, Nassau Macmillan Talks 12/62, Briefing Book; Transcript of McNamara–Thorneycroft Meeting, London 11 December 1962, in Declassified Documents Reference System, Microfiche 1891 (1996).

80 Record of a Meeting held at Bali-Hai, The Bahamas, 9.50 a.m. and 4.30 p.m., 19 December 1962, and 10.30 a.m and 12 noon, 20 December 1962, PRO, FO 371/173292.

81 Costigliola, *The Failed Design*, p. 249; 'Mr. Ball would almost certainly wish to lay greater stress on the multilateral aspect of the Nassau agreement than we should do … As the Americans consistently made plain, it was the multilateral element in the Nassau agreement which was attractive to them.' Sir D. Ormsby-Gore to Foreign Office, 2 January 1963, PRO, FO 371/173393; Points of Mr. Ball in NAC, 3 January 1963, NA RG 59 Lot 65 D 134, Deputy Assistant Secretary for Politico-Military Affairs, box 3, Mr. Ball's Presentation to NAC; Statement by the Honourable George W. Ball, Undersecretary of State, Before the North Atlantic Council, C-M(63)1, 11 January 1963, PRO, FO 371/173396; 'They attempted at Nassau merely to outline a general scheme that might provide a framework upon which an effective NATO nuclear capability could be erected. That scheme contemplated the creation of a NATO Nuclear force. But quite clearly the detailed planning for the development and organization of such a force is for the member governments to work out … the two Governments propose to work in consultation and cooperation with the other member nations of the alliance in the development of a multilateral force in which all members of NATO that choose to do so may participate. This force, which presumably will be based on the principles of mixed-manning, will also become a part of the NATO nuclear force.' UK Draft Statement, NATO Council, in Ormsby-Gore to Foreign Office, 8 January 1963, PRO, FO 371/173394.

82 Dixon to Foreign Office, 3 January 1963, PRO, FO 371/173394.

83 Maurice Vaïsse, 'Une hirondelle ne fait pas le printemps: La France et la crise de Cuba', in Maurice Vaïsse (ed.), *L'Europe et la Crise de Cuba*, Paris: 1999, pp. 89–108, here p. 106.

84 Dixon to Foreign Office, 4 January 1963, PRO, PREM 11/4151; 'Now that the demise of the SKYBOLT and the Nassau agreement have precipitated us into the full debate on Western defence which we hoped could be put off until after the decision about our entry into the EEC had been taken, it seems important for us to try to evolve a sort of general theory of independence and interdependence which can be used when we talk either of defence or of foreign policy … I believe that the evolution of a general theory of independence and interdependence on these lines would win us the respect of all and go some way to turning the eyes of the Europeans towards us as the modern internationalist leaders of Europe in contrast to the rather old-fashioned nationalism of the oracular figure in the Elysée.' Dixon to Home, 7 January 1962, PRO, FO 371/173398; Rolf Steininger, 'Grossbritannien und de Gaulle: Das Scheitern des britischen EWG-Beitritts im Januar 1963', *VfZ*, 44 (1996), 87–118, here p. 105; Richard Davis, 'The "Problem of de Gaulle": British Reactions to General de Gaulle's Veto of the UK Application to Join the Common Market', *Contemporary History*, 32, 4 (1997), 453–64, p. 461.

85 Macmillan to Kennedy, 19 January 1963, JFK, National Security Files, Countries, box 173, UK, Macmillan Correspondence, 1/63; Steininger, *Grossbritannien und de Gaulle*, pp. 96f.; Ministerkonferenz der EWG, Brüssel, 28/29 January 1963, AAPD 1963 I, no. 60; Schröder Aufzeichnung betr. Beitritt Großbritanniens zu den Europäischen Gemeinschaften, 30 January 1963, BA NL *Carstens*, N 1337, Bd. 650; 'We can at least be grateful to him [de Gaulle] for choosing to sabotage the negotiations in such a way as to take the blame squarely on himself … If the negotiations had to

fail, they could not have failed in a manner more advantageous to us.' Caccia, in Davis, *The Problem of de Gaulle*, p. 456; 'Edward Heath told his Cabinet colleagues on 25 January that the UK had a "moral advantage ... derived from the fact that if the negotiations broke down now, the responsibility for the failure would be seen to lie clearly with the French Government",' ibid., p. 453.

86 Protokoll über die deutsch-französische Zusammenarbeit, 7 January 1963, Erklärung des Bundeskanzlers und des französischen Staatspräsidenten (Entwurf), 7 January 1963, Aufzeichnung des Staatssekretär Carstens, 10 January 1963, Aufzeichnung des Ministerialdirektors Jansen, 12 January 1963, Gesandter Knoke Paris, an AA, 1 January 1963, Gespräch des Bundeskanzlers Adenauer mit Staatspräsident de Gaulle, Paris, 21 January 1963, Elysee Konferenz, 21 January 1963, Knappstein an Schröder, 23 January 1963, AAPD 1963 I, Nr. 6, 7, 13, 18, 21, 37, 38, 49; 'He [JFK] said that the Franco-German treaty had created a new situation. He felt that de Gaulle, certain of our willingness to go to the defense of Europe, was attempting to exploit us. He wondered whether de Gaulle's next move would be a treaty with Italy. Conceivably, de Gaulle might try to organize the Six and create a nuclear force responsible to this grouping.' NSC Meeting, 31 January 1963, cit in Kosthorst, *Unerwünschte Liaison*, p. 185; Dr Carstens, Aufzeichnung betr. Deutsch-französische Zusammenarbeit, 24 January 1963, StBKAH III/7; McGeorge Bundy, Memorandum for the Record, 28 January 1963, JFK, National Security Files, countries, box 72, France General 1/24/63–1/3/63; 'The most canvassed opinion was at present that the rest of the Allies should agree to isolate France. Signor Fanfani did not think that this was the best way to proceed. It would be better to forestall de Gaulle by coming to terms with Khrushchev before he could do so. Such a policy would isolate the French and aim at the very heart of their plans ... He thought that the rest of the alliance should now go on the offensive via Moscow. This would take away from de Gaulle the hope and the card of a Soviet alliance, and his policy would then be finished.' Record of the First Meeting at the Palazzo Chigi, 5 p.m., 1 February 1963, PRO, FO 371/173297; Aufzeichnung über Gespräch des Herrn Bundeskanzlers mit Botschafter Dowling, 4 February 1963, StBKAH, Doc. 13-18.A/63.

87 'If the Bundestag ratified the treaty unamended, this would be the end of Berlin' [translation], Lucius D. Clay, cit. in Knappstein an AA, 28 January 1963, AAPD 1963 I, Nr. 58; Carstens Tyler Talks, Memorandum of Conversation, 5 February 1963, Dean Rusk to AmEmbassy Bonn, 8 February 1963, JFK, National Security Files, box 80, Germany, Subject, Carsten's Visit, 2/63; Klein Memorandum of McGeorge Bundy–von Gassel Meeting, 25 February 1963, JFK, National Security Files, box 80, Germany Subject, Von Hassel Visit, 2/63; Kusterer, *Intention und Wirklichkeit*, pp. 189f.

88 'The United Kingdom Government consider, as they have often said, that the European members of the Alliance are naturally going to develop a European point in defence matters, and it is from a European point of view that we welcome the opportunity which Nassau provides for greater European participation in NATO's nuclear defence.' Statement in the North Atlantic Council on 30 January 1963, by Sir Evelyn Shuckburgh on the Nassau Agreement, 30 January 1963, PRO, FO 371/173399; Dixon to Foreign Office, 31 January 1963, PRO, FO 371/173340; Aufzeichnung betr. Zusammenarbeit der Sechs mit Großbritannien im Rahmen der Westeuropäischen Union, 2 February 1963, PA-AA, Referat IA1, Bd. 443; Note de Travail, 6 February 1963; Bentinck aan Ministerie van Buitenlanse Zaken, 5 February 1963, B.Z., WEU Archief, Periode 1955–1964, Inv. Nr. 14, 999.0. Politicke consultatie WEU 1959–1964; Foreign Office to Brussels, 7 February 1963, Shuckburgh to Foreign Office, 8 February 1963, Nicholls to Foreign Office, 8 February 1963, PRO, FO 371/173341; Shuckburgh to Foreign Office, 18 February 1963, PRO, FO 371/173400; Visit of Officials in Brussels, 14 February 1963, PRO, FO 371/173342; Botschafter von Etzdorf an Staatssekretär Lahr,

5 February 1963, AAPD 1963 I, Nr. 79; Foreign Office to The Hague, 5 Sepember 1963, PRO, PREM 11/4735.

89 Botschafter von Etzdorf an Auswärtiges Amt, 15 February 1963, AAPD 1963 I, Nr. 93; Sir P. Dixon to Foreign Office, 16 March 1963; PRO, FO 371/173477; Foreign Office Minute, Future of WEU, 22 March 1963, PRO, FO 371/173484; Record of a Conversation between the Lord Privy Seal and the German Ambassador, 1 April 1963, PRO, FO 371/173478.

90 Extract from a Letter dated 1 March 1963 from Thomson to Barnes, 1 March 1963, PRO, DEFE 10/548; Summary Record of a Conversation at Admiralty House, 4 March 1963, PRO, FO 371/173292; Roberts to Foreign Office, 9 March 1963, PRO, FO 371/173405; Livingston Merchant to the Secretary of State, 20 March 1963, JFK, National Security Files, Regional Security, box 217–220, Multilateral Force, General, Merchant, 3/9/63–3/28/3; Runderlaß des Ministerialdirektors Krapf, 12 March 1963, AAPD 1963 I, Nr. 120; Adenauer an Kennedy, 4 April 1963, StBKAH III/4; Rumbold to Hood, 25 June 1963, PRO, FO 371/173308; Adenauer an Kennedy, 30 April 1963, AAPD 1963 I, Nr. 156.

91 'What was needed was a new European initiative by the British Government, and he [Quaroni] felt that the most hopeful field for such an initiative was that of nuclear defence. He had heard reports of Anglo-American discussions on the possibility of Britain providing at least some of the warheads for the multilateral force. He personally thought that, if the warheads could be provided by a European country, this would be a most important step towards satisfying the European desire for a more equal defence partnership between Europe and North America. Such an initiative would be universally recognised in Europe as a sign of the British Government's devotion to European integration and would make the contrast between the two views of Europe more apparent.' Record of a Conversation between the Lord Privy Seal and the Italian ambassador, 10 June 1963, PRO, FO 371/173345; 'The American proposal for a multilateral force went some way to meet the requirements but suffered from the vital defect that if the Americans insisted on maintaining a veto, the force would not be truly European ... The Italians hoped therefore that Britain would be prepared to take an initiative. They did not see this as an anti-American move. Indeed, they hoped the Americans would contribute to the force. Since Congress would never surrender the veto on the use of American warheads these would have to be supplied by Britain ... The Italians readily accept that the UK should have a veto on the use of the European force but beyond this point their ideas on the system of control had not been worked out in detail.' Ward to Foreign Office, 21 June 1963, PRO, FO 371/173300; Runderlaß des Staatssekretärs Carstens, betr. Cattani Besuch, 9 July 1963, AAPD 1963 II, Nr. 222 and Aufzeichnung der Politischen Abteilung II, 23 January 1964, AAPD 1964 I, Nr. 23; cf. Carlo Masala, 'Deutschland, Italien und die nukleare Frage 1963–1969. Das Problem der nuklearen Mitsprache im Rahmen der Atlantischen Allianz', *Militärgeschichtliche Mitteilungen*, 56 (1997), pp. 431–70, here pp. 439ff.

92 'No-one in Europe really wanted a mixed-manned NATO force, except perhaps some Germans who thought membership might give them a special relationship with the Americans. From every other point of view, the proposal was nonsense. His own solution to the Western nuclear dilemma was to establish a European deterrent based on collaboration between British and French nuclear forces ... It was in the American interest that the British should be the vehicle of American help because this would help build British influence in Europe.' Record of a Conversation between the Lord Privy Seal and Professor Henry Kissinger, 21 May 1963, PRO, FO 371/173308.

93 Kennedy–Couve de Murville Talks, 25 May 1963, JFK, National Security Council, box 72, France General, 5/29/63–5/31/63; cf. Memorandum of Conversation between French Foreign Minister Couve de Murville and Under Secretary Ball, 25 May 1963, ibid.

94 Caccia Minute, 8 July 1963, PRO, FO 371/173294.
95 Aufzeichnung des Ministerialdirektors Krapf, 3 July 1963, AAPD 1963 II, Nr. 215.
96 'Let me say first of all how much we welcome your approach and the bold sweep of your proposals. We entirely agree that there is a great opportunity here with profound consequences for the East-West relations and also for restoring the full unity of the Western Alliance by bringing France back into partnership … We would hope therefore that the French Government would agree to participate in private talks with the two of us designed to determine whether we could, without any injury to the French programme, find means by which the need for French tests at least in the three environments covered by the treaty could be avoided. We could say that if this idea appealed to him, we would make specific proposals for private tripartite talks when the Moscow discussions had made more progress.' Harold Macmillan to Kennedy, 18 July 1963, PRO, FO 371/173308; Possible Anglo-American Nuclear Offer to France, 20 July 1963, PRO, FO 371/173309; Macmillan to de Gaulle, 23 July 1963, PRO, FO 371/173308; Paul de Zulueta to Prime Minister, 24 July 1963, PRO, PREM 11/4151; Rumbold to Foreign Office, 6 August 1963, PRO, FO 371/173308; Krapf Aufzeichnung, Nichtverbreitung von Kernwaffen, 8 August 1963, StBKAH II/12.
97 Aufzeichnung des Botschafters Grewe, Gibt es Alternativen zum MLF-Projekt? 26 July 1963, Gespräch des Bundesministers Schröder mit dem amerikanischen Außenminister Rusk, 20 September 1963, Gespräch des Bundeskanzlers mit Staatspräsident de Gaulle, 21 Sepember 1963, Gespräche des Bundesaußenministers Schröder mit Präsident Kennedy, 24 Sepember 1963, Gespräch des Bundesministers Schröder mit dem ehemaligen amerikanischen Außenminister Acheson, 19 October 1963, Aufzeichnung des Ministerialdirektors Krapf betr. Gegenwärtiger Stand der MLF Verhandlungen, 15 November 1963, AAPD 1963 II, Nr. 240, 349, 356, 361, 394, 414 (III); Memorandum by the Secretary of State for Foreign Affairs, French Nuclear Policy, October 1963, PRO, FO 371/173310; 'The United States hinted that their possible withdrawal from the MLF will depend on the formation of a EPU and the establishment of a close link between European and American Nuclear Forces' [translation], Vermerk betr. atomare Verteidigung Europas und namentlich der Bundesrepublik, 12 November 1963, BA, NL *Hallstein*, N 1266, Bd. 1115; Aufzeichnung für W. Hallstein, Fortschritte im MLF Projekt, 28 April 1964, BA NL *Hallstein* N 1266, Bd. 1115; 'When I had got through my list of topics with Dr. Schröder this morning, he said he wanted to say a word about current propaganda in favour of a European nuclear force as an alternative to the MLF. There were some people in Germany who had completely misunderstood the very ambiguous and tentative propaganda emerging from Paris on this subject. They thought that the French might now be offering Germany partnership in the development of the force de frappe. This was of course nonsense ….' Roberts to Foreign Office, 22 October 1963, PRO, FO371/1773300.
98 Aufzeichnung des Ministerialdirektors Krapf betr. Vorschlag Präsident Johnsons, die Kernwaffen in Ost und West einzufrieren, 6 February 1964, AAPD 1964 I, Nr. 38.
99 Aufzeichnung des Staatssekretärs Carstens, 10 February 1964, AAPD 1964 I, Nr. 39 – cf. 'Mr. Gromyko stated that the Soviet Government attached importance to a non-dissemination agreement, but it was impossible for the West to conclude such an agreement and at the same time proceed with the formation of a NATO multilateral force. A non-dissemination treaty must be an honest measure to limit the number of nuclear powers to those already in possession of nuclear weapons.' Visit of the Foreign Secretary to the United Nations General Assembly, 25 September–5 October 1963, PRO, FO 371/173295.
100 Gespräch des Bundeskanzlers Erhard mit Ministerpräsident Moro, 27 January 1964, Deutsch–Italienische Regierungsbesprechung in Rom, 27–28 January 1964, Gespräch des Bundeskanzlers Erhard mit dem italienischen stellvertretenden Außenminister

Nenni, 28 January 1964, Deutsch-niederländische Regierungsbesprechungen, 2–3 March 1964, Gespräch des Bundeskanzlers Erhard mit dem amerikanischen Botschafter McGhee, 6 March 1964, Gespräch des Bundeskanzlers Erhard mit dem amerikanischen Botschafter Finletter, 16 April 1964, AAPD 1964 I, Nr. 27, 28, 29, 59, 63, 98.

101 Gespräch des Bundeskanzlers Erhard mit Staatspräsident de Gaulle, 3 July 1964, Gespräch zwischen Bundesaußenminister Schröder und Couve de Murville, 4 July 1964, AAPD 1964 II, Nr. 180, 185; cf. [De Gaulle:] 'One day Europe will be organised politically to an extent allowing the formation of a European Government and Europe to command its own nuclear forces. Up to that day Europe will not have nuclear forces but will include France with its national nuclear forces and possibly those of Britain in its structure' [translation], Gespräch des Bundeskanzlers Erhard mit Staatspräsident de Gaulle, 4 July 1964, ibid., 187; 'When de Gaulle replied that the *force de frappe* will be French and not European, he [Ludwig Erhard] told the General that if this were the case Germans would always have to depend on someone for their security – on either the French or the Americans – and it does not need further elaboration who will be a better protector' [translation], Gespräch des Bundeskanzlers Erhard mit dem amerikanischen Botschafter McGhee, 6 July 1964, ibid., 189.

102 Generalkonsul Ruete an die Botschaft in Neu Delhi, 24 August 1964, AAPD 1964 Nr. 238; Botschafter von Keller an das AA, 21 Sepember 1964, AAPD 1964 Nr. 253; 'The MLF project is approaching its critical phase … A *débacle* – similar to the defeat of the EDC project of 10 years ago – is not entirely impossible … The MLF is the only means by which Germany can get closer to becoming a nuclear power … Those forces are the appropriate means not only to bind the United States into Europe, but also for the advancement of Europe to a politically and militarily viable entity … The MLF is currently the only path allowing at least a partial implementation of the MRBM program of the SACEUR … In short, the MLF treaty has to be signed before the General Assembly of the United Nations starts its deliberations on *non-dissemination*' [translation], Memorandum des Botschafters Grewe, 22 September 1964, AAPD 1964, Nr. 254; cf. Deutsch-niederländische Regierungsbesprechungen, 30 September–1 October 1964, Carstens and Grewe, 19 October 1964, AAPD 1964, Nr. 266, 288.

103 Susanna Schrafstetter and Stephen Twigge, 'Trick or Truth? The British ANF Proposal, West Germany and US Non-Proliferation Policy, 1964–1968', *Diplomacy and Statecraft*, 11, 2 (2000), 161–84, here pp. 162, 167; 'The MLF would be essentially a military solution to a political problem. We realize that the United States Government put the project forward with tough political motives and that the German Government had reacted to it on the same basis. But opinion in Britain is by no means universally convinced in favour of the MLF … Her Majesty's Government have expressly stated that we have entered these talks without commitment to participate in such a force', Visit of the Secretary of State to Bonn and Berlin, 9–11 December 1963, PRO, FO 371/173465; Aufzeichnung des Vortagenden Legationsrats I. Klasse Luedde-Neurath, 21 April 1964, AAP 1964 I, Nr. 104.

104 'Aufzeichnung betr. Ihr Zusammentreffen mit Staatssekretär Ball, hier: MLF, 14 November 1964, BA NL *Hallstein*, N 1266, Bd. 1184; Gespräch des Bundesministers Schröder mit dem britischen Außenminister Gordon Walker, 15 November 1964, Gespräch des Bundesministers Schröder mit dem britischen Außenminister Gordon Walker, 11 December 1964, Gespräch des Bundesaußenministers Schröder mit Außenminister Rusk, Gordon Walker und Couve de Murville, 14 December 1964, AAPD 1964, Nr. 334, 382, 389; Atlantic Nuclear Force, Memorandum Handed to the United States, December 1964, PRO, FO 371/179079; Saki Dockrill, 'Forging the Anglo-American Global Defence Partnership: Harold Wilson, Lyndon Johnson and

the Washington Summit, December 1964', *Journal of Strategic Studies*, 23,4 (2000), 107–29, here pp. 113ff.

105 Schrafstetter and Twigge, *The British ANF Proposal*, p. 169; Saki Dockrill, 'Britain's power and influence: dealing with three roles and the Wilson government's defence debate at Chequers in November 1964', *Diplomacy and Statecraft*, 11, 1 (2000), 211–40, here pp. 229ff.; cf. 'I called on Gromyko … referring to the Atlantic nuclear force and non-dissemination. I drew Mr Gromyko's attention in particular to the sentence in the communiqué issued after the PM's talks with the President, which referred to the agreed Anglo-American objective of maintaining existing safeguards on the use of nuclear weapons in any new force, which was set up. This referred to the need for the maintenance of the American veto on the use of the force which the British regarded as extremely important.' Lord Harlech to Foreign Office, 9 December 1964, PRO, FO 371/179078.

106 Schrafstetter and Twigge, *The British ANF Proposal*, p. 170.

107 Heuser, *European Nuclear Force*, p. 75; Schrafstetter and Twigge, *The British ANF Proposal*, pp. 165, 172.

10

De Gaulle's France and the Soviet Union from Conflict to Détente[1]

Georges-Henri Soutou

When de Gaulle returned to power in 1958, he already had a long-term blueprint for France's relations with the USSR and for European security. Even if in the short term and especially during the Berlin crisis of 1958–1962, he realized that Soviet policy was very aggressive and dangerous, in the long term he was convinced that Russia would ultimately discard communism and return to a traditional great power diplomacy. France would seek a profound revision of the Atlantic Alliance, suppressing NATO integration. NATO would be reformed and greater independence of the Europeans from the Americans would enable France to launch a new détente policy towards Moscow. At the same time, the reduction of tension would diminish the dependence of Eastern Europe on the USSR. Germany (through tacit Franco-Soviet cooperation) would be forced to accept its Potsdam boundaries and to give security guarantees to its neighbours, especially renouncing nuclear weapons; thus reinsured and able to dispense with the need for Soviet protection against Germany, the countries of Eastern Europe would overcome the artificial ideology of communism and revert to their traditional national interests. The Soviet Union, no longer confronted with the danger of an integrated Western alliance and especially with a strong German–US pairing, but having to address the Chinese menace, would also revert to its long-term national interests. Thus it would be possible to rebuild a European security order freed from ideological tensions, resting on a tacit Franco-Soviet understanding for controlling Germany. The USA would revert to their former role of outside guarantor of the new European order, as a form of reinsurance. This would be a return to the Concert of Europe before 1914, but of course, at least in de Gaulle's view, a modernized one, taking into account the political, strategic, and democratic necessities of the twentieth century.[2]

De Gaulle's Basic Tenets

Contrary to a commonly held opinion at the time, de Gaulle did not have in mind any kind of neutralism, nor did he wish to reverse France's alliances.

But he contemplated a new European system which would overcome the Cold War and establish a new European balance between a de-ideologized Russia, on the one hand, and a Western Europe led by Paris, on the other. In this new Concert of Europe, Germany might ultimately be reunited (but once again within the borders decided at Potsdam and with security guarantees for its neighbours, such as denuclearization). The counterweight to Soviet power, which de Gaulle felt was absolutely necessary, would be provided by the USA (from afar) and first of all by the grouping of Western Europe, including Germany, around France. In this web of interlocking balances, France would balance Germany with the help of the Soviet Union. With the help of Germany, the Soviet Union would remain at the apex of the European system, thus multiplying its actual power and allowing it to go on playing a world role.

Such a blueprint was largely explained by de Gaulle himself to Soviet diplomats in Paris in 1958 and 1959, just before and just after assuming power.[3] He actually published its main lines in the third volume of his *Mémoires de guerre*, which came out in 1959 and were as much a programme for future action as an account of the past.[4] He explained it to Alain Peyrefitte, a minister in his government and for four years its official spokesman and one of the Elysée's main links with the media.[5] He told Khrushchev in March 1960 that only a European détente from the Atlantic to the Urals would solve the German problem by 'controlling the German body in a Europe of peace and progress', regretting at the same time that Stalin had not allowed France in 1944 to transform the German Reich into a loose confederation; this reveals much about the basic continuity of his thinking.[6]

De Gaulle's basic views about France's relationship with the USSR derived from three major considerations. First, the historical necessity for France to control Germany and the German problem. Apart from the Franco-German *rapprochement* initiated by de Gaulle in 1958, which very clearly was devised to draw the FRG away from the USA and closer to Paris, the only country which would be ready to help France control the German problem was the USSR.[7] The second consideration was his very strongly held views about the permanence of nation states, despite internationalist ideologies, as the building blocks of the international system and, beyond that, as repositories of history, civilization and progress.[8] The third was his will to restore the unity of Europe. The Continent would overcome the division induced by the Cold War, would include Russia, and would rest on a system of cooperation between sovereign states evoking a modernized Concert of Europe.[9]

Complex Overlapping Tactical Moves

De Gaulle followed different successive tactical steps to implement this basic strategy. From 1958 to 1960, he tried to reach an agreement with Washington (and London) to reform the Atlantic alliance and hence the whole international system in accordance with his views; he felt there was no immediate possibility to deal with Moscow under the pressure of Khrushchev's Berlin ultimatum.[10] From 1960 to 1964, he tried to establish a privileged political and strategic relationship with Germany. Then in 1964 and 1965, he decided to approach Moscow directly.[11]

But the basic blueprint of interlocking balances remained the same all along and those different steps did not supersede each other but overlapped in a complex and subtle way. Even as he was taking a firm stand on the Berlin crisis, de Gaulle did not hesitate, in March 1959, to recognize the Oder–Neisse line, which was a clear signal to the Soviets, supported by subtle feelers in the background.[12] As early as 1959, de Gaulle spoke publicly of a 'Europe from the Atlantic to the Urals' and told French diplomats and Chancellor Adenauer that Soviet communism was mellowing, spoke of an inevitable Russian–Chinese rift, and evoked a new European security order including Russia.[13] In May 1962, he stressed publicly that close Franco-German cooperation would make possible the establishment of a new European balance between East and West, and thus of a European cooperative system from the Atlantic to the Urals.[14] In this way, in one sentence, he revealingly linked steps two and three of his programme! At the same time, de Gaulle's positions were not to be taken always at face value but could be instrumentalized to further his aims. As soon as the Berlin Wall was erected in 1961, for instance, he was convinced that West Berlin was potentially lost; his uncompromising stance (refusing to associate himself with Anglo-American negotiation offers to Moscow) was probably not so much directed against Moscow as devised to draw an isolated FRG to Paris and thus to 'create Europe'.[15]

1958–1963: Frosty Franco-Soviet Relations

Until 1964, Franco-Soviet relations were basically bad. Apart from the Berlin crisis and especially the failure of the Paris summit in May 1960, there were three basic reasons for this. First, the war in Algeria and Moscow's support of the rebels, culminating in the recognition of the FLN government 24 hours after the signature of the Evian agreements in March 1962 but months before the actual accession of Algeria to independence.[16] Second, there was Soviet opposition to the Franco-German *rapprochement* culminating in the Elysée Treaty of 22 January 1963, which brought accusations that Paris was promoting an anti-Soviet and revanchist military bloc.[17] Third, de Gaulle was furious about the signing of the Moscow Treaty in July 1963 banning nuclear tests in the atmosphere, which for him epitomized US–Soviet hegemonic collusion.[18]

At the same time, there were some subtle indications that the Soviets did not write off the big hopes that they had formed about de Gaulle in 1958 (as stated by Venedict Erofeev in his already quoted articles). On 22 and 23 March

1961, the French Communist Party's newspaper *Humanité* published articles on Franco-Soviet relations very critical of de Gaulle but expressing the hope that those relations could get better, a sentiment which did not escape the attention of the Quai d'Orsay.[19] In February 1961, the Soviets had published excerpts of the *Mémoires de guerre*, with a commentary going in the same direction.[20] The same could be said of a speech by Khrushchev in Stalingrad on 10 September of the same year.[21]

And even inside the Quai d'Orsay, there was discreet opposition to the official policy line of diffidence towards Moscow and *rapprochement* with Bonn. Maurice Dejean, ambassador to Moscow since 1955, historically a Gaullist and since the war a proponent of a Franco-Soviet understanding to control Germany, suggested that there might be some valid reasons behind Moscow's opposition to the Franco-German treaty, which could be seen as promoting Franco-German military and perhaps nuclear cooperation. He was convinced that despite the Elysée Treaty, the Soviets still wished an understanding with France on the basis of de Gaulle's policy of 'national independence'.[22]

1963–1964: The Thaw

From the summer of 1963, there were discernible beginnings of a thaw. Economic and scientific relations began to evolve in a positive way; Economics Minister Valéry Giscard d'Estaing went to the USSR in January 1964.[23] His trip marked a turning point in Franco-Soviet trade. On 16 July 1963, Khrushchev had a not unfriendly conversation with Maurice Dejean. He said that he would be happy to invite de Gaulle to Moscow, and he stressed, in a none too subtle insinuation, that he feared the Federal Republic would be the leading member of the Franco-German pair and would use France to further its own agenda.[24] The Quai d'Orsay noticed the change: in March 1964 the Department of Eastern Europe concluded that Moscow wanted to re-establish a dialogue with Paris. Three motives were adduced. First, France was standing aloof from the general atmosphere of détente which had existed since the end of the Cuban crisis; by engaging Paris and using the deterioration of the relations between France, the US, Great Britain and Germany, Moscow could hope to facilitate détente and to achieve its aims – such as recognition of the German Democratic Republic (GDR) and security agreements in Europe – and also to divide France and Germany. The second motive was the need to play the different Western powers against each other in order to obtain better trade and loans terms, which the USSR badly needed given the sorry state of its economy. The third motive was the Sino-Soviet rift.[25]

De Gaulle still remained very prudent[26] but he basically shared that analysis. In his press conferences of 31 January and 23 July 1964, he stressed the growing rift between Beijing and Moscow, both relinquishing ideology and returning to their traditional national interests, including potential rivalry about Siberia. He also stressed the ultimate failure of the Soviet system to provide for the well-being and dignity of mankind, the end of the totalitarian monolith, the opportunity now for Europe (both East and West) to regain its world role.[27] The point being not so much emphasis on the Sino-Soviet rift (which was a fact) but the conclusion that communism itself was becoming irrelevant for the Soviet Union and that a new European order was now possible. For the twentieth anniversary of the liberation of Paris in August 1964, Khrushchev sent a warmly worded message to France. De Gaulle modified the answer prepared by the Quai d'Orsay, making it much more amicable and adding his hopes that the combined Soviet and French efforts could lead 'to a lasting peace in Europe and in the world'.[28]

At the same time, de Gaulle was keenly aware of the evolving balance of power in the world and was quite ready to use it. On 27 January 1964, he had recognized the People's Republic of China. That move was as much a proclamation of independence from Washington as a discreet reminder to the USSR that it had now better come to terms with Western Europe.[29] This was an important part of the system of interlocking balances for which he was striving. And his choice of words about 'a Europe from the Atlantic to the Urals', often derided, actually had an obvious meaning for a man of his generation (the same problem had arisen in 1891 and 1944 at the time of the two Franco-Russian alliances): in the future European security framework, France was ready to collaborate with Moscow about European affairs, but not about Asia.[30]

The Problem of International Communism

Much attention was devoted in Paris during those years to the problem of international communism and its eventual unravelling in the aftermath of de-Stalinization and of the ideological turmoil which world communism was experiencing. There were interesting considerations close at home: the French Communist Party (PCF) appeared divided, some leaders maintaining a hard anti-Gaullist line, others judging that de Gaulle's foreign policy included 'positive' (that is, anti-US) aspects.[31] This latent convergence with the PCF on some issues of foreign policy was probably one of the ulterior motives of some Fifth Republic leaders, a strategy to keep the left divided, but with hard-to-assess effects; anyway, it did not prevent a united presidential candidature of the left by François Mitterrand in the election of 1965, with potent political consequences. But more research still needs to be done on the issue of how de Gaulle used his foreign policy to gain political support at home on the left of the political spectrum: for example, it has been said that on his orders (and certainly not without his consent) the very leftist and neutralist Emmanuel d'Astier de La Vigerie was granted a weekly television programme in 1964.

All this of course did not escape the Soviet Union, which apparently stepped up after 1958 its effort to penetrate the French political world and to establish all sorts of links with the new *régime*, in the hope that something useful could come out of the new political situation in France.[32]

As early as 1961, the Quai d'Orsay and French embassies abroad began a systematic and worldwide study of the effects of ideological divisions and especially of the Sino-Soviet rift (which had become noticeable the previous year) on the different communist parties all over the world.[33] That study was also made at the Atlantic level, inside the Consultative Group for Atlantic Policy; major themes were the Sino-Soviet rift, 'revisionism' in the USSR and in the Italian Communist Party, the 'autonomy' of the Rumanian party, the 'neo-communism' of the Cubans, the links with the Afro-Asiatic movement, and the impact of all those developments on East–West relations.[34] A conference initiated by Prof. Alexander Dallin in Washington in March 1962 about the final end of united international communism met with great interest in Paris.[35]

The secret services contributed to that effort. The notorious 'Renseignements généraux' (the secret police of the Interior Ministry) obtained the proceedings of the Moscow meeting of the communist parties' representatives in November–December 1960. The 'Secrétariat général de la Défense nationale', which collated open and secret intelligence, circulated a monthly bulletin about European communist countries.[36]

The Quai d'Orsay had numerous reasons to feel that Moscow was incapable of resolving the problems of the world communist movement. Evidence came from the growing disorganization of the movement in 1964, the publication of 'Togliatti's Will' in August of that year, the failure of the communist conference that Khrushchev had scheduled for December, his own fall in October, and the limited scope of the conference of the communist parties of the European capitalist countries held in Brussels in June 1965.[37] The mainstream conclusion was that the process of differentiation among communist parties determined to defend their own national interests had now become irreversible, particularly in Eastern Europe.[38]

But this conclusion was disputed. Specialists on the Soviet Union at the Quai d'Orsay, such as Jean Laloy, Jean-Marie Soutou and Henri Froment-Meurice, felt that despite the crisis of world communism the USSR and its satellites remained deeply ideological and had not reverted to a traditional style of realist foreign policy. It was also felt that Moscow had not lost its full control over Eastern Europe and that there was no way to drive a wedge between Eastern Europe and the USSR in the name of a new European security order, of a Europe from the Atlantic to the Urals, which could only lead to a fragmentation of the West, to a difficult situation for Western Europe, and to dangerous temptations for the FRG.[39] A close study of the papers may show signs of this rift.[40] But Jean Laloy, 'directeur-adjoint des affaires politiques' since 1961, became 'conseiller diplomatique du gouvernement' in

Autumn 1964. That is, he was effectively side-tracked. Henri Froment-Meurice, head of the Eastern Europe Department, was sent to Egypt in 1963; Jean-Marie Soutou, director of the European Department since 1961, moved in 1963 to the Africa and Middle East Department. Apart from the case of Laloy, those personnel changes were not directly motivated by the differences about the policy towards the Soviet Union, but the result all the same was that the three men mainly responsible for inspiring the previous policy towards the USSR (with close links to the Western diplomatic establishment devoted to Soviet affairs and with many Western and Eastern anti-communist intellectuals) had now been shunted aside. Those internal discussions and shifts were of course closely linked to the deep reorientation French foreign policy experienced from 1963 to 1966, first towards Bonn to the detriment of the links with London and Washington, and then towards Moscow. One litmus test was the perception of the Soviet Union either as an ideologically motivated power or as a 'realist' one. Another litmus test was the concept of a common Soviet–French interest in balancing Germany.

Those internal changes inside the Quai d'Orsay were reflected in French society at large. During those years, a sea-change took place in French opinion. Before 1958, Atlanticism had certainly been weaker in France than in other European countries, and the USSR always retained a higher level of sympathy than elsewhere (aside from Italy). But there was a powerful anti-communist and anti-Soviet sentiment, and a strong Atlanticist constituency encompassing the moderate left and the moderate right. After 1958 and the founding of the Fifth Republic, the Gaullists, who were now ascendant and would remain so until 1981, were mostly in favour of a Franco-Soviet *rapprochement* to enhance the French agenda while remaining staunchly anticommunist on the domestic level. It was particularly the case regarding Germany and the USA in order to balance those two countries and to further France's international role. On the other side, the socialists, until that time rather Atlanticist, were pushed into permanent opposition, which led them after 1965 to ally themselves with the communist party and generally to follow a more radical course, evident in the 1970s. They thus became much more hesitant about the Atlantic alliance if not, as was the case for many in their ranks, outright neutralistic. This meant that there was no longer a majority which had a positive attitude toward the Atlantic alliance, as there had been in the 1950s, and the constituency of Atlanticism, although it never disappeared, remained a minority one. The Cold War was often seen as the result, as much or even more, of US imperialism than of Soviet provocations. At the same time during the 1960s and until the 1980s, French opinion about the USSR and its system was quite often positive; at least the Soviet system was generally seen as a valid option, not too different from the dirigist, state-centred French one.

It is sufficient to read Raymond Aron's articles of the time in *Le Figaro* to understand those changes and the discussions and divisions in France – for instance, his two-part piece of 8 and 11 February 1963 ('Y a-t-il un grand dessein gaulliste?') and his article from 12 April 1966 ('Vingt ans après'), describing the main lines of de Gaulle's blueprint and stressing its basic continuity.[41]

1965: The Turning Point and the Convergence

In the period from 1964 to 1966, all the major problems of French foreign policy (relations with Washington, Bonn and Moscow) came to a head together and were deeply interlocked: now was the time to try to implement the Gaullist blueprint. In October 1964, France launched a massive attack against the Multilateral Force (MLF) project, which was now seen as the major tool of US policy to thwart the French 'European Europe' concept. In December, the MLF was effectively killed by de Gaulle.[42] On 23 December 1964, Soviet Prime Minister Alexei Kosygin told the French ambassador Philippe Baudet that France and the Soviet Union agreed about the necessity of promoting 'security in Europe' in order to forestall the dangers of German ambitions and of US–German privileged cooperation. This was an evident offer of cooperation, in the wake of the MLF failure, tailored to French fears about an eventual Bonn–Washington axis.[43] Paris immediately decided to take up the offer, despite the deep differences remaining with Moscow (especially the problem of the recognition of the East German regime, the necessity of retaining the Atlantic alliance, and the building up of Western Europe). But, for Paris, the most important point was that both states agreed that the main problem, the division of Germany, was a 'specifically European' one that could only be resolved within the framework of a European détente in which the European countries should play the leading role, in other words marginalizing the US.[44] De Gaulle himself told Vinogradov as much on 25 January 1965: France would not recognize the GDR or be drafted into an anti-US coalition, but Paris was ready to discuss with Moscow a European solution to the German problem.[45] During his press conference of 4 February, de Gaulle explained very clearly his whole concept: the USSR and Eastern Europe freed from communist totalitarianism; the German problem solved in the framework of a European security agreement; European cooperation from the Atlantic to the Urals; the grouping of Western Europe to balance the continent; cooperation between this new European system and the USA, 'Europe's daughter'.[46] (But let us note here that one month before, on 2 January, de Gaulle had told the French ambassador to Washington, Hervé Alphand, that he contemplated a European security system from the Atlantic to the Urals in which the USA would not participate.)[47] During the following weeks, careful soundings between Paris and Moscow took place, until it was announced on 2 March that Soviet Foreign Minister Andrei Gromyko would visit Paris in April, and Couve de Murville would fly to Moscow before the end of the year.[48] On 23 March, de Gaulle toasted departing ambassador Vinogradov by evoking 'the centuries old sympathy and natural affinity' between the two countries.[49] This was widely noted and it became evident that something was afoot.

On the eve of Gromyko's visit, French diplomats noticed that French and Soviet views about some international problems, and particularly about Laos and southeast Asia, were now converging. But, above all, they were very sanguine about the evolution of Eastern Europe toward the reaffirmation of national interests and more independence from Moscow, which they believed the USSR was obliged to accept. In their view, the only way to slow down this development would be for Moscow to achieve a solution of the German problem in a European security framework, but one which would include the recognition of the GDR by the West. The aim of the Soviets was to bring the French to accept, in exchange for a liberalization of Eastern Europe, the existence of the GDR and thus recognize the partition of Germany. That is why Vinogradov had been replaced as ambassador by Zorin, a specialist on the German question and with much more influence in the party.[50] But French diplomats were quick to note that the Soviets in their conversations and memoranda were distorting the meaning of the 4 February press conference: de Gaulle had evoked a solution of the German problem in a European security framework, but this solution would include the reunification of Germany, which has always been the official French position.[51]

But in his talk with Gromyko on 27 April, de Gaulle went beyond that. He believed that the partition of Germany was 'abnormal' and would not last for ever, but he was 'in no hurry' to overcome it. And for the time being, partition was 'an accomplished fact'. Gromyko and de Gaulle agreed on the idea of a European security framework, established among Europeans (that is, without the USA). Interestingly enough, Gromyko stated that France 'laid more stress on reunification' than did the USSR, but that Moscow was not against re-unification, provided it was agreed between both German states (which had always been Moscow's position). There was now certainly a measure of over-lap between the positions of both countries.[52] This led to an ambiguous communiqué at the end of the visit, in which the French did not expressly reaffirm their adherence to German reunification. The West Germans were furious.[53] Let me add that Gromyko suggested the conclusion of a bilateral treaty. De Gaulle answered that it was too soon, but he certainly did not reject the idea despite the fact that his diplomats realized that Moscow was trying to play France and Germany against each other.[54]

When Couve de Murville went to Moscow at the end of October, he was actually more reserved in his talks with Gromyko, Brezhnev and Kosygin than de Gaulle had been in April with Gromyko. Certainly France did agree that there was no solution to the German problem outside a general détente in Europe (but he did not allude to an actual European security framework); certainly the USA was no European power and certainly Germany should not possess any nuclear weapons and should be contained in the borders decided upon in 1945. But he added, much more forcefully than de Gaulle had done, that at the end of the process of détente Germany should be reunited, that reunification should be achieved not through a direct agreement between both Germanies but by the four powers (therefore including the USA), and he stressed the importance of good relations between France and the FRG.[55] A close study of the different versions of the final communiqué (issued on 2 November) shows that Couve de Murville resisted the Soviet wish to include the expression 'already existing realities' and refused a paragraph stating that any resolution of the German problem should be achieved 'by all interested states from East and West' and include the 1945 borders and dispositions about German armaments. There remained a call for détente and cooperation in Europe and for a solution to European problems by 'all interested parties'.[56] Thus prudently worded, the communiqué met with no objections in Washington or Bonn.[57]

Toward a New European Security Order?
De Gaulle's Visit to Moscow in June 1966

At the beginning of 1966, there was a general acceleration of de Gaulle's foreign initiatives. He was now convinced that for the time being no real agreement was possible with Bonn, which was still harbouring nuclear ambitions, was still keeping too close to Washington, and still did not accept the 1945 borders or the concept of détente. At the same time, he still desired political and strategic cooperation with Germany, which was necessary to achieve the security of Western Europe and the overall balance in the new Europe which would emerge anyway.[58] But the order of precedence in the French–German–Soviet triangle now changed: the new European system would not rest primarily on the Franco-German relationship, but on the Franco-Russian one. The whole point now was to build, by means of a basic agreement with Moscow, a new European order in which Germany would eventually be reunited, but would in any event be kept subject to a system of European security controlling its borders and armaments – in fact controlled in a system led by Paris and Moscow. De Gaulle explained most clearly in his press conference of 28 October 1966 that Bonn's reluctance to follow him and the new situation in the East had changed the whole situation.[59]

At the same time, de Gaulle decided to enforce NATO reform. In March 1966, he announced that France would withdraw from the integrated NATO command and that NATO organizations and US troops would have to leave France.[60] He was convinced that France's initiative would compel the other members to undertake a thorough reform of NATO. He envisioned its transformation into a classic alliance without military integration, especially given the 1969 treaty deadline, after which the members could leave the alliance. Evidently, his move was decided upon with his scheduled June trip to Moscow in mind: by eroding the Western 'bloc', France would set the example for an equivalent eroding of the Eastern one; in overcoming the two opposing blocs and in the climate of confidence thus created, a new European security system would become possible.

But de Gaulle did not forget what were in his view the necessary inter-locking balances. He had first contemplated leaving the alliance altogether and substituting a system of bilateral alliances. But he finally decided to leave not the alliance itself but only the integrated command: it was the only way to be sure that French troops could remain in Germany, and that France could retain its control of the German question and of an eventual reunification, and thus to retain control of the interlocking links with Germany, the USSR, the USA and the UK.[61]

De Gaulle probably never explained his whole concept more vividly than he did for US Senator Church on 4 May 1966. The USSR would have to come to terms with the West due to fears about China and eroding ideologies. The German problem could be solved only after the estau.:shment of an overall détente in Europe, which would appease Eastern Europe's fears about Germany, provided it forswore its ambitions and accepted its new borders and non-nuclear status. But, as we shall see, de Gaulle was perhaps less than candid with his US host when, in response to a pointed question, he stressed the necessity of the continuing presence of US troops in Europe in order to balance the USSR and stated that the USA should participate fully in the negotiations leading to the new system.[62]

When de Gaulle left for Moscow in June 1966, the situation papers prepared by the Quai d'Orsay for the Elysée largely supported his views. The USSR was beset with economic and systemic problems; it would have to be reformed. Eastern Europe was evolving toward greater autonomy. The evolution of NATO enforced by de Gaulle would compel the USSR to modify the Warsaw Pact toward more equality among its members. In his view, 'a hostile China pushed Soviet leaders to realize their kinship with the Western world'. Their former German and European policy having failed, it was in the Soviets' interest to agree with France about Europe and Germany, especially in order to prevent Bonn from achieving nuclear status.[63] At the same time, French diplomats understood that even if it might be in Moscow's best long-term interest to accept a reunited Germany in a European security framework, in fact and for the time being the Soviets were ready to discuss such a European security system with the French only if it led to recognition of the GDR and to the confirmation of Germany's partition.[64]

Let us add that the two main and crucial problems raised by de Gaulle's concept had emerged very clearly in his declarations to the press, to Senator Church, in the previous conversations with the Soviets, as well as in the internal papers of the Quai d'Orsay. Would the new European security system allow the reunification of Germany or not? Would the USA have a role in this new European order or not? The answers given by Paris up to then had been outwardly and officially yes to both questions, but we have noted that on some private occasions (especially with Hervé Alphand and with Gromyko) de Gaulle had already answered 'no' or 'perhaps' to both.

De Gaulle's trip to the Soviet Union took place in an especially warm mood. Apart from the atmospherics, there were some important agreements on economic and scientific matters concluded on that occasion and, even more important, an agreement for a permanent political exchange and consultation process between the Quai d'Orsay and the Soviet embassy in Paris.[65] But most important was the talk between Brezhnev and de Gaulle on 21 June.[66] Brezhnev began with his usual boilerplate about the German menace. De Gaulle agreed that Germany should not possess any nuclear weapons and should finally recognize its 1945 borders. He added that he had discussed German borders with Stalin in 1944 in the same room of the Kremlin, and that at the time the Soviet leader had not accepted his views about the western boundary of the former Reich being on the Rhine and in the Ruhr. 'I was not powerful enough at the time to prevail with my views.'

At the same time, he stressed the necessary balance between the USA and the USSR. Without this balance France would fall victim to the hegemony of either one power or the other: 'We are therefore quite happy with your might, and also with American might.' All this was not new. More important was the repeated statement that the French were 'neither very sanguine, nor in a great hurry' to see Germany reunited. Reunification should be a 'hope', a 'perspective', to prevent dangerous developments in Germany. Reunification was no longer a firm (if hypocritical) element of French foreign policy aims. And anyway the German problem should be discussed among Europeans, so as to take it out of the Soviet–US rivalry, which Germany, as de Gaulle implied, was using in a dangerous way for its own purposes.

At this point Brezhnev suggested a European security conference without the USA. De Gaulle then equivocated; it was too soon for such a conference, but if 'one should go in that direction', the conference would be the result of détente. As for the Americans, they certainly had rights regarding Germany that had resulted from the war, but there was ground to believe that the USA might accept a settlement arrived at among Europeans and that allowed the USA to disengage itself from Europe. At another point, de Gaulle agreed explicitly with Brezhnev's statement that the Europeans should collaborate among themselves without the USA.

As stated above, those two questions – German reunification and US participation in a European security conference – were the most important. De Gaulle's position, as sketched rather ambiguously to the Soviets, now went far beyond the previous French stance, explained for instance by Couve de Murville in Moscow the year before. As explained to Senator Church, there was to be a European détente including the mellowing of Soviet communism in Eastern Europe, the reunification of Germany, and a continuing US military presence in Europe, even with a completely transformed NATO. Quite another proposition was a European security system with a severely controlled Germany, with its reunification only a distant prospect and without US presence. The two pillars of such a system would have been the USSR and France. With its nuclear weapons and its leadership of Western Europe, France would provide a counterbalance to Russia, which would be contained on one side by China, on the other by the peripheral power of the USA. De Gaulle's diplomatic counsellor at the Elysée at the time, Pierre Maillard, sensed in those speculations a certain return to his views of 1944, when he had gone to Moscow to sign the Franco-Soviet pact: France and Russia would control Germany together and thus achieve European security, and at the same time a 'Western bloc' led by France would balance the USSR.[67]

The Aftermath

In the following months, France played its part in the Franco-Soviet détente and took it seriously; the celebration of 1917 on the French radio and television system (at the time nearly completely controlled by the state) reached unprecedented heights in 1967. The Germans were told to follow France's example and to negotiate with the Soviets.[68]

But actually Moscow was more interested in entering a round of negotiations with the USA, as the Glassboro meeting between Johnson and Kosygin in June 1967 showed. The Americans concluded, quite rightly, that the Soviets were interested in the fact that de Gaulle's policy was harming NATO, but not in his long-term views about European security; despite their public stance, they did not really wish the Americans to evacuate Europe, because they were in fact counting on them to contain any German revanchism.[69]

This did not prevent Moscow from celebrating France's withdrawal from the NATO command and the weakening of the Western alliance. As Brezhnev told his Warsaw Pact partners in 1966:

> Take, for instance, de Gaulle. Did we not achieve, thanks to him and with no risk at all, a breach into American capitalism? De Gaulle is our enemy and we know that. The French Communist Party, narrow-minded and thinking only of its interests, has tried to drive us against him. And still, what have we achieved? A weakening of the American position in Europe. And it is not yet finished.[70]

Actually, Moscow knew how to instrumentalize France's 'politique d'indépendance'. In 1967, for instance, the Soviets used the French stance on the Middle East conflict to reinforce their own policy. Both countries were united against the USA and Israel and both were demanding a four-power conference on the Middle East – which did not prevent Moscow from negotiating directly with

Washington later on. The same could be said about French opposition to the war in Vietnam.

But concerning the two main paradigms of de Gaulle's policy, the mellowing of Soviet ideology and the growing independence of Eastern Europe, it became evident, as early as 1967, that both were for the time being merely an illusion. When de Gaulle went to Poland in 1967, he told the Poles to overcome the ideological division of Europe. He was publicly rebuked by Gomulka, who reaffirmed the solidarity of socialist Poland with the USSR.[71] As for the Prague Spring and the Soviet invasion of Czechoslovakia in 1968, they definitively proved the point. But apparently, de Gaulle felt those events were only an episode in an inescapable evolution, and he reaffirmed the validity of his concept.[72] Paris felt that the Germans had been too pushy in Prague and had thus upturned the applecart of détente.[73] The conclusion was that, more than ever, Paris and Moscow should discuss European security together. As Michel Debré, then in charge of the Quai d'Orsay, told Soviet diplomats in January 1969:

> Neither in Moscow nor in Paris ought one to forget the lessons of history and geography. The French and the Russians must help each other. That is the price of Europe's peace![74]

The *Ostpolitik* and SALT were soon to show that other countries could play the game of détente with Moscow, that there were alternative European security concepts, and that there was no way to decouple European security from the USA. France's policy between 1962 and 1966 took place in a sort of historical *entredeux* between the height of the Cold War and the general détente of the late 1960s and early 1970s, making full use of the security and balance achieved by the Atlantic alliance in the previous years for its own ends.

NOTES

1 For a general account, see Maurice Vaïsse, *La grandeur: Politique étrangère du Général de Gaulle (1958–1969)*, Paris: Fayard, 1998, and Marie-Pierre Rey, *La tentation du rapprochement: France et URSS à l'heure de la Détente (1964–1974)*, Paris: Publications de la Sorbonne, 1991. See also Institut Charles de Gaulle, *De Gaulle en son siècle, vol. V, Europe*, Paris: Plon, 1992, and Jean Lacouture, *De Gaulle, vol. III, Le souverain*, Paris: Le Seuil, 1986.

2 Cf. Georges-Henri Soutou, 'Le général de Gaulle, le Plan Fouchet et l'Europe', *Commentaire*, 52 (Winter 1990–91); Georges-Henri Soutou, *L'Alliance incertaine*, Paris: Fayard, 1996, chapter VIII; Pierre Maillard, *De Gaulle et l'Allemagne*, Paris: Plon, 1990, pp. 247–52.

3 See the fascinating account by V. Erofeev, an important Soviet diplomat in Paris at the time: 'De Gaulle, sa clairvoyance et ses illusions', *Vie internationale* (Moscow) (October and November 1988), pp. 143–53 and 152–60.

4 See particularly page 62 of the Presses Pocket edition, vol. III, *Le Salut.*
5 See particularly Alain Peyrefitte, *C'était de Gaulle*, vol. III, Paris: Editions de Fallois/Fayard, 2000, pp. 195–207.
6 Charles de Gaulle, *Mémoires d'espoir*, Paris: Plon, 1970, pp. 239–42. For his 1944– 45 ideas, see Georges-Henri Soutou, 'Le général de Gaulle et l'URSS, 1943–1945: idéologie ou équilibre européen', *Revue d'Histoire Diplomatique*, 4 (1994).
7 Georges-Henri Soutou, 'Frankreich und die Deutschlandfrage 1943 bis 1945', in Hans-Erich Volkmann (ed.), *Ende des Dritten Reiches – Ende des Zweiten Weltkrieges*, Munich: Piper, 1995; Georges-Henri Soutou, *L'Alliance incertaine: Les rapports politico-stratégiques Franco-allemands, 1954–1996*, Paris: Fayard, 1996.
8 Fondation Charles de Gaulle, Cahier 7, 2000, *L'idée de Nation chez Charles de Gaulle.*
9 Fondation Charles de Gaulle, Cahier 6, 1999, *Coudenhove-Kalergi/De Gaulle: Une certaine idée de l'Europe.*
10 Henri Froment-Meurice, *Vu du Quai: Mémoires 1945–1983*, Paris: Fayard, 1998, pp. 202–3.
11 I have described those different steps in Soutou, *L'Alliance incertaine.*
12 Thierry Wolton, *La France sous influence: Paris–Moscou 30 ans de relations secrètes*, Paris: Grasset, 1997, pp. 272 ff.
13 Froment-Meurice, *Vu du Quai*, p. 213.
14 Charles de Gaulle, *Discours et messages*, Paris: Plon, 1970, vol. III, p. 411.
15 Henri Froment-Meurice, *Vu du Quai*, pp. 228, 234–5, 237–8.
16 Very cool talks between de Gaulle and Soviet Ambassador Vinogradov on 23 November 1960 (Ministère des Affaires étrangères, Cabinet du Ministre, entretiens) and on 23 February 1961 (MAE, Europe 1961–1965, URSS, carton 1930) and 'note pour le secrétaire général a. s. Relations Franco-soviétiques' from 29 March 1962, same box.
17 Note from 21 September 1962, telegrams from the French embassy in Moscow from 5 and 6 February 1963, round telegram from Paris on 8 February 1963, note from 14 February 1963, MAE, carton 1930.
18 Maurice Vaïsse, 'La France et le traité de Moscou (1957–1963)', *Revue d'Histoire Diplomatique*, 1 (1993), 41–53.
19 Note from 30 March 1961, MAE, carton 1930.
20 Note from 24 April 1961, MAE, carton 1930.
21 Note from 21 September 1961, MAE, carton 1930.
22 Telegram of 15 February 1963, MAE, carton 1930.
23 Account of his conversation with Khrushchev on 27 January, MAE, carton 1931. See Marie-Pierre Rey, *La tentation du rapprochement.*
24 Telegram from 17 July 1963, MAE, carton 1931.
25 Note of 2 March 1964, MAE, carton 1931.
26 See, for instance, his conversation with Soviet Ambassador Vinogradov on 18 June 1964, MAE, carton 1931.
27 Charles de Gaulle, *Discours et Messages*, Paris: Plon, 1970, vol. IV, pp. 179, 227; and also his remarks to Hervé Alphand on 2 January 1965, *L'étonnement d'être*, Paris: Fayard, 1974, p. 445.
28 MAE, carton 1931.
29 He told Senator Church as much on 4 May 1966, see below. See Fondation Charles de Gaulle, Cahier 1, *L'établissement des relations diplomatiques entre Paris et Pékin en 1964.*
30 Institut Charles de Gaulle, *De Gaulle en son siècle*, vol. V, pp. 509 ff.
31 Note from 22 February 1961, MAE, carton 1926.
32 Thierry Wolton, *La France sous influence.*
33 MAE, cartons 1926 and 1927.

34 Notes of 3 March 1964, and 30 October 1965, MAE, carton 1927.
35 Telegram from Washington on 7 March 1962, MAE, carton 1926.
36 MAE, carton 1927.
37 MAE, carton 1927.
38 Note of 9 April 1965, from the Eastern Europe Department, with wide circulation, including to the Elysée, MAE, carton 1927.
39 See Froment-Meurice, *Vu du Quai*, pp. 217, 247.
40 See, for instance, critical remarks by Laloy on a report by Burin des Roziers, ambassador to Warsaw, on 30 January 1961, MAE, carton 1927. Or handwritten corrections to the instructions given to Philippe Baudet, the new ambassador to Moscow, in February 1964, MAE, carton 1931.
41 Raymond Aron, *Les articles de politique internationale dans Le Figaro de 1947 à 1977, vol. II, La Coexistence (juin 1955 à février 1965)*, Paris: Editions de Fallois, 1993, pp. 1144–9 and *vol. III, 1997*, pp. 201–4.
42 Soutou, *L'Alliance incertaine*, pp. 277–80.
43 Note from 5 January 1965, MAE, carton 1931.
44 Telegram to the French embassy in Moscow from 8 January 1965, MAE, carton 1931.
45 Note from 25 January 1965, MAE, carton 1931.
46 *Discours et messages*, vol. IV, pp. 338–42.
47 Hervé Alphand, *L'étonnement d'être*, Paris: Fayard, 1977, p. 445.
48 Different notes, MAE, carton 1931.
49 *Discours et messages*, vol. IV, pp. 348–9.
50 Two notes of the Eastern Europe department, 20 April 1965, MAE, carton 1932.
51 Notes from 17 and 22 February, MAE, carton 1932.
52 Transcript in MAE, carton 1932.
53 Different documents in MAE, carton 1932, and transcript of a talk between the Political Director Lucet and German diplomats in Bonn on 3 May, MAE, carton 1932.
54 Note from 20 April, 'L'URRS, l'Allemagne et la sécurité européenne', MAE, carton 1932.
55 The transcripts of his talks with Gromyko on 29 October, with Kosygin on 31 October, with Brezhnev on 1 November are to be found in MAE, carton 1933.
56 MAE carton 1933.
57 Note from the Eastern Europe Department, 16 December 1965, MAE, carton 1933.
58 De Gaulle explained his views to a Cabinet committee on 4 February 1966, Charles de Gaulle, *Lettres, Notes et Carnets 1964–1966*, Paris: Plon, 1987, pp. 246 ff.
59 *Discours et messages*, V, pp. 101–2.
60 See *La France et l'OTAN 1949–1996*, Maurice Vaïsse, Pierre Mélandri and Frédéric Bozo (eds), Brussels: Complexe, 1996.
61 Georges-Henri Soutou, *L'Alliance incertaine*, pp. 287 ss.
62 *Lettres, Notes et Carnets 1964–1966*, pp. 295–6.
63 Notes from 25 May, 1 June and 10 June, and note without date, 'Réactions de l'URSS et des pays de l'Est aux décisions françaises concernant l'OTAN', Direction des affaires politiques, MAE, carton 2672.
64 Note from 26 May, MAE, carton 2672.
65 Olivier Wormser, 'L'occupation de la Tchécoslovaquie vue de Moscou', *Revue des Deux Mondes*, 1978, pp. 590–605 and 631–45.
66 Transcript in MAE, carton 2672.
67 Pierre Maillard, *De Gaulle et l'Allemagne*, Paris: Plon, 1990, p. 241. For de Gaulle's views in 1944–45 see Soutou, 'Le général de Gaulle et l'URSS, 1943–1945'.
68 Mémoire de Maîtrise under my supervision by Wanig Neveu, 'La politique de la RFA vis-à-vis de l'URSS de 1966 à 1969 vue par les responsables français', September 2001.

69 See a very interesting CIA report, 'France, the USSR and European Security', 20 May 1966, Johnson Library, National Security File, France.
70 E. Weit, *Dans l'ombre de Gomulka*, Paris: Laffont, 1971, p. 188.
71 Isabelle Renaud, 'Le voyage du général de Gaulle en Pologne en 1967', Mémoire de Maîtrise under my supervision in 1999, from French and Polish sources.
72 Press conference of 9 September, *Discours et messages*, V, pp. 332–5. See also Wormser, then ambassador to Moscow, 'L'occupation de la Tchécoslovaquie vue de Moscou'.
73 Neveu, 'La politique de la RFA vis-à-vis de l'URSS de 1966 à 1969 vue par les responsables français'.
74 Michel Debré, *Mémoires*, Paris: Albin Michel, 1993, vol. IV, pp. 260–1.

11

Khrushchev: Contemporary Perspectives in the Western Press

Elena Dundovich

A Hollywood le chef du Kremlin fournit lui-même le spectacle ... Tout est arrivé en effet, y compris l'étonnant spectacle de Shirley McLaine et des quinze autres girls lancées dans un 'can-can' endiablé, levant haut leurs jupes et montrant leurs dessous blancs et noirs à son excellence Nikita Khrouchtchev ... Le premier ministre soviétique ne paraissait pas souffrir de la situation ... Quel chemin parcouru depuis les jours difficiles dans les champs, dans la mine, durant la révolution bolchevique, les purges, le stalinisme, pour aboutir aux froufrous des danseuses d'un monde inconnu et hostile! (*Le Monde*, 22 September 1959).

In the two most recently published essays on Nikita Khrushchev (including the only one up till now based on new findings from Russian archives), F. Shakhnazarov and P. Reddaway[1] take opposing viewpoints when reflecting on the only two Soviet leaders who are generally presumed to have been reformers: Nikita Khrushchev and Mikhail Gorbachev. In the reformist intentions of each leader, the two historians find a starting point for comparing their differences and similarities.

Reform is indeed a central issue when approaching or debating a figure such as Khrushchev. The discussion is between those who accuse him of having missed or rejected an opportunity for a more radical transformation of the Soviet system and those who praise his efforts to reform the old Stalinist system in both foreign and domestic policy.[2] Often enough, and especially in the absence of documentary evidence, interpretation may transcend reality to the point of myth-making. Roy Medvedev once wrote that the process of de-Stalinization and freedom from the 'Gulag' were enough to justify any other mistake Khrushchev might have made.[3] Conversely, the latest historical considerations, which are based on new findings in the former Soviet archives, have expanded our horizons concerning Soviet history in the 1950s, redefining some of the key moments in Khrushchev's advocacy of reforms. For example, we now know that de-Stalinization was not his own personal initiative and that, after 1956, he welcomed a return to old repressive methods in order to contain a dangerous and unpredictable reaction in Soviet society to the beginnings of liberalization following the Twentieth Party Congress.[4]

The political and literary aura that has formed around that congress was enough to make Khrushchev the iconoclast of the Stalinist cult and the innovator in establishing a new era in international relations. The Cuban missile crisis sanctified his persona in the eyes of his supporters. Thanks to his temperance and openness to compromise, the world had been saved from catastrophe, but is that enough to provide substance to the Khrushchev myth? If so, on what basis? How did the myth overcome moments of crisis, and how did it survive over time?

Contrary to the Stalin myth, there is no single and complete answer about the one surrounding his successor. For example, Paul Hollander, who considers 'political pilgrimage' by Westerners to the Soviet Union one of the most effective ways by which the prestige of the USSR and of Stalin grew in the West, claims that following the Hungarian uprising in 1956, such journeys became fewer and fewer, revealing a clear disinterest in the Soviet Union and its allies.[5] The myths of the October Revolution and the anti-fascist struggle, which had both given stature to Stalin, gradually faded away over the years. In the 1950s, economic recovery in Europe, first and foremost in West Germany, belied the Marxist forecast of the collapse of the capitalist system. In contrast, the economic crisis which began in 1929 had highlighted the success of the economic processes of modernization in the USSR during the 1930s. Just as post-1945 pride in the victories of the Red Army had healed the wounds inflicted by both the Great Terror and the pact with Germany (and had once again united the people around their leader), so the economic crisis emerging in the 1950s transformed that pride into a mere relic of the past.[6]

But Khrushchev had to deal with more than just a diverse domestic policy. Stalin, 'laconic' as a god, had observed an international scene dominated by a handful of traditional players. Khrushchev, 'endlessly loquacious',[7] was forced to keep up with the challenges of a new era of rapidly expanding technological and scientific developments, the appearance of new players on the international stage, and the role of the mass media – a completely new phenomenon making its first appearance during the 1950s – and its influence on public opinion.

Building an Image: Khrushchev and the Mass Media

One of the key issues which remains unclear in the personal and political history of this Soviet leader is his concept of mass media and the importance he may have attributed to it. There are, however, numerous clues that allow preliminary observations, provisional as they may be.[8] For example, from the very beginning of his political career, when between 1953 and 1954 he was only a 'political name', he had readily understood the importance of an 'image' in international relations. His own son Sergei, in one of his last indirect accounts, remembers how embarrassed Khrushchev was when he arrived in Geneva in July of 1955:

> Until the day he died, he never forgot how humiliated he felt when the delegation's modest two-engine IL-14 landed. It looked like an insect next to the planes that delivered … Eisenhower, … Eden, … Faure.[9]

His presence and his obstinacy in drawing attention to himself are expressions not only of his exuberant albeit unpredictable personality but also of his conscious acknowledgement of the importance of projecting a personal image. This consciousness grew parallel to his status as a leader and international statesman. And the attention paid to him by the Western mass media and especially the press in the early 1950s grew as well. In this sense, three phases in Khrushchev's political career can be identified, each embodied by a single key episode recorded in the Western press and indicative of the relationship between this Soviet leader and the mass media at the time: his rise to power between 1953 and 1957; the years of power, 1958 to 1961; and his downfall from 1962 until he resigned in October 1964.

In each of these phases, Khrushchev built up his public image in different ways but always relied on 'visibility', a tactic very far removed from Stalin's custom. While struggling for power during 1955 and 1956, his trip to Belgrade offered him a chance to appear before the international public for the first time. In effect, little was known about him, even though he had played a part in Stalin's entourage for years and had held key roles at the very heart of the Stalinist regime.[10] At the time of Stalin's death and in the months immediately following, the European media ascribed to him very little importance.[11] In that meeting with Tito in Belgrade, it was also the case that the European press did not afford him a place of honour. No one could have imagined at that time the political influence Khrushchev would have. Although upon his arrival at the Belgrade airport, the future leader recited a Soviet 'mea culpa' for Lavrenti Beria's guilt, this was not bound to be recognized as indicating any important position held by Khrushchev within Soviet leadership.[12] In journalists' reports,[13] his name was always accompanied by that of Nikolai Bulganin,[14] who signed the Soviet–Yugoslav Treaty with Tito, while 'Mr. Khrushchev, in his eternal black suit, sporting a gray tie with odd spiral patterns, had his elbows on the table'.[15] On this occasion, only the correspondent of the Italian journal *Il Corriere della Sera*, the well-known and trenchant Indro Montanelli, focused on him as a ridiculous figure in this close-up: 'Khrushchev's whole attitude yesterday evening was marked by a deference that bordered upon humiliation and flattery. In front of the imposing marshal, highly decorated and imperturbable, who smoked a cigarette in a long holder, chubby little Khrushchev, shambling about with his light-coloured jacket unbuttoned, made a miserable impression'.[16]

Khrushchev's success was no greater in Geneva, where reporters at the conference were no more indulgent than they had been before. The most important European newspapers dedicated long articles to the meeting between Eisenhower and the old Marshal Georgi Zhukov,[17] and European journalists concentrated their attention mostly on the figure of Bulganin, who then held the position of prime minister and who was unanimously considered by all to be the true spokesman for Soviet interests at the conference.[18] Of Khrushchev, however, there were very few traces to be found in the press,[19] aside from the articles in *Il Corriere della Sera* once again, the only one among the newspapers to recognize some importance in his awkwardness:

> Khrushchev, dressed in grey-green with a horrible brown tie, appeared very small and round in the vast square.[20]

> The heads of state and their ministers ... pose smiling in front of the jungle of photographers and cameramen. Edgar Faure has Bulganin to his right and Molotov to his left. Khrushchev springs out suddenly from between Eden and Foster Dulles and, on his big pale-pink face, anxious in his manoeuvre of drawing near, a huge smile explodes, pierced by two malicious green eyes. With Khrushchev happy, the guests ... are invited to the table.[21]

It is probable that Nikita was not particularly worried about the situation. It was more important for him just to be there; his battle had been won when a few months earlier, despite the opposition of Molotov, Bulganin and Zhukov, he was appointed to the Geneva delegation. As his son Sergei recalls, Khrushchev's name was not on the list of delegates for the reason (or excuse) that he was only the first secretary to the Central Committee of the party and did not hold an official position in the government.[22]

It was the renowned secret speech delivered during the Twentieth Party Congress of the Politburo that definitively brought him into the international limelight. His attacks on Stalin's crimes, however, had much greater effects in his own country and in the general communist sphere: for example, the reactions of the French and Italian communists and the resistance from the Chinese Communist Party. It had less impact on the moderate European press, which had been very cautious with its judgments. The conclusions reached by the Twentieth Congress[23] and the following process of so-called de-Stalinization caused great amazement but did not raise too many hopes.[24] With these few lines, *Il Corriere della Sera* commented sententiously on the clamour that historians later made about news of Stalin's crimes:

> One finds no satisfactory answer to the question formulated after Khrushchev's statement by the universal public conscience: Why in the world have Stalin's successors waited for the death of the dictator to denounce so many errors? ... [They] were accomplices and collaborators in that interminable sequence of errors and depravity. With what authority,

with what ascendancy, do these accomplices set themselves up today as judges and executioners?[25]

From the beginning, Khrushchev's reputation as a reformer, despite the inevitable curiosity he aroused, was not regarded as well-founded. In the years of his rise to power and purging of adversaries (from about 1953 to 1958), European public opinion received via the press the slightly faded image of a leader who, although no longer clad in the diabolical vestments of Stalin, neither represented a new Soviet political direction[26] nor signified profound changes on the international political scene.[27] If Khrushchev had had the intention of presenting to the world the image of a leader totally different from Stalin, he obviously succeeded. At the time of the Geneva conference, for example, no journalist missed the delicious opportunity to sketch the Soviet troika that travelled carefree in luxurious convertible automobiles. *Le Monde* wrote, for example:

> The delegation from Moscow ... settled into a dozen cars ... more or less registered in the USSR, with little curtains in the back to keep dignitaries hidden from indiscreet gazes. But these precautions perhaps seemed superfluous to Mr Khrushchev and his two marshals since a little later we were able to see them driving along in a convertible.[28]

As Georges-Henri Soutou emphasizes, 'the extravagant personality of Khrushchev ... disrupted the conventional network inside the Soviet leadership'.[29] Who would have been able to picture Khrushchev's terrifying predecessor in a similarly futile and foppish circumstance? But – and this remains to be proved – if Khrushchev had had the intention of promoting on the international scene not so much a diplomacy different from that of the past, but, rather, a new Soviet Union in a period of thaw and as a guarantor of peace, he had failed. Reading the major Western European newspapers from the 1950s, one has the impression that the mythologizing of Khrushchev, symbol of a new era, was due much more to later memoirs and historiography than to any feeling or judgment by his contemporaries. In fact, there is no way it could have been any different. As Vladislav Zhubok and Constantine Pleshchakov wrote in their book *Inside the Kremlin's Cold War*, because of Khrushchev's Communist orientation, the ideological and revolutionary dimension was of basic importance for him. Khrushchev strongly believed in the 'revolutionary–imperial' paradigm. He simply tried to attune it to the new international situation.[30] Because of this perception, the invasion of Hungary obviously provoked harsh negative criticism[31] but not particular disappointment:[32] None of the reporters writing on the subject at that time was particularly surprised by the arrival of Soviet tanks in Budapest.

Although in the mid-1950s the press represented mass communication *par excellence*, things began to change slowly but radically with the introduction of television into European homes. This transformation coincided with the Khrushchev years, and its initial effects became evident when the Soviet leader decided to take his first trip to the USA in September of 1959. Even here, it is not clear whether or how the Soviet masters of ceremonies had actually prepared for that trip nor is it clear whether Khrushchev had truly planned to take advantage of television coverage. Although not comprehensively documented, some parts of the trip are revealing: his decision, for example, to travel with his family and allow his wife the role of first lady and his decision to visit cities and farms in the USA prior to meeting Eisenhower at Camp David. From a highly semiotic point of view, his trip to the United States in 1959 was a triumph especially after the first few days.[33] It certainly was successful from the point of view of mediation, if not of content. Preceded, not accidentally, by the launching of the first Soviet rocket to the moon,[34] the reception the Americans gave him was not particularly warm at the start. As French correspondent and future Cold War historian André Fontaine remarked:

> The last gestures of the Soviet prime minister had certainly not dispelled the mental reservations of the public on the other side of the Atlantic towards a person that, until recently, they had seen as a reincarnation of the devil. The gift to President Eisenhower of a copy of the Soviet emblem sent to the moon was in questionable taste, and Mr 'K.' in his speech at the airport, insisted too much on Soviet accomplishments in order not to aggravate, in some way, American self-esteem.[35]

The atmosphere improved little by little while the European press dwelt at great length on his suits, the First Lady[36] and her first press conference[37] as well as their family. Khrushchev's image became more and more familiar and as *Le Monde* observed:

> No one was converted to communism, but Mr Khrushchev seemed to be making small amounts of progress in his attempt to seduce. The public ... is getting used to seeing him in newspapers or on television screens. A familiar enemy is less frightening.[38]

But in the end, exactly as on all the other occasions in which history had set Khrushchev in the international spotlight and in front of the photographers, political judgment about basic Soviet choices remained unchanged in this case too.[39] In the lead article of 28 September 1959, *Le Monde* noted:

> Once again, an international meeting upon which general attention has been concentrated for days concludes with a press release that does not have any importance ... None of its results seem spectacular. If the ice has begun to melt between the two great nations, it is happening very slowly.[40]

With greater caution, *The Times* also noted that 'Mr. Khrushchev seems to have left the image of a man who genuinely wants peace, but also of one who is very confident and is unshakably convinced that history is on his side ... When he boasted so often of the eventual triumph of communism, he must have left most of his audiences either perplexed or suspicious about the means'.[41]

Despite enthusiasm displayed this time too by the moderate European press, not much had changed. And no one was surprised when the Soviet leader broke up a summit in Paris in May of 1960[42] or when he pounded his yellow shoes on the table of the United Nations. Strangely enough, that episode was barely covered in the papers at the time, with no more than a few lines dedicated to it.[43]

The Cuban crisis[44] and the signing of the 1963 Nuclear Test-Ban Treaty were the events that, for the last time, put Khrushchev in the headlines of newspapers worldwide. Now, however, the press changed its tune: the determination first to avoid a nuclear war with the USA[45] and the direct negotiation on nuclear weapons afterward redefined the authority of the Soviet leader. During the time of the Moscow Treaty (an event obviously less dramatic[46] than the first one) little gossip and few allusions were generated by the eccentric behaviour that had been reported in articles of the previous years. It was as if, using Georges Soutou's words, the press had understood some-how that, after Cuba, Khrushchev would never be the same:

> I think that from 1963 (this could be the reason for his downfall) his idea of peaceful co-existence (at first ambiguous) was more profound, not only tactically, but strategically. The historical development of the revolutionary process would continue to be an objective, but it would depend more and more on the domestic evolution of the Western world and less on the international role of the USSR.[47]

Shortly afterwards, Nikita Khrushchev was obliged to retire. The news was barely covered by the European press cited here. But, as often occurs, it was only after 14 October 1964 that Europeans realized to what extent Nikky[48] might have been a champion of peace. It was *The Times,* a newspaper which had praised him very little in the previous decade, that dedicated numerous articles to him in 1964. On 16 October, this British paper commented on the ousting of the Soviet leader: 'His pursuit of relaxation between the two great camps was his greatest – and most substantial work.'[49] And on the following day:

> Mr. Khrushchev brought the tactics of a flamboyant showman to the personal diplomacy that characterized his conduct of Soviet foreign affairs. He traveled widely abroad and received many of the world's statesmen in Moscow ... Mr. Khrushchev has made a deep impression at home and abroad in the eleven years since Stalin's death permitted him to enter the limelight.[50]

But the time for myth-making had already passed. The Western press had always been almost cold toward him. In this sense, over the following years, some intellectuals, commentators and historians sought to magnify this image of a new man and create the myth of Khrushchev as symbol of peace. European public opinion received and perhaps embraced that stereotype in a much more critical way. In the judgment of many journalists of his time, Khrushchev was in fact regarded as a great mass communicator rather than a real reformer.

NOTES

1 'Khrushchev and Gorbachev: A Russian View' and 'Khrushchev and Gorbachev: An American view', in William Taubman, Sergei Khrushchev and Abbott Gleason (eds), *Nikita Khrushchev*, New Haven, CT, and London: Yale University Press, 2000, pp. 301–20, 321–33.

2 Khrushchev is probably the most discussed of the Soviet leaders, beginning with his rise to power. In the late 1950s and particularly in the following decade, three biographies and numerous publications centred around Soviet history under Khrushchev were published in the West. Among those see: Lazar Pistrak, *The Grand Tactician: Krushchev's Rise to Power*, New York: Praeger, 1961; Edward Crankshaw, *Khrushchev: A Career*, New York: Viking Press, 1966; Mark Frankland, *Khrushchev*, New York: Stein & Day, 1967; Myron Rush, *The Rise of Khrushchev*, Washington, DC: Public Affairs Press, 1958; Robert Conquest, *Power and Policy in the USSR: The Study of Soviet Dynastics*, New York: St Martin's Press, 1961; Carl Linden, *Khrushchev and the Soviet Leadership*, Baltimore, MD: Johns Hopkins Press, 1966; Michel Tatu, *Power in the Kremlin: From Khrushchev to Kosygin*, New York: Viking Press, 1969; Priscilla Johnson, *Khrushchev and the Arts: The Politics of Soviet Culture 1962–1964*, Cambridge, MA: MIT Press, 1965; Roman Kolkowicz, *The Soviet Military and the Communist Party*, Princeton, NJ: Princeton University Press, 1967; Myron Rush and Arnold L. Horelick, *Strategic Power and Soviet Foreign Policy*, Chicago, IL: University of Chicago Press, 1966; Sidney Ploss, *Conflict and Decision-Making in Soviet Russia: A Study of Agricultural Policy, 1953–1964*, Princeton, NJ: Princeton University Press, 1965; William Hyland and Richard Wallace, *The Fall of Khrushchev*, London: Pitman, 1970; A. Brumberg (ed.), *Russia under Khrushchev: An Anthology from Problems of Communism*, New York: Praeger, 1962; Alexander Werth, *Russia Under Khrushchev*, New York: Hill & Wang, 1962; Roy A. Medvedev and Zhores A. Medvedev, *Khrushchev: The Years in Power*, New York: Columbia University Press, 1976; George W. Breslauer, *Khrushchev and Brezhnev as Leaders: Building Authority in Soviet Politics*, Boston, MA: Allen & Unwin, 1982.

3 Roy A. Medvedev, *Khrushchev*, Oxford: Blackwell, 1982, p. 260.

4 On this point, see the different opinion of Elena Zubkova, 'The Rivalry with Malenkov', pp. 82–3, and Oleg V. Naumov, 'Repression and Rehabilitation', p. 101 in Taubman, Krushchev and Gleason (eds), *Nikita Krushchev*. Certainty about Khrushchev's central role in de-Stalinization is the hallmark of the excessively romanticized volume by Roman Brackman, *The Secret File of Joseph Stalin*, London: Frank Cass, 2001, pp. 404ff.

5 Paul Hollander, *Pellegrinaggi politici: intellettuali occidentali in Unione Sovietica, Cina e Cuba*, Bologna, 1988, p. 15.

6 On the myth of the USSR, see Marcello Flores and Francesca Gori (eds), *Il mito dell'URSS*, Milan, 1990 and the two articles of Giorgio Petracchi, 'L'immagine della

rivoluzione sovietica in Italia, 1917–1920' and Marcello Flores, 'Il mito dell'URSS nel secondo dopoguerra', in Pier Paolo D'Attorre (ed.), *Nemici per la pelle: Sogno americano e mito sovietico nell'Italia contemporanea*, Milan, 1991.

7 Taubman, Khrushchev and Gleason (eds), *Nikita Khrushchev*, p. 1.

8 See Georges-Henri Soutou, *La Guerre de Cinquante Ans: Les relations Est–Ouest, 1943–1990*, Paris: Fayard, 2001, p. 325.

9 Sergei Khrushchev, *Nikita Khrushchev: Creation of a Superpower*, University Park, PA: Pennsylvania State University Press, 2000, p. 83. Some reporters at the conference impassively highlight his unease and in general, as the Soviet troika looked provincial, lost, and, inelegant in Geneva: 'They are awkward in their unlikely costumes – noted the French journalists – and the fault for this lies, evidently, in the fact that the profession of tailor was done away with in the first days of the Soviet regime … The day that Moscow learns how to make a pair of trousers or a suit again, then we will be able to say without a doubt that everything has returned to normal.' *Le Monde*, 'Le déjeuner Eisenhower–Joukov est l'événement du jour', 21 July 1955.

10 On the years before 1953, see William J. Tompson, *Khrushchev: A Political Life*, New York: St Martin's Press, 1995, pp. 1–130.

11 No articles were published by *Corriere della Sera*, *Le Monde* or *The Times* about Khrushchev when Stalin died or when, in September 1953, he was elected the Party's Central Committee Secretary. Other men under the dictator were much more famous in Europe than Khrushchev – Molotov, for example, or Zhukov, the great Soviet war hero.

12 'C'est la faute à Beria', *Le Monde*, 28 May 1955; J. Schwoebel, 'Les déclarations de M. Khrouchtchev ont provoqué à Belgrade un certain mécontentement', *Le Monde*, 29 May 1955; J. Schwoebel, 'Les entretiens russo-yugoslaves se poursuivent dans l'île de Brioni', *Le Monde*, 31 May 1955; 'Mr. Khrushchev', *The Times*, 27 May 1955; Indro Montanelli, 'Sorprendenti dichiarazioni di Kruscev all'arrivo all'aeroporto di Belgrado', *Il Corriere della Sera*, 27 May 1955.

13 They really saw very little of the closed-door meetings between the Soviets and the Yugoslavs, which dismayed all the foreign reporters present in Belgrade, J. Schwoebel, 'La déclaration de Belgrade s'en tiendra a des formules très générales', *Le Monde*, 3 June 1955; 'Irritation over Mr Khrushchev', *The Times*, 28 May 1955.

14 J. Schwoebel, 'Le voyage des dirigeants soviétiques en Yougoslavie touche à sa fin', *Le Monde*, 2 June 1955; 'End of Belgrade Discussions', *The Times*, 2 June 1955; Piero Ottone, 'La rinnovata amicizia con Mosca rafforzerà la neutralità di Tito', *Il Corriere della Sera*, 2 June 1955.

15 J. Schwoebel, 'Les dirigeants soviétiques sont arrivés a Sofia', *Le Monde*, 4 June 1955; 'Marshal Bulganin Signs for Russia', *The Times*, 3 June 1955.

16 Indro Montanelli, 'La clamorosa ritrattazione di Kruscev ha colto Tito completamente di sorpresa', *Il Corriere della Sera*, 28 May 1955. And still in the same tone a few days later: 'Khrushchev … head sunk between his shoulders and upper torso thrust a bit forward. From under his little dark gray shapeless jacket, the arms of which swallowed his hands to half-way down his fingers, emerged the wrinkled collar of his white shirt, a bit worn at the edges, and a light tie strangled into a tight knot … Khrushchev's little eyes looked like a blind mole's', 'Tito e Kruscev (in muto)', *Il Corriere della Sera*, 31 May 1955.

17 André Fontaine, H. Pierre, 'Le déjeuner Eisenhower–Joukov est l'événement du jour', *Le Monde*, 21 July 1955; V. Roberti, 'Eisenhower invita a colazione il "compagno d'armi" Zukov', *Il Corriere della Sera*, 21 July 1955.

18 'Heads of Government meet To-day', *The Times*, 18 July 1955; L. Barzini, 'Pacato inizio del grande dialogo fra Est e Ovest', *Il Corriere della Sera*, 19 July 1955.

19 'L'Espoir', *Le Monde*, 19 July 1955; 'Préséance soviétique', *Le Monde*, 22 July 1955.

20 V. Roberti, 'I quattro grandi riuniti a Ginevra', *Il Corriere della Sera*, 18 July 1955.

21 V. Roberti, 'Kruscev fra i delegati russi ostenta la maggiore affidabilità', *Il Corriere della Sera*, 20 July 1955; 'Khrushchev – as reported two days later by an Italian journalist – is described as an uncouth but intelligent man, with the political instinct of a democratic leader, that is, someone who must be aware of public opinion. He rides around Geneva in his free time like a tourist straight out of a mining camp, who wants to see and understand everything.' L. Barzini, 'I Russi hanno paura di ripetere gli errori commessi da Stalin', *Il Corriere della Sera*, 22 July 1955.

22 He was eventually sent to Geneva as a member of the Soviet Supreme Presidium, that is, as a representative of the USSR's highest legislative branch, in Sergei Khrushchev, *Nikita Khrushchev*, p. 81. Khrushchev himself wrote about this event in Strobe Talbott and Edward Crankshaw (eds), *Krushchev Remembers*, London: Deutsch, 1971.

23 'L'optimisme de M. Khrouchtchev', *Le Monde*, 16 February 1956; 'Retour à Lenine', *Le Monde*, 21 February 1956; 'Moscow critics of Stalin', *The Times*, 20 February 1956; 'Soviet Party Leadership', *The Times*, 27 February 1956; Piero Ottone, 'Il Congresso del PC sovietico condanna i metodi dello stalinismo', *Il Corriere della Sera*, 18 February 1956; D. Bartoli, 'Sospetti inglesi sui fini della sconfessione di Stalin', *Il Corriere della Sera*, 21 February 1956.

24 'Malgré le rapport', *Le Monde*, 19 June 1956.

25 'Un'ombra incomoda', *Il Corriere della Sera*, 17 June 1956. The same opinion was expressed by Camillo Caleffi in the article 'Stalin non fu un genio strategico ma Kruscev è un po' troppo disinvolto', *Il Corriere della Sera*, 29 June 1956; more optimistic and in favour of 'Khrushchev the innovator' were articles published during those days in *Il Corriere della Sera* by the Italian Moscow correspondent, Piero Ottone, see, for example: 'Dialoghi con la folla nell'URSS', 17 June 1956, 'Distrutta dal rapporto di Kruscev "l'unità monolitica" dei tempi staliniani', 22 June 1956, and 'Anche Bela Kuhn riabilitato in odio al "culto dell'individuo"', 22 February 1956.

26 M. Caputo, 'La sostituzione di Kruscev ritenuta imminente a Bonn', *Il Corriere della Sera*, 10 November 1956; V. Roberti, 'Molotov ritorna in primo piano come ministro del Controllo di Stato', *Il Corriere della Sera*, 22 November 1956; P. Ottone, 'Molotov potrà far cadere Kruscev ma difficilmente sarà l'uomo di domani', *Il Corriere della Sera*, 23 November 1956; P. Gentile, 'Disorientamento comunista', *Il Corriere della Sera*, 9 November 1956; 'In two Minds?', *The Times*, 19 November 1956; 'Mr. Molotov's New Post', *The Times*, 23 November 1956.

27 A laconic comment by the director of *Le Monde* on the results of the Geneva Conference: 'The conference closes just as we expected: euphoria, reconciliation, embraces, all that is in contrast with the reality of the final outcome which leaves unsolved the great problems of today', 'Armistice', 26 July 1955; about this, see also 'First Day', *The Times*, 19 July 1955, and also 'Leaders' Main Achievement', value of personal contacts', 25 July 1955; and also the two articles of L. Barzini, and A. Guerriero, 'La formale cordialità russa si alterna con la sostanziale rigidezza', *Il Corriere della Sera*, 23 July 1955, and 'Ginevra', *Il Corriere della Sera*, 26 July 1955.

28 'Le président Eisenhower a recueilli les acclamations les plus nourries', *Le Monde*, 19 July 1955; J. Schwoebel, 'Le Maréchal Tito n'a pas repondu aux excuses de M. Khrouchtchev', *Le Monde*, 28 May 1955; J. Schwoebel, 'Les conversations de Brioni ont porté sur l'avenir des relations russo-yougoslaves', *Le Monde*, 1 June 1955.

29 Soutou, *La Guerre de Cinquante Ans*, p. 317.

30 Vladislav Zhubok and Constantine Pleshakov, *Inside the Kremlin's Cold War*, Cambridge, MA: Harvard University Press, 1996.

31 'Repression', *The Times*, 5 November 1956; 'No Liberty', *The Times*, 8 November 1956.

32 André Fontaine, 'Retour au stalinisme?', *Le Monde*, 29 November 1956; 'Due linguaggi' and 'Censurate dalla "Pravda" le escandescenze di Kruscev', *Il Corriere della Sera*, 19 November 1956.

33 Walter L. Hixson, *Parting the Curtain*, New York: St Martin's Press, 1997, pp. 215–19.

34 'Dépasser la compétition', *Le Monde*, 15 September 1959.

35 André Fontaine, 'M. Khrouchtchev se soumet à l'épreuve traditionnelle du déjeuner au National Press Club', and by the same author 'Une foule immense et silencieuse a regardé passer les deux maîtres du monde', *Il Corriere della Sera*, 19 September 1955.

36 'Mr. Khrushchev to make a Disarmament Proposal', *The Times*, 17 September 1959.

37 H. Pierre, 'Les réussites russes sont en train de retourner l'opinion publique américaine', *Le Monde*, 15 September 1959; 'Nina Petrovna conquiert l'Amérique', *Le Monde*, 18 September 1959; 'La Conferenza stampa della Signora Kruscev', *Il Corriere della Sera*, 26 September 1959.

38 H. Pierre, 'La conviction et le tempérament combatif du leader russe ont impressionné les téléspectateurs américains', *Le Monde*, 18 September 1959. And also by the same journalist, 'Le chef du Kremlin est rentré à Washington', 26 September 1959. On this aspect, see also 'Mr. Khrushchev in Sunnier Mood', *The Times*, 23 September 1959; 'Mr. Khrushchev spends Day on Iowa Farms', *The Times*, 24 September 1959 and 'Mr. Khrushchev at Strike-Bound Pittsburgh', *The Times*, 25 September 1959.

39 H. Pierre, 'Le Voyage du chef du Kremlin n'a donné jusqu'à présent aucun résultat positif', *Le Monde*, 20 September 1959; 'L'Occident réserve un accueil mitigé aux dernières propositions russes de désarmement', *Le Monde*, 20 September 1959; H. Pierre, 'La visite a réveillé les Américaines', *Le Monde*, 22 September 1959; H. Pierre, 'Découverte de l'adversaire', *Le Monde*, 23 September 1959; H. Pierre, 'M. Khrouchtchev se rend au Camp David', *Le Monde*, 26 September 1959; 'Le président Eisenhower et M. Khrouchtchev confèrent au Camp David', *Le Monde*, 27 September 1959; 'Disarming Total and Complete', *The Times*, 19 September 1959 and 'Rough Going', *The Times*, 20 September 1959.

40 'La discussione continue', *Le Monde*, 29 September 1959.

41 'After the Barn-storming', *The Times*, 26 September 1959.

42 Behind the astounding and unexpected Soviet decision, according to *The Times*, were conceivable political considerations: the decision against signing an agreement with the outgoing President Eisenhower; pressure from the Politburo and the international communist community for an act of determination *vis-à-vis* the US; hope to split the United States and its allies, many of which had already condemned the reconnaissance aircraft flights over Soviet territory, 'Offensive', 17 May 1960, cf. also 'Mr Khrushchev Refuses to Give Way' and 'On the Brink', 18 May 1960. The same interpretation of the event is also in 'Le sens d'un éclat', *Le Monde*, 18 May 1960.

43 'Session at UN Adjourned in Uproar', *The Times*, 13 September 1960; André Fontaine, 'M. 'K' brandit son soulier', *Le Monde*, 14 October 1960.

44 On the role of Khrushchev during the crisis, see the volume by Alexsandr Fursenko and Timothy Naftali, *One Hell of a Gamble*, New York: Norton, 1997, pp. 158–315.

45 The moderate media reacted differently towards the Caribbean crisis. *The Times* gave unsensational, detached coverage of the events in a clear analysis of the international context and the reasons the Soviets may have had for stirring up a crisis: see, for example, the articles 'Calling a Halt', 24 October 1962, 'Russian Probing', 25 October 1962, 'Terms for Talk', 26 October 1962. On 29 October 1962, the British paper gave a clear view of the end of the tensions that had brought humanity to the brink of a third world war: 'Whatever else he wanted out of Cuba it is certain that Mr. Khrushchev did not want nuclear war. Faced with that risk, he has swung right round and ordered a withdrawal. The swing is so sudden – and apparently so complete – that it almost looks as though two schools, the "hards" and the "moderates", were alternating in Moscow

... The truth is more likely to be that there was a duality in the agreed Cuban policy from the beginning. The Soviet leaders saw in it an obvious way of extending Soviet striking power and humiliating America and at the same time a means of getting talks going after a period of tension. Both motives would be in Mr Khrushchev's mind, each to be used as the need arose. Now, when the first objective has failed in face of American determination, he plays the second – getting talks going – for all he is worth. Being a Russian, he does not use half measures ... In a sense it is Nikita Sergeyevich asserting himself against Mr Khrushchev, the prudent peasant', 'Withdrawal', 29 October 1962. *Le Monde*, on the contrary, heavily criticized the Americans, 'who find perfectly normal that a state such as Turkey, situated on the Soviet border, places missile launch pads threatening the entire basin of the Donets, [but] contests the USSR's right to make a similar agreement for installations in Cuba', 'Négocier plutôt que renchérir', 24 October 1962. But following the crisis, which in view of the French press had been cut surprisingly short, all attention was once again drawn to Khrushchev: 'We still need to find out', states an article on 30 October, 'what really happened at the Kremlin in those last few days and what triggered Mr Khrushchev's "about-face", what conditions were set, and how that has affected his reputation', 'Un dénouement inespéré', 30 October 1962. The Italian journal *Il Corriere della Sera* reported similar doubts in articles by A. Guerriero, 'Perché ha ceduto' and Arrigo Levi, 'Manovra non riuscita', 29 October 1962. Very interesting on this aspect too is the unsigned article 'Kruscev aveva scelto Cuba come banco di prova per Berlino', 31 October 1962.

46 See *The Times* articles 'Test Ban Agreement to be Signed Today', 5 August 1963, 'Three Ministers sign Test Ban Treaty in Moscow', 6 August 1963, and 'Cold War Economics', 7 August 1963. And also Michel Tatu, 'Le traité sur l'arrêt des expériences nucléaires a été signé au Kremlin', *Le Monde*, 6 August 1963, and V. Roberti, 'Firmato a Mosca il Trattato nucleare', 6 August 1963, and 'Si cercano a Mosca vie per altre intese', 7 August 1963, *Il Corriere della Sera*.

47 Soutou, *La Guerre de Cinquante Ans*, p. 319. Intriguing, too, is the change in Italian public opinion where, after Cuba, Khrushchev became popular, put in the ranks of Kennedy and Pope John, the Saviour of peace in the world. When he resigned, the *Corriere della Sera*, as compared to *Le Monde* or *The Times*, dedicated the most space to this leader. Among others, Piero Ottone, 'Kruscev sostituito da Breznev e Kossygin, Gloria e declino di Kruscev', and Enzo Bettiza, 'Breznev e Kossighin', 16 October 1964. Many articles were also written in the following days.

48 This is the nickname used for him by Americans during his travel in the USA, P. Viansson-Ponté, 'L'Amérique est en train d'admettre que le monde a changé et qu'il lui faut en tenir compte', *Le Monde*, 23 September 1959.

49 'Khrushchev Goes', *The Times*, 16 October 1964.

50 'Departure of Mr Khrushchev ends a Flamboyant Era', *The Times*, 16 October 1964.

12

The Western European Communist Parties in the Cold War, 1957–68

Marie-Pierre Rey

From the first Congresses of the Comintern in 1919–20 to the very end of the Stalinist years, the Western communist parties were used as parallel and obedient tools of Soviet diplomacy. During that time, Soviets could indeed rely on a double structure unique in the world: an official apparatus – the governmental one, the Ministry of Foreign Affairs – and an unofficial one, the communist structure which, through the Western European parties, was supposed to influence public opinion in a favourable direction and, possibly, to facilitate the establishment of communist regimes in Western Europe. In 1956 and the following years, de-Stalinization introduced new concepts into the diplomatic field, such as 'peaceful coexistence'. In this new context of de-Stalinization, do we observe essential changes in the relation between the Soviet leadership and the Western European communist parties or not? Did de-Stalinization and peaceful coexistence bring some freedom to the Western communist parties or did the Western European parties remain obedient tools of Soviet diplomacy?

To answer this question, this chapter will make use of archival sources and cite examples from the major Western parties: the Italian one and, of course, the French. With 340,000 members in 1956 and 330,000 in 1964, the French Communist Party remained an important force in French political life,[1] even if not as important as it had been at the end of the Second World War. But this chapter will also take into account the case of much smaller parties, such as Britain's Communist Party, which counted 56,000 members in 1945 and 30,000 in 1960 and which won less than a half percent of the vote.[2] This diversity will allow us to make useful comparisons and see whether the size, the authority and the political weight of the communist parties made a difference in relations with the Soviet leadership.

The chapter is divided in two parts: first, we will study the nature of the relation between the Soviet leadership and the Western communist parties; second, we will focus on the precise role which the Soviet leadership assigned to the Western communist structures during the period from 1956 to 1968.

I. The Western Communist Parties and the CPSU: Between Loyalty and Dependence

Evidence from Soviet archives and Western communist newspapers and other publications makes clear that for the period from 1956 to 1968 two concepts dominated the relationship between the Western European communist parties and the Soviet leadership: loyalty and dependence.

True Loyalty

During these years, the ideological and political bonds remained extremely strong. In April 1956, the Kominform was dissolved, but the Soviet leadership did not give up its authority in the international communist movement. On the contrary, at that time the International Department (ID) of the Central Committee of the CPSU, in charge of relations with all the non-governmental communist parties, became an essential organization, even preceding in the Soviet hierarchy the Ministry of Foreign Affairs led by Andrei Gromyko.

From June 1957 to the end of our period and beyond, the ID was led by Boris Ponomariov, a specialist in propaganda matters who had served in the Comintern from 1936 to 1943 and had then become Director of the Marx Engels Institute before heading the International Department. A few years later, Ponomariov was assisted by Vadim Zagladin who, after graduating from the Institute of International Relations, became a specialist on Western European matters and was from 1954 to 1964 a member of the editorial committee of two magazines, *Novoie Vremia* (*New Times*) and *Problemy mira i sotsializma* (*Problems of Peace and Socialism*). Throughout our period, some leaders who were members of the party apparatus but who did not belong to the International Department regularly took part in the work of the ID: for example, that is the case with Michail Suslov, head of the Culture and Propaganda Department of the Central Committee from 1946.

During the 1950s and 1960s, the ID and its main leaders developed a common communist education through many publications, all distributed in the various national languages to the different Western European communist apparatuses. These publications – *Problems of Peace and Socialism* was the most important one – aimed at giving the Western communist parties an 'official truth' on two kinds of matters: international problems and the socialist community.

This written education was reinforced by frequent official meetings between the Soviet and the Western European communist apparatuses. Whenever the CPSU held its congress or a world conference – in 1960, 1961, 1965 and 1966 – the Western communist parties staged their own congresses. When the First Secretary of the Soviet Party was visiting a Western country, as Khrushchev did Great Britain in 1956 and France in 1960, parallel meetings between Soviet and Western communist delegations were systematically organized. Of course, the most interesting and fruitful meetings were not the official ones, but rather the discreet or even secret ones.

Until the mid-1970s, the national and the regional staff of the Western European communist parties often spent one or two years at the Moscow International Party School[3] where they were given a special ideological training and education in conformity with Soviet political references and perceptions.

Ideological loyalty was also secured by permanent, frequent and secret exchanges with the Soviet ambassadors. The archives of the Soviet Ministry of Foreign Affairs show that, at the end of the 1950s and in the first half of the 1960s, the Soviet ambassadors in Paris and Rome met French and Italian communist leaders at least every two or three weeks.[4] During these meetings, the Soviet ambassador had almost no freedom and simply transmitted the instructions he had received from the ID. On this point, the testimony given by the former Soviet diplomat Nicholas Polianski is quite clear:

> The ambassador regularly received 'information' or rather 'instructions' from the Central Committee of the CP [Communist Party] to be given to the 'friends', as we called the communists in the diplomatic telegrams.
>
> This 'information' was approved during the meetings of the Politburo, which were held every Thursday. So the information was sent to the embassy every Friday evening in principle. The ambassador used to ask his collaborators to translate the text (which could sometimes amount to twenty pages) from Russian to French on Saturday and Sunday … The ambassador used to read the text word for word because he didn't have the right to change anything in the instructions of the Central Committee. Then he used to ask the opinion of his visitor, which was immediately transmitted to Moscow.[5]

The conversations dealt quite often with international questions: the Soviet leadership was taking advantage of these meetings to give the Western staff its position on sensitive matters and to define 'common attitudes' among them. During the second half of the 1950s and the first half of the 1960s, the Soviet rejection of West German rearmament and the Soviet opposition to the FRG's access to nuclear weapons were constantly at the heart of these secret meetings. The 'nature' of the EEC – that is, as an imperialistic weapon in the hands of West German and US big business – was also frequently described. Through its ambassadors, the Soviet leadership sent detailed and frequent reports to the Western communist chiefs on complex matters: during the Algerian war, for example, the Soviet Communist Party quite often addressed reports to the French communist leaders describing and explaining the Soviet strategy on the question. This would remain the case even after the end of the Algerian war. In July 1967 the Central Committee sent a report expressing the hope of bringing a 'progressive' regime to Algeria.[6]

This ideological dependence was only one aspect of a much larger dependence: It was the case that from 1956 to at least 1975[7] all Western communist parties were generously financed by the Soviets through the International Department of the Central Committee.

Financial Dependence

Financial assistance was both indirect and direct. The former[8] included subsidies to communist newspapers, holiday trips in the USSR for Western leaders and their families and invitations for delegations of Western workers who were shown the communist paradise. Throughout the decades, the process remained the same: financial decisions were discussed by the Presidium (and later by the Politburo) and, when the Presidium gave its agreement, the ID organized the payment. And there was direct financial aid as well.

The Kominform adopted the principle of direct and large-scale financing in 1947, and the structure was implemented in 1950, that is, during the Stalinist years. Officially, funds were given through an International Trade Union Fund; this fiction, maintained until 1966, was aimed at hiding the political dimension of the action. In 1966, that fiction disappeared and the fund became an International Fund to help workers' and leftist organizations. The reports produced by the International Department and presented for discussion and adoption by the Presidium give quite precise information about this direct aid.[9]

During the period from 1950 to 1968, the amounts of financial support continually increased. Expressed in 1996 constant French francs,[10] the total amount given to all non-governmental communist parties in 1958 represented three times the amount given in 1950; and, in 1968, the amount was more than six times that given in 1950 (see Table 12.1).

Table 12.1. Total of the amounts given to leftist parties and organisations through the International Trade Union Fund

Year	In current US dollars	In constant 1996 francs
1950	2,000,000	104,250,000
1954	5,000,000	222,025,000
1955	6,424,000	285,257,000
1957	6,450,000	286,412,000
1958	6,800,000	301,954,000
1959	9,000,000	361,620,000
1961	10,500,000	406,969,000
1962	11,000,000	426,349,000
1963	14,650,000	567,819,000
1964	15,750,000	610,454,000
1966	15,750,000	610,454,000
1968	16,550,000	641,461,000

The alleged international origin of the funds was supposed to express internationalist solidarity. The reality, however, was that the Eastern European Countries and Communist China played a minor role in this financing as shown in Table 12.2.

Table 12.2. Origin by country of the amounts given through the International Trade Union Fund.
(Amounts expressed in constant 1996 million francs)

	1957	1963	1966	1968
USSR	164.298	372.08	511.61	542.62
China	71.048	96.89	0	0
Bulgaria	0	13.56	13.56	13.56
Hungary	0	19.38	19.38	19.38
Poland	11.10	19.38	19.38	19.38
GDR	13.32	7.75	7.75	7.75
Romania	13.32	19.38	19.38	19.38
Czech.	13.32	19.38	19.38	19.38
Total	286.406	567.80	610.44	641.45

The amount given by the Eastern European democracies together represented only 18 per cent of the total in 1957, whereas the USSR provided 58 per cent and Communist China 25 per cent of the funds. In 1963, the Chinese Communist Party was supposed to provide 17 per cent of the total and the Soviet party 65.7 per cent. Actually in 1962,[11] however, the Chinese party stopped contributing and the CPSU began to increase its own participation. In 1966, for example, the Soviet Communist Party provided 84 per cent of the funds.[12] The distribution of the money is quite interesting (see Table 12.3).

Table 12.3. The destination of the funds: the communist parties benefiting from the aid. (Data are given in percentages)

Communist Party (CP)	1957	1966	1973
Italian CP	41.2	36.2	28.2
French CP	18.75	12.7	12.2
Finland CP	7.8	5.7	0
Austrian CP	6.25	5.7	1.1
Italian PUSP	5.0	6.1	0
GB CP	2.96	1.5	0
Danish CP	1.0	0.4	0.7
Greek CP	0.78	0	0.9
Portuguese CP	1.1	0	0.3
Luxembourg CP	0.62	0.4	0.8
Trieste CP	0.78	0	0
Belgium CP	0	0.44	0
Swiss Workers' Party	0	0.63	0.6
Progressive Party of Cyprus	0	0.44	0.7
% of non-European CP	13.7	33.8	54.1

In 1957, the Western European parties received 86.3 per cent of the total amount. To explain this high percentage, we have to take into account the strategic importance of Western Europe for Soviet strategy, which rejected West German rearmament and tried to encourage neutralism in Western public opinion. In the following years, this percentage decreased to 66.2 per cent in 1966 and 45.9 per cent in 1973. These figures show that the Third World was important for Khrushchev's diplomacy but not as important as was

Europe. We have to wait for the Brezhnev years to see the Third World becoming a priority.

In 1957 as in 1973, the Italian Communist Party received the biggest share among the Western European parties: 41 per cent in 1957, 36 per cent in 1966 and 28 per cent in 1973. It was followed by the French Communist Party but the amount given to the French communists was much smaller: 19 per cent in 1957, 13 per cent in 1966 and 12 per cent in 1973. These figures clearly show that if the Italian Communist Party appears from an intellectual point of view as the 'enfant terrible' of the communist family, the child was obviously not independent from a financial point of view. The last point to be noted in the table is the surprising absence of the Spanish and West German Communist Parties. However, this absence does not mean that these two organizations were financially independent. In his book *Les aveux des archives: Prague–Paris–Prague,* Karl Bartosek quotes a letter coming from the Central Committee in 1956 which confirms that part[13] of the funds given to the French and to the Italian parties was transmitted to the Spanish and the West German parties.[14]

In this context of extreme dependence, let us focus now on the precise role assigned by the Soviet leaders to the Western European parties. For if the Soviet leadership did not believe any more in the revolutionary potential of the Western communist parties, it nevertheless kept assigning them specific functions on the international scene.

II. The Role of Western European Communist Parties in the Cold War

The roles of Western communist parties were quite diverse. First of all, they were asked to promote Soviet perceptions and goals in their meetings, speeches, newspapers and public declarations.

The Promotion of Soviet Perceptions and Goals

Four main directions can be identified in the promotion of Soviet perceptions and goals.The Western communist parties were asked to fight against the FRG's rearmament and West German access to nuclear weapons as well as to promote Molotov's plan for an international treaty on European security. But they were also supposed to fight against two Soviet objects of fear: 'Atlanticism', that is, European dependence on NATO and the powerful influence of the United States on the European continent and 'Europeanism', that is, the EEC process, which was totally negative from the Soviet point of view.

In these four directions, the Western communist parties were quite active during the period. In particular, they actively supported the pacifist campaigns developed by the Soviet leadership: in 1956, when Nikolai Bulganin called for general disarmament and in 1957, when Adam Rapacki's plan was issued, and when Bulganin called this time for a balanced reduction of forces. In 1966, they strongly promoted the new project of a European Conference on Security and Cooperation. These four topics were also constantly and repeatedly developed in the Western communist press, for example in English communist magazines such as *Labour Monthly* or *Marxism Today*.

This role assigned to the Western communist parties aimed at influencing Western European public opinion in a 'favourable' direction. But this open action was not the only one. During this period, the Soviet leaders also called on their 'friends' to get information on the political, economic, social situation of their country, on the political balance, or on the future of one politician or another.

Underground actions

During the frequent and regular meetings mentioned above, the Soviet ambassador in Paris, Vinogradov, and the General Secretary of the French Communist Party, Maurice Thorez, often discussed the French situation and the de Gaulle 'enigma'. They were trying to answer a crucial question: Could de Gaulle be a good ally and could he help the Soviets achieve their main goals – that is, the weakening of NATO and the departure of US troops from the European continent?

On 1 February 1958 Vinogradov and Thorez met in Cannes, and spoke in detail about the French situation. In his long report to Gromyko, Vinogradov wrote:

> Thorez said that it would be useful for the Soviet Union to promote again, in one form or another, the question of the reduction of conventional weapons, which is a quite important matter for France, which has now more than one million of people in its military forces. This could be useful also against the political circles which are hostile to us and who pretend that the Soviet Union wants to ban nuclear weapons but wants to keep conventional armaments. That is the reason why, repeated Thorez, we have to make new offers on the reduction of conventional weapons. Then Thorez spoke about the military alliances and he emphasized that French public opinion is not ripe enough to think about exiting NATO. That is the reason why, said Thorez, the French Communist Party does not express any demands on this question. Thorez repeated that even if the communists entered the French government, they still would be unable to achieve an immediate break between France and NATO. Under these conditions, Thorez is in favour of our proposals which do not tend toward the immediate dissolution of the military alliance but to an agreement between them.[15]

This report is quite rich: it shows that Thorez makes proposals, offers directions – in a word, that he is active. And the function assigned to him is clear.

In contrast to the Stalinist period when the Western communist leaders had to obey Soviet directives, in Khrushchev's years they were supposed to inform, to analyse and to make proposals. But the most interesting fact about this meeting is the following. At the end of the discussion, Thorez emphasized de Gaulle's focus on French national interests and stressed that during the 'Hungarian events', the General remained silent and did not make any public anti-Soviet declarations. Five days after this discussion, Vinogradov met de Gaulle in his private house in Colombey les deux Eglises and, during the meeting, de Gaulle declared to the Soviet ambassador that 'the French dependence on the United States will not be eternal'.[16] This important declaration is of course emphasized in Vinogradov's report to Gromyko and explains why the Soviet diplomats and French communists were quite optimistic about de Gaulle's return to power. In June 1958, during a new meeting with Vinogradov, Thorez expressed his confidence in the promotion of regular and official contacts between de Gaulle's France and the Soviet Union.[17] However, these initial hopes did not last. In June 1960, a new meeting between Vinogradov and Thorez revealed the disappointment of the general secretary about de Gaulle's foreign policy:

> Comrade Thorez said that from now on their goal would be not only to unmask the American government but also to unmask de Gaulle's foreign policy which, on paper, strives to improve international relations, but which is actually supporting the current American policy and conducting a policy of reconciliation with West German militarism.[18]

Of course, Maurice Thorez was not the only interlocutor coming from the French Communist Party, and we could mention many others, such as René Andrieu, who was the editor-in-chief of the communist daily *L'Humanité*. Meeting Vassili Kuznetsov, who was a political adviser at the Soviet embassy in Paris, in September 1960, Andrieu was asked by the Soviet diplomat about the Franco-German reconciliation and about the neutralist feelings of the French people; he replied rather frankly that the neutralist consciousness had not made progress in France.[19]

The information and judgements expressed by the Western communist leaders were not always interesting: sometimes these leaders were led to misperceptions because of their ideological convictions; sometimes they told the Soviet leaders what they wanted to hear. But in general, this information was quite useful; during the years 1956–68, the Western European communists were good informants. They were also quite good agitators, as could be seen in the Algerian crisis.

Between 1958 and 1961, the Soviet state adopted moderate positions on the Algerian question. Since Soviet diplomacy was engaged in a privileged dialogue with President de Gaulle, the Soviet state had to show its willingness toward the French government. But at the same time, the French Communist

Party promoted very harsh criticism of de Gaulle's Algerian policy, which aimed at seducing the supporters of Algerian independence. And of course, Moscow assigned this role to the French Communist Party: in December 1960, for example, Jacques Duclos declared in a conversation with Ambassador Vinogradov: 'We will do everything to compromise de Gaulle's Algerian policy.'[20]

The Algerian example shows a clear 'casting' of roles: on the one hand, the Soviet state wanted to appear as a respectable partner and used diplomatic tools for this purpose; but, on the other hand, it asked the Western communist apparatus to fight against the international order. We observe the same process regarding the United Nations Organization (UNO): on the one hand, the Soviet leadership used the UN General Assembly to promote disarmament plans and to present a respectable and pacifist image of itself; but, on the other hand, the Western communist newspapers develop the idea that the UNO is only an 'American rubber-stamp'.[21]

So, from 1956 to 1968, and despite de-Stalinization, the Western European communist parties remained very useful tools of Soviet parallel diplomacy. Did they easily accept the role the Soviet leadership assigned to them or do we see inside the parties the birth of some protest?

Obedient Parties?

As a matter of fact, if the Western communist parties did faithfully adopt all the Soviet positions and perceptions on international questions, they were much more reluctant to accept Soviet perceptions and positions related to the communist movement.

In 1956, the hierarchy of the French Communist Party remained deeply attached to Stalinism and did not easily accept Khrushchev's Secret Report. After some internal discussions, the party leadership adopted on 22 March a resolution taking a clearly favourable position on Stalin's legacy. This declaration put a special emphasis on

> Stalin's role and merits, as a theorist and as a leader in the development of the Communist and Workers' Parties, in the ideological and political fight against all the enemies of the October Revolution (Trotskyite, Bukharinist, Nationalist) and Stalin's role in the construction of socialism, in the defeat of German fascism.[22]

At the same time, the leadership of the Italian party as a whole and despite Togliatti's reticence seemed to adopt a more moderate attitude, condemning the excesses of Stalinism and trying to take advantage of the situation to win more freedom in the international communist movement. In contrast, the small English Communist Party was enthusiastic about the congress, speaking through its general secretary, Harry Pollitt, of a 'splendid vision' and 'the immortal youth of Marxism–Leninism'.[23]

During the Hungarian tragedy, the leaderships of both the French and the Italian Communist Parties adopted quite conservative positions which contrasted with the criticisms voiced by some intellectuals who were members of the two parties. We now know that Togliatti was in favour of a firm response to the 'counter-revolution'. And, after the Soviet intervention, the Western communist hierarchies once again adopted conservative positions, much more conservative than Khrushchev's own. In November 1956, Thorez declared to the Central Committee of the French Communist Party:

> Our party will keep its eyes on the glorious experience of Lenin's party, which inspires all the revolutionary workers' parties in the world. As for us, we think that several centres could not exist in the international workers' movement because it would lead to the dislocation of the movement.[24]

And on the same day, he declared that

> somebody told me: Stalinism was a necessity. I think this expression is wrong. For there was no Stalinism; this expression belongs to our enemies' vocabulary.[25]

As these quotes show, the French and Italian leaderships were reluctant to adopt official Soviet de-Stalinization and remained attached to the Stalinist approach in 1956 and 1957. Step by step however, the following years brought some changes in their positions.

In 1966, the famous communist writer Louis Aragon began to express in the official communist daily newspaper *L'Humanité* a strong protest against Andrei Siniavski's and Yuli Daniel's condemnation to seven years in a labour camp. But the strongest criticism came from Italy: During the Prague Spring of 1968, the leadership of the communist party began to condemn Soviet military intervention and to contest the Soviet leadership of the international communist movement. However, and this point is quite interesting, the Italians' critical behaviour was not taken seriously by the Soviet leadership, which obviously misunderstood the nature of the dispute. In November 1968 in Moscow, an Italian delegation led by Enrico Berlinguer was received by such figures as Kirilenko, Pelshe, Ponomariov and Beliakov. The disagreement between the two parties clearly appeared in the discussion because Berlinguer declared:

> We want to emphasize that we do not want to exacerbate our discord, that we do not want to use this discord for propaganda, that we do not aim at a schism between our parties; but on the Czechoslovakian question, our point of view is different from yours. And we ask you to admit that our point of view is different from yours ... The Italian party never hesitated to support all the actions taken by the socialist countries which in its mind were in conformity with the interest of the international communist movement. We do

not hesitate to swim against the stream when we think it necessary. That was the case in regard to the Hungarian events. But now the situation is different. We adopted a position different from yours, not because we were afraid to swim against the stream but because our judgement of the situation, which is based on our own information, was and is different.[26]

In his answer, Kirilenko appears very inflexible and even shows some paternalism:

> The common point between 1956 and 1968 is the existence of the counter-revolution. In 1956, the counter-revolution was an armed one; now the tools are different. Nobody would have forgiven us if we had let Czechoslovakia become our enemy. We did what we could ... We are convinced that in due time, the Italian Communist Party will change its mind about the question. The Italian Communist Party is a creative one, which knows how to analyse the situations from a dialectical point of view; it showed this ability more than once in the past. We think that you will not always maintain the positions which were taken by your Central Committee ... We believe in your party, in the direction of your party. That is the reason why, and we speak frankly, we think that in due time, you will change your mind.[27]

The meaning of this declaration is clear: the Soviet leaders wanted to minimize the dispute, considering the attitude of the Italian Communist Party as a temporary mistake; they spoke to the Italian representatives with the authority of a father, of a *paterfamilias*. But this behaviour was not adequate: for the first time in the international movement, a dispute was the expression of a strong desire for radical change in the relationship between Moscow and the Italian Communist Party. It led to the Eurocommunist adventure.

Until 1968, criticism remained strictly limited to questions related to the socialist community. Under the authority of the International Department, ideologically and financially dependent on it, the Western European communist parties remained active tools of Soviet diplomacy. Were they efficient tools? Yes, if we think of their role as informants and agitators. But it is not easy to measure their impact on Western public opinion. The Western European communist parties obviously did not succeed in preventing German integration into NATO or in driving US troops out of the European continent; they did not prevent the EEC process; nor did they succeed in promoting neutralism in Western Europe. But they did have some influence on Western European public opinion and leaders, inducing them to accept at the end of the 1960s the principle of a forthcoming Conference on European Security and Cooperation, which would lead to the Helsinki process. Was it worth all this mobilization and all this energy? That remains an open question.

NOTES

1 In the legislative elections of November 1958, the French CP got 19 per cent of the votes; four years later, it won 22 per cent. Stéphane Courtois and Marc Lazar, *Histoire du Parti Communiste français*, Paris: PUF, 1995, *passim*.

2 Willie Thompson, *The Good Old Cause*, London: Pluto Press, 1992, *passim*.

3 Philippe Robrieux, *Histoire du parti communiste français, 1972–1982*, vol. 3, *Du programme commun à l'échec historique de Georges Marchais*, Paris: Fayard, 1986, pp. 75–6.

4 Archives of the Soviet Ministry of Foreign Affairs, AVP RF, referentura po Frantsii and referentura po Italii, years 1958, 1959, 1960, 1961, besedy posla, *passim*.

5 On this precise point, see Nicholas Polianski's testimony in *MID, Douze ans dans les services diplomatiques du Kremlin*, Paris: Belfond, 1984, pp. 177–8.

6 Excerpt from the protocol no. 29, 119g, adopted by the General Secretary of the Central Committee, 11 July 1967, in Party archives, RGANI, collection no. 6.

7 I was not allowed to look at the post-1975 archives related to this sensitive question.

8 Archives of the Parti, RGANI, General Secretary of the Central Committee, collection no. 6.

9 These reports are located in collection no. 89, protocols of the Politburo, peretchen' no. 38, in Party archives, RGANI. To this direct financing, we should have to add all the amounts which were circulated through numerous Western European businesses established by Communist leaders, such as Interagra, which was created in France by Jean-Baptiste Doumengue. But, unfortunately, Soviet archives related to these sensitive matters are still closed. However, some Czechoslovakian archives confirm the existence of these transfers. See Karl Bartosek, *Les aveux des archives, Prague-Paris-Prague, 1948–1968*, Paris: Éditions du Seuil, 1996, *passim*.

10 The amounts were originally given in US dollars in the Soviet archives. To transform these dollars into French francs, I used the *Annuaire rétrospectif de la France*, Paris: INSEE, 1990, which gives on page 592 the official exchange rates in Paris from 1948 to 1987. I then transformed these current francs into constant francs of 1996, using the coefficient of transformation given in the magazine *Liaisons sociales* issued on 20 February 1997. To put these amounts into perspective, I add that for the entire year of 1957, sales of the newspaper *L'Humanité* represented about 109,500,000 constant 1996 francs; in 1966, some 147,000,000 constant 1996 francs.

11 Cf. the written note from Boris Ponomariov, in the excerpt of the protocol no. 76 adopted by the Presidium, 7 January 1963, in Party Archives, RGANI, collection no. 89, peretchen' no. 38, document no. 25.

12 Report of the International Department, 26 December 1966, in Party archives, RGANI, collection no. 89, peretchen' no. 38, document no. 9.

13 But which part? For the moment we cannot answer this question because the Soviet archives are still closed concerning this matter.

14 Bartosek, *Les aveux des archives*, p. 138.

15 Report of the meeting between Ambassador Vinogradov and Maurice Thorez on 1 February 1958, 18 March 1958, no. 752, in MID archives, AVP RF, referentura po Frantsii, opis' no. 48, por no. 4, papka no. 276, in 'Zapisi besed posla SSSR vo Frantsii', 27 January–23 April 1958.

16 Report of the meeting between Ambassador Vinogradov and de Gaulle on 6 February 1958, 7 March 1958, no. 93, in MID archives, AVP RF, referentura po Frantsii, opis' no. 48, por no. 4, papka no. 276.

17 Report of the meeting between Ambassador Vinogradov and Maurice Thorez on 27 June 1958, 3 February 1959, in MID archives, AVP RF, referentura po Frantsii, opis' no. 49, por no. 11, papka no. 280, 'Politicheskie voprosy'.

18 Report of the meeting between Ambassador Vinogradov and Maurice Thorez on 13 June 1960, 12 July 1960, in MID archives, AVP RF, referentura po Frantsii, opis' no. 50, por no. 4, papka no. 282, 'Zapisi besed posla SSSR vo Frantsii', 5 January–22 December 1960.

19 Report of the meeting between the diplomat Kuznetsov and René Andrieu on 26 October 1960, in MID archives, AVP RF, referentura po Frantsii, opis' no. 50, por no. 6, papka no. 282, 'Zapisi besed sotrudnikov posol'stva SSSR vo Frantsii', 2 August–28 December 1960.

20 Report of the meeting between Ambassador Vinogradov and Jacques Duclos on 3 December 1960, 21 December 1960, in MID archives, AVP RF, referentura po Frantsii, opis' no. 50, por no. 4, papka no. 282, 'Zapisi besed posla SSSR vo Frantsii', 5 January–22 December 1960.

21 This expression is used in the English communist *Daily Worker*, 4 June 1955.

22 Quoted by Marc Lazar, *Maisons rouges: les partis communistes français et italien de la Libération à nos jours*, Paris: Aubier, 1992, p. 91.

23 Quoted in *Labour Monthly*, April 1956.

24 This declaration is reported in a note coming from the Quai d'Orsay archives: 'Note sur les répercussions des événements de Pologne et de Hongrie dans le monde communiste', 2 January 1957, in French Ministry of Foreign Affairs archives, série 'Europe 1944–1960', sous-série 'URSS', carton no. 261, 'Politique extérieure; action générale du communisme à l'extérieur, janvier 1957–décembre 1960'.

25 Ibid.

26 Excerpt of the meeting between Enrico Berlinguer and representatives of the CPSU, 13–14 November 1968, in Presidential archives of the Russian Federation, collection no. 3, opis' no. 77, delo no. 132, pp. 8–149. The text was published in *Istochnik*, 1994, no. 4, pp. 77–86.

27 Ibid.

13

Détente, the Superpowers and their Allies, 1962–64

Vojtech Mastny

The improvement of the international situation that followed the October 1962 Cuban missile crisis, whose aftermath coincided with the terminal stages of both the Kennedy and the Khrushchev leaderships, has generally been regarded as the formative period of East–West détente. As with other such sweeping generalizations, however, this observation raises more questions than it answers. What was the nature of the détente that took place? Was it intentional or incidental? Did it occur despite, because, or regardless of the incipient crisis in the relations between the superpowers and their allies? Did the outcome have the effect of precipitating the eventual end of the Cold War or delaying it?

Both Khrushchev and Kennedy could claim to have won something in the crisis over Cuba – the former the shelving of US plans to invade the island, the latter the withdrawal of the threatening Soviet missiles from there. In their relations with their allies, however, they both had to pay a price for what they had allowed to happen. The respective allies were alarmed about how close they had come to getting embroiled in a war not of their making but because of a confrontation between the superpowers over which they had no control. At a secret briefing on 2 November, Khrushchev admitted to the stunned Eastern European leaders that the outbreak of a war had been the question of but 'a few minutes'.[1]

Within the communist world, the impact of the Cuban crisis was the greatest on China which, though not a member of the Warsaw Pact, was tied with Moscow by a bilateral mutual defence alliance, signed in 1950. The effect was further complicated by the Sino-Indian border war, which coincided with the crisis and initially elicited Soviet verbal support for Beijing – in its view a bid for Chinese support in the forthcoming Soviet confrontation with the USA. Through East German and Hungarian diplomats, the Kremlin tried to impress upon the Chinese leaders the need for solidarity during the confrontation. However, once the confrontation climaxed and then resulted in Soviet retreat – while Moscow had switched its support to India in trying to block further Chinese advance and end the war – Beijing staged mass rallies ostensibly in support of Cuba but implicitly to condemn 'those who were frightened in the face of imperialist aggression' and 'bartered with the freedom and independence of another people'.[2] The Chinese criticized Moscow for not having consulted with them about an adventure which, by making the 1950 treaty operative, could have brought their country into war with the USA – the reverse kind of accusations Moscow used to level against them. They condemned Khrushchev for the dual sin of 'adventurism' and 'capitulationism'. Eventually, Mao Zedong's representative, Deng Xiaoping, memorably told the Kremlin leaders:

> you committed two errors: in shipping the missiles to Cuba you indulged in adventurism, and then, showing confusion in the face of nuclear black-mail from the USA, you capitulated ... For Cuba's defense no missiles are necessary at all. And so, in shipping missiles to Cuba, did you want to help her or ruin her? We have become suspicious that you, in shipping missiles to Cuba, were trying to place her under your control ... You daily speak about the danger of thermonuclear war. But in the given case you rashly played with nuclear weapons. You justify your actions by saying that you wanted to obtain some sort of 'promise' from the USA, and you say that you truly received such a 'promise'. But what are the facts? The facts are that under threat from the United States you were obliged to remove your missiles.[3]

The tensions within the communist world did not translate into détente with the Western one. The decompression that followed the climax of the Cuban crisis did not immediately change Soviet policy. Unprepared for the kind of dénouement that had taken place, Khrushchev rather let developments that had previously been in progress proceed regardless of the outcome of the crisis. That did not give Soviet policy much coherence or consistency.

On the one hand, on 28 November Khrushchev told the Canadian ambassador to Moscow that 'a new round of talks [about Berlin] should begin soon, and gave the impression that he meant within the next few months'. In a letter to Prime Minister Macmillan on the same day, he described Berlin and Germany as the most important questions, requiring 'urgent solution'. On the other hand, however, he

> warned that failure to reach a Berlin agreement would create a 'very dan-gerous situation' which could get out of hand, and he revived the threat of a separate peace treaty with East Germany. He emphasized that 'Berlin is not Cuba' and that it would be 'dangerous madness' to expect a further Soviet retreat ... Khrushchev warned that the USSR's local tactical and strategic position is vastly stronger in Berlin than it was in Cuba, and that 'if people think the Cuban affair will restrain us, they don't know us'.[4]

Moscow's wrangling with the USA over the presence of Soviet forces on the island continued until Khrushchev sent his trusted and experienced aide, Anastas Mikoian, to Washington to test the water, and found Kennedy unexpectedly forthcoming on the Soviet idea of a NATO–Warsaw non-aggression pact. Rusk subsequently qualified the president's posture by reminding Mikoian that 'the United States has not been delegated authority by the other countries to negotiate a pact on their behalf. Nevertheless, we were prepared to discuss the idea informally.'[5]

At the end of 1962 and the beginning of 1963, Moscow watched warily the dramatic developments within the Western alliance that marked the final demise of Kennedy's 'grand design' for Europe. After difficult negotiations, the USA agreed to compensate Britain for cancelling the delivery of US Skybolt missiles, intended to prolong the lifespan of the country's ageing nuclear bombers, by supplying instead the more-advanced Polaris missiles that Washington originally did not want to share.[6] The outcome of the controversy may have been an embarrassment for Kennedy but it was no gain for the Soviets either, who regarded the British nuclear force in any case as an extension of US power. Moreover, the December 1962 Nassau agreement between Kennedy and Macmillan that ended the Skybolt affair called for advancing the Multilateral Force nuclear-sharing plan that Moscow abhorred and offer the Polaris to France as well.

On 14 January, de Gaulle rejected the offer together with British membership in the Common Market – the 'double non' understandably was greeted in Moscow as evidence of both a crisis within NATO and the doubtful viability of European economic integration.[7] The latter was the more gratifying from the Soviet point of view since the plans for the Soviet bloc's own economic integration had recently been foundering, particularly on Romanian resistance. But de Gaulle's next step in reasserting France's right to its own security policy independent of the 'Anglo-Saxons' – the conclusion a week later of the Elysée treaty with West Germany[8] – was not reassuring by Soviet lights.

Far from substantiating rumours in the West that the German–French rapprochement would lead to a German–Soviet rapprochement,[9] the treaty was incongruously regarded in Moscow as a scheme by West German chancellor Konrad Adenauer, abetted by the USA, aimed at providing Bonn with access to nuclear weapons through the French back door.[10] Closer to the truth, though not quite at it, Polish party chief Vladyslav Gomulka interpreted the Elysée treaty as Adenauer's manoeuvre calculated to show that his country had an alternative if the US was not willing to support its ambitions.[11] The Soviets rightly judged de Gaulle as being unwilling to negotiate with them as long as their Berlin posture remained threatening. Soviet ambassador to Paris Vinogradov reported home that the Paris–Bonn 'axis' was unequivocally hostile to the Soviet Union.[12]

The disarray within the Western alliance thus did not foster détente between the superpowers which remained limited to tentative feelers between Washington and Moscow. In January, Soviet deputy foreign minister Kuznetsov on one day told Kennedy of Soviet desire for improved relations, whereas on another day, his boss, foreign minister Andrei Gromyko, showed his usual sour face to US ambassador Foy Kohler, taking a dim view of the ongoing discussions about the end of nuclear testing.[13] Those discussions had been going on and off since 1958 without significant progress. The Soviet publication in mid-January, without prior consultation with Washington, of the secret correspondence between Kennedy and Khrushchev on the subject did not help matters.[14] Evidently, the Soviet Union was not prepared to move forward on the test ban.

Instead, Moscow renewed on 20 February its proposal for a NATO–Warsaw Pact non-aggression treaty that it had been intermittently advancing since May 1958.[15] However, it did not do so in a manner suitable to make the idea attractive to the West. It presented the proposal at the Eighteen-Nation Disarmament Committee (ENDC), a United Nations forum, and accompanied it by Kuznetsov's 'long, propagandistic, and inflexible speech'.[16] Unlike the vaguer 1958 version, the proposal specifically provided for signature by all members of the two alliances, including East Germany. The USA dismissed it as a ploy calculated to force international acceptance of East Germany, loathed by West Germany, while sowing doubts within NATO about the alliance's continued utility.[17] Washington took the sensible position that such a treaty should be the culmination of détente rather than its beginning.[18] Moscow's move could have well been aimed at reassuring its own allies as well, rankled by the after-effects of the Cuban missile crisis, and the Soviet military, irritated by Khrushchev's troop cuts. At the June 1962 meeting of the PCC, Khrushchev had deliberately misled the Warsaw Pact allies by describing the USA as being more favourably disposed to the non-aggression treaty than he had reason to believe.[19]

Throughout March, the ENDC negotiations were languishing. Kohler believed to have detected 'an unmistakable change in the Soviet posture during the past six weeks' – for the worse. The ambassador speculated that Khrushchev was 'a tired man ... overwhelmed by his burdens ... [and suffering from a] depression [that] seems clearly to result from his difficulties with a complicated world which no longer fits his earlier confident analysis'.[20] Khrushchev's son Sergei retrospectively concurred with this diagnosis, recalling that 'father was tired. Immensely tired, both physically and psychologically. He no longer had either the strength or the desire for a power struggle' – a striking change from the previous years.[21]

The widening Sino-Soviet rift had reached a critical stage at that time. Khrushchev decided to make one last effort at conciliating the Chinese by inviting them for talks in Moscow. Nothing indicated that they were ready for reconciliation, however, thus opening the prospect of a dire and unpredictable confrontation with a hostile communist power, which was on the verge of acquiring nuclear weapons. Judging prospects for arms control agreements to be slim, the CIA estimated plausibly that 'the present unyielding Soviet stand is based on the judgment that, with the Chinese charging a sell-out and the

Soviet populace being called upon for sacrifices, this is no time to encourage hopes for an East–West détente'.[22]

At the beginning of April, Khrushchev sent Kennedy through Soviet ambassador Anatolii Dobrynin so insulting a message that the president's brother Robert, when hearing it from the envoy's mouth, refused to accept it.[23] The Soviet leader ruminated about the USA's failure to treat the Soviet Union with a respect supposedly due to it as a great power, complaining bitterly about having been misled by the chief US disarmament negotiator, Arthur Dean, about how many inspection sites the United States insisted the Soviet Union must accept in order to make the conclusion of a test ban treaty possible. Dean had indeed been imprecise and misleading in his statements, for which transgression he was subsequently fired, and Khrushchev had ample reasons to be concerned about the intrusiveness of the proposed US inspections on Soviet territory. Yet, the reason for his concern was not fear of US espionage, as he was proclaiming and some Western interpreters have been willing to take at face value.[24] The real fear was that of opening the closed Soviet society to international scrutiny, which in turn would open him for criticism by the Chinese for compromising the integrity of the socialist camp in its struggle with the capitalist enemy.

The prudent US response to Khrushchev's intemperance conformed with a subtle and convincing analysis of his predicament by the State Department's Policy Planning Council, presented by its chairman, Walt W. Rostow, to the National Security Council on 19 March.[25] 'Seldom has anyone produced so little with so much', the document observed by voicing the strictures of Khrushchev's putative domestic and Chinese critics, pressing him to show a success and consequently offering the USA an opportunity to score success, too. Not only are there 'presently strong forces operating on the Soviet leaders to make them want a change in relations with the US, but not to compel them to seek that change', but the same is true about the United States, albeit for different reasons. Washington must not miss an opportunity for accommodation, which the authors of the document believed had happened in 1953 when 'we stood as a mere onlooker while the Soviet leaders went through a bewildering succession of policy innovations and reversals'. In trying to shift away from what divides the two countries toward exchanges that could lay the groundwork for their better understanding, the State Department planners favoured starting talks without a rigid agenda rather than aiming at a breakthrough in areas where agreement was most difficult, such as disarmament or the Berlin question.

In an initiative coordinated with British Prime Minister Harold Macmillan, Kennedy nevertheless chose to focus on disarmament while leaving aside the Berlin question on the assumption that Moscow had already acquiesced in leaving the status quo in the divided city undisturbed. This was, indeed, a correct assumption, since Khrushchev had been trying to impress on an unhappy East German leader, Walter Ulbricht, that a separate peace treaty with

East Germany was no longer needed. The Soviet leader confirmed that 'Berlin is no longer a source of any trouble' to the president's emissary W. Averell Harriman during their Kremlin meeting on 26 April. 'I will give my word', Khrushchev vowed to Harriman, 'that I will find a basis for a test ban agreeable to both sides provided you agree to work out the basis of a German settlement which would recognize the two Germanies as they now exist.'[26]

In a lengthy message to Kennedy three days later, Khrushchev added what was the clearest indication that his much touted concern about the MLF pertained not so much to a fear of the Germans ever using nuclear weapons on their own as to West Germany's growing influence within NATO:

> We firmly believe that the Government of the USA will strive to arrange it so that the multinational and multilateral nuclear forces of NATO, no matter how their creation comes out in practice, could never be used without the Government of the USA. But one way or another states which are included in the nuclear pool of NATO, including the FRG, will have a vote there and will participate in the formulation of opinions and, as a consequence, of the final decisions concerning the utilization of nuclear armaments. Indeed, we all witnessed the fact that in NATO the voice of Western Germany is increasingly listened to.[27]

In another message sent jointly to Kennedy and Macmillan, Khrushchev demanded complete prohibition of nuclear tests while opposing any inspection as unnecessary because of the supposed adequacy of other means of detection[28] – a position that promptly caused negotiations to stall. In retrospect, the Kennedy administration may be fairly criticized for insisting so adamantly on intrusive inspections as supposedly necessary to monitor all tests, both underground and in the atmosphere, for other means of doing so already existed and would further improve with the passage of time. In his memoirs, Dobrynin mused that if a comprehensive test ban treaty had been concluded in 1963, the later runaway development of nuclear missile technology, which aggravated the Cold War, might have been avoided.[29] This is uncertain; what is certain is that even 40 years later and with the Cold War ended, the US Senate's opposition to a comprehensive test ban treaty prevented its ratification and with it the progressive reversal of the development of nuclear weaponry.

Khrushchev had reasons to desire a comprehensive ban, thus making Chinese nuclear armament more difficult, and therefore to be exasperated by US insistence on inspections that implied that the Soviet Union wanted to cheat in order to surreptitiously build up its own arsenal. 'Give them an inch and they take a mile', he complained to his son.[30] The pressure for a limited ban, allowing for underground testing to continue, came from both US and Soviet nuclear scientists. Much though they warned against the catastrophic consequences of a nuclear war, they had a stake in the continuation of their programmes for technical rather than political reasons.[31] The Kennedy administration, by fixing on the inability rather than unwillingness to cheat, tended to take, unlike Khrushchev, a technical rather than political view.

Rightly sensing that the Chinese were Khrushchev's major concern, presidential aides Chester B. Bowles and McGeorge Bundy in conversations with Dobrynin made bids for a US–Soviet nuclear deal against Beijing, without specifying details, but were rebuffed.[32] Pending conversations with the Chinese delegation, expected in Moscow in early July, Khrushchev evidently still wanted to give reconciliation with Beijing a chance while trying not to show his vulnerability to Washington. Kennedy's 'American University' speech on 10 June, delivered with the intention to break the deadlock in the test ban talks by dramatically reassuring the Soviet Union of US good will and asking it to reciprocate, has since been lauded for achieving that effect and making the conclusion of the test ban treaty possible.[33] The president would have hardly succeeded, however, without the Chinese unwittingly lending their hand.

Although the speech was received favourably in Moscow,[34] no Soviet action in response to it had ensued by the time Beijing's blistering 25-point written denunciation of Khrushchev's policies, not yet made public, arrived in the Soviet capital four days later, all but destroying what remained of his hopes for reconciliation. Still, it was not until 2 July, while keeping the Chinese letter secret, that Khrushchev first publicly suggested the workable solution of the impasse with the US by declaring himself in favour of a partial rather than a comprehensive test ban.[35] The suggestion had for him the advantage of both raising the prospect of an agreement with the USA as a possible bargaining point with the Chinese delegation on the eve of its arrival and, in the probable case that the collision course with Beijing would not be reversed, subsequently concluding the agreement in a fashion that would allow for continued underground testing, believed to be necessary in order to stay ahead in the looming nuclear confrontation with hostile China. Concurrently, Khrushchev promoted hopes for East–West détente as he understood it by again pushing for a NATO–Warsaw Pact non-aggression treaty, although he left the West guessing whether he intended to link the two covenants together.

Underlining the critical importance of the Sino-Soviet rift for progress toward the test ban treaty, Khrushchev on 9 July indicated to the visiting former NATO secretary-general Paul-Henri Spaak that there was no linkage.[36] This was the day after the closed-door meetings with the Chinese delegation had ended in disarray, Deng Xiaoping having lambasted the Soviet leader for assorted 'revisionist' treachery and the desire 'to bind China by the hands and feet through an agreement with the USA'.[37] Adding to the significance of the timing, the day after the Spaak visit Khrushchev sent to the Warsaw Pact allies a 'recommendation' to admit Mongolia as full member of the alliance.[38] This would have extended its validity, and with it their obligation to assist the Soviet Union militarily, to the region of possible hostilities with China.

On 14 July, Moscow chose to reveal the full extent of the break by making the 25-point Chinese denunciation public, along with its rebuttal.[39] The next day Mongolia formally requested admission into the Warsaw Pact, Khrushchev called for its political consultative committee to meet in as little as two weeks, and the test ban negotiations resumed.[40] They were quickly concluded in the Soviet capital on 25 July, just as the Warsaw Pact party secretaries were converging there for their meeting, in time to discuss the implications of the US–Soviet treaty against the background of the breakdown of the relations with China. In praising the treaty to Harriman, Khrushchev expressed the desire to move 'from [the] particular to [the] general' – not only in disarmament but also with regard to NATO–Warsaw Pact relations and the German question.[41]

The test ban treaty was an accomplishment of the superpowers, in which their allies – with the notable exception of the Chinese, whose opposition facilitated it – had played no substantive role. With hindsight, the test ban treaty has been described as the capping stone of the 'constructed peace' built since the onset of the Cold War and lasting for the rest of it, and even beyond.[42] More modestly, it has been characterized as the solution of the Berlin question in disguise.[43] It was, as the treaty's chief British negotiator Quinton Hailsham rightly noted, 'the biggest step forward in international relations since the beginning of the Cold War'; he added, however, that no détente ensued, nor did the Cold War end for another quarter of a century.[44] Foreign minister Maurice Couve de Murville of France – France joined China in denouncing the treaty as designed to perpetuate superpower predominance and restrict their own independent nuclear policies – warned at the time that 'the mere fact that these talks were taking place before the elements of a real détente were present could lead … to a deterioration of the political climate in Europe'.[45] By focusing on the secondary issue of nuclear arms race rather than the primary one of the political rivalry that underlay it, the treaty sidetracked détente. It generated a false appearance of détente in an area where technological developments were running out of control without addressing the political issues that remained within the superpowers' control. Nevertheless, both sides wanted to proceed beyond the modest confines of the treaty, although only Khrushchev tried to do so in a radical way conducive to creating the opportunity to terminate the conflict. Why did the opportunity not come about?

In February 1963, when the prospects for the test ban treaty looked the gloomiest, Khrushchev convened his top military brass for a defence council meeting at Fili, one of the Soviet missile design centres. His son Sergei was present, and later recounted what happened as follows. Reminding the generals that the army is for the people and not the other way round, his father announced at the meeting the need for further reductions of military spending to ease its pressure on the economy and allow for a rise in the standard of living. The Warsaw Pact supreme commander, Marshal Andrei Grechko, pleaded vainly for mass production of tactical nuclear missiles and artillery. 'Two cannons are enough for you, Marshal, and for the Americans', Khrushchev snapped. Berating the chief of the general staff, Marshal Zakharov, for planning for a nuclear war with hundreds of targets, he argued 'that even a dozen of missiles with thermonuclear warheads are enough to make the very thought of war senseless'.[46] He scorned defence minister Marshal Rodion Malinovskii's proposal for abolishing draft deferments for students as 'unforgivable waste' – a prescription for stymieing Soviet scientific advance. Khrushchev sent a chill down the bones of his generals by suggesting that a small professional army, supported by territorial militia, might be all that the country needed.

Even if Khrushchev may not have been as outspoken as his son – our only source on the Fili meeting – has reported from memory a third of a century later, what he writes is consistent with other sources as well as with Khrushchev's behaviour. Having bluffed dangerously with the deployment of nuclear weapons before the Cuban missiles crisis brought him to the brink, he had incentives to think harder about the implications of the doomsday weaponry than did his Western counterparts who had never gone as far in brinkmanship as he had done. Unlike the strategic planners in the Kennedy administration and their European clients, he was particularly concerned about proliferation of battlefield nuclear weapons as lowering the moral and practical inhibitions against their use. But he also went farther than any other Kremlin leader before Gorbachev in questioning the justification of oversized Soviet conventional forces and the concomitant militarization of Soviet society.

The long-classified history of US–Soviet strategic competition, completed in 1980 with the benefit of access to US intelligence data, noted that in February 1963 Khrushchev had to reverse policy to accelerate missile development, attributing the reversal to opposition within Soviet leadership.[47] Indeed, on 30 March the Soviet government issued a secret decree providing for mass production of intercontinental ballistic missiles.[48] Yet, the classified US history also noted that the pattern of Soviet missile deployments remained defensive rather than offensive, indicating no other strategic purpose beyond seeking parity with the USA.'[49] Although this was not necessarily correct, it casts doubt on the significance of the reversal.

Whatever opposition Khrushchev may have encountered within the Soviet leadership at that time, he was able to proceed toward the test ban treaty. Upon its conclusion on 25 July, however, he showed unusual caution by requesting that its actual signing be postponed until the foreign ministers of the three powers would meet two weeks later. In the meantime, he would be able to assess the repercussions of the predictably outraged Chinese reaction, complemented on the Western side by the French rejection of the treaty, as well as the extent of support given to it by Moscow's Warsaw Pact allies. Attesting to the importance of not only the political but also the economic ramifications of the issue, the meeting of the alliance's political consultative committee was preceded immediately by a meeting at the highest level of the Comecon, the Soviet bloc's organization for economic cooperation – pairing to be continued in the future.

The Comecon gathering revealed how much the high expectations of Soviet-directed economic integration and 'division of labour' among member states, entertained by Moscow during the organization's previous meeting a year earlier, had fallen victim to the fallout of the Cuban missile crisis and its aftermath. To Romania's increasingly persistent opposition to the kind of division of labour that would have perpetuated its backwardness was the added tension between East Germany and the countries its leaders expected to help subsidize its ailing economy, particularly Czechoslovakia and Poland. The concept of centralized allocation and implementation of capital projects by the Comecon was discarded in favour of the principle of 'interested party' in determining the extent of collaboration and its limits.[50]

As distinguished from the discord that Ulbricht's insistent demands for aid had fomented at the economic forum, it was a 'pleasure' for him, as put to the East German politburo, to report about the consequent meeting of the Warsaw Pact's political body.[51] There was no sense of urgency among the allies as they had welcomed the conclusion of the test ban treaty, although Ulbricht could not resist emphasizing that it meant no 'truce' (*Burgfrieden*) in the ongoing struggle with the capitalists. In the spirit of Khrushchev's earlier, though not so much latest thinking, he stressed that détente required more persistent competition to make 'socialism' beat capitalism by non-military means.

Behind the façade of unanimity, however, the different weight attributed by Moscow and its Eastern European allies to the conflict with China hinted at growing tension within the Warsaw Pact. Poland opposed unconditionally the Soviet attempt to bring Mongolia into the alliance. Polish foreign minister Adam Rapacki argued, subtly but irresistibly, that Mongolia's admission into the alliance would bring no advantages but only risks to either, while providing China with ammunition for accusations that an ideological conflict was being expanded into the military area. Rapacki pointed out the inconsistency of wanting to give military guarantees only to Mongolia and not to North Korea, North Vietnam, indeed China itself – all of which were supposedly threatened by Western imperialists. He warned that since the Warsaw Pact was limited to Europe, changing its terms would require unanimous consent by all its members, which in turn would raise the tricky question of the Albanian and perhaps also Romanian vote, thus fueling further discord.[52]

The Western powers regarded Moscow's interest in following up the test ban treaty as a test of Soviet readiness for détente. When Rusk came to Moscow for the signing of the document, he found Khrushchev repeating standard Soviet positions without indicating any wish to advance beyond them, and concluded that the Soviet leader did not want to tackle 'difficult issues'.[53] Khrushchev's reticence was soon to suggest that he had German settlement very much on his mind but was undecided about how to proceed. On the one hand, he made his most candid allusion in a conversation with a Westerner to his troubles with Ulbricht when asking Rusk the rhetorical question of

> whether time had not come when we, mature people who knew life and had seen war, should try move things from rails of war to rails of peace, namely, record situation as it existed now and forget about Adenauer and other people opposing such course. It was not only US who had such allies, for God had not forgotten USSR either and had given it allies who did not understand its policy. He believed however all such allies would eventually realize they had been wrong and unrealistic.[54]

On the other hand, Khrushchev still displayed his residual predilection for brandishing bombs as a method, according to his son, 'of exerting pressure, threats, and even blackmail'.[55] Having taken Rusk aside after luncheon, the Soviet chief wanted to know why, since Adenauer, de Gaulle and Macmillan had all told him they would never fight a nuclear war over Berlin, could he be expected to believe that the Americans would. 'Mr. Chairman', the Secretary of State memorably replied, 'you will just have to take into account the possibility that we Americans are God damn fools', after which remark the subject was changed, never to surface again.[56]

In the discussion with Soviet officials, the United States took the position that consolidating the recent gains in mutual relations was more important than moving ahead fast.[57] Confirming the US predilection for addressing the military rather than political dimensions of the East–West rivalry, Rusk stated publicly that, instead of a 'comprehensive discussion … looking toward some negotiated détente across the board', specific issues ought to be explored, for example, 'in the surprise attack field'.[58] In contrast, Gromyko re-introduced the NATO–Warsaw Pact non-aggression treaty as an alleged generator of proper atmosphere for further disarmament talks.[59] The idea was congenial to Harriman, who favoured the treaty as well as recognition of the GDR and of the Oder–Neisse line as Poland's western border, but not to Rusk and the majority of US officials.[60]

Following the ratification of the test ban treaty by the US Senate on 24 September, Moscow shifted its position in favour of the US emphasis on arms control, particularly non-proliferation. Again, there was a coincidence with a new development on the Chinese side. The Soviet shift occurred after Beijing had responded to the test ban treaty by urging general and complete disarmament – the declaratory policy Moscow itself had previously pursued in trying vainly to slow down the growth of Western armaments and only abandoned once it had managed to narrow the USA nuclear preponderance because of its own accelerated buildup. Now Moscow and Washington had common interest in checking Chinese nuclear buildup.

In a conversation with Rusk and the British foreign secretary Alexander Douglas-Home at the United Nations on 28 September, Gromyko broached the non-proliferation issue while remaining silent about the non-aggression treaty and Berlin.[61] He subsequently briefed his Eastern European colleagues who had come to New York for the opening session of the UN General Assembly, letting them know that the Berlin question was no urgent matter.[62] Behind its diminished urgency were remarkable developments within the Warsaw Pact, which remained hidden from public eye until after the Cold War was over. They involved the special interests of Romania and Poland.

On 4 October, Romanian foreign minister Corneliu Mǎnescu met with Rusk at the UN in deepest secrecy to reassure him that in case of a Soviet–American military conflict arising from a confrontation such as that over Cuba, his country would remain neutral.[63] This stunning breach of loyalty to the Soviet alliance may or may not have become known in Moscow – no written record of the conversation was apparently kept – but was not out of character for a regime bent visibly on loosening its ties with the Soviet Union. In contrast, Moscow's hidden disputes with Poland as well as with East Germany were of Soviet making, related to Khrushchev's new interest in defusing the German question by accommodating the USA.

Confirming that Khrushchev's professed alarm about nuclear weapons in Germany was not nearly as great as pretended, the Soviet foreign ministry on 2 October notified the Polish party chief, Gomulka, of Moscow's intention to drop its demand for including a prohibition of joint nuclear forces from the non-proliferation agreement that was to be negotiated with Washington.[64] The proposed omission amounted to Soviet acceptance of the prospective sharing of US nuclear weapons by NATO allies, including West Germany, within the framework of the MLF. The acceptance would have sent a warning to Beijing about the possibility of US–Soviet collaboration against its nuclear ambitions – collaboration in which the Kennedy administration had been signalling to Moscow it was interested.[65]

Yet, at a meeting with Rusk and Douglas-Home on 3 October, Gromyko showed no interest in exploring cooperation against China, thus suggesting that his ministry's message to Gomulka on the previous day had been primarily intended to test Polish reaction to a policy that was still in the making.[66] Gomulka was appalled by the message. He immediately convened an emergency session of the Polish politburo, which unanimously rejected what he regarded as a Soviet attempt to compromise on Germany with the USA at the expense of Poland. In a message to Khrushchev informing him on the politburo's position, Gomulka advised the Soviet leader that he should seek a compromise with the Chinese instead, adding the gratuitous comment that the Soviet Union was not without blame in antagonizing them. He condemned any acceptance of West Germany sharing in NATO's nuclear weapons as contradictory to the spirit of the test ban treaty and injurious to the prestige of the Soviet Union and its allies.[67]

Gomulka was obsessed by what he regarded as the incessant German threat to Poland's unrecognized western border, the defence of which was the centrepiece of the Polish communist regime's dubious claim to legitimacy in the eyes of its people.[68] His Germanophobia, unlike Khrushchev's, was genuine rather than pretended, and his mistrust of the USA, too, was deeper. In Gomulka's view, the MLF was 'a military-political transaction between the USA and the FRG based on the FRG's committing itself to the maintenance of US hegemony in Western Europe in return for the USA's committing itself to supporting the FRG's efforts to annex the GDR'. Echoing the Stalin–Molotov strategy, he insisted that 'everything that contributes to the weakening and decay of NATO is in the interest of the socialist states',[69] and went as far as suggesting that the proper response to the MLF should be a joint Soviet–Chinese nuclear force.

On 14 October, deputy foreign minister Vasilii Kuznetsov broke the news of the intended Soviet acceptance of the NATO nuclear sharing plan to the East German politburo, eliciting a similarly negative, if more subdued, reaction as in Poland. Ulbricht lamented that the West German threat was growing regardless of Bonn's access to nuclear weapons and suggested that Soviet acquiescence in it would be interpreted as a concession bound to have disruptive internal repercussions in East Germany. Showing little sympathy, the Soviet diplomat concluded the conversation by hinting at the possibility that Moscow's earlier 'proposal to withdraw all foreign troops from Germany and the GDR' might 'have to be resuscitated' – an alarming perspective for Ulbricht and his regime.[70] A week later, an official Soviet statement charging that the MLF contradicted 'the spirit' of the test ban treaty struck US officials as 'notably restrained'.[71] Rusk may not have realized how pertinent was his observation that 'we might be on the threshold of important developments' provided 'the real problems the Soviets were facing would lead them to seek genuine détente'.[72]

Such an outcome, however, was far from certain. New incidents on the Berlin autobahn, with Soviet forces harassing British and US military convoys, not to mention the arrest in Moscow of Yale University Soviet specialist Frederick C. Barghoorn on phony spying charges, seemed to contradict Rusk's assessment.[73] Yet, Washington chose to play down the incidents on the premise that they were not indicative of a reversal of Soviet commitment to détente, whereas Moscow sought to reaffirm the commitment when it saw the danger of a reversal on the US side when Kennedy was assassinated and succeeded by Lyndon B. Johnson on 22 November. By all accounts, Khrushchev was deeply affected by the tragedy that could not fail to remind him of the fragility of his power as well.

Dobrynin later reminisced that Kennedy and Khrushchev had been set on détente when the president's death interrupted the process. He cited Kennedy's supposed remark to his wife on the morning of his death expressing the belief, after 'deep reflection', that 'everything should be done to get things under way with Russia'.[74] Whatever the substance of the belief, Khrushchev himself in his first message to President Johnson credited his predecessor with having 'laid down the unseen bridge of mutual understanding which, I venture to say, was not broken to the very last day in … [his] life'.[75] Contradicting these lofty postmortems is the warning delivered to Dobrynin on the eve of the assassination by ambassador-at-large Llewellyn Thompson, the experienced former US envoy to Moscow, who characterized the recent developments in mutual relations as 'not good'.[76]

In fact, the change of the guard in Washington did not affect adversely the US–Soviet relations. Rusk remained optimistic, believing the USA had been given a 'hunting license for means to develop détente'.[77] Johnson, to reassure sceptics, went out of the way to emphasize the continuity of US policy despite the inevitable change in style resulting from the change of personnel.[78] Uncharacteristically, Soviet diplomats welcomed the 17 December NATO communiqué as an invitation to détente.[79] As the new year dawned, Khrushchev announced a 4.5 per cent cut in the Soviet defence budget, to which Johnson responded by a 2 per cent cut in US defence spending and a 25 per cent reduction in the procurement of enriched uranium for use in nuclear weapons. Khrushchev then reciprocated by stopping the construction of two new plutonium plants, designed for the same purpose, and scaled down other nuclear programmes for the military. According to Dobrynin, Khrushchev considered reduction of military budgets the necessary first step toward effective disarmament.[80]

At the beginning of 1964, the relations between the superpowers were thus more relaxed than at any other time since the onset of the Cold War and seemed to be getting closer. Such a prospect was not welcomed without reservations by their respective allies. To West Europeans, no matter how much they desired détente, its management by the superpowers raised the spectre of the abandonment by the USA of their nuclear protection. De Gaulle had, in any case, already concluded that the US nuclear umbrella was a fiction, and drawn the conclusion that France must take the responsibility for its own security, preferably in a special relationship with West Germany. Yet the Elysée treaty he had designed proved a 'pale imitation' of what he had wanted,[81] once the Bonn parliament appended to it a clause reaffirming West Germany's loyalty to the USA. Nor did rapprochement with the Soviet Union seem an option for France as long as Moscow displayed preference for dealing with Washington.

The MLF was the key issue in US relations with NATO in 1964.[82] Yet just as the Soviet Union was getting ready to acquiesce in the implementation of the project, the European allies that were originally intended to be its principal beneficiaries were developing doubts about it. Adenauer, its foremost advocate, was succeeded as chancellor by Ludwig Erhard, more susceptible to pressure for 'change through rapprochement' in relations with the East – the formula enunciated by Social Democratic politician Egon Bahr on the eventful day in July 1963 when the negotiations leading to the test ban treaty were resumed.[83] The British, and even less the smaller NATO members, were never enthusiastic about Germany sharing nuclear weaponry and remained uncomfortable with the absurd complexity of the MLF scheme, with its multinational crews on nuclear-armed surface warships.

On the Warsaw Pact side, the prospect of West Germany rising to become NATO's strongest European power rankled both East Germany and Poland, straining not only their relations with Moscow but their mutual relations as well. In December 1963, Poland unveiled the 'Gomulka plan' for freezing nuclear armaments in Central Europe, designed particularly to prevent the entry of NATO's German-manned vessels into the Baltic.[84] East Germany resented the plan because it ignored the GDR's primary goal of achieving international recognition as a sovereign state, and tried to pre-empt it by proposing the alternative plan for denuclearization of both German states. Although such a project stood little chance of being accepted, it at least served to undermine the Polish initiative. Nor was Moscow enthusiastic about Gomulka's idea of a nuclear freeze conducive, according to Gromyko, to recreating 'the thick icy frost of the Cold War'.[85] When Rapacki tried to come to Berlin to clarify matters, Ulbricht sent word that 'the leading comrades at the foreign ministry' were not in town to receive him, and the Poles responded in kind by snubbing East German representatives in Warsaw.[86] More to the point, Khrushchev infuriated Gomulka at their January meeting by revealing his intention to visit Bonn and to improve relations – a telling sign of the direction in which Khrushchev's policy was moving. Not without reason, Gomulka berated him for pursuing Soviet interests at Poland's expense, in response to which the Soviet leader hinted menacingly that Gomulka's position in the party was 'not forever'.[87] In fact, it was to outlast Khrushchev's own by seven years.

So frayed had Moscow's relations with the Warsaw Pact's northern members become – in addition to the fraying of those with Romania and China – that Khrushchev found it appropriate to propose regular consultation and exchange of information to coordinate policies.[88] This appeared particularly urgent in view of the forthcoming ENDC negotiations on the spread of nuclear armaments and the divergent opinions on the subject. He proposed consultations at the level of foreign ministers – the beginning of the arduous Soviet effort to streamline and institutionalize the Warsaw Pact's policy-making bodies in a fashion comparable to that of NATO.

Ulbricht responded by calling for a meeting of the alliance's political consultative committee, ostensibly to follow up Khrushchev's New Year's Eve appeal to the heads of the world's governments for the renunciation of the use of force but in reality to line up the allies' support for the GDR's drive for international recognition.[89] Wanting to meet as early as March, he insisted there was danger in delay since 'some' of them, meaning the Poles, had already advanced disarmament proposals on their own. The Romanians demurred, pleading inconvenient timing, and proceeded issuing in April what came to be known as their 'declaration of independence', asserting the intention to conduct their own policy without foreign interference.[90] As a result, neither the planned foreign ministers' meeting nor the PCC session took place during Khrushchev's remaining days in office, indicating that his days were numbered.

In June, the Soviet Union signed a mutual defence and friendship treaty with East Germany, the absence of which had been one of the last features that distinguished the status of East Germany from that of other members of the Warsaw Pact. The gesture was designed to reassure the edgy Ulbricht, and he was duly gratified. At the same time, under the circumstances, the normalization of East Germany's status within the alliance carried the disturbing implication of Moscow wishing to normalize its relations with the other German state as well, as Khrushchev had hinted to Gomulka he wanted to do. The USA did not show it considered the treaty an unfriendly act.[91]

The situation evolving in 1963 resembled in important ways that of the Cold War's terminal stage 25 years later; at the same time, there were crucial differences. Soviet authority in Eastern Europe was eroding as the Khrushchev leadership was losing steam, showing disposition toward appeasement and accommodation. Yet, the pressure from Eastern Europe to which Moscow was responding emanated from the ruling oligarchies, which by posing as defenders of national interests were asserting their own power, rather than from their constituents challenging the discredited rulers. East European populations were quiescent, reluctant to endanger the tangible improvements in their lives that had taken place under Khrushchev. This was still the generation shaped by the memories of Stalin and Hitler, fearful of another war – and no people were more resigned to the prospect of another war than the Poles, the people that in 1989 would be in the forefront of the struggle that brought down the Soviet empire.[92]

Nor were the superpower relations the same then as they would be in the late 1980s. Major arms control agreements had been signed on both occasions, but the 1963 test ban treaty was not followed up by Western pressure on the Soviet Union to address its political vulnerabilities. Instead, the USA deliberately focused on arms control as presumably more important as well as more manageable than the systemic differences underlying the Cold War. Johnson's landmark speech of 23 May 1964, was about 'building bridges' rather than knocking down walls.[93] The ultimate reason why the Cold War did not end in the 1960s, however, concerned Soviet leadership, despite superficial similarities between Khrushchev and Gorbachev.

Khrushchev's son has maintained that if the planned Soviet armed forces reductions had been carried out the USA would have reciprocated, and the Cold War would have ended earlier. Although this cannot be proved, his father, like Gorbachev, became appalled at the cost of his country's militarization and sought to reverse it, even unilaterally. In the summer of 1963, he further antagonized the Soviet military by ending the separate status of the ground forces within the command structure and threatened to downgrade them by curtailing drastically the production of tanks – the mainstay of Soviet offensive strategy in Europe and the main ingredient of the Warsaw Pact's numerical superiority over NATO, the abandonment of which by Gorbachev eventually broke the confrontation.

Besides demands for additional cuts in the defence budget, Khrushchev jolted his generals by his cavalier pronouncements about matters of military expertise, such as his wisecracks about tanks supposedly going the way cavalry had gone.[94] Nevertheless, the traditionally docile Soviet generals did not conspire against him; it was the party coterie, consisting largely of his protégés and acolytes, that did, with indispensable help from Khrushchev's appointee as the head of the secret services, Vladimir Semichastnyi.[95] By that time, unlike Gorbachev, Khrushchev was a tired man while his opponents were spoiling for action. He had not come to power, like Gorbachev, after the rest of the politburo had acknowledged the bankruptcy of its policies, but was himself widely regarded as politically bankrupt after his ambitious domestic reform plans had failed to meet expectations. His foreign policy, which had taken a stable course after the Berlin and Cuban adventures, was not the main issue, yet it became the main casualty of his forced dismissal on 14 October.

The extent of his prospective opening to West Germany, which has tantalized interpreters of his downfall, is not sufficiently documented – *prima facie* evidence of its having been in the realm of intentions rather than specific plans. In summing up Khrushchev's failings in a prosecutorial speech to the party central committee, its chief ideologist, Mikhail A. Suslov, alluded to the recent mission to Bonn by Khrushchev's boorish son-in-law, Aleksei Adzhubei, as something that 'could have brought harm to our relations with friendly socialist countries'.[96] He was referring to Adzhubei's indiscretions that could have been interpreted by his West German hosts as implying Soviet readiness to sacrifice East German and Polish interests for the sake of normalization of relations with Bonn – indiscretions monitored by Polish intelligence and passed on to Moscow.[97]

Whatever were the opportunities inherent in Khrushchev's attempted demilitarization of the Cold War along with a prospective compromise settlement in Germany, they were missed because of his dismissal. This did not occur, as French government estimates at the time and other interpreters later on wrongly assumed, because of the adventurism Khrushchev had shown in provoking the Cuban missile crisis but, on the contrary, because of the common sense that had been increasingly showing since.[98] The détente he sought was suspect to his rivals not only because of his style but also, more importantly, because of its substance. They were men who sought comfort in Soviet military might, which – contrary to Khrushchev – they believed could offset the Soviet system's other deficiencies and, above all, secure their own power. They could easily gain support from the disgruntled Soviet generals, in return for which they were prepared to countenance the generals' dreams that he had threatened to disturb.

NOTES

1 Speech by Novotný to the Czechoslovak party central committee, 2 November 1962, ÚV KSČ, 01/98/85, SÚA.
2 Mikhail Yu. Prozumenshchikov, 'The Sino-Indian Conflict, the Cuban Missile Crisis, and the Sino-Soviet Split, October 1962: New Evidence from Russian Archives', *Cold War International History Project Bulletin*, 8–9 (1996–97), 251–7, at p. 255.
3 Stenogram: 'Meeting of the Delegations of the Communist Party of the Soviet Union and the Chinese Communist Party', 8 July 1963, *Cold War International History Project Bulletin*, 10 (1998), 175–9, at p. 178.
4 *Current Intelligence Weekly Review*, 7 December 1962, FRUS (*Foreign Relations of the United States*) 1961–1963, vol. 5, no. 271.
5 Memorandum on Rusk–Mikoian conversation, 30 November 1962, FRUS 1961–1963, vol. 5, no. 270.
6 Richard E. Neustadt, *Report to JFK: The Skybolt Crisis in Perspective*, Ithaca, NY: Cornell University Press, 1999.
7 *Current Intelligence Weekly Review*, 25 January 1963, FRUS 1961–1963, vol. 5, no. 284.
8 Jacques Bariety, 'De Gaulle, Adenauer et la genèse du traité franco-allemand du 22 janvier 1963', *Revue d'Allemagne*, 22 (1990–91), 539–64.
9 George W. Ball, *The Past Has Another Pattern: Memoirs*, New York: Norton, 1982, p. 271.
10 'Moscow Assails Paris–Bonn Pact as Peace Threat', *New York Times*, 6 February 1963.
11 Gomulka to Khrushchev, 8 October 1963, in Douglas Selvage, 'The Warsaw Pact and Nuclear Nonproliferation, 1963–1965', Cold War International History Project Working Paper no. 32, Washington, DC: Woodrow Wilson International Center for Scholars, 2001, pp. 22–9, at p. 25.
12 Marina Ts. Arzakanian, 'Plan 'edinnoi Evropy' de Gollia i SSSR (1958–1962)' (De Gaulle's Plan of 'One Europe' and the USSR), in A.S. Namazova and B. Emerson (eds), *Istoriia evropeiskoi integratsii (1945–1994)* (History of European Integration), Moscow: Institut vseobshchei istorii RAN, 1995, pp. 197–205, at pp. 201–2.
13 Kuznetsov–Kennedy meeting, FRUS 1961–1963, vol. 5, no. 277, vol. 11, pp. 658–62, vol. 15, pp. 474–5, and vol. 7, pp. 630–1; Gromyko–Kohler discussion, 18 January 1986, *Current Intelligence Weekly Review*, 25 January 1963, FRUS 1961–1963, vol. 5, no. 284.
14 FRUS 1961–1963, vol. 5, nos 281 and 284.
15 *Documents on Disarmament*, 1963, pp. 57–8.
16 US Delegation to Secretary of State, 22 February 1963, Def 4, 2/1/63, Box 3697, RG-59, NARA.
17 Rusk to US Embassy in Paris, 28 February 1963, Def 4, 2/1/63, Box 3697, RG-59, NARA.
18 Arms Control and Disarmament Agency to US Embassies, 1 April 1963, Def 4, 4/1/63, Box 3697, RG-59, NARA.
19 Record of PCC meeting in Moscow, 7 June 1962, file 'Novotný, zahraničí, Varšavská smlouva', k č. 20, SÚA.
20 Kohler to Department of State, 16 March 1963, FRUS 1961–1962, vol. 5, no. 304.

21 Sergei N. Khrushchev, *Nikita Khrushchev and the Creation of a Superpower*, University Park: Penn State University Press, 2000, p. 732.

22 Memorandum by Central Intelligence Agency, 18 March 1963, FRUS 1961–1963, vol. 5, no. 305.

23 FRUS 1961–1963, vol. 6, no. 94.

24 Deborah Welch Larson, *Anatomy of Mistrust: US–Soviet Relations during the Cold War*, Ithaca: Cornell University Press, 1997, pp. 150–1.

25 'Khrushchev at Bay', 21 March 1963, Pol US–USSR, 2/1/63, Box 4121, RG-59, NARA.

26 FRUS 1961–1963, vol. 15, pp. 510–11.

27 Khrushchev to Kennedy, 29 April 1963, FRUS 1961–1963, vol. 6, no. 988.

28 Khrushchev to Kennedy and Macmillan, 8 May 1963, FRUS 1961–1963, vol. 7, pp. 693–9.

29 Anatoly Dobrynin, *In Confidence: Moscow's Ambassador to America's Six Cold War Presidents*, New York: Random House, 1995, p. 104.

30 Khrushchev, *Nikita Khrushchev and the Creation of a Superpower*, p. 693.

31 Oliver Kendrick, *Kennedy, Macmillan and the Nuclear Test-Ban Debate, 1961–63*, London: Macmillan, 1998.

32 Memorandum on Bowles–Dobrynin conversation, 17 May 1963, Memcon, Pol 1 General Policy US–USSR, Central Foreign Policy File, Box 4122, RG-59, NARA; memorandum on Bundy–Dobrynin conversation, 17 May 1963, FRUS 1961–1963, vol. 5, p. 673.

33 See, in particular, Arthur M. Schlesinger, *A Thousand Days*, Boston: Houghton Mifflin, 1965, pp. 900–2.

34 Raymond L. Garthoff, *A Journey through the Cold War: A Memoir of Containment and Coexistence*, Washington, DC: Brookings Institution Press, 2001, p. 165.

35 *Documents on Disarmament, 1963*, pp. 244–6.

36 FRUS 1961–1963, vol. 7, p. 793.

37 Stenogram: 'Meeting of the Delegations of the Communist Party of the Soviet Union and the Chinese Communist Party', 8 July 1963, *Cold War International History Project Bulletin*, 10 (1998), 175–9, at p. 178.

38 Khrushchev to Gomulka, 10 July 1963, KC PZPR, 2662/521–22, AAN.

39 *New York Times*, 15 July 1963.

40 Khrushchev to Gomulka, 15 July 1963, and Cedenbal to Cyrankiewicz, 15 July 1963, KC PZPR, 2662/523–26, AAN; Khrushchev to Ulbricht, 15 July 1963, ZK SED, J IV 2/202–245 Bd 2; DY 30/3387, SAPMO.

41 Record of Khrushchev–Harriman conversation, FRUS 1961–1963, vol. 7, pp. 856–63, at p. 861.

42 Marc Trachtenberg, *A Constructed Peace: The Making of a European Settlement, 1945–1963*, Princeton: Princeton University Press, 1999, pp. 382–402.

43 Christof Münger, *Ich bin ein West-Berliner: Der Wandel der amerikanischen Berlinpolitik während der Präsidentschaft John F. Kennedy*, Zurich: Forschungsstelle für Sicherheitspolitik und Konflikanalyse, 1999, pp. 190–9.

44 Quinton Hailsham, *The Door Wherein I Went*, London: Collins, 1975, p. 219.

45 Memorandum on conversation with Couve de Murville, 7 October 1963, FRUS 1961–1963, vol. 5, no. 360.

46 Khrushchev, *Nikita Khrushchev and the Creation of a Superpower*, p. 675.

47 Ernest May, John Steinbrunner and Thomas Wolfe, *History of the Strategic Arms Competition, 1945–1972*, ed. Alfred Goldberg, Washington, DC: Office of the Secretary of Defense, 1981, pp. 686–7. Copy at NSA.

48 Khrushchev, *Nikita Khrushchev and the Creation of a Superpower*, p. 671.

49 May, Steinbrunner and Wolfe, *History of the Strategic Arms Competition*, pp. 732–3.

50 Michael Kaser, *COMECON: Integration Problems of the Planned Economies*, London: Oxford University Press, 1965, pp. 110–12.
51 'Wie soll es in der Zusammenarbeit zw. den Mitgliedsländern des RGW weitergehen?', ZK SED J IV 2/202–233 Bd 2, SAPMO; report by Ulbricht, undated, ZK SED, J IV 2/202–204 Bd 7, SAPMO.
52 Memorandum by Rapacki, 20 July 1963, KC PZPR, 2662/527–30, AAN.
53 Memorandum on Rusk–van Roijen conversation, 14 August 1963, Pol US–USSR 6/1/63, Box 4121, RG-59, NARA.
54 Rusk to Secretary of State, 5 August 1963, FRUS, 1961–1963, vol. 5, no. 344.
55 Khrushchev, *Nikita Khrushchev and the Creation of a Superpower*, p. 670.
56 Rusk to Slany, 21 May 1963, Pol US–USSR 6/1/63, Box 4121, RG-59, NARA.
57 Memorandum on Beam-Kornienko conversation, 6 August 1963, Pol US–USSR, 6/1/63, Box 4121, RG-59, NARA.
58 *Department of State Bulletin*, 2 September 1963, p. 358.
59 Thompson to Department of State, 10 September 1963, FRUS 1961–1963, vol. 5, no. 354.
60 David Kaiser, 'Men and Policies, 1961–69', in Diane B. Kunz (ed.), *The Diplomacy of the Crucial Decade: American Foreign Relations During the 1960s*, New York: Columbia University Press, 1994, pp. 11–41, at p. 23.
61 US delegation to the United Nations to Department of State, 18 September 1963, Pol 1 General Policy US–USS, Cen. For. Policy File, Box 4122, RG-59, NARA.
62 Note by Hájek on briefing by Gromyko, 5 October 1963, in Michal Reiman and Petr Luňák (eds), *Studená válka, 1954–1964: Sovětské dokumenty v českých archivech* (The Cold War, 1954–1964: Soviet Documents in Czech Archives), Brno: Doplněk, 2000, pp. 373–6.
63 Raymond L. Garthoff, 'When and Why Romania Distanced Itself from the Warsaw Pact', *Cold War International History Project Bulletin*, 5 (1995), 111. Cf. Mircea Suciu, 'Criza rachetelor din Cuba şi apropierea româno-americană' (The Cuban Missile Crisis and the Romanian–American Rapprochement), *Dosarele istoriei* (Bucharest), 6 (1997), 30–1.
64 Soviet memorandum, transmitted 2 October 1963, in Selvage, *The Warsaw Pact and Nuclear Nonproliferation*, pp. 20–1.
65 William Burr and Jeffrey T. Richelson, 'Whether to "Strangle the Baby in the Cradle": The United States and the Chinese Nuclear Program, 1960–64', *International Security*, 25, 3 (2000–2), 54–99, at pp. 67–78.
66 Summary of meeting between Rusk, Douglas-Home and Gromyko, dated 4 October 1963, FRUS 1961–1963, vol. 7, pp. 887–9.
67 Gomulka to Khrushchev, 8 October 1963, in Selvage, *The Warsaw Pact and Nuclear Nonproliferation*, pp. 22–9.
68 Marcin Zaremba, *Komunizm, legitymizacja, nacjonalism: Nacjonalistyczna legit-ymizacja władzy komunistycznej w Polsce* (Communism, Legitimation, Nationalism: Nationalist Legitimation of the Communist Regime in Poland), Warsaw: Trio, 1991, pp. 305–13.
69 Selvage, *The Warsaw Pact and Nuclear Nonproliferation*, pp. 24–5.
70 Excerpt from the record of Kuznetsov's discussion with the SED politburo, 14 October 1963, in Selvage, *The Warsaw Pact and Nuclear Nonproliferation*, pp. 31–5, here at p. 35.
71 *Current Intelligence Weekly Review*, 25 October 1963, FRUS 1961–1963, vol. 7, no. 367.
72 Memorandum on Rusk–Cecil King conversation, 29 October 1963, King, Pol 1 General Policy US–USSR, Cen. For. Policy File, Box 4122, RG-59, NARA.
73 FRUS 1961–63, vol. 7, no. 365.

74 Dobrynin, *In Confidence*, p. 110.
75 Khrushchev to Lyndon Johnson, 24 November 1963, FRUS 1961–1963, vol. 6.
76 Memorandum on Thompson–Dobrynin conversation, 21 November 1963, FRUS 1961–1963, vol. 5, no. 377.
77 Memorandum on Rusk–Paul Martin conversation, 4 December 1963, Pol US–USSR, 10/1/63, Box 4121, RG-59, NARA.
78 After Johnson's assumption of office, Kennedy's former intimate, William Walton, reportedly went to Moscow to reassure the Kremlin that Johnson would soon be replaced by Robert Kennedy, as a result of which succession any deterioration of US–Soviet relations under Johnson would be reversed. See Jeff Shesol, *Mutual Contempt: Lyndon Johnson, Robert Kennedy, and the Feud that Defined a Decade*, New York: Norton, 1997.
79 Memorandum on conversation between Assistant Secretary of State Robert Manning and Soviet Embassy counsellor Aleksandr S. Zinchuk, 20 December 1963, Def 4, NATO, Box 3696, RG-59, NARA.
80 Dobrynin, *In Confidence*, p. 147.
81 Gérard Klein, 'Les relations franco-allemandes et la sécurité de l'Europe occidentale sous la présidence du Général de Gaulle', *Etudes gaulliennes*, 6, nos 23–34 (July–December 1978), p. 60.
82 Massimiliano Guderzo, *Interesse nazionale e responsabilità globale: Gli Stati Uniti, l'Alleanza atlantica e l'integrazione europea negli anni di Johnson, 1963–69*, Florence: Aida, 2000, pp. 43–144.
83 A. James McAdams, *Germany Divided: From the Wall to Reunification*, Princeton, NJ: Princeton University Press, 1993, p. 539.
84 Selvage, *The Warsaw Pact and Nuclear Nonproliferation*, p. 8.
85 *Izvestiia*, 3 March 1964.
86 Ulbricht to Gomulka, 25 January 1964, KC PZPR, XIA/103, AAN; Gomulka to Ulbricht, 13 February 1964, ZK SED, J IV 2/202–246, Bd 3, SAPMO.
87 Andrzej Albert, *Najnowsza historia Polski, 1918–1980* (Recent History of Poland), London: Puls, 1991, pp. 822–3.
88 Khrushchev to Ulbricht, 2 January 1964, ZK SED, DY 30/3387, SAPMO.
89 Ulbricht to Khrushchev, 24 January 1964, ZK SED, J IV 2/202–246 Bd 3, SAPMO; Ulbricht to Gomulka, 28 January 1964, KC PZPR XIA/103, AAN.
90 Gheorghiu-Dej to Ulbricht, undated (March 1964), ZK SED, J IV 2/202–246, Bd 3, SAPMO; *Statement on the Stand of the Romanian Workers' Party Concerning Problems of the World Communist and Working-Class Movement*, Bucharest: Agerpress, 1964.
91 Dobrynin, *In Confidence*, p. 121.
92 George Kolankiewicz and Ray Taras, 'Poland: Socialism for Everyman?', in Archie Brown and Jack Gray (eds), *Political Culture and Political Change in Communist States*, New York: Holmes & Meier, 1977, pp. 101–30, at p. 106.
93 *Public Papers of the Presidents of the United States: Lyndon B. Johnson, 1964*, Book I, pp. 708–10.
94 Khrushchev, *Nikita Khrushchev and the Creation of a Superpower*, pp. 717–21.
95 *Ljubjanka III. patro: Svědectví předsedy KGB z let 1961–1967 Vladimíra Semičastného* (Liubianka, Third Floor: Testimony by Vladimir Semichastnyi, the KGB Chairman in 1961–1967), ed. Tomáš Sniegoň, Prague: Dauphin, 1998, pp. 176–95.
96 Speech by Suslov to Soviet politburo, 2/1/749/7–24, RGANI.
97 Daniel Kosthorst, 'Sowjetische Geheimpolitik in Deutschland? Chruschtschow und die Adschubej-Mission 1964', *Vierteljahrshefte für Zeitgeschichte*, 44 (1996), pp. 257–93.
98 Frédéric Bozo, *La France et l'OTAN: De la guerre froide au nouvel ordre européen*, Paris: Masson, 1991, p. 79.

PART IV:
DIRECT NEGOTIATIONS BETWEEN
EASTERN AND WESTERN EUROPE

14

Soviet Union, Finland and the 'Northern Balance', 1957–63

Seppo Hentilä

The term 'Northern Balance' was introduced in 1966 by the Norwegian political scientist Arne Olav Brundtland to describe the foundations of the existing situation in the North of Europe.[1] The phrase means two different things at the same time: on the one hand, it served as a description of the prevailing constellation including a special presence of the superpowers in the area and a description of relations between the four countries Denmark, Finland, Norway and Sweden. On the other hand, the theory of 'Northern Balance' has also been used as a general explanatory model for the geo-political changes in the North of Europe.

Brundtland did not actually invent the idea of a 'Northern Balance' although he might have been the first to use the term. Since 1949, when the constellation of security policy of the four Nordic countries had been formed, the predominant explanation for the geopolitical situation had in fact been based on this kind of 'balance' thinking. Brundtland admitted this when, in the same periodical of the Norwegian Institute of Foreign Policy in which he had originally presented the term, he once again returned to the idea of 'Northern Balance' in 1976. On that occasion, he argued that the model had not lost its value as a theoretical approach to geopolitics in the North of Europe over the previous ten years.[2]

The 'Northern Balance' as a Geopolitical Theory

The key word 'balance' means that every possible effort to change the constellation would almost automatically lead to countermeasures by the opposite side in order to regain the original balance. The imagined existence of this kind of automatic correction mechanism is actually the core of the theory of 'Northern Balance'. Thus, the term 'balance' also includes an explanation of the so-called 'relative moderation' of Soviet policy toward Finland and the Nordic countries in general – and this primarily because of possible countermeasures by the Western powers if Soviet policy were to become more aggressive toward Finland. Also, the behaviour of the

Scandinavian countries – the issue of how close Norway's and Denmark's ties with NATO would be and whether Sweden would continue its neutrality policy or bind itself more closely to the Western bloc – this all could be understood and explained from the point of view of the theory of 'Northern Balance'.[3]

The fundamentals of geopolitics in the North of Europe, often described as 'Northern Balance', were as follows:

1 Denmark and Norway were members of NATO under so-called 'minimum conditions', which meant that they refused to allow the stationing of nuclear weapons or foreign troops on their territories in peacetime. This also included Norway's voluntary demilitarization of the area bordering on Murmansk on the Arctic Ocean, where the Soviet Union had built numerous naval bases.
2 Sweden's neutrality policy, 'non-alignment' in peacetime, aiming to preserve neutrality in wartime as well, supported by a relatively strong national defence.
3 Finland's neutrality policy in the framework of the 1948 pact of friendship, cooperation and mutual assistance (FCMA) between Finland and the Soviet Union. Most important in this treaty were articles 1 and 2, the so-called military articles, which obligated Finland to defend its own territory with all its strength if Germany or some country allied with Germany attempted to invade the Soviet Union using Finnish territory. In the event it were unable to resist the invader alone, Finland undertook to negotiate for military assistance from the Soviet Union. This so-called 'consultation article' was from the Finnish point of view the most dangerous part of the FCMA Treaty.

Possible changes in the 'Northern Balance' could be caused by certain initiatives of either superpower involving new military strategies or arms systems (especially the issue of deploying tactical nuclear weapons or missiles in this area). Withdrawing or defusing of military potential in the area would logically lead to changes in the 'balance' as well. Specific proposals and plans for nuclear-free zones (NFZ) put forth during the 1950s and 1960s were very important for exactly that reason.

In the North of Europe, the Iron Curtain did not seem to be as stiff as it was in Central Europe. Finland's position between the blocs and the reservations of Denmark and Norway on the nuclear and base policies of NATO made it possible for both sides to use the North of Europe as a kind of testing ground where the reactions of the opposite side could be observed.

A major change in the geopolitical situation in the North of Europe was caused by West Germany's joining NATO in 1955 and its military presence in the area (especially West German participation in NATO's naval manoeuvres in the Baltic Sea). The new role of the Federal Republic was important, on the one hand, because of the NATO membership of Denmark and Norway and, on the other, because of the Finnish–Soviet FCMA Treaty, which was premised on a potential military threat from (West) Germany.

The theory of 'Northern Balance' seems to offer a fruitful approach for researching Finnish–Soviet relations during the late 1950s and early 1960s. On the basis of 'balance thinking', we can assume – and this is the main hypothesis of this article – that the Soviet Union's policy toward Finland always had a certain Scandinavian dimension. The Soviet Union may have used Finland – and especially Finland's President Urho Kekkonen – as a tool of its Scandinavian policy. The opposite is also true: the behaviour of the Scandinavian countries, their relations to each other, and, even more, to the policies of the Western powers – especially their attitudes toward NATO's nuclear and other strategic plans in the area – might well have had a substantial influence on the Soviets' Scandinavian policy and Finnish policy as well.

The Ambivalence of Soviet Views on Neutrality

The attitudes of Soviet foreign policy toward neutrality always remained ambivalent. The Soviets' dualistic world-view left little room to deal with a phenomenon such as neutrality. According to the 'Two Camps doctrine' presented by A.A. Zhdanov in 1947, national liberation movements could still be included in the 'Camp of Peace and Democracy'. Neutrality, on the other hand, was just an 'imperialist deviation'. Staying on the sidelines was interpreted as giving active support to the 'imperialists'.[4]

In the first phase of the Cold War, the Soviets allowed Finland very little freedom. Since the summer 1947, when the Soviet Union had actually hindered Finland's participation in the Marshall Plan (ERP), it had been jealously watching every Western contact with Finland. Thus, the Finns were not allowed to join such European bodies as the Organization for European Economic Cooperation (OEEC), the European Council or even the Nordic Council, founded in 1952 as an interparliamentary organization of the Scandinavian countries. Obviously, the NATO membership of Denmark and Norway was literally too much for the Soviet Union at that time and did not fit with its interpretation of the 'Northern Balance'.

With the Soviet Union seeming to view the Nordic countries so suspiciously in the 1950s, Finland's chances of maintaining its democratic system and establishing its trade relations with the market economies seemed to be very dismal. Finland was not allowed to cooperate with or become a member of international organizations or arrangements which were dominated by the NATO countries. Since the mid-1950s, this ban meant more precisely organizations of which the Federal Republic was a member. This was naturally based on the Soviet interpretation of the military articles of the FCMA Treaty of 1948.

The first détente emerged after Stalin's death in 1953 as a transition in Soviet domestic and foreign policies. The Soviet Union soon began to use the concept of 'peaceful coexistence' to describe its relations with the West, though this became the official Soviet foreign policy doctrine only in February of 1956 at the Twentieth Party Congress of the CPSU.[5]

In the spirit of Geneva, during the fall of 1955, the Soviet Union surprisingly waived its 50-year lease and handed back its naval base on the Porkkala peninsula – as near as 15 miles to Helsinki – as compensation for extension of the FCMA Treaty for an additional 20 years. The departure of foreign troops from the vicinity of the Finnish capital enhanced the credibility of Finland's neutrality in the eyes of the Western powers. In October of 1955, Finland succeeded in joining the Nordic Council; identification with the Scandinavian countries was important for Finland's image in the wider world. In December of the same year, it was also finally accepted as a member of the United Nations.

N.S. Khrushchev was the first Soviet leader to achieve practical results through use of the neutrality concept, especially in the case of Austria in 1955. Then Khrushchev made a remarkable theoretical reinterpretation at the Twentieth Party Congress when he announced that, along with the world's two known camps, there also existed a third one, a zone of peace; he went on to praise the policies of the neutral countries of Europe and Asia. Surprisingly, though not accidentally, Finland was mentioned as a neutral state, comparable to Sweden and Austria.

Soviet scholars soon added to Khrushchev's remarks by asserting that the existence of the socialist camp was a prerequisite for non-alignment and active neutrality. Active neutrality or neutralism was seen to have emerged after the Second World War as the threat of nuclear war had grown. Neutralism differed from the tradition of permanent neutrality in three ways: (1) it was based on peaceful coexistence; (2) it was anti-imperialist and active, and was based on a broad popular interest; and (3) the countries adhering to it would abstain from possessing nuclear weapons. As traditional neutrals, they would also prohibit foreign military bases and the use of their territory by foreign aircraft.[6]

Even though the neutrals were no longer seen as harmful 'fellow travellers' or 'hidden allies' of the enemy, the ambiguity in Soviet feelings toward neutrality did not disappear. For a socialist country, in any case, neutrality would be a step back toward US imperialism and its sphere of influence, a move which in the final instance should be prevented through 'brotherly help' to the communist party of the friendly nation. Although a European collective security organization guaranteeing the status quo had been one of the main issues of Soviet foreign policy, the possible neutrality of certain countries was seen as an important objective too – especially Germany and Austria, and in Scandinavia, the NATO members Denmark and Norway.[7]

In Scandinavia, promoting neutrality instead of NATO membership became Moscow's general policy. The earlier Soviet policy on Scandinavia was no longer regarded as very satisfactory; the Soviet foreign ministry now perceived that attitudes toward these countries had to move beyond a state of stagnation. The main objective still remained eliminating Scandinavia as a military bridgehead against the USSR. But now the best way of achieving this seemed to be by steering Scandinavia toward neutrality. Larger Soviet foreign policy objectives were reflected in the expected consequences of détente. It was seen as strengthening the position of the neutral countries and also furthering the aspirations of many countries to leave aggressive military alliances, a hope which clearly referred to Denmark and Norway.[8]

The new Soviet approach to international relations and neutrality was noticed in Finland as early as the summer of 1953. The first major evaluation of the changes was made by the Finnish Ambassador to Moscow, Eero A. Wuori. His central concern was to analyse whether the international situation had altered so much that it should be taken into consideration in Finnish foreign policy. Despite the easing of tensions between the superpowers, no changes were perceived that would make it advisable to alter substantially Finland's relations with the Soviet Union. New possibilities were seen, however, to change Finland's policy toward the West – in certain respects, it could become more open and positive in tone.[9]

Consequently, the moment was advantageous for both the public image of Soviet foreign policy and for Urho Kekkonen as defender of Finland's manoeuvring room to tie together the FCMA Treaty and neutrality. Already in March 1956, Kekkonen had privately stated that 'our own success depends on the fact that we are able to safeguard our position as a display window of peaceful coexistence'.[10] This was supported by K.M. Voroshilov's statements during his visit to Finland in 1957, where he underscored the importance of peaceful coexistence as the foundation of Soviet foreign policy and also stressed the exemplary nature of Soviet–Finnish relations.

Kekkonen, who had emerged as J.K. Paasikivi's trusted ally, was an exceptionally gifted and ambitious, if controversial, leader. It is well known that the Soviet Union and especially the KGB had regarded it as necessary to intervene in the 1956 Finnish presidential elections to ensure the victory of the most suitable candidate, Kekkonen, in order to guarantee good relations.[11]

Kekkonen certainly knew how to make the most of his powers as president of the republic, even going further than the articles of the constitution allowed (when interpreted narrowly). His autocratic style of leadership was well suited to the management of relations with the Soviet Union, where personal contacts were everything. It was especially notable that Kekkonen was soon able to build a close personal friendship with Khrushchev. Soon after Kekkonen had won the presidential election in February 1956, the Soviets analysed the fundamentals of the new situation carefully. It was observed that as Kekkonen had won by only the closest of margins, his freedom of action as well as his re-election in six years' time would be dependent on how much support he could gain outside his own party, the Agrarian League.[12]

This being the case, it was expected that the Soviet embassy in Helsinki would follow with keen interest developments among Kekkonen's main competitors in the socialist and bourgeois camps. As well as opposing Kekkonen in domestic politics at least since the late 1940s, these groups had different, more Scandinavian and Western, emphases in their foreign policies. In the reports of the Soviet embassy, they were often labelled as 'unfriendly,' 'rightist' or at times simply as 'certain circles'.[13]

Stationing Nuclear Weapons in the North of Europe?

The development of arms technology was extremely rapid in the first half of the 1950s, especially in the Soviet Union. In 1957, the Soviets made their first successful test with intercontinental missiles. The most spectacular demonstration of this new technology was the launch of the first Sputnik into orbit around the earth in October of 1957. By that year, the Western powers seemed to have lost their lead in the development of nuclear weapons technology. Stationing missiles equipped with tactical nuclear warheads in European NATO countries seemed to be the only way to prevent Soviet military supremacy.

The USA offered two types of short-range missile, 'Nike' and 'Honest John', to NATO countries including Denmark and Norway. The governments of those two countries were considering serious changes in their security policy during the spring of 1957. There were, for example, plans for building a joint NATO staff in command of the North Sea and the Baltic Sea and to start joint manoeuvres with the newest NATO member, the Federal Republic.[14]

When West Germany joined NATO, military tensions in the North of Europe had inevitably increased. The Soviet Union was very worried about the growing strength of West Germany. When we see the situation from the point of view of the theory of 'Northern Balance', the appearance of a strong new player on the Western side almost automatically had to lead to serious Soviet pressure on the opposite side of the field. This was the geopolitical fate of Finland. Developments in the Baltic Sea began to concern Finland when West Germany became a member of NATO in 1955. From 1957 at least, the USSR was sounding out Finnish support for its policy of opposing naval cooperation between West Germany, Denmark and the UK.[15]

In this phase, Denmark and Norway were inclined to accept missiles but absolutely did not want nuclear warheads. Soviet Prime Minister N.I. Bulganin wrote to his Norwegian and Danish counterparts, warning them of serious consequences. Bulganin's advice to the Danish prime minister was that a small country such as Denmark would be wise to leave NATO as soon as possible. The Norwegian parliament, the Storting, decided in April of 1957 to prohibit the stationing of nuclear weapons in Norway. Prime Minister Gerhardsen's letter to Bulganin confirmed this.[16]

The official newspaper of the Soviet government, *Izvestia*, harshly attacked Finland in March of 1957 and claimed that militarism and war propaganda had recently gained strength there as well. The Soviet propaganda campaign against the Nordic countries was continued in June of 1957 by Prime Minister Bulganin and Secretary-General Khrushchev, both of whom paid a one-week visit to Finland. 'The guests are coming when love is blooming in nature' – with this phrase Khrushchev praised the beauty of the Finnish summer. The aim of this visit by the highest Soviet leadership was obviously to influence the Nordic countries, especially Denmark and Norway. In talks with Finnish leaders, Khrushchev advised them to tell the Norwegians that it would be very wise for them to resign from NATO.

In his speech at the Great Fair Hall in Helsinki, Khrushchev told a large audience about his plan to make the Baltic Sea a neutral area by means of a treaty among all the coastal states. The Baltic should be and for ever remain a sea of peace. To what extent was this a serious proposal? Was it mere rhetoric? We can only note that it was easy for Soviet leaders to promise any-thing and everything, knowing that the opposite side would never agree to such proposals.

In the final press conference of the visit, Khrushchev said that he was very worried about the situation in Denmark and Norway. And, although Sweden was a neutral country, he said that a new kind of war hysteria was to be seen even there. Khrushchev obviously meant the ongoing Swedish debate as to whether the country should strengthen its national defence with nuclear weapons of its own. 'We know that the Danish and Norwegian leaders are at the moment negotiating on stationing nuclear weapons in their countries. May God give their leaders enough courage to refuse this kind of plan', Nikita said prayerfully.

Contemporaries were not aware of the power struggle among the Soviet leadership during Khrushchev's and Bulganin's visit to Finland in June of 1957. The hardliners, a group around Malenkov and Kaganovich, were removed and Khrushchev's position became stronger. But, even later on, he too occasionally showed that he was able to put the 'Western imperialists' under severe pressure. The criticism of détente in connection with the attempted removal of Khrushchev in 1957 created a serious need for a significant foreign political breakthrough for the Soviet Union. The lead the Soviets had gained in missile technology was demonstrated by the launching of Sputnik in late 1957, and this created preconditions for the breakthrough. Sputnik simultaneously symbolized planet-wide striking capability and helped portray the socialist system as the Wave of the Future. The Soviets saw the international system tilting toward the superiority of the socialist camp.[17] In the autumn of 1958, the global context worsened again due to growing superpower confrontation, as the Soviets were heading toward a conflict over Berlin, and the Americans were planning to station tactical nuclear missiles in West Germany.

The Soviet Union answered those US plans with intensive peace propaganda. One of the key issues was a proposal to establish a neutral zone between Western and Eastern Europe. The Baltic Sea and the North of Europe were most favourable for this kind of project. During his visit to Finland in June of 1957, Khrushchev had painted a wonderful picture of the Baltic as a sea of lasting peace. A little later, he proposed to the Western countries a peace treaty with Germany, and, when they rejected it, he threatened to make a peace treaty with the GDR alone and to give all authority over Berlin to East German officials. In January of 1959, the Soviet peace initiative for Germany was sent to the Finnish government as well, which was no surprise at all. With polite but firm words, the Finns rejected the plan, as they did the Soviet invitation to a summit conference on the German question some months later.[18] In this case, as in other similar situations, Finland could refer to the introductory chapter of the FCMA Treaty, which not only entitled but also obliged Finland to remain aloof from disputes between the great powers. If anything qualified as such a dispute, the German question did.[19]

From the point of view of the Nordic countries, the neutralization of the Baltic would have made it a closed sea, the Soviet Union's Mare Nostrum, which only would serve the strategic aims of the USSR, creating a kind of Pax Sovietica. As Swedish Foreign Minister Östen Undén emphasized, it was extremely important that the Baltic remain free for the ships and aircraft of all nations.

Domestic and International Aspects of the 'Night Frost' Crisis of 1958 and 1959

During the latter half of the 1950s, instability had grown in both Finnish domestic politics and in the politics of foreign trade. The consolidation of the European Economic Community (EEC) without Great Britain had led to negotiations on the European Free Trade Association (EFTA). As the main customers of Finnish products and Finland's main rivals would belong to this organization, it was necessary for Finland to make some kind of arrangement toward the end of the 1950s.[20]

At the economic level of Soviet–Finnish relations, there seemed to be problems connected to Finland's growing economic ties with the West. The Soviet Union had seen Western economic organizations as a security and political threat since the time of the Marshall Plan. This attitude remained practically unchanged even during détente. The OEEC was regarded only as a 'US tool' whose influence was not confined to the Western bloc alone. Its function was seen as luring the neutral countries into supporting the overall interests of the West. The Finnish Cold War historian Kimmo Rentola has discovered that clear reasons for the Night Frost crisis were the Soviet Union's economic interests and concerns about the liberalization of Finland's trade with the West since 1957; along with this, there were Finland's strengthening ties with the Western countries. The Soviet Union became worried because the proportion of Finland's trade with Eastern countries began to decrease. According to Rentola, another ideological interest was the Soviet Union's need to get the Finnish Communist Party into the cabinet again; it had been in the opposition since 1948. The participation of the communists in the government would potentially turn Finland into a model country transforming itself into a socialist society on the basis of peaceful coexistence and an alliance of the workers' parties.[21]

In Finnish domestic politics, the main Soviet interest was always only this: continuity. Concerns related to that interest were present in the evaluations of Soviet policy toward Finland in the spring of 1958. The policy of good neighbourly relations had so far been based on a large coalition, in which the main partners had been the Agrarian Party, the Social Democratic Party (SDP) and the Finnish People's Democratic Union. In 1958, the Soviets were blaming the breakdown of the government coalition on the return of the right-wing socialists to the leadership of the SDP during the previous year. According to Moscow, this activated the Finnish conservative circles, which were now trying to create a government of bourgeois parties and right-wing socialists. These circles aimed to bring Finland closer to the Western countries and ultimately to prepare the abandonment of the policy of co-operation with the USSR.[22]

A majority government was then formed in August 1958 by Kekkonen's opponents, the SDP and the Coalition Party (Conservatives) with the participation of the Agrarian Party. This seemed to threaten not only Kekkonen's position but also Soviet investments, given the rising level of international confrontation. The Soviets' view that the new majority government was politically unreliable caused the so-called 'Night Frost' crisis in Soviet–Finnish relations. The Soviets' moves were unexpectedly harsh. They broke off trade negotiations and withdrew their ambassador from Helsinki, an act which in international diplomacy is generally a prelude to severing diplomatic relations. After sufficiently heavy Soviet political and economic pressure, the Finnish government had to resign in early December of 1958.[23]

The crisis was eased in January when President Kekkonen met Khrushchev in Leningrad and reassured him that there would be no changes in Finland's foreign policy. The Night Frost crisis was a practical demonstration of just how little room for manoeuvre Finland had in its foreign policy, and even to an extent in its internal affairs. Together with the obvious foreign political reasons – tensions over the German question and the need to give a serious warning to the Scandinavian NATO members Denmark and Norway – the crisis between Finland and the Soviet Union had some objectives which were aimed solely at Finland.[24]

By far the most dangerous of the reasons for the Night Frost crisis was the Soviet anger at Finland's Western trade relations. More than 50 per cent of the market for Finland's paper and wood products lay in the OEEC countries. When steps were taken at the end of the 1950s to set up a free-trade area encompassing all of the 16 OEEC countries, Finland faced the threat of being left totally out in the cold. At that time, Finland would not have been able to join any organization dominated by members of NATO and especially those including West Germany. It was Finland's good fortune that French President Charles de Gaulle thwarted the British proposal for a broad free-trade area. This led in 1959 to the birth of EFTA, which the Scandinavian countries duly joined in Britain's wake. Finland negotiated a separate deal with EFTA. This could not, however, be signed immediately due to opposition from the Soviet Union. When we think about the future of the Finnish market economy at the time, it is no exaggeration to say that such an agreement was a matter of life and death.

In September of 1960, Khrushchev then unexpectedly turned up at President Kekkonen's sixtieth-birthday celebrations in Helsinki and indicated that he fully understood Finland's efforts to arrange its trade relations with the West.[25] This gesture of benevolence was not done for the sake of the Finns but rather out of the Soviets' own economic interest. On the basis of the Finn–EFTA arrangement, the Soviet Union was guaranteed the status of most favoured nation by EFTA. In April of 1961, Finland became an associate member of EFTA, and, in practice, the treaty offered the rights and duties of full membership following an initial period of transition. With hindsight, Finland's joining EFTA at that time can be considered a stroke of luck because barely six months later Finnish–Soviet relations once again entered into a crisis.

The 'Note Crisis' of 1961: Warning to Finland and Message to the Scandinavian Countries

The Berlin crisis in the summer of 1961 had led to an extremely tense international situation just as both parliamentary and presidential elections were approaching in Finland. The re-election of the controversial Kekkonen looked far from certain. Then on 30 October 1961, the Soviet Union sent the Finnish government a note which, referring to the 'imperialist threat' from West Germany, proposed defence consultations in accordance with the military article of the mutual assistance treaty. President Kekkonen was at the time on a visit to the USA, and, when the note arrived, he was sitting in Hawaii with a lei around his neck.

On the very same day they sent the note to Finland, the Soviets detonated a 50-megaton nuclear device in Novaya Zemlya; this was by far the most powerful in nuclear history.[26] This test was probably a mere coincidence and not meant to be a sign to Finland of a coming doomsday, but the timing was horrifying in any case. The Soviet Union aimed the note at the government of

Finland but its motivations were first of all an attack against the Federal Republic of Germany and partly against Denmark, Norway and Sweden as well. Soviet rhetoric was extremely harsh: West Germany was accused of harbouring plans for revenge, and it was claimed in the Soviet note that the Bundeswehr had been established to carry out the military plans which Hitler's Wehrmacht had not been able to fulfil two decades earlier.[27] Bonn rejected these accusations, regarding them as totally absurd and as a sign of the Soviet Union's own imperialistic plans in the North of Europe.[28]

In the files of the East German foreign ministry, there is a detailed explanation of the aims of the Soviet note to Finland; this had been given to the East German government by the head of MID's Scandinavian department, N.M. Lunkov. In the first place, the Soviet government wanted to express clearly its view to Finns in general and to the reactionary forces in particular, which were led by the right-wing social democrat leader Väinö Tanner. In the second place, the aim was to influence attitudes in Denmark and Norway such that 'these countries would not be hooked by West German imperialists'.[29]

As much as 47 per cent of the text of the note (which ran to 15 pages) dealt with West German militarism, 24 per cent with West German influence on Denmark and Norway, 15 per cent with the military cooperation between West Germany and Denmark, and 4 per cent with Sweden. Only the remainder of the note, about 10 per cent, actually concerned Finland itself. The last sentence was, however, the most dangerous: on the basis of the military articles of the FCMA Treaty, the Soviet Union was proposing consultations on possible Soviet aid to Finland in repulsing the increasing military threat in the North of Europe.[30]

Kekkonen did not interrupt his visit to the USA in the face of the Soviet initiative but rather sent Foreign Minister Ahti Karjalainen to Moscow to find out what the Soviet Union was trying to achieve with the note. When this failed to ease the crisis, Kekkonen had to go and talk with the Soviet leadership in person. The sense of drama was heightened by the fact that the meeting was held at Novosibirsk in Siberia, deep within the Soviet Union. At this point, Kekkonen's main rival in the presidential election, Olavi Honka, indicated his intention to withdraw his candidacy for the sake of national interests.

Tensions seemed to abate rather easily in Novosibirsk. Khrushchev promised to postpone consultations but wanted Kekkonen to keep a closer watch in future on developments in the Baltic area and in the North of Europe. The engagement of the Finnish president was by far the most important aspect of the resulting Novosibirsk communiqué. Kekkonen had to pay this debt again and again in the 1960s and 1970s. It was just this phrase which was used against Kekkonen by his domestic opposition and his foreign critics. Kekkonen had promised to serve Khrushchev as his 'watchdog' in the North of Europe.

There was a feeling of relief in Finland once the crisis had passed. Even in the eyes of many of his opponents, Kekkonen had become the saviour of the nation. There has since been debate in Finland over whether the note resulted from genuine Soviet fears over the situation in Europe, or from a desire to interfere in Finland's internal affairs so as to ensure Kekkonen's re-election. Did Kekkonen himself request the note, as has been claimed? No one has been able to produce conclusive proof of this theory, and it seems more likely that the Soviet Union launched the operation of its own accord to support Kekkonen's re-election.[31]

In any case, Kekkonen certainly benefited enormously from the 'Note Crisis'. It marked the beginning of his unchallenged dominance of both foreign and domestic policy, which some critical contemporaries derided by reference to 'Kekkoslovakia'. Kekkonen never again had to face a serious challenge. He gradually crushed his political opponents and during the 1960s and 1970s constructed a presidential system in Finland. Just as in Gaullist France, Finland also saw the emergence of an unofficial party of Kekkonen supporters which spread from the Agrarian Party in the centre to both the left and the right.

At about the same time that Kekkonen and Khrushchev met in Novosibirsk, Denmark and West Germany were planning to build a joint command centre, the so-called COMBALTAP, for their cooperation in the Baltic Sea. The Soviet Union responded by immediately sending a note with very harsh wording. The Norwegian government publicly announced that pressure from the Soviet side would only lead Norway to more intensive cooperation with NATO and would not have the opposite effect. Foreign Minister Halvard Lange, during his visit to Moscow a couple of weeks after the Note Crisis, said that Norway would possibly revise its former negative attitude toward allowing NATO bases and nuclear weapons on its territory if the Soviet Union continued putting pressure on Finland. The hardline Soviet attitude would automatically increase the fear of war in the North of Europe and would also influence Sweden to seek security in the West.[32]

That the Soviet Union appealed to the military articles of the FCMA Treaty was by no means mere rhetoric or a pretext for interfering in the internal affairs of its small neighbour. We should not forget that the Mutual Assistance Treaty was actually the only arrangement for the security and defence of the Soviet Union's north-western border, which was some seven hundred miles in length.

In the early 1960s, Finland's defence suffered from a lack of modern military equipment. For example, the armed forces did not have the slightest possibility of controlling Finnish airspace if aircraft were flying at high altitudes; this is not even to mention their inability to defend against modern missiles. The armed forces of Finland were seriously limited by the articles of the Paris peace treaty of 1947; for example, Finland was not allowed to acquire missiles of any kind. In this respect, the Soviet Union was very liberal and did not hinder the acquisition of arms when Finland wanted to buy them from the right sources. During the 1960s, the Soviets, especially military leaders such as Minister of Defence Marshal Rodion Malinovski, wanted to interpret the FCMA Treaty literally as a military agreement. Finland bought MiG jet fighters and even surface-to-air missiles from the Soviet Union.[33] Whenever the Finnish armed forces conducted war games on maps, however, the enemy was always portrayed as attacking from the east.

The 'Kekkonen Plan' for the Nordic Nuclear-Free Zone, May 1963

Various initiatives to reduce military forces in Europe were made beginning in the mid-1950s. The first concrete proposal for a nuclear-free zone (NFZ) was presented in 1957 by Polish Foreign Minister Adam Rapacki. He suggested that Poland and both German states create such a zone and forbid nuclear weapons on their territories.

As we have seen earlier, it was one of the main objectives of Soviet Scandinavian policy to encourage Denmark and Norway to continue their relations with NATO under so-called 'minimum conditions', which meant that these two countries refused to station nuclear weapons and foreign troops on their territories in peacetime. Every effort to change this state of affairs was harshly attacked by the Soviets. Concerning future developments in Scandinavia, they had political expectations which ran in exactly the opposite direction. There is much evidence in the sources for the conclusion that the long-term political objective of the Soviet Union in Scandinavia was neutralization. In practice, this would have required some kind of a 'roll-back' of NATO from Denmark and Norway.[34]

In his 1959 speech in Stettin, Khrushchev attacked the leaders of these two countries because their attitude was so negative to his proposal for creating a neutral zone around the Baltic Sea. 'If war breaks out in this area, millions of people in these countries will be swept away, and the cause of this catastrophe will be the nuclear arms and other bases which will be destroyed by the counterblows of Soviet H-bombs and A-bombs', Khrushchev threatened.

Ireland's foreign minister Frank Aiken was one of those who had a positive attitude toward Rapacki's plan and suggested that a club of non-nuclear powers should be created. In 1961, his Swedish colleague, Östen Undén, prepared a detailed plan on the basis of Aiken's idea. According to Undén, the club of non-nuclear powers should be open to the aligned countries as well if they did not allow the deployment of nuclear weapons in their territories. This part of the proposal obviously referred to Denmark and Norway. The Undén Plan was accepted in the autumn of 1961 by the UN General Assembly.[35]

As early as 1952, when Kekkonen was Finland's prime minister, he had reinterpreted the introduction of the FCMA Treaty, which mentioned Finland's desire to remain aloof from great-power conflicts, as a justification for – or even as a guarantee of – 'neutrality of a certain kind'. The actual substance of his remarks at the time had dealt with the separation of Denmark and Norway from NATO through a Nordic neutrality alliance. Despite Finland's participation in the alliance, it would still have the FCMA obligations toward the Soviet Union. The speech mainly supported the objectives of Soviet Scandinavian policy, and its formulation had been begun together with the Soviet ambassador in Helsinki, Viktor Lebedev. Interestingly enough, this was initiated even before President Paasikivi had been informed.[36]

In March of 1962, then Soviet ambassador in Helsinki Andrei Zakharov informed Kekkonen about Foreign Minister A.A. Gromyko's visit to the Scandinavian countries. Acting on behalf of his government, he then proposed that Kekkonen make an initiative for establishing a nuclear-free zone in the North of Europe, referring to the Undén Plan as a model. One of the objectives of the plan should be that Denmark and Norway resign from NATO. Kekkonen seemed to be very doubtful and reluctant to do anything, but still he answered Zakharov that 'he would keep it in mind in discussions with Nordic leaders, among them Lange',[37] meaning the Norwegian foreign minister, whom he considered to be the most NATO-minded of all the Scandinavian ministers.[38]

A couple of weeks later, in April of 1963, Kekkonen paid a visit to Yugoslavia where his host Marshal Tito encouraged him to make a plan for an NFZ. Kekkonen immediately ordered his political assistant Max Jakobson to prepare such an initiative. On 28 May 1963, Kekkonen presented his plan in a speech to the Paasikivi Society.[39] The President made reference to the Undén Plan and addressed himself to all countries which did not yet have nuclear weapons and would refrain from obtaining them in the future. They could bind themselves with real agreements, in which they would promise to make neither nuclear weapons nor means of transport for them, nor would they allow stationing of this kind of military equipment on their territories. These countries could begin serious efforts to get international approval for this kind of commitment. The final aim of Kekkonen's plan was that only those countries which already had nuclear weapons would be left outside the group of the nuclear-free.

The situation in the North of Europe was, according to Kekkonen, most favourable for practical steps toward realizing an NFZ. Although Finland and Sweden had chosen the policy of neutrality, and Denmark and Norway were members of NATO, none of them had wanted nuclear weapons. This meant that the Nordic countries in reality were already building an NFZ. This state of affairs was, however, based on unilateral statements only. Therefore, it was high time to confirm this state of affairs with agreements in accordance with the Undén Plan. He suggested that announcing the establishment of an NFZ in the North of Europe would not change the policy of the Nordic countries or weaken their security positions.

Kekkonen justified his proposal by reference to turmoil in the world – especially the Cuban crisis seven months earlier – and by pointing out that the North of Europe was still free of nuclear weapons. The US rearmament policy begun by the Kennedy administration would mean either that the Nordic members of NATO, Denmark and Norway, would become participants in the multilateral nuclear force or that NATO nuclear weapons would be stationed on their territories. Preventing West Germany from acquiring nuclear weapons either from NATO or on its own initiative was naturally one of the most important aims of the Kekkonen Plan. Another, less immediate objective was to get the USA to withdraw its nuclear weapons from Central Europe.

Kekkonen was well informed about the so-called MLF Plan, the Multilateral Forces of NATO, which was intensively prepared from 1961 to 1963. This plan was also known as the McNamara Plan and was preliminarily accepted at the NATO summit in Nassau. The idea of the MLF was to share the command responsibility of NATO between the USA and the other member countries. The aim was also to establish a NATO nuclear submarine fleet equipped with nuclear warheads. One part of the plan was for West Germany and Denmark to establish a joint fleet which would carry nuclear missiles of the 'Polaris' type. The MLF Plan was exactly the kind of agreement that could have offered West Germany the opportunity to acquire nuclear weapons, that is, if the plan had been realized.[40]

The new developments of NATO's nuclear strategy concerning possible participation of West Germany could well have motivated the Soviets to stress again the need for military consultations with Finland. This was for the Finns a very dangerous vision of the future. Perhaps Kekkonen's initiative of 1963 was meant to be a warning to his Scandinavian neighbours that the development of nuclear strategies in the North would inevitably lead to a situation in which Kekkonen would be compelled to make good on his promise in Novosibirsk and to suggest consultations on Soviet military aid in accordance with article 2 of the FCMA Treaty. Otherwise, Kekkonen's Eastern policy would suffer a serious credibility crisis. In accordance with the conception of the Northern Balance, the behaviour of NATO members Denmark and Norway could lead to Soviet pressure on Finland's security policy.[41]

The governments of Denmark and Norway could by no means accept Kekkonen's plan.[42] They pointed out that their membership in NATO could not even in theory allow their participation in an NFZ. Norwegian Foreign Minister Halvard Lange explained that the reluctance of Norway and Denmark should be understood simply as a sign of their willingness to maintain the Northern Balance. Sweden's reaction was not much friendlier, especially because Kekkonen had not informed his Scandinavian neighbours beforehand that he would propose an NFZ for the North of Europe.

The reactions of the Scandinavian press to the Kekkonen Plan were extremely critical as well. On the one hand, Finland's president had been compelled to make this initiative. On the other hand, what kind of concessions would the Soviet Union give? When the Soviets were demanding that Denmark and Norway resign from NATO, they did not promise anything in return, such as the dissolution of the FCMA Treaty with Finland. Only if that occurred would Finland gain the status of a neutral comparable to that of Sweden.

West German Minister of Defence Kai-Uwe von Hassel stated that the Kekkonen Plan was directed against the NATO membership of the Federal Republic of Germany. According to him, that 'poor man Kekkonen' was again being forced to play the role of the Kremlin's watchdog; of his own free will, Kekkonen would never have made such a ridiculous proposal.

Conclusion

During the so-called 'First Détente' in the years immediately after Stalin's death, relations between Finland and the Soviet Union were made into an example of neutral and peaceful relations. This was done especially to influence the Nordic Countries but was also intended for a wider context. The nature of this neutrality that the Soviet Union was ready to support in Scandinavia was defined very carefully. A clear difference was made between the manoeuvring room allotted to Finland and that of other Nordic countries. Given that Norway and especially Denmark were seen as the 'weakest links in the NATO chain', any support for their possible future neutrality was desirable. It was not, however, in the Soviet interest to promote the formation of a Scandinavian neutrality bloc resembling the earlier Scandinavian Defensive Union (SDU) plans of 1948 – not even as an alternative to NATO membership. It was perfectly clear to the Soviets that it would be difficult to expect real neutrality from such a bloc. Moreover, from the Soviet point of view, Finland's participation in that kind of association would have been a clear step backward. Finland's status differed decisively even from that of Sweden because on the basis of the FCMA Treaty, Finland was clearly a part of the Soviet security sphere, rejecting neutrality in case of war between the blocs. So, from the Soviet viewpoint, neutrality elsewhere in Scandinavia was worth supporting, but only neutrality without any kind of alliance, as there were suspicions that an alliance would be too Western oriented.

Everything that served to lessen the Soviet Union's fears and doubts was important for Finland's national interests. If the Soviet proposition created controversy between the parties concerned, then support for the Soviets would endanger other, even more important interests: Nordic cooperation and the confidence of other Western countries. From the Finnish point of view, growing international tension would lead to a conflict between the country's Soviet and Scandinavian policies.

A clear turn for the worse in Finnish–Soviet affairs took place during the late 1950s: the Night Frost crisis of 1958–59 was to signify a structural change in Soviet–Finnish relations. If 'Finlandization' is understood to mean that Soviet relations were used to achieve domestic political objectives in the country, then the significance of the Night Frost crisis was to be decisive in the birth of this phenomenon. As a consequence of the crisis, foreign political reliability became a generally accepted criterion in Finland, not only concerning the political makeup of the government but also in lower-level political decisions.

At the beginning of the 1960s, Finland's position in international politics was extremely difficult and narrow. The main factors that Kekkonen had to take seriously into account were as follows: (1) The Soviet Union seemed to appeal unscrupulously to the military articles of the FCMA Treaty in order to exercise influence on NATO's northern flank; (2) Finland's position could be maintained only if the Soviet leadership trusted the will and ability of the Finnish government to adhere to the FCMA Treaty under any circumstances; (3) Finland's foreign-policy leaders had to be very careful, and they could not even by accident give the impression that Finland wanted to avoid enforcement of the treaty; and (4) it was therefore in the vital interest of Finland's foreign policy to try to prevent situations in the North of Europe which would demand the implementation of the FCMA Treaty. On this basis, it is clearly understandable that Finland's policy toward its Scandinavian neighbours tended to be more and more preventive beginning in the early 1960s.

The participation of Denmark and Norway in the Western bloc also linked Finland's and Sweden's positions when Soviet leaders evaluated the motives behind Swedish neutrality. It was asserted that Sweden's non-alignment was based to a great extent on fear of possible Soviet countermeasures against Finland, which the USSR could implement in the case of Swedish participation in the Atlantic alliance. When the Swedish position of non-alignment and neutrality is compared with Finland's position toward the Eastern superpower, the Soviet assessment clearly supported the idea of 'Northern Balance'.

NOTES

1 Arne Olav Brundtland, 'Nordisk balanse før og nå', *Internasjonal Politikk*, 5 (1966), pp. 491–541. *Internasjonal Politikk* is published by Norsk utenrikspolitisk Institut (Norwegian Institute of Foreign Policy) and is one of the leading periodicals in Norway with articles on research in international relations.
2 Arne Olav Brundtland, 'Nordisk balanse på nytt', *Internasjonal Politikk*, 3 (1976), 599–639, see esp. pp. 627–33. Another remarkable Norwegian political scientist dealing with the concept of 'Northern Balance' is Johan Jørgen Holst in his two-volume work, *Norsk sikkerhetspolitikk i strategisk perspektiv*, Oslo, 1967, see esp. vol. 1, pp. 129–40. See also Erik Moberg, 'The "Nordic Balance" Concept', *Cooperation and Conflict*, 3 (1968), pp. 210–14.
3 Brundtland, 'Nordisk balanse', pp. 497–501, 530.
4 Margot Light, *The Soviet Theory of International Relations*, Brighton: Wheatsheaf Books, 1988, pp. 299–334.
5 Ibid., pp. 25–31, 64–5.
6 Ibid., pp. 45–65, 172.

7 Ibid., p. 234.
8 Jukka Nevakivi, *Miten Kekkonen pääsi valtaan ja Suomi suomettui*, Helsinki: Otava, 1996, pp. 206–10.
9 Archives of Finland's Foreign Ministry, UM L 12, Eero A. Wuori's Memo 'Ulkopolitiikkamme arviointia', 22 July 1953.
10 Juhani Suomi, *Kriisien aika. Urho Kekkonen 1956–1962*, Helsinki: Otava, 1992, p. 53.
11 Kimmo Rentola, *Niin kylmää että polttaa. Kommunistit, Kekkonen ja Kreml*, Helsinki: Otava, 1997, pp. 354–60.
12 Nevakivi, *Miten Kekkonen*, pp. 94–7.
13 Ibid., p. 156.
14 Pekka Visuri, *Totaalisesta sodasta kriisinhallintaan*, Helsinki: Otava, 1989, pp. 102–6.
15 Osmo Apunen, *Paasikiven – Kekkosen linja*, Helsinki: Tammi, 1977, pp. 142–4.
16 Nevakivi, *Miten Kekkonen*, p. 211.
17 Vladislav Zubok and Konstantine Pleshakov, *Inside the Kremlin's Cold War*, Cambridge, MA: Harvard University Press, 1996, pp. 187–8.
18 UM 7 D 2, Box 304, 'Suomen vastaukset Neuvostoliiton nootteihin', 21 January 1959 and 26 March 1959.
19 UM 7 D 2, Box 305, Y. Väänänen's memo 'Suomen kannanotot Saksan kysymyksestä vuodesta 1959', 16 August 1961. The negative response of the Finnish government to the Soviet initiative was naturally noted with satisfaction at the US State Department, see NA, College Park MD, State Dept., RG 59, CDF, Box 3490, Joint Week 4, 23 January 1959.
20 Jukka Seppinen, *Suomen EFTA- ratkaisu yöpakkasten ja noottikriisin välissä*, Helsinki: Suomen Historiallinen Seura, 1997, pp. 47–52.
21 Rentola, *Niin kylmää*, p. 488.
22 Nevakivi, *Miten Kekkonen*, pp. 157–81.
23 Hans Peter Krosby, *Kekkonen linja*, Helsinki: Kirjayhtymä, 1974, pp. 194–206.
24 Apunen, *Paasikiven*, pp. 146–64.
25 *Urho Kekkonen päiväkirjat 1. '58–'62*, ed. Suomi, Helsinki: Otava, 2001, pp. 356–8 (3 and 4 September 1960).
26 Pekka Visuri, *Puolustusvoimat kylmässä sodassa: Suomen puolustuspolitiikka 1945–1961*, Porvoo: WSOY, 1994, pp. 187–8.
27 For the text of the Soviet Note to the Finnish government on 30 October 1961, see, for example, Krosby, *Kekkonen linja*, pp. 399–406 (appendix).
28 Archives of President Kekkonen (Tasavallan Presidentin Arkistosäätiö, TPA), Orimattila,. Urho Kekkosen Arkisto (UKA), Kekkonen's Yearbooks, UKKn vsk. 1961, 'Ulkomaisten hallitusten virallisia kommunikeoita Neuvostoliiton nootin johdosta (I)', Bonn, 31 October 1961.
29 Politisches Archiv des Auswärtigen Amtes, Aussenstelle Berlin (PAAA), Bestand MfAA (Ministry of Foreign Affairs of the GDR), A 14053, Note on the appointment with Comr. Lunkov in Moscow on 11 December 1961.
30 Jukka Tarkka, *Suomen kylmä sota: Miten viattomuudesta tuli voima*, Helsinki: Otava, 1992, p. 84.
31 On the dispute concerning the origin of the Soviet note, see Suom, *Kriisien aika*, and Hannu Rautkallio, *Novosibirskin lavastus: Noottikriisi 1961*, Helsink: Tammi, 1992.
32 Brundtland, 'Nordisk balanse', pp. 605–7.
33 Visuri, *Totaalisesta*, pp. 174–8.
34 On the basis of the files in Archives of the Soviet Foreign Ministry, Jukka Nevakivi, 'Kekkonen, the Soviet Union and Scandinavia – Aspects of Policy in the Years 1948–1965', *Scandinavian Journal of History,* 22 (1997), pp. 74–6.
35 Brundtland, 'Nordisk balanse', pp. 608–10.
36 Nevakivi, *Miten Kekkonen*, pp. 68–70.

37 UM Kc 10, Kekkonen's memo on Foreign Minister Gromyko's visit to Scandinavia in 1963, 17 April 1963.
38 Nevakivi, *Miten Kekkonen*, p. 74.
39 The Kekkonen Plan is published in *Ulkopoliittisia lausuntoja ja asiakirjoja* (ULA), Helsinki, 1963, pp. 28–30; the original in UM 89 H, Tasavallan Presidentin lausunto Paasikivi-Seuran kokouksessa Helsingissä 28 May 1963.
40 Visuri, *Totaalisesta*, pp. 107–8.
41 Jukka Nevakivi and Juhani Suomi have disputed about the originality of the Kekkonen Plan. On the basis of Soviet archival sources, the former states that Kekkonen was at least persuaded by the Soviets to make his proposal. Suomi, Kekkonen's biographer, absolutely denies this – see Jukka Nevakivi and Juhani Suomi, 'Kaksintaistelu: Tekikö Kekkonen PYV-ehdotuksen Neuvostoliiton aloitteesta?', *Ulkopolitiikka*, 3 (1996), 55–8.
42 On Scandinavian reactions to Kekkonen's Plan, see UM 89 H, Max Jakobson's Memo 'Keskusteluja ydinaseetonta Pohjolaa koskevasta Tasavallan Presidentin lausunnosta', 1 June 1963; UM 89 H, Compilation Memo of Juhani Suomi, 'Pohjoismaisia näkökantoja ydinaseettomasta Pohjolasta', 12 December 1974.

15

Western Europe and Negotiations on Arms Control: The Anglo-Americans and the Evolving Concept of European Security, 1963–68[1]

Marilena Gala

To speak of disarmament negotiations during this period requires that we examine the question of nuclear non-proliferation as a kind of imperative pre-liminary condition for the success of any other arms control initiative. In fact, especially after the Cuban missile crisis, the necessity of ensuring stability during a crisis and of reducing the reciprocal fear of a surprise attack found an increasing consensus in both East and West. Arms control, as a concept broader than disarmament, could better serve the purpose of attempting to regulate or stabilize the conflict between East and West and thereby over-coming the divisions of the Cold War.[2]

To understand the major Western European countries' attitudes toward and roles in arms control and thus also non-proliferation, the first point to stress is that the negotiations involved the Europeans more as allies of the two superpowers rather than as protagonists themselves. This is not only related to the limited dimensions and reduced threat, if any, posed by the Western European countries' nuclear arsenals but to the essentially political – rather than military – meaning that arms control began to acquire during the 1960s

This was the decade in which the two superpowers gradually agreed on shifting the focus of their security policies away from expansion of their nuclear arsenals – the arms race – to an arms control process aimed first of all at checking the potentially destabilizing spread of national nuclear capabilities. According to this approach, a more stable and thus more secure international context was required in order to stem the tide of nuclear proliferation because effective deterrence between the two blocs required that the two superpowers exercise centralized control over the respective nuclear deterrents.

Non-Proliferation as a Divisive Factor

Difficulties within both the Eastern bloc and the Atlantic alliance inevitably arose due to the converging interests of the two main adversaries in promoting cooperation rather than confrontation and their decision to inaugurate a new era with agreements on the very sensitive question of improved nuclear capabilities resulting from test activity. In fact, with the signing of the first agreement aimed at regulating the testing of nuclear devices, the Limited Test-Ban Treaty of 1963, not only was it the case that France and Communist China refused to adhere (Beijing characterized the agreement as a 'big fraud'),[3] but even the Federal Republic of Germany and Italy showed very little enthusiasm.[4]

The emergence of a community of interests between the US and the USSR seemed to contradict the traditional concept of security – at least as Western Europe had interpreted it since the birth of the Atlantic alliance. According to the USA, the future belonged to new and more intensive efforts at collective security and to the collective search for arms control and disarmament measures; only success in these ways of handling the nuclear issue would make it possible to build effective economic and political institutions that promoted interdependence. Conversely, if other nations claimed the right to use nuclear weapons independently of tight collective security arrangements with the USA, the Americans might well pull back from their defence commitments. A US withdrawal from the critical field of security would, however, entail a perceptible reduction of US total influence on affairs in other parts of the world.

In short, as a memorandum for the US president underlined in 1965:

> whether the United States solved the nuclear proliferation problem on a collective security basis, with the US playing a key role in each area, or whether the US let national nuclear capabilities rip, would shape the whole political and economic bone structure of the world in the future.[5]

In other words, the US government was conscious of at least three issues at stake on the question of nuclear proliferation: the way the world was organized, US power and influence, as well as the balance of power in Europe and Asia. This was the reason nuclear proliferation was considered a vital concern but not primarily an East–West issue in the eyes of US policy makers but rather a question of whether the Atlantic world would eventually fragment into separate components.

But if this was the US 'side of the coin' and the Arms Control and Disarmament Agency in Washington saw a non-proliferation agreement as the occasion for the USA to engage in the type of joint activity with the Soviet Union essential to prevent the proliferation of nuclear weapons,[6] what was the Western European reaction to this different approach to the concept of

Atlantic security and Western security overall as promoted by the United States?

First of all, we should mention a couple of paradoxical aspects distinguishing the status of Western European countries and with which those countries inevitably had to cope. On the one hand, they had the political difficulty of renouncing the acquisition of the very means that would enable them to participate in a negotiation process devoted to the elaboration of a different notion of security. On the other hand, the same Europeans could not afford to boycott a process – such as the arms control initiative – which promised to free the Cold War of one of its most dangerous features. To put it differently, the larger Western European countries had to come to terms with the challenge of trying to increase their weight and their influence on the two superpowers engaged in negotiations for the sake of European security, while at the same time renouncing what seemed to represent the only means of attaining such a capability: a nuclear arsenal or at least the possibility of acquiring one. Since the beginning of the Kennedy administration, this had thus been the context in which, on the one hand, de Gaulle opted for the kind of French autonomy he had been claiming for his country in the nuclear field as the only element essential to *la grandeur de la France*,[7] and, on the other, Britain pursued its traditional 'independence in concert' with its most powerful ally,[8] whereas the Federal Republic of Germany and Italy kept requesting and waiting for a collective Atlantic solution to the ever-critical European defence question.[9]

The Central Issue of Germany

Within NATO, success in what actually was an attempt to 'square the circle' required first the evaluation of a number of elements indispensable for the existence of the Atlantic alliance and then efforts to provide the West with sound development on the international scene. True, the European allies had not forgotten the evidence of past Soviet hostility toward the West nor did they assume that the Soviet Union had abandoned the traditional great-power ambitions of the Russian state. By the mid-1960s, however, the key factor was that the fear of an armed attack that had prevailed ten or fifteen years before no longer existed in Europe. The experience of the West European leaders over the previous decade had suggested to them that the danger of any deliberate war in Europe was small so long as the USSR believed that its aggression might lead to a nuclear response and so long as the availability of the US nuclear force to Western Europe appeared credible to Moscow.[10] If these two conditions were met, Western Europeans believed that US force would effectively deter aggression. But this was only the first crucial component of the puzzle that NATO members had to deal with. On the other hand, the US military presence in Europe continued to be essential not only for security reasons in a narrow sense but also because the ultimate purpose of Washington's predominant European policy in the postwar period was to find a constructive place for Germany in the Western World. The stability of Germany and its firm adherence to NATO would, moreover, remain vital elements of the security of the alliance until an overall East–West adjustment had been reached.[11]

At least since the last year of the Eisenhower presidency, the US government had been seeking to strengthen NATO politically through more effective political consultation and militarily through the Multilateral Force (MLF) proposal as well as the NATO Force Planning Exercise. In fact, a major influence on US security policy in Europe during the 1960s was the well-known ambitions of the German Defence Minister Franz-Josef Strauss – neither completely disowned nor denied by the Chancellor, Konrad Adenauer, who sought the political advantage of occasional ambiguity on nuclear defence questions with the FRG's most powerful ally.[12] They made the US government quite conscious of the ever-present German nervousness over the possibility that the US interest in achieving a peaceful and stable world might one day lead to some betrayal of German interests.[13] At the same time, however, no one in either Washington or Bonn – and especially the latter – could afford to forget that any measure capable of reducing the risk of war and lowering tensions, if promoted by Washington and negotiated with the USSR, could be useful. This was especially because such measures, once accomplished, could contribute to the solution of other problems, including the division of Germany.

This concise exposition of the principal constraints faced by the USA and its most important European allies during the 1960s makes clear the importance of the crucial issue of Germany, especially in regard to the process of arms control negotiations. In fact, the gradual shifting of security matters from a paradigm oriented toward defence deterrence to one centred on arms control gave rise to a paradox which was even more evident to Germany than to the other Western European countries. After the fear of Soviet attack had decreased among the European allies, the credibility of the US guarantee as well as the reason for US presence in Europe had to be considered more than ever in relation to Germany and its aspirations to equality with the other allies because Germany, as a divided country, was the symbol of the Cold War in Europe.[14] In other words, any deal with the Soviets aimed at regulating the contest between the two blocs had to face the German question both inside and outside the alliance.

Since 1964, most of the officials at the State Department had felt certain that reviewing possible arms control measures for Central Europe would be useful as part of the process of elaborating adequate European security provisions to accompany a future initiative toward a German settlement. This was the case even though they recognized that the public airing of such proposals in the absence of a changed Soviet attitude on the German question would profoundly disturb the Germans.[15] The acquiescence of the Federal Republic was essential to any important progress toward a solution of the problems of Germany and of European security simply because it was not politically feasible to treat the former separately from the latter. Both the Rapacki Plan and the Gomulka Plan[16] had failed because they sought an answer to European security in the field of arms control without taking into account the need for a political settlement. In a background paper prepared in Washington for the visit of West German Chancellor Ludwig Erhard in June of 1965, the analysis made at the State Department confirmed that the 'Federal Republic of Germany could play an important and useful role in increasing Western relations with the countries of Eastern Europe'.[17]

Meanwhile, on the other side of the ocean, the British cabinet had been discussing Her Majesty's government's proposals on disarmament with the US secretary of state and had come to the conclusion that it ought to give

> further thought to the possibility of a Western initiative taking the form either of: a) more limited proposals combining observation posts with freeze of nuclear delivery vehicles in Central Europe, or b) comprehensive pro-posals covering German reunification as well as European security.[18]

Khrushchev had displayed interest in drawing the Federal Republic into more active relations with Moscow. After his eviction,[19] his successors had not manifested the same level of interest. Faced with the need first to consolidate their position at home and within the communist movement, the new leadership had frozen Soviet–West German relations. Later on, the Kremlin had made it clear that any significant improvement in the relations between the Federal Republic and the Soviet Union could occur only if Bonn gave up some major foreign-policy objectives such as nuclear sharing, and, in any event, no improvement could come at the expense of Soviet relations with East Germany.

This means that the crux of the problem – as a State Department analysis already observed in September of 1965 – was 'to get the German government to feel that its short- and long-term interest did not lie in possession of an independent nuclear capability'.[20] The prospect of European countries acquir-ing their own nuclear arsenals had always been disruptive particularly in the case of Germany. The proposal for a NATO Multilateral Force had been first envisaged by the Eisenhower administration and then developed by the State Department during the Kennedy presidency, with the very goal of preventing the rise of any problem connected with bilateral nuclear sharing or the emergence of many uncontrollable nuclear powers in Europe.

The Anglo-American Approach to Non-Proliferation

Actually, the US government under Kennedy repeatedly tried to share its own perceptions and apprehensions about the general danger of proliferation with its main European allies. Not only had the president and Secretary of State Dean Rusk often and clearly referred to US concerns about the likelihood that more and more nations would develop nuclear weapons during the next decade unless some action was taken to prevent it, in December of 1962, during the Anglo-American summit in Nassau.[21] Kennedy attempted to make the provision of Polaris missiles to Great Britain conditional upon a specific requirement:

> if we could work out a solution in regard to Polaris which would move Europe away from national deterrents, we would be prepared to consider such a move, but it should be in that context.[22]

The idea of a force created on the basis of multilateral ownership, financing and control, with mixed staffing to the extent considered operationally feasible by the Supreme Allied Commander, Europe (SACEUR), had seemed the only practical way of stopping nuclear dissemination. This was especially because it seemed to be the only way out for both Germany's aspirations not to be kept down forever and the French government's determination to obtain a national nuclear deterrent.[23] In particular, nationalistic trends set in motion by de Gaulle, especially after 1962, had proved to be extremely dangerous since they could create insurmountable barriers to European supranational integration and disrupt the US postwar policy of incorporating Germany into a developing European community closely allied to the USA.

There was a close connection between the negotiations for a test-ban treaty and the inter-allied discussions about NATO deterrence and non-dissemination which marked the efforts of the Kennedy administration for promoting non-proliferation. This was to be reproduced forcefully during the Johnson years when the US commitment to a policy of non-proliferation increased together with conflicting aspirations and persisting dissatisfactions within the Atlantic alliance.

Previous experience had shown that the US impetus to strengthen NATO's military role would elicit the cooperation of the West Europeans to the extent of their joining in a common military effort on terms tolerable to Washington: since 1964, an ill-defined Atlantic Nuclear Force (ANF) had thus gradually emerged as the appropriate tool

> to deter nuclear proliferation by making it possible for non-nuclear members of the Atlantic alliance to participate in the ownership, management and control of NATO's nuclear forces through collective action and without the creation of new independent national nuclear systems.[24]

According to the Wilson cabinet, the new force proposal – which Great Britain considered preferable to the mixed-manned option envisaged in the MLF – was aimed at bringing the Altlantic alliance closer together.[25] Actually, this proposal was much more the result of the British intention to resist any hypothesis of nuclear sharing that implied the joint management of a surface fleet armed with nuclear weapons. The proposal was not the consequence of a real commitment on the part of the United Kingdom to achieve some sort of common Atlantic deterrent for Europe.[26] This is clearly seen in the record of discussions in November of 1964 between British Foreign Secretary Gordon Walker and German Foreign Minister Gerhard Schröder.[27]

Again, the core of the problem was ensuring confidence and cooperation in maintaining effective nuclear defence of the alliance as a whole while keeping the road open for strenuous efforts toward arms control. To the Johnson administration, however, this objective proved extremely difficult to reach, as the USA now aimed at soliciting West European countries to cooperate in a course of action that many of them did not agree with, albeit for conflicting reasons and to different degrees.

Although Britain too was looking for a means of escaping the dichotomy of 'have' and 'have-not' powers in the nuclear field, the British government did not contemplate giving up control of their nuclear weapons even if faced with the creation of an Atlantic Nuclear Force which had no purpose but to impede development of national nuclear forces.[28] This had been quite clear at least since the point when in December 1964, Defence Minister Denis Healey advanced proposals for an ANF. To the Wilson government, it was a matter of seeking to prevent any form of nuclear sharing without renouncing Britain's independent deterrent, which fixed its status as a great power in relation to the other European countries. What London was suggesting was a force containing two elements: national contributions from the USA and the United Kingdom as well as joint, or mixed-manned, contributions on the part of other European countries, both irrevocably tied together as long as the alliance lasted. What London could not accept was the hypothesis that the Americans were unwilling to make such a contribution, and, consequently, that British bombers and submarines were seen merely as an appendage to a Multilateral Force of surface vessels.[29]

The alternative that the USA were ready to support in 1965 was instead an Atlantic Collective Force made up initially of mixed-manned V-Bombers and four UK Polaris submarines. These weapons systems would be owned and financed by a group of countries exerting political control; this group would have to include at least the USA, Britain and the Federal Republic. This was the solution which, in accordance with US interests, would allow pursuit of a threefold objective: (1) to eliminate the UK national strategic deterrent in Europe, (2) to adopt policies not open to plausible French criticism, and (3) to give the Germans a standing in all nuclear matters (except national production and control of warheads) which would be equal to that of Great

Britain, and equal to the empty chair which was waiting for France. According to the US government, in other words, the creation of some sort of Atlantic Nuclear Force had to be conceived not as an addition to strategic forces that would have been otherwise provided but as a partial substitute for US forces in Europe.[30]

In fact, as a State Department memorandum on the Atlantic nuclear problem emphasized in October of 1965, 'any nuclear sharing arrangement had to deal with disarmament' because the object of the whole exercise was 'to control, not to build up, nuclear arms'.[31] The Americans were so deeply convinced of this choice that they were even willing to reassure the Soviet leadership – through a private letter, if necessary – that the USA had no intention of allowing their nuclear weapons out of their ownership or control, and that the US administration was prepared to negotiate a non-proliferation agreement based on the understanding that an ANF/MLF would hardly be able to come into existence. But the USA were not prepared to give the Soviet Union a veto over NATO nuclear arrangements not involving proliferation to Germany. As the US government did not regard the creation of a NATO collective force as proliferation, it could not accept that the Soviet Union successfully pressed this false issue at the end of 1965; consequently, a detailed analysis of the State Department underlined that the USA

> would not be prepared to enter into any treaty that would foreclose such a force in the future. There is every reason to believe that the conclusion of any non-proliferation treaty which sought to preclude the creation of such a force would never win the adherence of the Federal Republic – even in principle – and would only endanger the future of the alliance and the objective of non-proliferation itself.[32]

The idea that the Germans 'needed to be included precisely because they were dangerous'[33] resulted from fear of a resurgent German nationalism springing from resentment over inequality and the possibility that this independent power might eventually be used to make a deal with the Soviet Union. But this was not the opinion of the British prime minister. According to Wilson, the important thing was to decide whether the rootless generation of Germany wanted reunification or not. The question of access to nuclear hardware would 'knock reunification out of court'. But if they wanted reunification, then they could only have it at the end of a long period of détente with the Soviet Union. 'The problem was whether they could be induced to become détente-minded.'[34]

A divergence was clearly emerging between the British and US assessments of the price worth paying to secure Germany's Western orientation. Further, the fact that in these specific circumstances, Britain shared with France a mistrust of a nuclear-armed Germany as well as a desire to promote an East–West détente[35] risked making the situation even more complicated.

Moreover, during the same period when Washington and London were deeply engaged in the MLF/ANF negotiations, de Gaulle was trying to promote a Franco-German axis aimed at counteracting a US-dominated NATO. The French president offered Bonn vaguely defined German participation in the *force de frappe* as an alternative to the Anglo-American plans.[36] Against this background, the possibility of eventually alienating France for pursuing a pro-German policy was considered conterproductive in London especially as Wilson had no intention of renouncing the British nuclear deterrent and also remained totally opposed to any kind of access to nuclear hardware for Germany.[37]

Such access was exactly what Chancellor Erhard and other important members of the government of the Federal Republic had been asking for.[38] In November of 1965, Kurt Birrenbach, a CDU member of the Bundestag and adviser to the chancellor, told Secretary Rusk not only that the Federal Republic had to be an integral part of a common nuclear weapons system but specified that the MLF provided the best answer to the problem concerning Germany. The ANF, put forward by the British, was not acceptable without modifications but could become the basis for discussions.[39] In short, Germany wanted a greater voice in US decisions, and since it knew that it could not achieve this through a bilateral relationship with the USA – which would be dangerous politically – Bonn was looking for a share in the decision on the use of nuclear weapons in a way which increased both its own security and the deterrent effect on the enemy.

Foreign Minister Gerhard Schröder – following the trail blazed by Adenauer's policy – had repeatedly and publicly stated that he was interested in having a share in a weapons system. He also seemed keen to convince European partners and adversaries that the Germans were prepared to go ahead with the hardware solution despite what was, predictably, the strongest opposition on the part of the allies.[40] According to several US State Department reports in late 1965 and early 1966, the government of the Federal Republic was thinking of a common nuclear weapons system which had to involve strategic and not merely tactical weapons, had to be placed under SACEUR, and had to be jointly owned and mixed-manned. Even a British embassy report in January 1966 confirmed that

> it was of course true that the Germans took the view that they could not accept a non-proliferation agreement which closed the door on a nuclear sharing agreement of the kind now under discussion and that they also feared that this might in fact be the effect of a non-poliferation agreement, if it were signed before any further progress had been made on nuclear sharing.[41]

A different attitude could thus be expected only from the Social Democratic Party (SPD), which had been expressing interest in taking part in discussions on strategy and planning within NATO and which was expected to be more supportive of a non-proliferation agreement.[42]

Actually, when the attempt to promote Atlantic nuclear consultation arrangements eventually prevailed in the form of the Nuclear Planning Group, it became evident that even Schröder's position was not inflexible. To the Federal Republic, the idea of a Nuclear Planning Group as a permanent body in NATO had the great advantage of letting common doctrines and mutual confidence develop over the years so that agreed action would flow naturally if ever nuclear weapons had to be used.[43] Since it would involve both consultation and hardware, the creation of the Nuclear Planning Group offered a solution capable of assuaging the Germans' frustrations in particular but also the Italians' dissatisfaction at being excluded from direct control of a nuclear NATO deterrent.

In fact, it had become indisputable especially after 1966 that the creation of a collective Atlantic Force, instead of fostering unity inside the alliance, represented a divisive factor, which furthermore promised to make the achievement of a non-dissemination agreement more 'expensive' in terms of political payoff. As long as the Soviets thought that they could exploit Western differences over nuclear sharing and thus reduce the price of a non-dissemination agreement, they had an interest in delaying its conclusion.

It was axiomatic: a prerequisite to the search for East–West stability was to work toward stability within the Western alliance. Consequently, the adamant refusal of the British to abandon their special nuclear status in Europe, the obstinacy of the French in following their independent path with the subsequent termination of their participation in the integrated commands of NATO,[44] as well as the relatively meagre level of Italian involvement in any kind of collective nuclear force which could be envisaged, made non-proliferation and arms control the key elements and the only choices available to the USA to prevent Germany's acquisition of a national nuclear capability together with a stable détente with the Soviet Union.

In January of 1966, Soviet leader Aleksei Kosygin wrote a message to President Johnson which testified to the great significance that the Soviet Union attached to the problem of preventing the dissemination of nuclear weapons and the belief that

> if the dissemination of these terrible weapons of mass destruction is not blocked and these weapons continue to spread more and more throughout the world, that would inevitably lead to the growth of the threat of a war and immeasurably increase the danger of the outbreak of a nuclear war.

In the same letter, however, the Soviet leader did not fail to emphasize that what the Kremlin considered especially dangerous was a policy of satisfying step by step the nuclear ambitions of the Bonn government, creating thereby the conditions which made it easier for the West German revanchists to get access to nuclear weapons.[45] In his reply, Johnson first of all reminded the Soviet leader that the situation would be different if the European NATO members were not threatened by nuclear weapons. To deny those countries the possibility of arrangements for participation in their defence might now only promote proliferation by encouraging states to develop national nuclear forces for their own protection. And the US president concluded his letter by stating that

> our Governments have a strong mutual interest in acting together to stop the proliferation of nuclear weapons and in achieving a closer understanding on other means to curb the nuclear arms race.[46]

Conclusion

During the second half of the 1960s, US security policy in Europe consisted first of non-proliferation negotiations with the Soviets and second of US pressure on the Western Europeans to sign the treaty that would eventually emerge.[47] After a time-consuming debate on the different possibilities available to the Atlantic alliance for making the Western European countries more active in and responsible for their own defence through a nuclear sharing alternative, the Europeans were left in a frustrating situation. They were expected not only to renounce a collective NATO nuclear deterrent (which for Germany and Italy was the sole possibility of gaining access to the nuclear club) but, above all, to promise not to allow national nuclear deterrents to proliferate. The controversial aspects of such a policy now had to be faced by each Western European country with what each of them considered the most effective means of preserving or strengthening its own influence on the international scene.

The range of attitudes was relatively broad and reproduced quite accurately the differences characterizing the international status and political interests of the major European allies. Thus, a year before the signing of the Non-Proliferation Treaty, Italian Foreign Minister Amintore Fanfani attempted to take advantage of the Italian 'resolute support of a treaty which would be acceptable to as many states as possible', suggesting collateral measures useful for encouraging adherence to the treaty. In particular, what the Italian government had in mind was for the nuclear powers to transfer periodically an agreed quantity of fissile material to non-nuclear signatories of the Non-proliferation Treaty.[48] If this was the understandable preoccupation of a country which had renounced any ambitious programme for developing an independent national nuclear capability – for defence as well as for peaceful purposes – Britain had to cope with the necessity of deciding its own policy toward the treaty while maintaining, if possible, a balance between

a) the position as a European power, and in particular the present position as an applicant for membership of the European Communities; b) the status as a nuclear power in which Great Britain shares special responsibilities with the United States; c) the strong desire to see the successful conclusion of a non-proliferation treaty.[49]

As France and Britain in the end opted for opposite courses of action, which led to a claim for 'national interpretation' of the non-proliferation policy, and Italy was too weak to obstruct the treaty overtly, the crucial factor in determining the success of that policy was thus Germany once again.[50] But in this case what had always been and continued to be essential was its dependence on the USA. Hence, it was highly unlikely, for both military and political reasons, that Germany would make the decision to produce or acquire nuclear weapons against US wishes, and failure to achieve an alliance nuclear force could not affect this posture. Only a radical change in the basic structure of the political relationships in the postwar world would permit – or force – a change in the German attitude on this issue. Thus, a fundamental reversal in Soviet policy toward Germany might permit the Federal Republic to feel that it was no longer dependent upon the USA for its security and therefore free of the restraints of a US policy against possession of nuclear weapons.

At the same time, as the US permanent representative on the North Atlantic Council wrote to Dean Acheson in June of 1966, 'If NATO was not to disintegrate' in the long run, 'it had to find some rationale beyond military deterrence'.[51] The logical area for this fresh emphasis lay in the search for real security through a European settlement or at least through intensified efforts to improve the climate for an eventual settlement. Consequently, the non-proliferation discussions as well as the increased emphasis on détente with the Soviet Union had created fears, especially in Bonn, that a Soviet–US arrangement was emerging as a substitute for the original NATO concept of an alliance based on equal partnership. That was why West Germany had been trying for so long to give priority to satisfactory nuclear sharing arrangements over any non-dissemination agreement and had reiterated that the signing of such a treaty somehow had to be related to progress on the German problem.[52]

In other words, the awareness that a German decision to develop a nuclear force could seriously undermine Germany's foreign relations even with its closest allies and destroy any hope of eventual reunification co-existed with the idea that in order to achieve German national goals, the Federal Republic had to be 'of interest' to the Soviet Union. This meant that, unless West Germany began to question the rigid guidelines of the policy it had been following since 1949, it could be useful to have something – for example, at least the freedom to become a nuclear power – to renounce in return for Soviet concessions on the question of reunification. Only when a 'new spirit of determination to seize the apparently favorable current opportunity to speak and deal with the USSR and Eastern Europe'[53] had prevailed as the main feature of West German international policy could adherence to the Non-proliferation Treaty finally become the choice in support of the Ostpolitik implemented by Chancellor Willy Brandt and, consequently, also a means of strengthening European security.

NOTES

1 Glenn T. Seaborg with Benjamin S. Loeb, *Stemming the Tide: Arms Control in the Johnson Years*, Chicago, IL: Lexington, 1987. See also Michael J. Brenner, *Nuclear Power and Non-Proliferation: The Remaking of US Policy*, Cambridge, MA: MIT Press, 1981; J.P.G. Freeman, *Britain's Nuclear Arms Control Policy in the Context of Anglo-American Relations, 1957–1968*, London: Macmillan, 1986; National Academy of Sciences, *Nuclear Arms Control: Background and Issues*, Washington, DC: National Academy Press, 1985; J. Samuel Walker, *Containing the Atom: Nuclear Regulation in a Changing Environment, 1963–1971*, Berkeley, CA: University of California Press, 1992.

2 Keith Krause and Andrew Latham, 'Constructing Non-Proliferation and Arms Control: The Norms of Western Practice', in Keith R. Krause (ed.), *Culture and Security: Multilateralism, Arms Control and Security Building*, London: Frank Cass, 1999, pp. 23–54.

3 Glenn T. Seaborg, *Kennedy, Khrushchev, and the Test Ban*, Berkeley, CA: University of California Press, 1981, p. 257; Maurice Vaïsse, 'La France et le traité de Moscou (1957–1963)', *Revue d'histoire diplomatique*, 107 (1993), 41–53; John F. Kennedy Library (JFKL), National Security File (NSF), Departments and Agencies, Arms Control and Disarmament Agency, Disarmament, Harriman Trip to Moscow, part A, Box 265, 31 July 1963, from INR to the Secretary of State, intelligence note: 'Peiping officially rejects test ban treaty', limited official use.

4 National Archives (NA) College Park, Record Group (RG) 59, Subject Numeric file 18–4, Box 3709, 6 August 1963, tel. from the State Department to Amembassy Bonn, secret; Box 3708, 7 August 1963, tel. from Amembassy Rome to the Secretary of State, confidential. See also Leopoldo Nuti, *Gli Stati Uniti e l'apertura a sinistra: Importanza e limiti della presenza americana in Italia*, Bari: Laterza, 1999, p. 641.

5 NA, RG 59, Lot file 69D150, Box 8, 8 November 1965, memorandum to the President, subject: Nuclear Proliferation: Erhard and Wilson, secret.

6 NA, RG 59, Lot file 69D150, Box 8, 10 November 1965, memorandum for the President, from William C. Foster, subject: Steps to Prevent the Spread of Nuclear Weapons – Erhard Visit, secret.

7 Institut Charles De Gaulle, *De Gaulle et son siècle: Vol. 4, La sécurité et l'indépendance de la France*, Paris: Plon, 1992, chs IV and V; Maurice Vaïsse, *La grandeur: politique étrangère du général De Gaulle, 1958–1969*, Paris: Fayard, 1998.

8 On the Anglo-American defence relationship, see John Baylis, *Anglo-American Defence Relations, 1939–1984*, London: Macmillan, 1984; Ian Clark, *Nuclear Diplomacy and the Special Relationship: Britain's Deterrent and America 1957–1962*, Oxford: Clarendon Press, 1994; Stephen Twigge and Alan Macmillan, 'Britain, the United States and the development of NATO Strategy, 1950–1964', *Journal of Strategic Studies*, 19, 2 (1996), pp. 260–81.

9 David N. Schwartz, *NATO's Nuclear Dilemmas*, Washington, DC: The Brookings Institution, 1983.

10 NA, RG 59, Lot file 69D150, Box 1, 25 October 1966, Trilateral Talks (US–UK–FRG), Background Paper, secret/no foreign dissem.

11 NA, RG 59, Lot file 69D150, Box 10, 23 February 1967, memorandum for the President, subject: Force Levels in Europe, secret.
12 On the Federal Republic of Germany's nuclear ambitions, and on Adenauer's and Strauss' attitudes toward this question, see Catherine M. Kelleher, *Germany and the Politics of Nuclear Weapons*, New York: Columbia University Press, 1975; A. Pertti, 'Franz-Josef Strauss and the German Nuclear Question, 1956–1962', *Journal of Strategic Studies*, 18, 2 (June 1995).
13 NA, RG 59, Lot file 76D170, Box 14472, 11 November 1964, 'The Undersecretary's Trip to Germany, November 1964', secret.
14 For a recent examination of the international political aspects of the division of Germany till the unification of the country, see William R. Smyser, *From Yalta to Berlin: The Cold War Struggle over Germany*, New York: St Martin's, 2000.
15 NA, RG 59, Lot file 76D170, Box 14472, 4 December 1964, 'Visit of the Prime Minister Harold Wilson, 7–8 December 1964', confidential.
16 On the Rapacky plan see in particular, Piotr Wandycz, 'Adam Rapacky and the Search for European Security', in Gordon A. Craig and Francis L. Loewenheim (eds), *The Diplomats: 1939–1979*, Princeton, NJ: Princeton University Press, 1994.
17 NA, RG 59, Lot file 76D170, Box 14471, 4 June 1965, background paper, 'Visit of Chancellor Erhard. FRG Relations with Soviet Union and Eastern Europe', secret.
18 Public Record Office (PRO), Foreign Office (FO) 371/181398, IAD 1057, 2 July 1965, European Security, secret.
19 Cfr. Sergei N. Khrushchev, *Nikita Khrushchev and the Creation of a Superpower*, translated by S. Benson, foreword by William Taubman, annotations by William C. Wohlforth, University Park, PA: Penn State University Press, 2000; William Taubman, Sergei N. Khrushchev and A. Gleason (eds), *Nikita Khrushchev*, New Haven, CT: Yale University Press, 2000.
20 NA, RG 59, Lot file 69D150, Box 10, 21 September 1965, 'The Nuclear Problem of the Alliance', secret.
21 On the Nassau summit of 1962, see in particular: Donette Murray, *Kennedy, Macmillan and the Nuclear Weapons*, London: Macmillan, 2000; Jan Melissen, 'Pre-summit Diplomacy: Britain, the US and the Nassau Conference, December 1962', *Diplomacy and Statecraft*, 7, 3 (1996); 'Summit Diplomacy and Alliance Policy: The Road to Nassau, December 1962', Diplomatic Studies Programme, discussion paper No. 12, December 1995.
22 NA, RG 59, Lot file 69D150, Box 7, 19 December 1962, memorandum of conversation, participants: US: The President, Secretary McNamara, Mr Ball, Ambassador Bruce, Mr Bundy, Ambassador Thompson; UK: The Prime Minister, Lord Home, Mr Thorneycroft, Ambassador Ormsby Gore, Mr De Zuleta, subject: Skybolt, secret.
23 Beatrice Heuser, 'European Strategists and European Identity: The Quest for a European Nuclear Force (1954–1967)', *Journal of European Integration History*, 2 (1995), 61–80; Marilena Gala, 'The Multilateral Force: A Brief History of the American Efforts to Maintain the Nuclear Status Quo Within the Atlantic Alliance', *Storia delle Relazioni Internazionali*, 13, 1 (1998), 121–49.
24 NA, RG 59, Lot file 69D150, Box 8, 14 December 1964, memorandum for the Secretary of State, the Secretary of Defense, the Under Secretary of State, Mr McGeorge Bundy, 'US Comments on the UK Proposal of a Project for an Atlantic Nuclear Force', top secret.
25 PRO, FO 371/184427, 89958, 26 October 1964, Record of the Meeting between the Foreign Secretary and the United States Secretary of State at the State Department, secret.
26 New evidence and an interesting interpretation of the British ANF proposal are in Susanna Schraftetter and Stephen Twigge, 'Trick or Truth? The British ANF Proposal,

West Germany and US Nonproliferation Policy, 1964–68', *Diplomacy and Statecraft*, 11, 2 (July 2000), 161–84.

27 PRO, FO 371/184427, 89958, 15 November 1964, Record of Discussions between Foreign Secretary and the German Foreign Minister in the Foreign Ministry, Bonn, secret.

28 PRO, FO 371/184427, 89958, 21 May 1965, from Evelyn Shuckburgh, UK Delegation to NATO, to E.J.W. Barnes, Western Organisations and Coordination Department, Foreign Office, secret.

29 PRO, FO 371/184427, 89958, 18 June 1965, from Evelyn Shuckburgh, UK Delegation to NATO, to the Viscount Hood, Foreign Office, confidential.

30 A memorandum of October 1965 signed by George Ball, and prepared for Secretary Rusk, Secretary McNamara and Mr Bundy clearly stated: 'We should develop this system not by creating a whole new set of weapons, but by the transfer to collective ownership and control (and financing) of the present British nuclear deterrent plus perhaps two or three nuclear submarines from our side … Moreover, by eliminating the British *national* deterrent, the plan would strike a blow for non-proliferation more significant than any piece of paper.' It is also interesting to note a short comment relating to Germany: 'The question facing us is the same question that faced the Allies between the wars: How can the extraordinary talents and energies of the German people be put to a useful rather than a destructive end?'; NA, RG 59, Lot file 69D150, Box 8, 27 October 1965, memorandum to Secretary Rusk, Secretary McNamara, Mr McGeorge Bundy, from the Undersecretary of State George W. Ball, 'The Case for a Strong American Lead to Establish a Collective Nuclear System That Would Help Save the Western World from Repeating an Old Mistake', secret.

31 NA, RG 59, Lot file 69D150, Box 10, October 1965, memorandum, subject: The Atlantic Nuclear Problem, secret.

32 NA, RG 59, Lot file 69D150, Box 8, 13 November 1965, 'The NATO Nuclear Problem Proposals and Background Papers', Talking Points for Wilson Discussions, top secret.

33 NA, RG 59, Lot file 69D150, Box 8, 18 October 1965, 'The Case for a Fresh Start on Atlantic Nuclear Defense (with Mixed Manned Forces or Plans for Such Forces)', secret.

34 PRO, Prime Minister (Prem), 13/805, 89932, 26 November 1965, Record of a Conversation between the Prime Minister and the United States Secretary of Defence, Mr Robert McNamara, at Luncheon at 10 Downing Street, secret.

35 PRO, Prem 13/805, 89932, 1 February 1966, to the Prime Minister, 'Policy toward France'.

36 The challenges and contradictions of the French policy toward the United States and the Atlantic alliance as well as de Gaulle's aspirations in Europe are effectively presented in: Frédéric Bozo, *Deux Stratégies pour l'Europe: De Gaulle, Les Etats-Unis et l'Alliance Atlantique, 1958–1969*, Paris: Plon, 1996; Georges-Henri Soutou, *L'alliance incertaine: Les rapports politico-stratégiques franco-allemands, 1954–1996*, Paris: Fayard, 1996.

37 NA, RG 59, Lot file 69D150, Box 9, 5 March 1966, tel. Bruce, Amembassy London for the President and Secretary of State, secret.

38 NA, RG 59, Lot file 69D150, Box 8, 20 December 1965, evaluation: 'The Nuclear Question', secret.

39 NA, RG 59, Lot file 69D150, Box 8, 8 November 1965, memorandum of conversation, subject: Collective Nuclear Arrangements in NATO, participants: Dr Kurt Birrenbach, CDU member of Bundestag and adviser to Chancellor Erhard, ambassador Knappstein, Secretary Rusk, Secretary McNamara, Undersecretary Ball, Mr McGeorge Bundy, secret, limdis.

40 NA, RG 59, Lot file 69D150, Box 8, 8 November 1965, to the Under Secretary, from

EUR John M. Leddy, subject: Hardware Solution to Nuclear Problem, Information Memeorandum, secret.

41 PRO, FO 1042/153, 10730 NATO Nuclear Defence, 13 January 1966, from the British Embassy, Bonn, to the Viscount Hood, Foreign Office, confidential.

42 NA, RG 59, Lot file 69D150, Box 1, folder Book 49 Germany, 'The United States and Germany – 1968', secret.

43 PRO, FO 1042/153, 10730 NATO Nuclear Defence, Washington January 1966, 'The NATO Nuclear Question', Brief for the Foreign Secretary, Washington, secret.

44 NA, RG 59, Lot file 69D150, Box 9, 7 March 1966, tel. from Amembassy Paris to the Secretary of State, De Gaulle letter to President Johnson, secret. In the letter, very similar to another one sent to Prime Minister Wilson (tel. from Amembassy Paris to the Secretary of State, 10 March 1966), President de Gaulle clearly stated: 'France considers that the changes that have occurred, or are in the process of occurring, since 1949, in Europe, Asia, and elsewhere, as well as the evolution of her own situation and her own forces, no longer justify, in so far as she is concerned, the arrangements of a military nature made after the conclusion of the Alliance, either jointly in the form of multilateral agreements, or by special agreements between the French Government and the American Government. That is why France intends to recover, in her territory, the full exercise of her sovereignty, now impaired by the permanent presence of Allied military elements or by the habitual use being made of its air space, to terminate her participation in the "integrated" commands, and no longer to place forces at the disposal of NATO.'

45 NA, RG 59, Lot file 69D150, Box 8, 11 January 1966, message on non-proliferation from Kosygin to President, handed to Acting Secretary by Ambassador Dobrynin, secret.

46 NA, RG 59, Lot file 69D150, Box 8, 24 January 1966, letter from President Johnson to Chairman Kosygin, secret.

47 A memorandum of a conversation between Secretary Rusk and the British Prime Minister in February 1968 is particularly illuminating about what the US government really intended to do with the Germans and Italians and the non-proliferation issue. Rusk, in reply to a question about the value of a Non-Proliferation Treaty, said that 'The US Government were resolved that other European powers, and particularly Italy and Germany – "the countries which had witnessed the rise to power of Mussolini and Hitler" – should never have them. If there were ever a question of Germany getting nuclear weapons it would be the end of NATO because "we can be counted out of that point"'; PRO, Prem 13/2442, 89932, 9 February 1968, 'The Non-Proliferation Treaty', secret.

48 PRO, Prem 13/2441, 1967–68 United Nations, 1 August 1967, Ukdis. Geneva, tel. N. 110 to Foreign Office.

49 PRO, Prem 13/2441, 1967–68 United Nations, 2 October 1967, letter from Foreign Office S.W.1, to A.M. Palliser, ESQ., CGM, secret.

50 Harald Muller, 'The Non-proliferation Treaty and the German Choice Not to Proliferate', in David Carlton, Mirco Elena, Klaus Gottstein and Paul Ingram (eds), Controlling the International Transfer of Weaponry and Related Technology, Brookfield, WI: Dartmouth, 1995, pp. 173–86.

51 NA, RG 59, Lot file 69D150, Box 8, 24 June 1966, letter from Harlan Cleveland, United States Permanent Representative on the North Atlantic Council, to Dean Acheson, secret.

52 PRO, FO 1042/153, 10730, NATO Nuclear Defence, 23 December 1965, British Embassy Bonn, incoming tel. N. 3418, secret; FO 953/2465, 26 April 1966, 'The Problem of Nuclear Proliferation: Discussion in APAG', secret.

53 NA, RG 59, Lot file 69D150, Box 1, 18 November 1966, Trilateral Talks, Background Paper, secret.

16

Gerhard Schröder and the First *'Ostpolitik'*

Torsten Oppelland

During most of the Adenauer era, there was not much of a German Eastern policy (*Ostpolitik*). Only during Adenauer's famous visit to Moscow in 1955 were diplomatic relations established with the Soviet Union. And even this step was most difficult for the German government to take – after all, the Soviet Union was the power that supported East Germany, which at the time the West had not yet recognized and which in the Federal Republic was usually referred to as the 'SBZ', the Soviet Occupation Zone. In order to conceal the inconsistency of not recognizing the GDR on the one hand and establishing diplomatic relations with its 'occupying' power on the other, the Hallstein doctrine was put into effect. This declared that the recognition of the GDR by any other state would be considered an unfriendly act by the West German government.[1] It was intended to block and in fact did block all attempts to improve relations between West Germany and Eastern Europe. It was only in light of that situation that the more flexible policies of Gerhard Schröder, who became foreign minister in the last Adenauer cabinet (1961) and stayed in office throughout the short-lived Erhard era, were interpreted by contemporaries and most historians as the first *Ostpolitik*.[2]

Yet, this term describes Schröder's policies only in a very limited sense because his main focus was in the West.[3] The reason for this is quite simple. Schröder shared Adenauer's conviction of the early 1950s that the only road to reunification – and that was the ultimate goal of all German foreign policy of the time – lay in firm alliance with the West, or more precisely, with the USA. Schröder's primary concern during his term as foreign minister and afterward was to keep the full weight of US power on the European scales and to maintain US support for German reunification.[4] In order to achieve this, he was much more ready than Adenauer to follow and adapt to the changes in US strategy that became apparent during the late Eisenhower years and that fully evolved in the Kennedy years. These differences over the USA were at the root of many conflicts between Adenauer and Schröder throughout the first half of the 1960s.[5] Schröder's secondary concern was relations with Germany's European allies and their support for the issue of German reunification. He put much less priority on relations with Eastern Europe and did so mostly with an eye to the effect this would have in the West. However sincere his wish to reduce the image of West Germany as an enemy in the eyes of Eastern Europeans and to begin a process of reconciliation, this was never much more than a side show of a foreign policy that was first and foremost oriented toward the West. Three episodes which reach back to the time when Schröder was still minister of domestic affairs can illustrate that the initial impulse for a new attitude toward Eastern Europe originated in the West, Schröder's priorities and his interpretation of West German vital interests, and why his strategy toward Eastern Europe ignored both East Germany and the Soviet Union.

The Anti-Semitic Incident of Christmas 1959

On Christmas Eve 1959, two members of a small right-wing party in Germany caught the attention of the world when they scrawled anti-Semitic propaganda phrases and swastikas on the Cologne synagogue.[6] There was an immediate and overwhelming propaganda reaction from East Germany and the Soviet Union, but Western public opinion was stirred as well. This was not a great surprise in the case of Great Britain; East German propaganda about an alleged 'renazification' of West Germany had gained much attention in Britain during the previous years, and the German government had more than once complained about the negative reporting on Germany in the British press. But the public reaction in the USA caused much more alarm in Bonn.[7] In the following days, Minister for Domestic Affairs Gerhard Schröder, more so than most other West German cabinet members, was busy giving interviews to foreign newspapers trying to calm the storm of mistrust against Germany. Unanimously, the members of the German government expressed disgust at the desecration of the synagogue and affirmed the determination of the German people never to allow the crimes of the past to recur. In fact, many rituals of the particular German way of dealing with the Nazi past (*Vergangenheitsbewältigung*) had their origin in the reaction to those anti-Semitic incidents.[8]

Yet, the apparent unanimity concealed a rift within the government and the leading party, the Christian Democratic Union/Christian Social Union (CDU/CSU), on the question of how to deal with the international public reaction, particularly in the Western world. The differences surfaced in the discussions of the CDU/CSU parliamentary group in mid-January. As the responsible cabinet member, Schröder opened the discussion. His speech referred to the possibility that at least the original Cologne incident, which had provoked many imitations, could have been instigated from East Berlin. There were, he claimed, quite a few hints pointing in this direction but very little proof. After all, the anti-Semitic incidents fitted all too well into the East German campaign against the Federal Republic that had been going on for some time. But that was not his main point. Rather, he looked at the question of why these incidents had received such enormous attention from the public in nations allied with Germany. The reason was, he thought, that there was a 'wave of peaceful coexistence all over the world'.[9] The peoples of the West were tired of the burdens of the Cold War which consumed so many resources. Schröder was afraid that this kind of feeling automatically focused attention on those, such as the Federal Republic, which seemed to impede the chances for a détente. The more Germany's allies would feel the weight of their obligations at the centre of the conflict, the more difficult the German psychological position would become. In the present situation, there were very few remedies he could suggest. The efforts West Germany had made to compensate Israel, the reconciliation with former enemies, the domestic efforts at *Vergangenheitsbewältigung* had to be continued, and all this should be properly used in a propaganda effort to counter the communist accusations.

Where Schröder basically opted for a defensive public relations strategy, his cabinet colleague, Minister of Defence Franz-Josef Strauss, took the opposite point of view. He argued for aggressive anti-communist rhetoric that would counter the Soviet and East German propaganda. The Federal Republic had nothing to apologize for and should meet the pressure of Eastern propaganda that was obviously designed to weaken its position particularly on the Berlin question. In a cabinet meeting the next day, Adenauer supported the argument of his defence minister while the foreign office took the same line as Schröder.[10]

This conflict within the West German government anticipated the much deeper and more passionate controversy between the 'Atlanticists' and 'Gaullists' of the following years which also saw Schröder on one side and Strauss and Adenauer on the other. As early as 1959 and 1960, it became apparent that Schröder had a better sense of the international 'winds of change'. The Federal Republic was not in the same position that it had been five years before. During the mid-1950s, the most important Western goal had been to integrate West Germany into the military structures of the free world. Almost no one wanted to put this in jeopardy by referring too much to what was conveniently dubbed the 'shadows of the past'.[11] By the end of the 1950s, the difficult task of integrating the Federal Republic into the Western world, which had made it necessary to treat the Germans very carefully, had been achieved. At the same time, 'Sputnik shock' demonstrated the dangers of the Cold War to the populations of Europe and the USA. The public reaction to the Cologne incident and the mistrust of Germany's democratic reliability were symptoms of the changed psychological position of West Germany. It demonstrated that the Federal Republic was not only militarily but also psychologically much more vulnerable than, for instance, France. Accordingly, Germany's ability to act independently was much smaller than that of France. Even before he became foreign minister, Schröder had displayed some sense of this. He had realized that the strategies of the 1950s – simple anti-communist Cold War-strategies – would not be sufficient any longer but that there was a need to adapt to the 'winds of change' in the Western world. His limited *Ostpolitik* as foreign minister was part of the effort to adapt to the changes in the political strategies and feelings of the Western allies. And already in 1959 and 1960, it had become apparent that such a course would be challenged by members of his own party.

Schröder and the Berlin Wall

The federal election of 1961 was overshadowed by the construction of the Berlin Wall. The consequences for Schröder personally were quite ambiguous. On the one hand, the fact that the CDU lost the absolute majority in the Bundestag, not least because of Adenauer's initial reaction to what had happened in Berlin,[12] helped him to become foreign minister in the renewed CDU–FDP coalition government.[13] In the very last moment, on the other hand, he almost lost the nomination for this office he had long desired because there were rumours that he was 'soft on Berlin'. In a background interview with a prominent journalist, he was alleged to have given the impression that it might become inevitable to give up the city and evacuate the population to some place in West Germany. Schröder himself claimed that his words had been misconstrued; he had discussed only possible options and, of course, he claimed that he did not favour that particular option.[14]

In his private papers, in fact, there are personal notes suggesting that he may have been carelessly frank with that journalist. West Berlin, he wrote in a personal memorandum, could be militarily untenable and thus useless for any political offensive on the German question. But since the USA had pledged all their prestige to keeping their position in Berlin, they might be forced to give up vital interests regarding German reunification.[15] Such concessions to Soviet and East German interests were in his view *de facto* recognition of the GDR, the recognition of the Polish western border (which he was ready to accept but only as a concession for German reunification), and a minor status for West Germany within NATO. The first concession was most important to him. To recognize the East German regime was almost equal to renouncing rights regarding German reunification. This was not only a matter of national self-respect, but it would, so he explicitly feared, over the long run undermine the will and determination of the German people to achieve reunification.

Schröder's thinking on the Berlin question in October 1961 was by no means a master plan for his policy as foreign minister. Rather, it was an improvised and certainly not a very deep or perceptive analysis of the situation.[16] This episode nevertheless shows to what lengths he was ultimately prepared to go in order keep full US support for the German position on reunification.

Schröder's First Encounter with Gromyko

In the spring of 1962, the foreign ministers of the great powers met in Geneva for the UN disarmament talks. Gerhard Schröder, foreign minister since November of the previous year despite the protests of the Berlin faction within the CDU, met his colleagues from the three Western powers to exchange views on the German question and its connections to the issue of disarmament. On this particular occasion, Schröder also made a courtesy call to his Soviet colleague, Andrei Gromyko. It was clear from the start that there would be no negotiations or even consultations since the two governments had only recently exchanged notes which had demonstrated that no common interests existed – except on trade.[17] So it did not come as a great surprise that in Geneva there was not much more than a dialogue of the deaf.[18] The uncompromising Soviet position was that the Federal Republic had to accept postwar realities, that is, the existence of the GDR and the Polish borders, before any negotiations between the Soviet Union and West Germany could even begin. Schröder of course followed the official government position that it was necessary to establish a just peace settlement – implying that the partition of Germany was unjust and unacceptable. This exchange of notes and the personal exchange of views demonstrated to Schröder that the two positions were completely incompatible. As long as the Soviet Union insisted on recognition of postwar realities, as their oft-repeated phrase went, as a precondition for any negotiations except trade, then there would be no bilateral negotiations. This intransigent Soviet position changed only in the spring of 1969 before the federal elections which finally made the SPD the leading government party. The Social Democrats could thus begin the 'second' *Ostpolitik* under much better circumstances.[19]

To sum up, these three episodes throw some light on the circumstances under which Foreign Minister Schröder had to develop his concept of *Ostpolitik*. The Berlin crises beginning with the Khrushchev ultimatum of 1958 had clearly demonstrated the vulnerabilities of the West German position. First, there was the pending danger of further Soviet blackmail over Berlin. Second, there was the difficult psychological position of West Germany, which more and more proved to be the main obstacle to achieving a *modus vivendi* between the Western powers and the Soviet Union. Third, this reawakened some mistrust of the Germans' democratic reliability in the eyes of the Western public and even in government circles, particularly in Britain. This kind of feeling was subconsciously boosted by the permanent pounding of Soviet and East German propaganda. To deal with these difficulties and, most of all, to preserve the chances for reunification, the Federal Republic needed the support of the USA. This was Schröder's deep 'Atlanticist' conviction and he therefore rejected Adenauer's idea of a close Franco-German special relationship to put pressure on the USA. 'If you absolutely depend on this great and strong partner [that is, the USA] to really keep being engaged in the way he has been engaged', then you cannot afford to keep criticizing him, but rather you have to prove your reliability and demonstrate a constructive attitude.[20] This was the essence of what Schröder wanted to do as German foreign minister. One important aspect of this was a more constructive attitude toward Eastern Europe than was favoured by the Kennedy administration. But here the options were of course extremely limited. The GDR could at this point not yet be a partner in negotiations and the Soviet Union refused any negotiations as long as the Federal Republic did not meet its preconditions.

The Evolution of Schröder's Concept of Ostpolitik

In 1962, it was clear to Schröder that West Germany could not afford to keep a Mephistophelian attitude of saying no to all proposals for a détente with Eastern Europe. At the end of May, he met with a very small group of confidants from the foreign office for some brainstorming ա a monastery in Maria Laach. Unfortunately there are only very few records oⲓ the deliberations on how Germany ought to proceed: 'new memoranda? diplom[atic] declarations? trade initiatives? cultural activities? Prognosis'.[21] A prominent role during this meeting was apparently played by Hans-Albert Reinkemeyer, the head of the Soviet desk at the foreign office, who at the time was not only regarded as one of the most brilliant younger diplomats but who was also a personal friend of the US political scientist Zbigniew Brzezinski.[22] Most probably it was Reinkemeyer who either at this meeting or at some other time showed Schröder Brzezinski's *Foreign Affairs* article on 'peaceful engagement'. The parallels between Schröder's policy and the policy suggested by the Polish–US scholar are striking.[23] Brzezinski, who was close to the Kennedy administration, argued for a realistic and constructive US policy toward Eastern Europe, which at least since 1956 was no longer the monolithic bloc that it had been perceived as earlier. Brzezinski set three goals for such a US policy: he wanted to stimulate further diversification within the Eastern bloc, and he wanted to encourage these states to gain more independence of the Soviet Union. These, he hoped, would help in the long run to establish a belt of neutral states which would be similar to Finland in ruling over their own domestic affairs but would not be allowed to join any alliance against the Soviet Union. Brzezinski was sceptical about the Federal Republic's possibilities of contributing to these policies. Germany could do little more than gradually reduce the enmity against it, particularly in Poland and Czechoslovakia. For this purpose, he suggested compensation of victims of the National Socialists similar to what had been done in the case of Israel. As the Hallstein doctrine should not be applied to 'captive nations', the Federal Republic should establish diplomatic relations with Eastern Europe. For the USA, he suggested a clear statement supporting the present Polish borders; this would be an indispensable precondition for German reunification, and it would to that extent be in the long-term interest of Germany. Non-recognition of the GDR should, however, be continued; 'peaceful engagement' should not apply in this case. Brzezinski was primarily concerned with Poland and the other Eastern European states, but his line of thinking was most interesting for German politicians such as Schröder who were looking for new ways to achieve German reunification. But of course a foreign minister of the CDU could not go quite as fast as a US scholar.

Less than two weeks after the deliberations in Maria Laach, the 11th federal party convention of the CDU began in Dortmund, where Schröder for the first time publicly discussed his ideas on the course of German foreign policy. He began his speech with a wide overview of the development of the Federal Republic from the smallest beginnings to the position of a major economic power.[24] Only toward the end of the speech did he reveal some new ideas:

> The peoples of the Warsaw Pact also belong to Europe. I think it would be good if the hateful communist propaganda and if the resentment disturbing the relations between the Eastern European peoples and the German people were overcome ... A beginning could be made, for instance, by improving cultural and human contacts between Germans in the Federal Republic and Eastern European peoples. We are seriously interested in the intellectual debate currently taking place in the Eastern bloc and we are convinced that it would be valuable for all open-minded, undogmatic people of Eastern Europe to get to know the cultural and political development of free Europe.

But Schröder remained cautious. He neither suggested establishing diplomatic relations with the Eastern European states nor mentioned any compensations for Nazi crimes. Yet it is obvious how close his ideas were to those developed by Brzezinski, even more so since he took steps to put his words into practice. The negotiations that eventually led to the establishment of West German trade missions in the Eastern European states began soon after the party convention.[25]

Why was Brzezinski's concept so attractive to Schröder? There are two reasons:

(1) Since the very beginning of his policies that led West Germany into NATO and the EEC, Adenauer had claimed that this was the road to German reunification. By the end of the 1950s, most commentators agreed that this road was actually a dead-end. Adenauer's famous 'policy of strength', whose core element was the linkage between any progress on détente between the superpowers to progress on the German question, had apparently yielded no results at all. Brzezinski opened a new perspective which had the great advantage that the previous policies would not have to be abandoned completely. It was

particularly the fact that his ideas for reconciliation with Eastern Europe explicitly excluded the GDR that made his concept compatible with Schröder's view on reunification.

From the beginning, the new 'policy of movement', as Schröder later labelled it, was designed as a new approach to German reunification. Since direct negotiations with the Soviet Union and the GDR were either not possible or not acceptable, there remained only the option of 'indirect means': 'Of course, it is part of these indirect means that we attempt to prevent the communist bloc from stabilizing and that we on the contrary make all possible efforts to support ... the natural tendencies of dissolution which are fed in part by national traditions.'[26] Even at the CDU party convention where he first went public with his new policy on Eastern Europe, Schröder had stressed that divided Germany would profit most from any relaxation of the tensions between East and West.

Yet, the record remains ambivalent as to what degree he really believed in this reunification element in his 'policy of movement'. Particularly in 1964, he seemed more optimistic than before and emphasized in public the first successes of his policy and spoke of the famous 'polycentric' development in Eastern Europe which might eventually increase the chances for reunification. His greatest fear was that there could be similar polycentric developments within the Western world. This was the reason why he opposed the anti-hegemonic policies of the French president General de Gaulle so rigidly. Only a year later, in 1965, Schröder discussed the chances for reunification very candidly with some journalists.[27] During this background talk, he appeared much more sceptical that progress on reconciliation with Eastern Europe alone, as important as it was, would bring about German reunification. Much more than before, he stressed the importance of US might in bringing about the fundamental change in power relations between East and West that would be necessary to allow any real progress toward German reunification. This points to the second great advantage of Brzezinski's concept.

(2) As an Atlanticist, Schröder never saw any choice for West Germany other than to follow the changes in US foreign policy. The Kennedy administration had implicitly abandoned the former linkage between détente policies and the German question. Adenauer and his many admirers saw this almost as a kind of treason, a sentiment which became quite popular in Germany when the USA at first reacted very passively to the construction of the Berlin Wall.[28] Adenauer and his German 'Gaullist' faction drew the consequence from US behaviour that they should look to Paris for support since de Gaulle had been hard as steel during the Berlin crisis. To Schröder, this reaction appeared almost foolish. After Adenauer's 'policy of strength' had failed on the German question, this course would have put at risk even the alliance with the USA which seemed to him the most important achievement of the Adenauer era. Schröder had always claimed he was continuing Adenauer's policies and in a

way this was true. Only his interpretation of what that policy had been differed from Adenauer's own. The old chancellor thought he had aligned Germany to a certain US policy toward the communist world and the German question. In Schröder's view, West Germany had been aligned to the USA and he sought to keep it that way.

As shown before, Schröder had a much more realistic view of German dependence on the USA and on the restrictions of German freedom of action. To him, there was no alternative to adapting to the US policy changes. And the advantage of Brzezinski's concept was that he could do so without being forced to give up any of the vital interests sketched out before, particularly non-recognition of the GDR. Rather, he could try to make the best of this new US course for improving the status quo in favour of West Germany and thus in the long run improve the chances for German reunification.[29] Whenever the Kennedy or Johnson administration tried to put pressure on the West German government for a more flexible attitude toward détente, he could point to his 'policy of movement' which was so much in line with US policy. And he could point to the domestic alternative to his policy which was represented by Adenauer, Franz-Josef Strauss and the other German Gaullists, who would be much less cooperative.[30]

Conclusion

At the end of 1963, Gerhard Schröder had an argument with his US colleague Dean Rusk on the policy of West Berlin Mayor Willy Brandt. Rusk approved wholeheartedly of the conclusion of the *Passierscheinabkommen* (transit permit agreement) between the authorities in West and East Berlin whereas Schröder was very critical. The East, he feared, would give the impression of being more humane, the public would come to say that it was possible to negotiate with these people and the results would be quite welcome as well. But this process would eventually stabilize the status quo. Unless, Schröder continued, 'it was practically the aim to come to a *de facto* recognition of the GDR in order to be able to have an impact within the GDR and effect changes there … this was absolutely the wrong course'.[31] Without actually quoting Egon Bahr, Schröder obviously referred to his famous formula 'Wandel durch Annäherung' (change through approach). No doubt, this kind of new *Ostpolitik* was not what Schröder had in mind.

His concept was to adapt to the American policy of détente in a very limited way. His 'policy of movement' was exclusively addressed to the states of Eastern Europe, not to the GDR. Against considerable resistance from various CDU factions, he wanted to modify the Hallstein doctrine to be able to establish diplomatic relations with Eastern Europe, but he never wanted to give up the doctrine completely.[32] The idea that the GDR might be represented in all capitals of the world was a nightmare for him; this became apparent during the crisis of spring 1965 when Walter Ulbricht visited Egypt.[33] These limitations on Schröder's *Ostpolitik* explain its limited success. In regard to *Ostpolitik* and détente policy, there was only little success – the trade missions were not the beginning of a West German offensive in Eastern Europe but its climax. Within a short time, Walter Ulbricht was able to counter the West German offensive when he forged the 'iron triangle' between East Germany, Poland and Czechoslovakia with Moscow's support.[34] The negative responses to the West German peace note of 1966 by most Eastern European states illustrate that there was little room for further progress along established lines. As a strategy for reunification the 'policy of movement' proved to be a dead-end street just as Adenauer's 'policy of strength' had been. A 'polycentric dissolution' of the Soviet sphere had not (yet) happened. Only as an adaptation to the US policy of détente was it successful. This had been Schröder's main objective all along, and his policies helped to steer the Western alliance through the difficult time of crisis in the mid-1960s.

NOTES

1 Rüdiger Marco Booz, '*Hallsteinzeit*': *Deutsche Außenpolitik 1955–1972*, Bonn: Bouvier, 1995.
2 For example, Franz Eibl, *Politik der Bewegung: Gerhard Schröder als Außenminister 1961–1966*, Munich: Oldenbourg, 2001.
3 The term is also misleading in so far as it suggests a continuity between the 'first' and the 'second' *Ostpolitik*, cf. Torsten Oppelland, 'Der "Ostpolitiker" Gerhard Schröder – ein Vorläufer der sozialliberalen Ost- und Deutschlandpolitik', *Historisch-Politische Mitteilungen* (*HPM*), 8 (2001), pp. 63–84.
4 Torsten Oppelland, *Gerhard Schröder (1910–1989): Politik zwischen Staat, Partei und Konfession*, Düsseldorf: Droste, 2002, pp. 681ff; Schröder's concern to keep the Americans in Europe paralleled the overriding Soviet aim to make them leave the continent, cf. the contribution by Marie-Pierre Rey to this volume.
5 Oppelland, *Gerhard Schröder*, pp. 483ff.
6 The incidents have often been described; for the international reactions cf. Ulrich Brochhagen, *Nach Nürnberg: Vergangenheitsbewältigung und Westintegration in der Ära Adenauer*, Berlin: Propyläen, 1999, pp. 345ff.
7 Ibid., pp. 299ff., 350f.
8 Manfred Kittel, 'Peripetie der Vergangenheitsbewältigung: Die Hakenkreuzschmierereien 1959/60 und das bundesdeutsche Verhältnis zum Nationalsozialismus', *HPM*, 1 (1994), pp. 49–67.
9 CDU/CSU parliamentary group, 19 January 1960, Archiv für Christlich-Demokratische Politik (ACDP), VIII-001-1008/2.
10 Brochhagen, *Nach Nürnberg*, pp. 338, 350ff.
11 The most noteworthy example is Eisenhower's famous apology to high-ranking German officers for the anti-German remarks in his autobiography, ibid., pp. 227ff.
12 Rolf Steininger, *Der Mauerbau: Die Westmächte und Adenauer in der Berlinkrise 1958–1961*, Munich: Olzog, 2001, pp. 277–9.
13 Oppelland, *Gerhard Schröder*, pp. 429ff.
14 Ibid., pp. 423, 430ff.
15 Memorandum 3 October 1961, ACDP, I-483-272/2.

16 For a more detailed discussion, cf. Oppelland, *Gerhard Schröder*, pp. 423ff.

17 Ibid., pp. 468ff.

18 Protocol of the discussions of 12 March 1962, ACDP, I-483-281/1.

19 Timothy Garton Ash, *Im Namen Europas: Deutschland und der geteilte Kontinent*, Munich, Vienna: 1993, p. 90. (Garton Ash interprets this Soviet change of position as a result of their 'success' in suppressing the Prague Spring of 1968 but also because of their interest in better economic relations with the Federal Republic; thus he sees Adenauer's hard-line strategy vindicated.)

20 Quoted from a speech at a local party convention, 20 May 1962, ACDP, I-483-140/1.

21 Note by Schröder, 23 May 1962, ACDP, I-483-272/2.

22 Interview with Schröder's assistant, Dr Klaus Simon, 19 September, 1995.

23 Zbigniew Brzezinski and William E. Griffith, 'Peaceful Engagement in Eastern Europe', *Foreign Affairs*, 39 (1960/61), pp 642–54.

24 Gerhard Schröder, 'Deutschland, Europa und die freie Welt', *Bulletin des Presse- und Informationsamtes der Bundesregierung*, Nr. 104/1962 (my translation).

25 For the details of the long and difficult negotiations, cf. Eibl, *Politik der Bewegung*, pp. 264ff.

26 Speech 10 April 1964, ACDP, I-483-141/1 (my translation).

27 He later made sure that the shorthand protocol of this background discussion would get into the wrong hands; 20 May 1965, ACDP, I-483-107/1.

28 Steininger, *Der Mauerbau*, pp. 262ff. To some extent, Steininger's perspective reflects that attitude.

29 Cf. for instance his conversation with Rusk, 20 September 1963, AAPD 1963, Doc. 349 (particularly pp. 1158–61).

30 For examples, see Oppelland, *Gerhard Schröder*, p. 536.

31 AAPD 1963, p. 1683 (my translation).

32 Cp. Booz, *'Hallsteinzeit'*, pp. 93ff., who describes Schröder's *Ostpolitik* as an offensive variation of the Hallstein doctrine.

33 Oppelland, *Gerhard Schröder*, pp. 625ff.

34 Peter Bender, *Neue Ostpolitik: Vom Mauerbau bis zum Moskauer Vertrag*, Munich: Deutscher Taschenbuch Verlag, 1989, p. 140.

17

The East–West Problem as Seen from Berlin: Willy Brandt's Early *Ostpolitik*

Gottfried Niedhart

The Other Foot Called Ostpolitik

When Willy Brandt became Governing Mayor of West Berlin in October 1957 he was convinced that the Federal government in Bonn should broaden the range of its foreign policy. After its creation as a product of the Cold War, the Federal Republic of Germany had to achieve one main goal, namely, the establishment of friendly relations with the USA and their neighbours in Western Europe. Stopping there, however, would mean standing 'on one leg' only. In Brandt's view Bonn, in accordance with the Three Powers and firmly adhering to the West, had to put down the other foot too, 'and that is called *Ostpolitik*'. It seemed to Brandt that the necessity to develop an *Ostpolitik* was felt more strongly in Berlin 'than on the left bank of the Rhine'.[1]

In Bonn Chancellor Konrad Adenauer also had thoughts on how to supplement the policy of binding the Federal Republic to the West. Both Brandt and Adenauer realized that the status quo, including the division of Germany, could not be changed in the foreseeable future. Neither was prepared to recognize the GDR but they both knew that they somehow had to come to terms with postwar realities. Both had to make an endeavour to persuade their respective parties and the public at large that a new approach to the German question was in the national interest. Eventually Brandt was more successful than Adenauer who, although he felt that his earlier concepts had failed, could not shake himself free from them. Brandt and the SPD lost the elections in 1961 and 1965 when Brandt campaigned as a candidate for the chancellorship in Bonn. But by the time Brandt left his post in Berlin in 1966 in order to become Foreign Minister in a Grand Coalition with the Christian Democrats in Bonn he had become a prominent figure in national politics. The new government with Kurt Georg Kiesinger (CDU) as Chancellor took up a number of the initiatives of its predecessors, notably those of Foreign Minister Gerhard Schröder,[2] and paved the way for what became known internationally as *Ostpolitik*.

The purpose of this chakpter is to describe the beginnings of *Ostpolitik* in Berlin. According to Brandt himself, the Grand Coalition had an enormous impact on West German politics and on *Ostpolitik* in particular. But he added that *Ostpolitik* was not invented in 1966, and he acknowledged the roles of Adenauer and his successor Ludwig Erhard who, each in his own way, tried to improve relations with the Soviet Union and the other Eastern European states.[3] But it is of considerable interest that Brandt remembers his time in Berlin, when the Soviet Union threatened to change the status of the city and gave way to Ulbricht's pressure and let him build the Wall in 1961,[4] as the period when *Ostpolitik* was conceived.[5] Indeed, the procedure by which the pass agreement (*Passierscheinabkommen*) of December 1963 was achieved served as a model some years later when Brandt pursued *Ostpolitik* as Federal Chancellor from 1969 onwards and when the Four Powers negotiated the Berlin agreement in 1970/71.

However, the original concept of *Ostpolitik*, as distinct from practical steps and operational policy, dates from the 1950s. Brandt's reaction to the Wall and his policy of small steps (*Politik der kleinen Schritte*) was based on his earlier ideas and perceptions.[6] Forced by the harsh reality of events during the Berlin crisis the concept of *Ostpolitik* was further elaborated and could be applied to the situation in Berlin and later on to the Federal Republic's pivotal role in East–West relations. The formulation of the concept of *Ostpolitik* and the practical experience of direct talks and negotiations with the GDR during Brandt's time as Governing Mayor in Berlin were to form the first act of a lengthy drama.

The Concept of Ostpolitik

When Brandt used the term *Ostpolitik* in January 1958 his main contention was that the East–West conflict could not be solved by the so-called policy of strength.[7] Contrary to the expectations of the late 1940s the Soviet Union was rapidly gaining in military strength. As it was striving for equality or even superiority within the coming years some kind of de-escalation was needed and a new approach towards conflict resolution had to be developed. The Cold War attitude of the early 1950s had to be replaced by a more realistic assessment of the international constellation and a more flexible response to postwar realities. Since the Soviet empire was a reality that could not be removed by military pressure, the West should not hesitate to open up various lines of communication to the East. Without accepting every aspect of postwar realities in Europe, and continually insisting on the right of self-determination for the Germans on both sides of the border, the guiding principles of a new approach towards the East were peaceful coexistence and political, economic and cultural exchange. The combination of the renunciation of force and of improved communication seemed to be essential in order to achieve a relaxation of tensions between East and West and initiate a process of détente (*Entspannung*).

Brandt and his team of advisers had specific purposes in mind as well as certain expectations with respect to the future attitudes and policies of the Soviet Union. In Berlin the conditions in and around the city had to be improved. The immediate aim was to improve the lot of ordinary men and women in both parts of the city of Berlin (*menschliche Erleichterungen*). On the national level the Germans in the Federal Republic and in West Berlin, in accordance with their Western allies, had to take the initiative in dealing with the German question. Its solution could not be regarded any longer as a precondition for détente – this had been the orthodox view in the 1950s – but was only conceivable as the end result of a long and difficult process of negotiation which would finally lead to détente. As to Brandt's expectations, he believed that the Soviet Union was also interested in some kind of cooperation. In a middle-range perspective there seemed to be a good chance for some relaxation of the Cold War tensions. The conflict would not be overcome, but at least there might be a degree of cooperation between the two hostile parties.

The concept of *Ostpolitik* was in no sense a secret affair. Its guiding lines were enunciated in public speeches and printed in newspapers and journals. The publicity was necessary because public opinion in Germany and the main-stream thinking of West German policy makers, the Social Democrats included, had to be changed. Furthermore, delivering speeches was the only possible way of political action, given that the West Berlin Senate lacked both competence and power in foreign affairs. Being dependent on the three powers Brandt was unable to pursue a foreign policy of his own. In addition to this he was aware that he had to be in step with the Federal government in Bonn. Confronted with these restrictions Brandt acted as a writer and speaker. Thereby he prepared the ground for later political action without knowing when the time for action would come and what kind of action would be possible and appropriate.

Again, it has to be stressed that the concept of *Ostpolitik* was outlined before the Berlin crisis. An early opportunity for Brandt to explain it to an international audience was provided by an invitation by the Royal Institute of International Affairs to give a speech at Chatham House in London. In March 1958 Brandt described 'The East–West Problem as Seen from Berlin'.[8] Regarding 'a speedy solution of the German problem unlikely', he pleaded for '*active* coexistence'.[9] He deplored the Western attitude of anxiously staring at the East. 'The West has been far too much on the defensive in its dealings with the peoples of Eastern Europe. Even in Western Germany there was for years a fear that we should be affected or even poisoned by our con-tacts with the other side. This fear and lack of self-confidence has caused us to assume a defensive attitude and to dig ourselves in.' In Brandt's view the West should advocate an 'open-door policy' with respect to 'human and cultural contacts'. It should 'strive for a degree of normalization in relations'. A more 'flexible policy' had nothing to do with 'wishful thinking' or with the 'idea of capitulation'. On the contrary, it would mean competition. It would provide a chance to enter the East and to work for peaceful change. Having ruled out force, 'only one course now remains: an unflinching, stubborn struggle for a peaceful solution by political action'.

As far as the GDR was concerned a more flexible policy could create the possibility of technical contacts between the two German states and hopefully would bring about 'change' in East Germany. 'Why not try?'[10] Why not begin an 'active *Ostpolitik*'?[11] Getting 'out of the trenches of the Cold War' remained Brandt's message before and during the Berlin crisis.[12] It goes without saying that Brandt had both sides in mind. Throughout his period of office in Berlin Brandt pursued a double-track course. On the one hand, he tried to build up as much resistance to the Soviet threat as he could organize. On the other hand he looked for ways and means beyond the actual clash of positions and interests. The outcome was a kind of elaborated theory of détente in East–West relations and peaceful change in Germany. Brandt and his close aide, Egon Bahr, explained it many times, the famous speeches by Brandt in Harvard in 1962 and by Brandt and Bahr in Tutzing in 1963 being the most notable occasions.[13]

The essence was to accept the status quo in order to overcome it. The Soviet Union was to be persuaded to cooperate and at the same time to accept peaceful change in Europe. A more cooperative Soviet attitude could be reached by recognizing the status quo. In the short run the Soviet Union seemed to be the winner. But the recognition of the status quo would prove to be the initial step towards changing it to the West's advantage. Once Moscow had lost its fear of being pushed out of Germany and Eastern Europe, it could feel able to enter into a process of communication with the West. A rapprochement between East and West might result in the 'transformation of the other side'. Bahr's famous formula 'change through rapprochement' (*Wandel durch Annäherung*) was meant to be a challenge to the Soviet empire, not by military force but by the more subtle power of economic strength, technological superiority and Western ideas. This was the only power at Germany's disposal and, furthermore, seemed suitable to avoid the dangers of a continual arms race. Weak militarily and dependent on allied protection, West Berlin and the Federal Republic could only hope that the Soviet superpower would refrain from using military force in Central Europe. However, a militarily weak and economically strong West Germany had something to offer, and the Soviet Union might possibly wish for cooperation from Germany as well as from the West in general.

The concept of *Ostpolitik* cannot be understood without taking into account Brandt's perception of the Soviet Union and of the Soviet empire in Eastern Europe. The underlying assumption which was absolutely crucial for the whole concept was that the Soviet leaders, though behaving in an aggressive way, were no adventurers. Furthermore, people like Khrushchev seemed to realize that Stalinist bureaucracy and sheer military power was no longer sufficient. In order to stabilize the Soviet empire its economic performance had to be drastically improved. Consequently a process of change and reform had to be introduced. As early as 1956 Brandt perceived an ideological crisis within the Soviet elite and a clash between reformers and orthodox communists which arose out of this constellation.[14] Brandt supposed that the Soviet Union would look for a solution by turning to the West for the purpose of economic and technological cooperation, provided the West recognized Soviet security interests and itself was prepared for communication, contacts and exchange. Obviously Brandt was guided by the theory of convergence of highly industrialized modern societies. With increased industrialization and in need of technological progress the Soviet Union would not be able to avoid a certain degree of de-ideologization and liberalization.

In addition to this Brandt believed that the Eastern bloc was increasingly confronted with 'divergent tendencies'.[15] From the late 1950s onwards until 1968, when the 'Prague spring' collapsed, the wish for more independence from Moscow in Eastern Europe was regarded as an important factor on which the Western policy of détente could count. In a lengthy memorandum of August 1964 Brandt recommended US Secretary of State Dean Rusk to encourage the reformists in the East by offering economic support and cooperation.[16] No doubt Brandt and his advisers overestimated the power of the forces of evolution and the actual room for manoeuvre of the Warsaw Pact states, but it clearly shows their political vision of a world in which they believed that the superpowers, including the USA, would reach the limits of their power. Looking ahead to the year 2000 it seemed to Brandt in 1963 that the twentieth century would prove to be neither a US nor a Soviet century.[17]

Opportunities and Constraints

As we have seen, the concept of *Ostpolitik* started from the fundamental assumption that both sides should talk to each other and search for overlapping interests. Communication was a key notion in Brandt's language of détente. One had to break the ice and begin somewhere, even without knowing the true intentions of the adversary. An early example of developing contacts was Brandt's meeting with Chamov, the Soviet commandant of East Berlin, on 10 January 1958.[18] It took place at the Soviet headquarters at Karlshorst in the Eastern part of the city. Brandt suggested establishing cultural contacts and raised the problem of how new ways of movement between West Berlin and the East could be found. The two-hour meeting, helped along by large quantities of vodka, was friendly but, not surprisingly, did not produce any concrete results. Nor was there any follow-up meeting, although it was agreed upon that there should be one. Nonetheless, the mere fact of the meeting, although it did not have any positive impact on the Soviet policy, seemed to be of some political relevance.

Brandt reported to the allied powers about the meeting but he had not asked for their consent in advance. He had merely informed them that he would be going to Karlshorst. At later stages Brandt was more cautious and even accepted objections put forward by the allies. Only after he had become Federal Chancellor in 1969 he did repeat this pattern. He informed the Western allies of the forthcoming negotiations with the Soviet Union, but he did not consult with them. A more active policy towards the East needed new initiatives and, at the same time, had to take into consideration all sorts of constraints. The Soviets seemed to be simultaneously both talkative and aggressive. The allies and the Federal Government in Bonn wanted to keep a close eye on any movement towards the Soviet or East German authorities. Last but not least Brandt's own party, the SPD in West Berlin and in the Federal Republic, was not altogether pleased. Two days after his trip to the East Brandt had to defend himself at a party convention in West Berlin.

The main precondition for putting the concept of *Ostpolitik* into effect was a change of attitude in the Soviet Union. Only Moscow could open windows of opportunity. As it turned out the Soviet leadership and the government in East Berlin did the opposite. Instead of taking up Brandt's proposal of June 1958 to establish technical contacts in order to improve the chances for the Berliners in East and West to move and communicate more freely,[19] the Soviet Union questioned the status quo in November 1958 by proposing a peace treaty with the two German states within six months. West Berlin was to become a 'Free City'. Contrary to Chancellor Adenauer, Brandt perceived the crisis not only as a threat, which it was, but also as an opportunity for negotiations.[20] In December 1958 he felt reassured when he won the election in West Berlin. Although the SPD share of the vote was 53 per cent the coalition with the CDU was continued. Also in December 1958 Brandt consented to the two-track decision of NATO. The Soviet ultimatum was rejected, but future discussions on both Germany and Berlin were not ruled out. In particular, Brandt's reaction to the crisis was 'very similar to that of the United States – a firm rejection accompanied by indications of compromise'.[21]

With the exception of a short period after the building of the Wall in August 1961, Brandt's views and the US approach largely coincided, even though Brandt suspected time and again that the USA might be inclined to compromise with the Soviet Union at the expense of the West Berliners. It also happened that the Americans decided for Brandt. When he was unsure whether to accept an invitation for a meeting with Khrushchev in East Berlin in March 1959, the negative attitude of the US representative in Berlin was decisive. The British government as well as the government in Bonn were willing to leave the decision to Brandt. The French were sceptical and so were parts of the SPD in West Berlin. Brandt himself wanted to avoid any political risk, but in retrospect he regretted that the opportunity to talk to the Soviet leader had been missed.[22]

In fact Brandt's readiness to establish contacts with the East on a working level did not change. But attempts to achieve this in late 1959 proved futile.[23] Again and again it became crystal clear that any improvement in East–West relations and any chance to launch a new *Ostpolitik* depended on the behaviour of the Soviets. In the meantime, however, the Germans themselves should prepare and should not shrink from taking their own initiatives. In Brandt's view the time had come for more independent action. The Germans should shed the remaining egg shells and should not expect the allies both to speak and to think for them. In short: continuity was vital in foreign policy and in the Western attitude towards the East, but so too was the introduction of 'fresh ideas'.[24] In practice, however, as the Berlin crisis went on, not much could be done by the West Berlin Senate. It was only after the Cuban missile crisis had been settled that the window of opportunity for any such 'fresh ideas' was slightly opened.

In the course of the difficult and dangerous year of 1962 Brandt tried to combine a new approach with old positions.[25] In order to alleviate the situation of the Berliners there was an urgent need for technical agreements between both sides under the supervision and responsibility of the four-powers, without recognizing the GDR or the division of Germany. The four power status of Berlin had to remain in force. To put it succinctly: one had to stick to the legal status, but work on the basis of the real status. The real situation was shaped by the presence of the Western allies in *West* Berlin only. Hence one should concentrate on improving the real status rather than stubbornly but fruitlessly insisting on the legal status. Improving the real status meant finding a satisfactory solution for the access to and from Berlin and to increase the ties between West Berlin and the Federal Republic. Khrushchev's attack on the legal position had to be rejected, but the hard facts of the situation could not be ignored. What really mattered was defending West Berlin. After the building of the Wall there was no alternative to this course unless the use of force was taken into consideration. Military action was ruled out, however. A Wall was 'not a very nice solution but … a hell of a lot better than a war', was President Kennedy's comment.[26] Kennedy wanted to support 'the *idea* of self-determination, the *idea* of all-Germany, and the *fact* of viable, protected freedom in West Berlin'.[27]

Once the initial shock of the Wall and the disappointment over the passivity of the West was over, Kennedy's view was shared by the West Berlin Senate. Kennedy's recommendation did not take the Senate by complete surprise. After all the idea that the Germans should base their thoughts and expectations on the status quo was, as we have seen, not new at all for Brandt and his advisers. But having experienced the brutality of the Wall the lesson had to be learned again. Now the stage, which prior to the Wall seemed to be full of dangers as well as of hopes, was completly 'empty'.[28] In order to start the play again one had to respect the status quo. According to Egon Bahr, Kennedy had pointed out that legal claims (*Rechtsansprüche*) might exist, but realities were something else. The status quo was the reality.[29]

Between August 1961 when the Berlin Wall was erected and the autumn of 1962 when it was feared that the Soviets could act against West Berlin in retaliation for US pressure on Cuba,[30] it was not clear whether the Soviet Union would be content with the status quo. Moscow still insisted on changing the status of West Berlin. Consequently Brandt, while offering negotiations on passes for the West Berliners who wanted to visit their relatives and friends in the East, did not stop demanding both the removal of the Wall and the securing of the status quo for West Berlin.[31] On balance, however, he stressed the necessity of practical steps in order to solve a variety of questions, such as access to and the resumption of freedom of movement in Berlin.[32] Brandt's emphasis on the factual rather than the legal position met with a mixed reaction in Bonn. On the one hand Foreign Minister Schröder's 'policy of movement' to Eastern Europe was similar to Brandt's approach. On the other hand, influential Christian Democrats abhorred the up-grading of the GDR: 'It all leads to coexistence.'[33]

In the end the Berlin crisis led to the enforced division of Berlin, but also to the survival of West Berlin. The Soviet Union was satisfied with a partial victory. This provided the fundamental precondition for launching new approaches in East–West relations on the basis of the status quo. Now the aim was not to remove the Wall but to make it less impenetrable. The Soviets and the GDR had to grant some alleviations to the West Berliners in return for the *de facto* recognition of the status quo by the West. A first result was the pass agreement (*Passierscheinabkommen*) which was signed in December 1963, just in time for Christmas.[34] Further agreements were to follow soon. Western and Eastern interests were not identical but, after the experience of the double crisis of Berlin and Cuba, there was a sufficient amount of joint interests. Both sides wanted an agreement without insisting on maximum goals. The Wall could not be removed, but nor were the GDR authorities legally recognized. Moscow told its East German ally to be content with some form of *de facto* recognition, even though it was somewhat less than judicial recognition. Hence no 'treaty' was concluded, only an 'agreement'. When the talks with East Berlin entered their decisive phase in December 1963, Bahr believed that Ulbricht was under pressure by the Soviet Union and the other Warsaw Pact states which seemed to be interested in a step forward towards détente.[35]

The contacts and negotiations of 1963 could be based on earlier contacts with East Berlin which had been established by various institutions and individuals, such as the Trust Office for Inter-Zonal Trade (*Treuhandstelle für den Interzonenhandel*), the International Red Cross, private persons (businessmen, journalists, churchmen) and government officials. These sorts of exchange continued in 1963, including semi-official or official contacts. Even at the top level a direct exchange of views seemed possible when Khrushchev visited East Berlin on the occasion of the SED conference in January 1963. A member of the Soviet Embassy in East Berlin informed Bahr about Khrushchev's interest in talking to Brandt. Brandt was as keen on the meeting as Khrushchev and consulted with the government in Bonn and the three powers in West Berlin. Adenauer pointed out that accepting the invitation would mean implicitly that the Soviets could feel confirmed in their opinion that West Berlin should have the status of a free and demilitarized city. Having to take a decision, however, Adenauer in the end did not advise against the meeting. The Allies took the same view, and yet Brandt cancelled the meeting at very short notice. He was stopped by the CDU in West Berlin, or rather had not the courage to go against his coalition partner. The CDU was afraid that Brandt might go too far to meet the Soviet position and threatened to withdraw its ministers from the Senate.[36] The answer to the veto was the defeat of the CDU in the up-coming elections in West Berlin. Brandt and his SPD gained 62 per cent of the vote in February 1963. In spite of this clear majority the SPD again formed a coalition government, this time with the liberal Free Democrats. The SPD/FDP government in West Berlin was a forerunner of the same coalition in Bonn in 1969 when Brandt became Federal Chancellor.

A comparison between March 1959 and January 1963, Brandt's two missed opportunities to meet Khrushchev, shows how much had changed. The Soviet Union no longer insisted on getting rid of the four-power status completely, and the West accepted the status quo as defined by Moscow. It had to be seen whether the Soviets could attain their goal and get the legal recognition of the GDR. For the time being the West Germans had their way, and still called the GDR the 'Zone' (Soviet Occupation Zone). At the same time, although Brandt was fully aware of the delicacy of the situation, he did not hide his conviction that the only chance to improve the condition of the West Berliners was to allow contacts and negotiations on an official level. Encouraged by Washington generally and particularly by the message which President Kennedy delivered during his visit to West Berlin in June 1963, Brandt demonstrated considerable flexibility in order to reach the first pass agreement in December 1963.

Egon Bahr is right when he calls Brandt's, and for that matter his own, 'policy of small steps' (*Politik der kleinen Schritte*) a model for the bigger steps of *Ostpolitik* which were possible a couple of years later.[37] To summarize the main features:

- A wide range of contacts and channels had to be used in order to exchange information and views and to bridge the gulf which separated both sides.
- Nothing could be achieved without or against the Soviet Union.
- The partners of the agreement concurred that they did not agree on legal and status questions.
- Any agreement of the West Berlin Senate with the authorities in East Berlin needed the support of the three powers and in particular the USA.
- At the same time West German initiatives and a certain degree of German self-reliance were called for.

The West Berlin Senate, and later the Federal Government in Bonn, had to keep the balance between the rights of the three powers and the wish to break new ground in East–West relations. In 1969/70 there was some fear in the West that the position of the three powers might be infringed by *Ostpolitik* or that the spectre of Rapallo might get out of the bottle. As early as 1963 the US Ambassador in Bonn, who regarded the pass negotiations as a 'quantum jump', warned that the allies had to be alert as to whether their competencies were affected. In his view, Brandt's 'new approach could settle some problems, and create others by projecting entire new dimensions of relationships'.[38]

NOTES

1 Brandt in a talk on *Betrachtungen zur internationalen Politik* in Berlin, 17 January 1958. Quoted from Wolfgang Schmidt, *Kalter Krieg, Koexistenz und kleine Schritte: Willy Brandt und die Deutschlandpolitik 1948–1963*, Wiesbaden: Westdeutscher Verlag, 2001, p. 219. I am grateful to Martin Kitchen for his editorial assistance.
2 Franz Eibl, *Politik der Bewegung: Gerhard Schröder als Außenminister 1961–1966*, Munich, Oldenbourg, 2001.
3 Willy Brandt, *Begegnungen und Einsichten: Die Jahre 1960–1975*, Hamburg: Hoffmann & Campe, 1976, p. 219.
4 Cf. Hope M. Harrison, 'Driving the Soviets up the Wall: A Super-Ally, a Superpower, and the Building of the Berlin Wall, 1958–61', *Cold War History*, 1 (2000), pp. 53–74. See also Hans-Hermann Hertle, Konrad H. Jarausch and Christoph Kleßmann (eds), *Mauerbau und Mauerfall: Ursachen – Verlauf – Auswirkungen*, Berlin: Links, 2002.
5 Brandt, *Begegnungen*, p. 17.
6 Willy Brandt, *Erinnerungen*, Frankfurt am Main: Propyläen, 1989, pp. 16, 64. On the early origins of the concept of *Ostpolitik* see Schmidt, *Kalter Krieg*, pp. 168ff., and Peter C. Speicher, 'The Berlin Origins of Brandt's Ostpolitik 1957–1966', thesis, University of Cambridge, 2000. Both works supersede the older literature (which will not be listed here) and are impressive examples of archival research. In addition to German material Speicher also made use of unpublished British and American sources.
7 For the following summary of the concept of *Ostpolitik* see also Brandt, *Begegnungen*, pp. 56ff.; Brandt, *Erinnerungen*, pp. 48ff.; Egon Bahr, *Zu meiner Zeit*, Munich: Blessing, 1996, pp. 108ff., 125ff.
8 Willy Brandt, 'The East–West Problem as Seen from Berlin', *International Affairs*, 34 (1968), pp. 297–304.
9 Emphasis in original.
10 Brandt in May 1958, Schmidt, *Kalter Krieg*, p. 231.
11 Brandt in September 1958, ibid., p. 235.
12 See, for instance, Brandt's interview for the *Süddeutsche Zeitung*, 22/23 August 1959. Brandt considered the establishment of diplomatic relations with Poland and other Eastern European states. Such a move could represent 'a not insignificant contribution to the further treatment of the German question'. Quoted from Speicher, 'Berlin Origins', p. 171.
13 The following is based on these texts. See Willy Brandt, *Der Wille zum Frieden*, Hamburg: Hoffmann & Campe, 1971; Willy Brandt, *Koexistenz – Zwang zum Wagnis*, Stuttgart: Deutsche Verlagsanstalt, 1963. For Brandt's and Bahr's speeches in Tutzing see also *Dokumente zur Deutschlandpolitik*, Reihe IV, vol. 9, pp. 565–75 and Brandt, *Begegnungen*, pp. 56f.; Brandt, *Erinnerungen*, pp. 73ff.; Bahr, *Zeit*, pp. 153ff.

14 Speicher, 'Berlin Origins', p. 151.

15 Brandt, 'East–West Problem', p. 301.

16 Memorandum for Secretary of State Dean Rusk, 26 August 1964. *Dokumente zur Deutschlandpolitik*, Reihe IV, vol. 10, part 2, pp. 877ff. See also a speech by Bahr on *Entspannung und Wiedervereinigung* at Hamburg University, 1 June 1964: 'Die Politik gegenüber den osteuropäischen Ländern ist darauf abgestellt, einen gewissen Liberalisierungsprozeß innerhalb dieser Länder zu fördern, ihre Eigeninteressen zu fördern und auf diese Weise die sowjetisch besetzte Zone Deutschlands zu isolieren oder zu zwingen, einen ähnlichen Kurs einzuschlagen.' The GDR, although being a special case, was to be included in the overall Western strategy: 'Ich glaube …, daß der … Weg allmählicher Veränderungen und Auflockerungen und verstärkter Bindungen und Verbindungen zur Zone ein Weg ist, der nicht nur die Zeit bis zur Wiedervereinigung überbrückt, sondern ihr dient und sie vorbereiten hilft', Archiv der sozialen Demokratie der Friedrich-Ebert-Stiftung, Bonn (AsD), Depositum Bahr, 1/EB AA 000145. In November 1965 Bahr put it in the succinct way which was typical of him: '1. Eine zunehmende Ost-West-Entspannung ist erwünscht. 2. Deutschland darf in dieser Entwicklung nicht isoliert werden. 3. Wir müssen den Prozeß der Wandlung im Ostblock fördern. 4. Dazu sind wirtschaftliche und kulturelle Kommunikationen, auch gemeinsame Projekte, nützlich. 5. Mit der Sowjetunion ist ein langfristiges Programm zur Normalisierung der praktischen Beziehungen zu entwickeln. 6. Innerhalb Deutschlands sollten faktisch die gleichen Kommunikationen errichtet werden wie zwischen der Bundesrepublik und Ost-Europa', Note by Bahr, 13 November 1965, ibid., 1/EB AA 000030.

17 Brandt in Tutzing, 15 July 1963: 'Jedenfalls hat es den Anschein, daß wir im Jahr 2000 weder auf ein amerikanisches noch auf ein sowjetisches Jahrhundert zurückblicken werden', *Dokumente zur Deutschlandpolitik*, Reihe IV, vol. 9, p. 570. See also Brandt, *Erinnerungen*, p. 75.

18 Schmidt, *Kalter Krieg*, pp. 216f.; Speicher, 'Berlin Origins', pp. 148f.

19 See the questionnaire by the West Berlin Senate, 16 June 1958, which was forwarded to the authorities of East Berlin, *Dokumente zur Deutschlandpolitik*, Reihe III, vol. 4, pp. 1254f.

20 Speicher, 'Berlin Origins', p. 166.

21 Ibid., p. 169.

22 Brandt, *Erinnerungen*, pp. 51f.

23 Speicher, 'Berlin Origins', p. 181.

24 Willy Brandt, 'Außenpolitische Kontinuität mit neuen Akzenten', *Außenpolitik*, 11 (1960), pp. 717–23.

25 On this amalgam see Speicher, 'Berlin Origins', pp. 180ff.; Schmidt, *Kalter Krieg*, pp. 271ff.

26 William R. Smyser, *From Yalta to Berlin: The Cold War Struggle over Germany*, Houndmills and London: Macmillan, 1999, p. 161.

27 Kennedy to Rusk, 21 August 1961, *Foreign Relations of the United States 1961–63* (FRUS), vol. 14, p. 360. Emphasis in original. See also Kennedy to Brandt, 18 August 1961, ibid., pp. 352f.

28 Brandt, *Erinnerungen*, p. 11.

29 Bahr, *Zeit*, p.136. On the ups and downs in West Berlin–US relations see Schmidt, *Kalter Krieg*, pp. 399ff. For the reactions of the three powers to the Berlin crisis see also Rolf Steininger, *Der Mauerbau: Die Westmächte und Adenauer in der Berlin-Krise 1958–1963*, Munich: Olzog, 2001.

30 In a letter of 8 May 1964 to the political scientist Kurt L. Shell who had asked Bahr to comment on a first draft of a book on the Berlin crisis (see Kurt L. Shell, *Bedrohung und Bewährung: Führung und Bevölkerung in der Berlin-Krise*, Cologne and Opladen:

Westdeutscher Verlag, 1965) Bahr referred to the threat which was felt in West Berlin. The possibility of a Soviet surprise coup against West Berlin (*handstreichähnliche Aktion gegen West-Berlin*) could not be ruled out. 'Es war eine Situation, in der Zusammenhalt der westlichen Allianz oder die Ernsthaftigkeit der Garantien für die Sowjetunion fragwürdig sein konnte. Die Kraftprobe kam dann zwar in Kuba und das brachte die Erleichterung. Sie hätte auch in Berlin erfolgen können. Dieses Moment hat uns wochenlang beschäftigt', AsD, 1/EB AA 000145.

31 Brandt in a report of March 1962 for the SPD leadership: 'Material zum 13. August 1961'. In any negotiations on Berlin one should insist on the removal of the Wall (*Beseitigung der Mauer*). The priority, however, had to be the opening rather than the removal of the Wall (*jede nur mögliche Anstrengung zu machen, um ein Minimum an Verbindungen zwischen den beiden Teilen der Stadt wieder herzustellen*) and the securing of the viability of West Berlin (*Lebensinteressen West-Berlins*), AsD, 1/EB AA 000346.

32 In March 1962, Brandt met the Soviet journalist Polyanov of *Izvestiya*. Brandt stressed that it was sensible to start with practical questions rather than with status questions. He did not fail to emphasize that he was prepared to adjust to the 'real' situation. The Americans were informed about this talk by Bahr. Speicher, 'Berlin Origins', p. 231.

33 Comment by Heinrich Krone, one of the most influential members of the CDU leadership, 6 October 1962. Speicher, 'Berlin Origins', p. 246.

34 It is not the purpose of this chapter to describe the complicated course of contacts and negotiations which led to the pass agreement. See Schmidt, *Kalter Krieg*, pp. 503ff., Speicher, 'Berlin Origins', pp. 278ff. and Gerhard Kunze, *Grenzerfahrungen: Kontakte und Verhandlungen zwischen dem Land Berlin und der DDR 1949–1989*, Berlin: 1999.

35 In a note for Brandt, 11 December 1963, Bahr suspected that Ulbricht wanted 'Passierscheine'. 'Er braucht sie als Nachweis seiner entspannten Haltung für die Russen, für seine Ost-Block-Kollegen und für das offene deutsche Gespräch, das ohne Passierscheine zu Ende ist, d.h.: wenn die sich auf Gespräche mit uns einlassen, werden wir über die Modalitäten hart verhandeln können. Wenn sie das Gespräch mit uns anfangen, *müssen* sie zu einem Ergebnis kommen. Sie werden zu Kompromissen bereit sein', AsD, 1/EB AA 000142.

36 Schmidt, *Kalter Krieg*, pp. 475ff.

37 Bahr, *Zeit*, p. 164: 'In der Nußschale ist die ganze Philosophie der Ostpolitik bei den Passierscheinen erprobt worden.'

38 McGhee to State Department, 11 December 1963, FRUS 1961–1963, vol. 15, p. 642. The Americans welcomed Brandt's flexible approach. At the same time their support was not unquestioning. See Speicher, 'Berlin Origins', pp. 267, 329, 340ff. This ambiguous attitude remained typical for US reactions towards *Ostpolitik*. See Gottfried Niedhart, 'The Federal Republic's Ostpolitik and the United States: Initiatives and Constraints', in Kathleen Burk and Melvyn Stokes (eds), *The United States and the European Alliance since 1945*, Oxford and New York: Berg, 1999, pp. 289–311.

Index